The Lifeblood o

LOGISTICS IN ARMED CONFLICT

The Lifeblood of War

LOGISTICS IN ARMED CONFLICT

Major General Julian Thompson

BRASSEY'S

LONDON ✳ WASHINGTON

First English edition 1991
Reprinted 1992, 1994

UK editorial offices: Brassey's, 33 John Street, London WC1N 2AT
orders: Marston Book Services, PO Box 87, Oxford OX2 0DT

USA orders: Macmillan Publishing Company, Front and Brown Streets,
Riverside, NJ 08075

Distributed in North America to booksellers and wholesalers by the
Macmillan Publishing Company, NY 10022

Library of Congress Cataloging in Publication Data
available

British Library Cataloguing in Publication Data
A catalogue record for this book is available
from the British Library

ISBN 0-08-041776-0

Printed in Great Britain by
BPC Wheatons Ltd, Exeter

Contents

Contents

Acknowledgements

I have many to thank for help with this book, but first I must express my gratitude to the Leverhulme Foundation without whose generous funding, the research and writing would have been impossible. I must also express my warm appreciation to Professor Lawrence Freedman for approaching the Leverhulme Foundation in the first instance, having suggested that I tackle the subject, and for according me the honour of allowing me to join his department. It has been a considerable privilege to work at King's College London, and especially in a department with such a high national and international reputation.

A very large number of people helped and encouraged me, but I must make mention of the following. Patricia Methven of the Liddell Hart Centre for Military Archives at King's College London and her staff, were most helpful and unfailingly patient. Mr John Andrews, Mrs Judith Blacklaw, and all the staff at the Ministry of Defence Whitehall Library were, as always, of great assistance in finding material. The Tactical Doctrine Retrieval Cell at the British Army Staff College Camberley, was very helpful in pointing me in the right direction at the start of my research, and for finding documents throughout. Dr Meyerson of the Operational History Branch at the Center of Military History Department of the US Army, Washington DC, gave me much encouragement, and answered inumerable questions. Colonel Mac-Garrigle of the Combat Operations Branch of the Centre of Military History, was also most helpful in suggesting that I contact the US Army Logistics Management College, Fort Lee, Virginia, where Terry Speights was of considerable assistance. I had encouragement and valuable information from Professor Martin van Creveld, of the Hebrew University, Jerusalem, whose book *Supplying War* is a masterpiece on the subject of military logistics. Christøpher Donnelly, head of the Soviet Studies Research Centre at the Royal Military College Sandhurst, at present the Sovietologist in Residence at the office of the Secretary General of the North Atlantic Treaty Organization, was most generous in allowing me access to his publications and in reading the typescript of the chapter on the Warsaw Pact and NATO logistics. Without his advice, it would not have been possible to have made any progress on Soviet logistics. Charles Blandy, a Soviet research consultant who contributes to the Soviet Studies Research Centre, has been of considerable assistance in the same field. Brigadier Alstead allowed me to see an early draft of his comprehensive work *Ten in Ten: a Study of the Central Region Transport Capability in Crisis and War*, which helped towards an understanding of the movement problems that would arise in transition to war in the Central Region.

I must also thank the following for giving their time and their encouragement: Miss Alex Ward of the Army Historical Branch, Ministry of Defence; Brigadier General Meyara, the Defence Attaché at the Embassy of Israel in London; General Sir Richard Trant, formerly Quartermaster General of the British Army; General Sir Martin Farndale, formerly Commander Northern Army Group and Commander-in-Chief British Army of the Rhine; General Sir Anthony Farrar-Hockley, formerly Commander-in-Chief Northern European Command, and British Official Historian of the Korean War; Major General Baxter, formerly Assistant Chief of Defence Staff (Logistics), Ministry of Defence; Major General Istead, formerly Director General Logistics Policy (Army); Brigadier Hunt, formerly Director NATO on the Staff of the Assistant Chief of Defence Staff (NATO/UK) Ministry of Defence; Brigadier Pitt, formerly Director of Movements (Army); Colonel Colston, formerly Director Defence Logistics (Movements); Brigadier Heath, formerly Director Support Planning (Army); Brigadier Hulme, formerly Director Logistic Operations (Army); Dr Pauline Creasey; Colonel Hellberg; Lieutenant Colonel Macdonald; Lieutenant Colonel Wells-Cole; Group Captain Empson of British Aerospace Commercial Aircraft Limited.

I am grateful to a number of authorities, publishers, and authors for permission to reproduce passages from their works in this book. The extracts on pages 352 and 353 are British Crown copyright of the Ministry of Defence and are reproduced with the permission of the Controller of Her Britannic Majesty's Stationery Office. Extracts from the papers of General Sir Humfrey Gale are quoted with the permission of the Liddell Hart Centre for Military Archives, King's College London. Professor van Creveld of the Hebrew University Jerusalem and the Cambridge University Press have kindly allowed me to quote passages from *Supplying War*. The passages from *Alexander the Great*, published by Penguin Books, are reproduced with the permission of the author, Dr Robin Lane Fox of New College Oxford. John Keegan, now Defence Editor of the *Daily Telegraph*, has allowed me to quote from his book *The Price of Admiralty, War at Sea from the Man of War to the Submarine*, published by Hutchinson. The notes on Alexander the Great's logistics are reproduced from *Alexander the Great and the Logistics of the Macedonian Army*, copyright © 1978 The Regents of the University of California, by permission of the publisher, The University of California Press. The distinguished historian, John Terraine has generously permitted me to quote extensively from *The Right of The Line, The RAF in the European War 1939–1945*, published by Sceptre London. The passage from *The Rise and Fall of the Great Powers*, published by Fontana, is reproduced with the permission of Professor Paul Kennedy, The J Richardson Dilworth Professor of History at Yale. Books published by the Center of Military History Washington DC are in the public domain, however I am grateful to Dr Meyerson for pointing this out to me. General Mathew B Ridgway kindly allowed me to quote a passage from his book, *The Korean War*, published by Doubleday & Company Inc, New York. Sidgwick and Jackson, the publishers of General Davidson's *Vietnam at War*, have been most generous in permitting passages to be reproduced. Professor Ronald Spector, now Professor of History and International Relations at the Elliot School of International Affairs, George Washington University, has permitted me to quote from his book, *Advice and Support, The Early Years, The US Army in Vietnam*, published by the United States Army Center of Military History. Lieutenant Colonel Gardiner, Royal Marines, has again allowed me to quote from his private diary. George Weidenfeld & Nicolson Limited have permitted me to quote from Walter Lacquer's *The Age of Terrorism*, which they published. Curtis Brown of Regent Street, London have permitted me to reproduce a passage from Sir Fitzroy Maclean's *Eastern Approaches*, published by Jonathan Cape. Jane's Information Group have allowed me to quote from Colonel Dupuy's *Elusive Victory*. The quote in note 52 of Chapter Five is reprinted with permission from Presidio Press, 31 Pamaron Way, Novato, CA 94949, from the book *Strategy for Defeat: Vietnam in Retrospect*, by Adm U. S. G. Sharp, Copyright © 1978. The passage from *The Battle for Khe Sanh*, by M. S.

Shore, is reproduced with the permission of the publisher, The Marine Corps Historical Center, Washington DC, and the Director of Marine Corps History and Museums, Brigadier General E. H. Simmons, USMC (Retd). Major General Lachman Singh Lehl has generously allowed me to quote from his book *Indian Sword Strikes in East Pakistan*, published by Vikas Publishing, New Delhi.

I am grateful to Mr Michael Willis of the Photographic Department of the Imperial War Museum, and Helen Menzies of the Hulton Picture Company for their patient assistance in finding photographs to illustrate the book.

I would especially like to thank Brigadier (Retd) Bryan Watkins of Brassey's. His profound knowledge of military matters, coupled with his extensive experience with sword and pen, made working with him a most stimulating and enjoyable experience. He suggested a number of textual amendments, all of which have been included.

Jane Harper was a tireless assistant, without her help progress would have been considerably slower. Her comments and criticisms of the typescript as it progressed were of inestimable value, as was her support throughout.

Finally I must emphasise that except where I quote another source, all the opinions expressed in this book are my own, and I take full responsibility for them.

Preface

The genesis of this book was back in late 1986, when I was about to leave the Royal Marines, and Professor Freedman asked me if I would research and write on the subject of logistics and armed conflict in the modern age. I readily accepted this offer, which among other things, would give me the opportunity to join the Department of War Studies at King's College London, a chance not to be missed. It was also a challenge to write about something that has attracted so few other authors, and yet is so central to the success or failure of any campaign. It was a subject about which I knew nothing during the early part of my career. It was only after graduating from the British Army Staff College at Camberley, that I was forced to take an interest in what, hitherto, I had regarded as something strictly for quartermasters, or 'blanket stackers'. I was posted to the headquarters of the Far East Land Forces, based in Singapore, on the staff of 'Q' Operations, the staff branch responsible for seeing that the logistic plans and operations in the theatre meshed in with the operations requirement; and for directing the efforts of all the theatre logistic services to that end. The colonel at Camberley responsible for my division commiserated with me on my ill fortune in not landing one of the more glamorous operations jobs, and I agreed with him. I could not have been more wrong.

At the time, the campaign of confrontation with President Sukarno of Indonesia was reaching its climax, and 'Q' Operations was kept very busy indeed ensuring that the supply system responded swiftly to the many demands. No sooner was the campaign over, than the withdrawal from Borneo was in full swing, and, as usual, long after the captains and kings had departed, the administrative services were still toiling. Riots in Hong Kong were the next to demand the attention of the logisticians, despatching quantities of defence stores and other material, by sea and air. A team to brush up the British plans in the event of trouble in the South-West Pacific, including Fiji, the Solomons, the Gilbert and Ellice Islands, and New Hebrides (said to have inspired the show 'South Pacific'), included me as the logistician. It transpired that there were few operational plans, and none for logistics. It required tact and persistence to prise out of local officials and contractors the figures for stock-holdings of fuel and food, the number of bulldozers and a host of other bread and butter matters. A trip to Aden followed on the heels of a month in the romantic setting of the South Pacific. Plans for the withdrawal were in full swing, and the Far East theatre was to become involved in the latter stages. As this would also include me when I returned to commando soldiering on completion of my staff tour, I took considerable interest in the plans, including the logistic arrangements.

I learned a great deal about logistics in that appointment, not least the critical importance of supply and the suppliers in any operation. Nothing that I have seen since changed that view. Often, the results of one's labours were more tangible, more easily measured than those of other staff departments, and therefore a greater source of satisfaction.

*   *   *

My original intention for this book was to carry on where Professor Martin van Creveld, in his scholarly work *Supplying War*, left off in 1944. However, the more I read and researched, the more I formed the opinion that there was much still left unsaid about logistics and armed conflict from antiquity up to the end of the Second World War, my original starting point. For example, there were campaigns that gave pointers for the future, such as the American Civil War and the First World War. The sea flank, and the logistic advantage it gave to generals who would, or could, make use of it was interesting to me; from Alexander the Great over 300 years BC, to Field Marshal Alexander in Italy in AD 1943/45. The campaign in Normandy 1944 included the greatest amphibious operation of all time and has been covered frequently, but there were many logistic lessons learned in the Torch landings in North Africa in 1942. Bringing in supplies from the sea adds another dimension to the logistic problem, one not readily appreciated by those whose professional horizons are bounded by continental experience. Finally, Burma, perhaps the logistic triumph of the Second World War, in the most daunting terrain; the longest land campaign fought by the Allies against the Japanese.

The post-Second World War campaigns and wars have been selected with an eye to bringing out certain lessons. I speak no language other than my own, and for this reason chose campaigns that are well documented in English.

In Korea, the initial unpreparedness of the United States was based on their experience in the Second World War, and the time allowed them to build up their defence industries, both before Pearl Harbor, and afterwards. This coloured their view of how any future war would unfold. They paid the price for placing too much faith in what is high on my private list of military sins; over-confidence in one's ability to foretell the future. Korea also provides an excellent example of the use of the sea flank, as well as the interplay between the effectiveness of interdiction of an enemy's lines of communication and the pressure being applied on his forces at the front. Unless the two are co-ordinated, the effort put into the former may be wasted. This was also the first time the Americans had taken on a Communist Asiatic enemy, and produced valuable lessons, many of which they failed to apply in Vietnam, the next war against Asiatics of the same political persuasion.

*   *   *

Vietnam, which is the longest chapter, provides a chance to look at four logistic phases (referred to in Chapter 5 as Rounds 1, 2, 3 and 4). Phase One, the French campaign, failed militarily, mainly because they did not possess the logistic means to flesh out their operational plans. Phase Two, the period between the French withdrawal and the committal of American forces in strength, held portents for the future, in the lack of administrative skills among the South Vietnamese, which were to prove a considerable drawback towards the end of the period of American involvement, and afterwards. In Phase Three, the Americans had logistic problems, but possessed the means to overcome them; as we shall see, their strategy, and hence their operational and tactical methods, were at fault. Finally, in Phase Four, the steady reduction of American logistic support to the South Vietnamese, post 1973, was a major factor in the latter's defeat.

Vietnam also provides an interesting example of the build-up of a guerilla army from a platoon to a force of several corps, with armour, artillery and all modern weapons. The logistic problems facing a guerilla commander, fighting a power equipped with sophisticated weapons and enjoying total air domination, is also interesting.

*   *   *

If those masters of mobile warfare, the Israelis, have an Achilles heel, it is logistics. Nevertheless, thanks to support from the Americans, and the brilliance of the Israeli generals, they managed to inflict defeat upon numerically superior enemies in the Yom Kippur War of 1973. Israeli fighting qualities have never been in doubt, but their free-wheeling, indisciplined methods could be their undoing logistically. It is difficult to obtain much hard information from the Israelis, who regard questions on any military matter with deep suspicion. However, some 'reading between the lines' in conversation, and much questioning of those who have made a study of the subject, has led me to the views expressed above.

*   *   *

The 1971 Indian campaign in Bangla Desh, provides a good example of the logistic problems to be encountered in an underdeveloped country, which is why it is placed out of historical context, after the Yom Kippur War of 1973, and right before the Falklands Campaign of 1982. The latter was fought in an even more underdeveloped country than Bangla Desh, from the point of view of a soldier, with the added complication that every bean, bullet, and drop of fuel had to come 8,000 miles and, having arrived, be carried into battle on the backs of soldiers, by helicopter, or in the handful of tracked vehicles capable of travelling over the peat bog.

In these days of *Perestroika* and *Glasnost*, a chapter on the logistics of NATO and the Warsaw Pact seems almost superfluous. However, it does provide an example of how logistics can be planned (Warsaw Pact) and the more *ad hoc* approach of the NATO Alliance. With luck, the two systems will never be put to the test, but perhaps future historians will find something on which to ponder. It also provides a convenient stepping-stone to lead into the chapter on future war.

*   *   *

Writing on war in the future in these fast-moving times, is like describing a game in which the goalposts are moved every day, and the rules changed every night. Here I have had to take the plunge and overcome my own distrust of those who claim to be able to predict the trend of future events. However, it seems to me that there is merit in seeing where we might be twenty or more years from now in defence terms. It is highly unlikely that we will be in a situation that bears much similarity to the present, and almost anyone's guess can be as good as the next person's.

*   *   *

It was originally my intention to include some low intensity operations. However, after preliminary research, it became clear to me, that they provided few examples where logistics played an important part in their success, or otherwise. Writers on the Borneo campaign, during confrontation, have used such words as logistics were 'important'. The answer of course is that they always are. However, with the huge Singapore base near the theatre of operations, plentiful shipping and air transport, and an adequate helicopter force, there was never, from my personal experience, nor as far as I can discover, anyone else's, any constraint on operations for logistic reasons. By their very nature, low intensity operations involve low ammunition expenditure, particularly shells, and compared with mobile warfare, little fuel. Such wars are usually decided politically, rather than militarily. The ragged, poorly equipped and trained guerilla forces, in what is now Zimbabwe, were consistently defeated by numerically inferior, but better equipped and trained Southern Rhodesian troops. The campaign was won, and lost, round a conference table in London, as a result of political pressure, and the drain on the Southern Rhodesian economy and morale, caused by a long war with no prospect of an end in sight.

*   *   *

One of the longest wars in modern times, the Iran/Iraq conflict, has ended too recently for any detailed study to be made of the logistic aspects. To do so would involve examining reports, which, apart from being written in Arabic and Farsee respectively, are, given the nature of the two régimes involved, unlikely to see the light of day for some time to come—if ever. What is known, is that there was heavy expenditure of all types of war-like resources on both sides. In this respect, the Iran/Iraq war does not differ greatly from any modern war fought by equally matched sides. On the Iranian side, however, they quickly found that, having ousted their American advisers, who had managed their computerised stores inventory, they were now unable to trace the vital spares they needed for tanks and aircraft. Very soon, large numbers of both were lying idle because they could not be repaired. The intensity of that war served to underline the need for holding large stocks of expensive war materials if one is contemplating war or intending to deter a potential aggressor. Such stocks offer little appeal to most politicians with their eyes on the electorate: nor to those who wish to cut defence spending for moral or economic reasons, or, indeed, to those who wish to be seen to have their country's defence interests at heart, by building up the shop-window with men and equipment. All too often, that shop window has pitifully small stocks of war reserves behind it, simply because to cut back on the holdings of war reserves represents an easy and invisible path to economy. Yet, to deter, stocks need not only to exist but be seen to exist.

*   *   *

The naval and air force logistician will look in vain for any substantial discussion on logistics in their operational environments. Because, as Professor Freedman stated in his submission to the Leverhulme Foundation, when seeking funds for this project, '[although] it is a practical art that must be mastered by navies and air forces as well, there is something distinctive about logistics in land warfare in that it requires territory to be held once taken, over an extended period'. What is also distinctive, and therefore interesting, about logistics in land warfare is that they are, to put it crudely, more difficult. A good example is provided by any amphibious operation. Shipping stores to the area off the beachhead is relatively simple in pure transportation terms, although enemy action may make matters more complicated. The real problems begin when supplies have to be landed, and transported, sometimes hundreds of miles inland. Even without enemy interference, the difficulties can be considerable. I hope this is illustrated in my short piece on naval logistics in Chapter 2 and the relevant notes, and in Chapters 3, 4 and 8. Logistics in support of the air battle have until recently been largely a naval or land problem. Fuel, ordnance, and spares for air forces were transported on the water by navies, and overland by courtesy of armies. Because it was in the interests of soldiers and sailors to have air support, if they were wise, they allocated the necessary movement resources to the airmen. But the problem of delivery, including maintaining routes, and protection, was largely naval or army. Although it might be argued that the air support of, say, the British in Burma was an air force problem, they were in effect acting as airborne truck drivers in response to an army requirement, as indeed are helicopters and fixed-wing transports now. The transportation of fuel, spares, and ordnance to the theatre of operations was, and still is primarily a naval or army responsibility. Even in the Falklands campaign, where the Royal Air Force played such an important logistic role, it was secondary, and less complicated than the part played by the other two services. Whether this will always be so is addressed in the final chapter.

Finally, I have no reason to believe that logistics will ever have much military sex-appeal, except to serious soldiers, but this book is written in the hope that I am wrong.

List of Illustrations

Plates

Maps

Figure

Glossary of Terms and Acronyms

AP	Ammunition Point, a place to which ammunition is delivered by logistic units for collection by the fighting units.
APC	Armoured Personnel Carrier, an armoured tracked or wheeled vehicle designed to carry infantry into battle. More lightly armoured than a Main Battle Tank. Some APCs have machine guns in a turret, in which case it is designated an Armoured Infantry Fighting Vehicle (AIFV) or Mechanised Infantry Combat Vehicle (MICV).
Army Group	A group of armies, or in NATO a group of corps.
ARVN	Army of the Republic of Vietnam (South Vietnam).
AVCAT/ AVTUR	Aviation fuel (paraffin) for jet and turbo-jet engines.
AFV	Armoured Fighting Vehicle, a general term to cover all armoured vehicles used in combat.
Bailey Bridging	A system of quickly assembled bridging invented by Professor Bailey, an Englishman, at the beginning of the Second World War. Often described as a 'war winner', it made a significant contribution to tactical mobility and to the maintenance of logistic support in North Africa, Europe and the Far East.
Battalion	An infantry organisation of about 500–1,000 men, usually commanded by a lieutenant colonel, in some armies by a major, in which case the battalion may be only about 300 strong, as in the Soviet Army. A battalion is made up of anything from four to eight companies. In most armies, other than the British,

	artillery and tanks are also formed into battalions and sub-divided into companies.
Battery	The smallest self-contained sub-unit of artillery. Normally of eight or six guns in two equal troops. Heavy and Medium batteries usually have fewer guns.
Bazooka	A United States recoilless (see RCL) anti-tank weapon used by infantry.
BEP	*Bataillon Étranger de Parachutistes*; French Foreign Legion Parachute Battalion.
BMA	Brigade Maintenance Area, located in the BSA (see below), but can move out to keep up with the move inland of the brigade it is supporting. (See FBMA).
BMI	*Bataillon de Marche Indochinoise*; French Indochinese Light Infantry Battalion.
BPC	*Bataillon de Parachutistes de Choc*; French Parachute Assault Battalion. Also *Bataillon de Parachutistes Coloniaux*; French Colonial Parachute Battalion.
BPVN	*Bataillon de Parachutistes Vietnamiens*; French Vietnamese Parachute Battalion.
Brigade	An army formation of two or more battalions. May have its own artillery, armour, and engineers. Usually commanded by a Brigadier (British), Brigadier General (United States and others), or Colonel (West German, Israeli).
BSA	Beach Support Area, the location for logistic units and stores in an amphibious operation. If more than one brigade is taking part, all BMAs may be placed under centralised control here.
BV 202	Bandwagon, a tracked oversnow vehicle made by Volvo.
Caribou C-7A	Twin engined, short take-off and landing, short-range transport aircraft, with tail-gate.
C-119	or Flying Boxcar. A United States Air Force transport aircraft of the immediate post-Second World War years. With twin booms and a tail-gate, it was an improvement on the Dakota, particularly for dropping supplies, and speed of loading.
C-123	Twin-engined, short take-off and landing, short to

	medium range transport aircraft, fitted with tailgate.
C-130	Four-engined, short take-off and landing, transport aircraft. Still a great workhorse aircraft, despite being largely 1950s technology.
CCF	Chinese Communist Forces, the name given to the Chinese forces who entered the Korean War in the winter of 1950/51 on the side of the North Koreans.
CFE	Talks on Conventional Forces in Europe.
Chinook	Large twin-rotor helicopter of United States manufacture with payload of ten tons.
CINCENT	Commander-in-Chief Central Europe, a NATO commander.
CIVGAS	Petrol.
COMNAVFE	Commander Navy Far East, the senior United States Navy Commander in the Far East during the Korean War.
Company	An infantry company varies in size from 100–200 depending on whose army it is in. In most armies it is about 100 strong. A company at full strength is made up of a minimum of three platoons, each of about 30 men.
Corps	An army formation of two, or more divisions. Usually commanded by a Lieutenant General (three star general).
Deadweight tons	2,240 pounds per ton (see Short Tons).
DAER	Daily Ammunition Expenditure Rate, the anticipated rate at which ammunition will be expended each day over a 30 day period. This is arrived at by assuming that the unit for which it is designed will be in action at intense rates for X days, at medium rates for Y days, and at low rates for Z days over a 30 day period. The expenditure is totted up and divided by 30 to give the DAER.
Dakota C-47	The great Allied transport aircraft of the Second World War. Adapted from the pre-war civilian two-engined DC-3. Could drop parachutists, and small loads from one side door.
Dieso	Diesel fuel.

Division	An army formation of two or more brigades. In some armies the lowest level at which supporting arms and services (artillery, engineers, logistic units) are organic to the formation. Usually commanded by a Major General (two star general).
DMZ	A nominally De-Militarised Zone between North and South Vietnam.
DP	Delivery Point, a designated point, forward of the BMA or FBMA to which combat supplies are delivered by logistic units for collection by the fighting units.
Dracone	A large, floating, rubber, sausage-shaped, container into which fuel can be pumped from a tanker.
DZ	Dropping Zone, area into which paratroopers and/or parachuted supplies are dropped.
EFHE	Emergency Fuel Handling Equipment. Kit for setting up a temporary bulk fuel installation ashore in an amphibious operation. Includes pipelines and pumps for pumping fuel ashore from a tanker, and large rubber tanks to hold fuel.
ETA	Basque terrorists.
FARP	Forward Arming and Refuelling Point, the place to which missiles, ammunition and fuel is delivered for armed and reconnaissance helicopters, who fly back to collect. The further forward this can be the better because it reduces the time the helicopter is out of action.
FBMA	Forward Brigade Maintenance Area. If it is not possible to move the whole BMA, for tactical or logistical reasons, an FBMA will sometimes be set up if the distances from the brigade back to the BMA have become so great that an intermediary stage is required to hold a limited amount of stock.
FSA	Forward Support Area. United States term for forward logistic base.
IRA	Irish Republican Army (see PIRA).
LCU	Landing Craft Utility. In the British service, a landing craft capable of carrying 200 men or 22 tons of stores or four large trucks. Four carried in the dock of each LPD (see below). United States LCUs are bigger, and there are at least two different types.

LCVP Landing Craft Vehicle and Personnel. In the British service a landing craft capable of carrying an infantry platoon (30 men), or a landrover and trailer. There are different designs of LCVP in the Dutch and United States Navies.

Liberator A United States Army Air Force bomber of the Second World War. Also in service with the British Royal Air Force. Very under-powered for a bomber. Sometimes used as a transport aircraft and to tow gliders.

LPD Landing Platform Dock, two in the Royal Navy, considerably more in the US Navy. An amphibious ship fitted with a dock aft, accessed by a tail-gate. By flooding ballast tanks, and opening the tail-gate, craft can enter and leave, loading and unloading at a ramp at the forward end of the dock. This is a big advantage, and quantum step forward from driving vehicles off roll-on-roll-off (ro-ro) ferries on to pontoons, or lowering trucks and other loads over the side by crane, particularly in a seaway. In the British service, each LPD has the command and control facilities for an amphibious and landing force task group commander to exercise joint command.

LSL Landing Ship Logistic, RFA (see below) roll-on-roll-off ships designed to carry tanks, trucks and logistic supplies for an amphibious operation. Can carry an assembled Mexeflote (see below) on each side, or in pieces on deck. Can land a helicopter amidships if the crane is stowed. Has a one-spot helipad on the stern.

LST Landing Ship Tank, designed during the Second World War for amphibious operations, and produced in large numbers in the United States. Could take about 50 trucks, depending on the size of vehicle, or about 8 main battle tanks. Had bow doors and a ramp. Had a flat bottom and shallow draught, and could beach, and even dry-out on a falling tide, to be re-floated on the next rising tide. Very robust, but rolled in a 'heavy dew'. Remained in service with the British Services until the mid 1960s.

Still used in some Third World navies. The United States and Soviet Navies have several more modern versions in service to this day.

MBAV   Main Battle Air Vehicle, a helicopter capable of destroying armour, with a high survivability, the successor to the tank, one day.

MBT   Main Battle Tank. Possesses sufficient fire power and protection to enable it to play a leading role in offensive operations in General War. Current examples include the German Leopard II, American Abrams M1-A, Soviet T80, Israeli Merkava II and the British Challenger. Its long-term future in the order of battle is a matter for controversy.

Mexeflote   Hollow metal pontoons which, when joined together, will make a 120 or 60 foot raft powered by large outboard engines. The rafts can also be joined together to make a causeway.

MHE   Mechanical Handling Equipment, e.g.: fork-lift trucks, mobile cranes.

Milan   Wire-guided, anti-tank missile.

MSR   Main Supply Route. The principal route by which the supplies for a formation will be moved.

NATO   North Atlantic Treaty Organisation.

NCO   Non-Commissioned Officer. Soldier or marine holding a rank between that of private and Warrant Officer.

NKPA   North Korean People's Army. The armed forces of North Korea.

NVA   North Vietnamese Army.

PIRA   Provisional Irish Republican Army, break-away group from IRA, and the main instigators of terrorism in Ireland, Britain, and Europe. The old IRA is dormant at the moment.

Platoon   The basic infantry tactical sub-unit. Normally has three Sections (see below) and a strength of about 30 men. Commanded by a junior officer or a senior NCO. The term is also used in some armies for a sub-unit of 3–5 tanks.

PNG   Passive Night Goggles, image-intensifying goggles mainly used by helicopter pilots to fly at night.

POL	Petrol, Oil and Lubricants.
Raiding Craft	Small, rigid, glass-fibre craft powered by a large outboard. Useful for raiding parties, and for communications.
Rapier	British surface-to-air missile.
RAS	Resupply At Sea. Divided into RAS(L) for liquids, i.e. oils and other fuels, and RAS(Solids), i.e. ammunition, stores, food, etc.
RCL	Recoilless weapon. To save the weight required by the mechanism to absorb recoil in a conventional gun, a recoilless gun works on the principle of the equal and opposite blast of the propellant charge escaping from a venturi in the rear. The penalty is lower muzzle velocity and hence range.
RCP	*Regiment de Chasseurs Parachutistes*; French Parachute Light Infantry.
RFA	Royal Fleet Auxiliary. The logistic ships for the Royal Navy—mainly storeships and oilers, but also LSLs.
ROK	Republic of Korea (South Korea).
RPG	Soviet anti-tank hand-held RCL.
RVNAF	Republic of Vietnam (South Vietnam) Armed Forces.
SACEUR	Supreme Allied Commander Europe.
SAGGER	Soviet wire-guided anti-tank missile.
SAM	Surface-to-Air Missile.
SEAC	South-East Asia Command. A command area set up in early 1944, which included India, Ceylon, Burma, Malaya, and the Dutch East Indies. The Supreme Commander SEAC was Admiral Mountbatten.
Sea King	British helicopter which comes in various forms. The Mark IV troop lift version can carry about twenty men in full battle order.
Section	Normally, eight to ten infantry soldiers commanded by a corporal or sergeant; at full strength there will be a minimum of three sections to a platoon.
SHAR	Sea Harrier.
Short Tons (tonnes)	2,000 pounds per ton (see deadweight tons).
Sortie	An operational flight by one aircraft.

Spot	The circle on a ship's flight deck marking the landing position for one helicopter. Thus a one-spot deck will take one helicopter at a time.
STUFT	Ship Taken Up From Trade. Merchant ship requisitioned for war service.
T-34	Russian tank. One of the most successful tank designs of the Second World War. Some still in service in Third World countries today.
TEZ	Total Excluson Zone, a maritime area designated as out of bounds for a potential aggressor.
TOW	Wire-guided anti-tank missile of United States manufacture.
USAF	United States Air Force.
USKMAG	United States Korean Military Assistance Group, set up in South Korea by the United States after the Japanese surrender in August 1945 to advise and assist the South Korean armed forces.
USMAAG	United States Military Assistance Advisory Group. Formed in Indochina in 1950 to act as the conduit for material assistance to the French fighting against the Viet Minh, and to monitor the distribution of equipment provided by the United States. It did not advise the French on operational matters. In 1954, after the Geneva Conference, which resulted in the partition of Vietnam into North and South, it took over responsibility from the French for training what became the South Vietnamese Forces. Changed its name to USMACV in 1962.
USMACV	United States Military Assistance Command Vietnam, the successor to USMAAG. It had far wider responsibilities than its predecessor, and ended up running the war in Vietnam until the withdrawal of the United States in 1973.
Viet Cong (VC)	*Viet Con Son* (Vietnamese Communist).
VTA	Soviet Military Transport Aviation.
Viet Minh	*Viet Nam Doc Lap Dong Minh Hoi*; Vietnamese Independence League.
Wessex	Obsolescent British helicopter. Over anything more than a short distance, payload about 10 men in full battle order.
WMR	War Maintenance Reserve. National stocks of fuel,

ammunition, food and spares from which formations in the field will be replenished during the early weeks of a major war. Normally expressed in terms of 'days' and calculated to cover the period needed to get national industry and other sources of supply 'on stream'.

Wombat   An obsolescent recoilless 120 mm anti-tank gun.

PART ONE

1

Principles: The Disciplines of War

Logistics 'the stuff that if you don't have enough of, the war will not be won as soon as'.[1]

General Nathaniel Green, when asked by George Washington to accept the post of the Quartermaster General of the American Army, is reputed to have said, 'Whoever heard of a Quartermaster in history as such'.

Thorpe in his book *Pure Logistics* propounds the view that 'the conclusion is irresistible that the military themselves know next to nothing about logistics'.[2] Perhaps he is being contentious in order to gain the reader's attention and to make him more receptive for the message which he puts across so lucidly. And yet, using the word 'know' in the sense, 'personally acquainted with', and as an American writing for the United States forces before his country entered the First World War, he was probably not stretching a point too far. For as experience of war recedes, so, with the passing of time, logistics tend to take a back seat to the more glamorous tactics and strategy. The experienced military, certainly the successful, know about, are all too well personally acquainted with, logistics. Although Napoleon may have said *'qu'on ne me parle pas des vivres'* ('let no one speak to me of provisions'),[3] he not only reorganised the logistic system of the French Army, but usually planned his campaigns so that they were logistically possible. His logistic system failed only twice; in Spain, where he was in command in person for a very short time, and in Russia in 1812 where his army had outgrown his staff system.

Clausewitz

From time to time the military, or ex military, have sounded forth on the subject; from Clausewitz: 'there is nothing more common than to find consideration of supply affecting the strategic lines of a campaign

3

and a war';[4] to Montgomery: 'during the last war 80 per cent of our problems were of a logistic nature'. Rather than a lack of knowledge, the problem may lie in a reluctance to acknowledge the importance of logistics in war and the need to lay sound foundations for supply in war while at peace, including a sound set of principles. This is partly what Thorpe was driving at. While tactical and strategic principles abounded, there were no principles to guide the logistician. Some writers have criticized Clausewitz for paying lip service to logistics. This is too dismissive. In *On War*, he has chapters on; 'Camps', 'Marches', 'Billets', 'Maintenance and Supply', 'Base of Operations', and 'Lines of Communication'. These, like most of the work, draw heavily on the experiences of Frederick the Great and Napoleon. He uses lessons from the past to illustrate such problems as the increased sickness rate in armies that have abandoned tentage in order to increase their mobility; and the wear and tear on soldiers on long marches, and in a long war. He outlines four methods of supply; the advisability of fighting in someone else's territory, and thus eating at their expense; and recommends that one does not stay too long in one place lest supplies run out. He mentions the dependency of the army on its base, and that supply is easier in defence, provided adequate preparations have been made. The need to make arrangements for stocks of weapons, ammunition, and equipment is also given a line or two. It is when he starts philosophising on the relationship between supply and what we would call the concept of operations, that a note of what in the British Army is called 'G snobbery'[5] creeps in.

In his chapter on supply[6] he asks the question:

> '. . . whether war governs the supply system or is governed by it? We would answer that at first the supply system will govern war insofar as the other governing factors will permit; but where these start to offer too much resistance, the conduct of war will react on the supply system and so dominate it'.

Having discussed how many men and animals can feed from given areas with varying sizes of population, taking into account towns, roads, rivers and so forth, he launches into another question:

> 'All this will indicate the general influence that questions of supply can exert on the form and direction of operations, as well as the choice of a theatre of war and the lines of communication.
>
> How far their influence will extend, and how much weight should in the final analysis be attached to the ease or difficulty of supply—those are questions that will naturally depend on how the war is to be conducted. If war is to be waged in accordance with its essential spirit—with the unbridled violence that lies at its core, the craving and the need for battle and decision—then feeding the troops, although important, is a secondary matter. On the other hand, where a state of equilibrium has set in, in which the troops move back and forth for years in the

same province, subsistence is likely to become the principal concern. In that case, the quartermaster general becomes the supreme commander, and the conduct of war consists of organising the wagon trains.'

His contempt for commanders who allow such situations to occur comes through, even in translation from German to English!

It is nevertheless important to remember that these chapters form part of Book Three, and the whole work, except Book One should be read as notes, or a draft. Even so Chapter 14 in Book Five is more specific on supply problems than anything in Jomini. It is conceivable that had Clausewitz lived to completely revise his work, the chapters which cover what we would call logistics, would have been revised and the emphasis changed. He might have given more space to logistics, and provided more solid data. But this can only be speculation, and there is a lingering suspicion that logistics would have been relegated to the blinding glimpse of the obvious department by Clausewitz; '. . . in about the same relationship to combat as the craft of the swordsmith to the art of fencing'.[7]

Jomini's Definition

Jomini, who had served as a staff officer to Ney in Napoleon's army, was the first to define the art of logistics. He set down logistics as one of the six branches of the military art, the other five being; statesmanship in its relationship to war, strategy or the art of properly directing masses upon the theatre of war, grand tactics, engineering (the attack and defence of fortifications), any minor tactics. He does not, however, use the word in the sense that we would use it today. His definition: 'logistics is the art of moving armies. It comprises the order and details of marches and camps, and of quartering and supplying troops; in a word, it is the execution of strategical and tactical enterprises'[8] sounds almost right to modern ears, until we read the chapter on logistics. It then becomes apparent that he is talking about the whole gamut of staff-work involved in campaigning. Of the eighteen principal points he includes, less than half are what we today would call logistical. And when he enlarges upon some of the points, it is only when he speaks of depots and material, that he covers matters which a modern military logistician would recognise as being in his department. In his examples he strays even further from logistics, into the realms of strategy and grand tactics, or the operational art.

The reasons are two-fold. First, by including the phrase 'it is the execution of strategical and tactical enterprises' in his definition of logistics, he is as it were, hooked on his own definition. Second, and more important, in his day, the dividing line between what we would call the operations staff and the logistic staff was not so clear as it became in the latter half of the last century. To begin with, the chief of staff and subordinate staff officers, were almost solely concerned with the supply and movement of armies in response to the commander's strategic, operational, and tactical plans, often drawn up by the commander alone, and frequently kept to himself. The quartermaster general was in effect the chief of staff. This persisted, in name only, into this century. Ludendorff's title, as chief of staff to Hindenberg, was First Quartermaster General; because in Germany, quartermaster generals were directors of military operations. As Jomini himself points out:[9]

> 'But when war began to be waged without camps, movements became more complicated, and the staff officers had more extended functions. The chief of staff began to perform the duty of transmitting conceptions of the general to the most distant points . . .'

Therefore, despite Jomini's including logistics as one of the six military branches, by his treatment of the subject in his work, he actually confuses the issue by bracketing logistical with operational and intelligence staffwork. It is not, therefore surprising that military men in the years that followed were more impressed with Jomini's strategic and tactical advice than what he had to say about logistics, which in practical terms was remarkably little; even less than Clausewitz.

Jomini gives no logistical diagrams, as companions to his detailed tactical drawings; no principles; no equivalents to his maxims on lines of operations and the like; no logistical lessons, or pearls of wisdom. The logistician would search in vain for the nineteenth century version of the modern weight and balance tables, with fuel consumption, weight and distance parameters, for a move by helicopter. There are no helpful statistics giving the daily consumption of water and fodder by mules, horses, donkeys, elephants or camels; or the balance to be struck between the number of animals taken and the forage and fodder requirement; and consequently the need for additional animals to carry the fodder; who themselves need feeding. Although Jomini was widely read for his advice on tactics and strategy, there is nothing sufficiently substantial to give a lead to others to write on the subject, or invest logistics with the same fascination that strategy and tactics has for most soldiers.

The Principles

If principles are what we seek, first the word itself. 'Logistics' derives from the French *'maréchal de logis'* in Louis XVI's army, in English, quartermaster[10] general (*logis* means lodging or quarters). The *maréchal de logis* was responsible for the administration of camps, billets and marches. The *maréchal general* later became responsible for all administration and, as has already been noted, was sometimes employed as a chief of staff. Although the term was dropped in the French Army, after the French Revolution, the word *Logistique* remained in use. It was picked up by Jomini and used rather loosely to cover staff work, some of it not logistical. The budding logistician, or general for that matter, might well ask for a few principles to act as 'markers' when faced with mobilising an army, planning a campaign, battle or minor skirmish. He might find the 'Principles of Administration' as laid down in the British Army Pamphlet 'Administration in the Field', as good a guide as any, because they are applicable at all levels from a nation preparing for war, to a company commander planning a training exercise. They are:

    Foresight
    Economy
    Flexibility
    Simplicity
    Co-operation

Or he might prefer to turn to the United States Army where there are no less than nine principles:

    Logistics Intelligence
    Objective
    Generative Logistics
    Interdependence
    Simplicity
    Timeliness
    Impetus
    Cost-effectiveness
    Security

It is obvious that there is a similarity between the two sets of principles. Without Logistics Intelligence it is difficult to bring Foresight to bear in forward planning. Similarly, it is necessary to have a clear and attainable Objective, such as the development of logistic plans for the transition to war phase in Europe; or the reinforcement of Northern Norway during a time of tension. The application of modern technology to meet the logistic support requirements of armies in the field requires Generative Logistics. The use of airlift in a number of campaigns, from the First World War onwards, is a perfect illustration of this principle. Finally, still in the 'Foresight' department, Interdependence requires that each part of the logistics system must be co-ordinated with the rest of the system as a whole. For example, a developer must design equipment which is easy to support on a logistic basis. A case of failure to follow this principle was the American M47 tank. When the tank made its first appearance in the field, it was found to have a number of logistic drawbacks, not least that in order to change the sparking plugs, the fitters had to remove the engine.

The need for simplicity in planning, in the design of supply systems, and in the maintenance and operation of equipment, if not its technology and functioning, goes without saying. It is a principle that has been followed more in the breach than the observance on more than one occasion.

Timeliness demands that logistic support must be provided in the proper quantity at the right place and time to enable the unit or formation to carry out the mission. To achieve this, in a fast moving battle, or when axes are being switched, or there are heavy material losses through enemy interdiction, the system must be supple and quickly and easily adaptable to meet the new circumstances. Hence the British principle: Flexibility. By Impetus the Americans mean the need to provide support well forward, right into, or close behind the fighting units' areas. This avoids units engaged in battle looking over their shoulders for resupply of resources without which they cannot continue to fight. The British logistic principle of Co-operation includes supply forward, but takes it further to mean the need for units and formations at all levels, right up to Army Groups, to co-operate logistically to avoid duplication of effort and waste, to maximise logistic resources such as transport, and to resupply across unit and formation boundaries.

Which brings us to Cost-effectiveness, or Economy. This can range from a programme of analysis to provide a systematic approach to the problem of allocating limited economic resources when procuring equipment, to decisions on stock levels and logistic priorities.

The British do not include Security as a logistic principle. Perhaps on the grounds that it is a principle of war, and that the need for rear area security goes without saying. This may be so, but the emphasis that the Soviets place on attacking key installations in rear areas, underlines the need for resources to protect the tail, lest it be cut off. The Soviets certainly have considerable worries about the vulnerability of their logistic tail to precision guided weapons. The wider aspect of Security is also important, that of the need to conceal one's logistic intentions from the enemy, lest by his interpretation of them he divines the overall plan. Soviet logistic principles have not been discussed here. They are less broad-brush than the British and American logistic principles, and discussion of them fits more logically in the chapter on Soviet Logistics.

Having briefly discussed the principles, the art of logistics must be examined by casting back into history, rapidly coming forward to the Second World War, then looking at case studies of conflict since the Second World War, discussing logistics in NATO and the Warsaw Pact; finally a look at logistics in future war.

2

The Assyrians 700 BC to the
Armistice AD 1918

*'Surely one of the strangest things in Military History is the almost complete silence
upon the problem of supply.'* [1]

Organised armies had their earliest origins in the emergence of hunting
bands and raiding parties, fighting over land, women or food. As other
drives, such as the urge to dominate others or to defend men's homes
and villages from marauders, or to seek independence from tyranny
became more general, so did the need to organise larger and larger
fighting groups emerge, and with that need the imperative for a system
of supply. As weapons became more sophisticated and arrows and
javelins superseded sticks and stones, so did metal armour replace the
wicker shield and the need for craftsmen to forge and repair not only
weapons but also the new means of waging war—chariots and, later,
siege engines. The now universal horse, the mules and oxen used for
pulling transport, needed fodder—which would ultimately become fuel
with the advent of mechanical vehicles. Men and beasts called for an
ever increasing range of warlike equipment and supplies and a system,
which we now call logistics, by which these essentials could be provided
and administered.

The Assyrians

In about 700 BC, the Assyrians had the earliest known standing
army in history. It was equipped with iron chariots; iron weapons and
armour replaced the bronze accoutrements of earlier soldiers. At about
the same time, the art of fortification of the larger cities in what we now
call the Middle East, had developed to a degree that their reduction had

FIG. 2.1   Assyrian infantry and charioteers. An encampment bottom left. From the portion of bronze band from the gates of the palace of Shalmaneser III, King of Assyria 860–825 BC (*Hulton Picture Company*).

become a considerable undertaking, involving trains of battering rams, wooden towers, and a plentiful supply of arrows and other missiles for protracted siege operations. The Assyrian army had a high degree of organisation, and displayed an ability to fight successfully over all kinds of terrain. It may have approached 50,000 men, and a formation of this size would require a large supply organisation for desert and mountain operations. It would also have been familiar with the problem of all armies up to the age of the railway and beyond which, put crudely, was: 'to live, keep moving'. If an army stopped, even in a well populated area, the available food was soon consumed; unless its commander had had the foresight to make arrangements to carry food with him or have it brought in. If armies stopped at any time of year from late spring to harvest, there was little food for the taking, as the inhabitants were at subsistance level themselves. Arrival just after the harvest was the best time for the army, although not for the local population; the complete harvest was available for requisitioning. The most voracious consumers of the grain were the increasing number of animals, mainly horses and mules, but sometimes bullocks, elephants, and camels, that accompanied armies as they grew in size and sophistication. In summer, these animals soon overgrazed the immediate area of the army, creating the need for foraging patrols to be sent progressively further and further afield. In winter, grain had to be provided from local resources or brought in. In one of the last wars in which animals still played a leading part, the First World War, whilst the British shipped 5,253,538 tons of ammunition, including over 170,000,000 shells, to France, the greatest single item shipped consisted of 5,438,602 tons of oats and hay. In this respect, the First World War was no different from the wars of antiquity, although it differed vastly in another logistic aspect, a huge increase in ammunition supply, thereby heralding a new era of warfare.

Alexander The Great of Macedon

Philip of Macedon, and his son Alexander advanced the art of logistics considerably. Philip, realising the limitations imposed on his mobility by large numbers of pack mules and wagons to carry baggage and supplies for the soldiers and their women, made the soldiers carry their own kit and some rations, and banned the women. His example was followed by Alexander, and, two hundred and fifty years later, by the Roman consul Marius, whose soldiers called themselves 'Marius's Mules'[2,3]. Other armies in Alexander's time eased their soldiers' loads by providing a large baggage train of carts and pack animals, accompanied by drivers and other followers, including forage cutters, women and, in that pre-birth-control age, hordes of children. The load carried by Alexander's soldiers only marginally reduced their daily mileage and some of that load could be dumped when fighting; as modern infantry divest themselves of rucksacks before assaulting an objective. By having fewer animals, the problem of providing forage was reduced.[4] The fewer the number of carts, the less of a hindrance they became in rough going, there were less drivers to feed and a reduction in the number of spare parts to carry or make out of local wood; this last was a genuine difficulty in the treeless terrain which was Alexander's objective.[5] Despite his policy on reducing carts and baggage, Alexander was, however, more lenient than his father over the question of women accompanying his army; which was sensible in view of the length of time his soldiers were away from home. Not only was he demonstrating his care for his men by allowing them to keep their women; but also, because he liked and respected women, it is possible, that he neither wished his army to abandon their women to their fate,

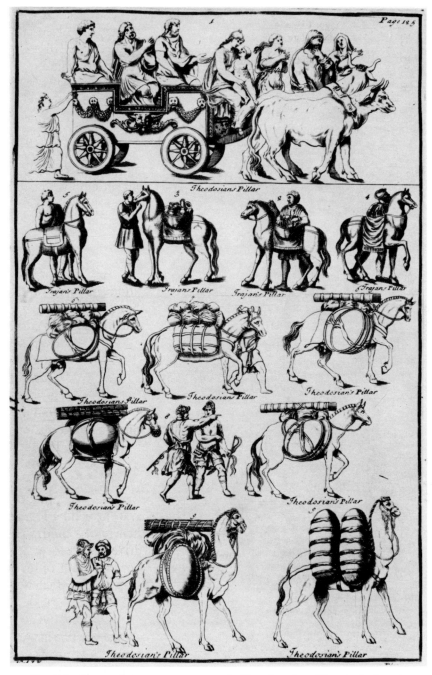

FIG. 2.2   Roman Army transport animals. Drawings from Theodosian's and Trajan's pillars. Animal transport would remain important in many armies until after the Second World War (*Hulton Picture Company*).

FIG. 2.3 Roman infantry crossing a pontoon bridge. Trajan's column. Each soldier carried his pack and other kit on a stick—see Notes 2 and 3 to this chapter. (*Hulton Picture Company*).

nor to satisfy their normal desires, perhaps by force, at the expense of the females in newly conquered territory.[6]

Seaborne Supply

He also made extensive use of ships to carry fodder, since a large merchant ship could carry about 400 tons,[7] while a pack horse carrying only 200 lbs would eat 20 lbs of fodder daily, thus consuming its own load in ten days.[8] Indeed, Engels concludes that Alexander never spent the winter, or even a few weeks, with his entire army in a region remote from a sea port or navigable river.[9] He was also astute enough to take advantage of the logistic weakness of his enemies' warships. As Robin Lane Fox has noted in his study of Alexander:[10]

'Like all warships in the ancient world, the Persians' men-of-war were like "glorified racing-eights", and had so little room on board in which to store provisions that they were forced to remain in daily touch with a land base. Meals could not be cooked on the move and fresh water had to be collected by putting into a nearby river-mouth. Sharp as ever, Alexander had anticipated them and sent several units by land to beat them off. Thwarted and thirsty, the Persian crews sailed away to the island of Samos where they stocked with stores, perhaps with the help of its resident Athenians. On their return to Miletus, they still fared no better for water, and so gave up the struggle in the interests of their stomachs, and sailed away south-wards.'

Having used these tactics in the Aegean, he was to use them again to force the Cypriot and Phoenician ships to surrender and join him. Alexander's grasp of the significance of logistics was not limited to matters of supply alone, but encompassed morale and reinforcements, as Lane Fox shows.[11]

'Before advancing (to the coast of Lycia and Pamphylia to hold the seaboard and render the enemy useless), he gave orders that all Macedonians who had married "shortly before his Asian campaign" would be sent back home to Macedonia to spend the coming winter with their wives. "Of all his actions, this earned Alexander popularity among his Macedonians", besides helping the homeland's birthrate and encouraging more reinforcements'.

Nowhere is Alexander's use of his merchant fleet to provide logistic support for the army more evident than at the end of his campaign in India. He planned to march from the mouth of the Indus at Pattala (120 miles north-east of present day Karachi) along the coast to Pasni on the coast of the Makran in Baluchistan. Engels tells us[12] that Alexander had collected four months provisions for his army, totalling about 52,600 tons. He would have to take little water, because the rivers that flowed to the coast would be full in the monsoon which was about to break, and wells could be dug on the coast. He could not carry the 52,000 tons of supplies overland, for after nine days the animals would have consumed it all, and the 30 lbs carried on the man would also have been eaten.[13] The bulk of his provisions would therefore be carried by the fleet, which would sail along the coast keeping pace with the army who, in their turn, would be responsible for supplying the fleet with water. Alexander set out in mid July, but the fleet never arrived off the coast. Unknown to Alexander the monsoon which provided the water, had prevented the ships from sailing, and would immobilise them until October. Alexander could not stay where he was in the hope that the ships would turn up, the area was already devastated, and for all he knew the fleet destroyed by the Indians. He could not return to Pattala, a journey of nearly 300 miles over territory which had been stripped bare, and would not support an army of 87,000 infantry, 18,000 cavalry and up to 52,000 followers. He marched through the inland inhabited regions of Gedrosia, where some fodder was available; but lost three-quarters of his army in the deserts of the Kolwa depression between the central and coastal Makran ranges. He eventually arrived at Turbat, where the remnants of his army were able to gather sufficient supplies for the march to the coast at Pasni. From here he marched to Gwadar, covering 136 miles in seven days. Now, at last, they could re-provision.

Logistics the Key

Alexander's strategy depended on logistics, indeed his mastery of it allowed him to conduct the longest military campaign in history. At the farthest point reached by his army, the river Beas in India, his soldiers had marched 11,250 miles in eight years, and there were three more years and many miles of marching before the campaign ended. Success depended on the ability of his army to move fast by depending on comparatively few animals, the use of the sea wherever possible, and last, but not least, good logistic intelligence. Advanced information about routes, climate and resources in the country he was intending to move through were critical to his plans. When his intelligence failed, in the case of the monsoon-bound ships, which he had not foreseen, the results were near disaster.

The Changing Scene at Sea

Alexander's exploitation of the weakness of the contemporary warship discussed earlier, is of interest; lack of endurance was inherent in its design. Fighting ships were even more difficult to sustain logistically than the armies of the time. The broader beamed, more seaworthy merchant ships of antiquity, and those in the centuries to come, could carry enough food and water to sustain their crews for several weeks, but were unsuitable for the fighting tactics practised in the Mediterranean then and for nearly another two thousand years, into the sixteenth century. As John Keegan has pointed out,[14] it was not until the European powers on the Atlantic seaboard put artillery in the stout, broad-beamed, deep-bottomed merchantmen of the early sixteenth century AD, thus combining fighting and logistic capability in one vessel, that ships became instruments of remarkable endurance and hitting power. They reached the pinnacle of their logistical potential in the Napoleonic Wars. In the mid-nineteenth century, the adoption by navies of a new means of motive power, steam, and coal fuel, considerably reduced the endurance of warships. For example, Keegan says[15] that HMS *Dreadnought* carrying 2,000 tons of coal, had an endurance of five days at 20 knots. However, warships were still able to carry ammunition for their guns, and food for the crews, over considerable distances at a higher speed than horse-powered armies, and hence, despite the need for coaling stations, they were logistically more independent than armies. The conversion to oil fuel increased endurance by about 40 per cent, because of its greater efficiency as an energy source. The coming of the fleet train and underway replenishment techniques from oilers and stores ships in the Second World War endowed navies with as great endurance as in Nelson's time; except that his ships could stay at sea for years, with longer intervals between dockyard maintenance periods than modern warships. Resupply at sea (liquids) and resupply at sea (solids), RAS(L) and RAS(Solids) in sailor's jargon, provides almost every commodity required by a fighting ship: from fuels for the ship and its aircraft, to missiles, food, and spares, from the smallest silicon chip for a fire control system, to a complete replacement turbo-jet engine for the ship's main propulsion system. RAS and the ability to distil water for drinking and other uses, enables even a complex modern warship to remain at sea for months, her endurance limited only by that of her crew, and those portions of her hull and machinery that cannot be repaired except in a dockyard.[16] Since the sixteenth century, navies have been considerably easier to maintain, and are logistically more flexible than armies. Which is why this book concentrates on land force logistics, they are more difficult; and explaining why is the reason that the narrative has jumped forward 2,000 years. It is time to return to it.

The Age of Charlemagne

With the decline of the Western Roman Empire and its military system in the fifth century AD, armies in Western Europe became smaller, as the tribal groupings that supported them became increasingly fragmented. Logistics descended to the plunder level as the art of war degenerated. Only with the advent of Charlemagne in the ninth century AD, did matters in Western Europe improve. He provided the basis for the feudalism of the Middle Ages, by establishing a system of calling men to service through noble vassals. For lack of a logistic organisation, his predecessors had been unable to keep armies in the field for long periods, and supply shortages usually caused the dispersal of Frankish armies after a few weeks of campaigning. Charlemagne instituted a logistic system including supply trains with sufficient food and equipment to maintain his troops for several weeks.[17] This enabled him to campaign 1,000 miles from the heart of France, and to maintain armies in the field, or in sieges, throughout the winter; almost unknown in Western Europe since the time of the Romans. A key element in his logistic system, was the use of fortified frontier posts, or burgs. These were built along the frontier of every conquered province, and connected to each other by a road. A road also led back to the old frontier from each burg. These forts were stocked with supplies, and became the bases from which the Frankish cavalry could sortie to maintain order in the conquered territory, and from which to make fresh advances.

The Byzantine Empire

In Eastern Europe, the Byzantines, the military heirs of the Roman Empire, owed their survival to the fact that their army was the most efficient military body in the world at that time. The Byzantine Empire maintained a standing army of between 120,000 and 150,000 men, about fifty per cent horse, the remainder foot. Except in the ninth century, when a series of great soldier Emperors led a counterattack against the Muslims, the Bulgars and the Slavs, Byzantine strategy was mainly defensive, foreign conquest being expensive in lives and treasure. They recognized that their wealth was a constant attraction to the barbarian tribes that surrounded them, and they adopted a deterrent policy, avoiding war if possible, but energetically repelling invaders, following up by punishing and harrassing their aggressors with a minimum expenditure of wealth and manpower, rather in the manner of the Israelis today. Their striking force consisted of heavily armoured horsemen, the cataphracts, highly disciplined and well drilled.

By operating a defensive strategy, the Byzantine's logistic problems were simplified. As Clausewitz noted over a thousand years later, supply is easier in defence than in attack, provided proper preparations have been made in advance. Communications were also made easier by being on the defensive; the army was able to switch from one base to another by changing its lines of communication in a way that was more difficult in enemy territory. Thanks to their excellent military organisation, in which logistics played an indispensable part, the Byzantines were able to turn back the Muslim invasion of Christian Europe from the East in the early eighth century; perhaps a more significant event than the battle of Tours, thirteen years later, which marked Islam's high water-mark in Western Europe.

Unlike the Moors operating from Spain, the Muslim armies in the East were closer to their own heartland, and logistically better positioned to drive deep into Eastern Europe, as they eventually were to do centuries later. If in the eighth century, they had defeated and advanced through the Byzantine Empire, they would have found the hodge-podge of petty kingdoms beyond easier to gobble up than the powerful combination of European powers, mainly Austria and Spain, that were later to bar their way from the end of the fifteenth century until the middle of the eighteenth. When Constantinople, held by seven thousand exhausted men, finally fell on 29 May 1453 to eighty thousand Turks, who had battered a breach in its wall, it had provided a bulwark against the tides of chaos and disorder for over a thousand years.

At a time when most of Western Europe was sunk in a state of brutal barbarism, the Byzantine Empire was a major world power, and centre of civilization. A significant setback occurred, however, at the battle of Manzikurt in 1071, when, mainly through treason, the Byzantine army was defeated by the Seljuk Turks. The subsequent loss of most of Anatolia was a stupendous blow. The Turks ravaged the countryside until what had been the main Byzantine recruiting ground, became virtually a desert, from which most of the surviving non-Turkish population had fled. When parts of the province were reconquered, the Byzantines were no longer able to raise any worthwhile force from the region.[18] In consequence they were forced to resort to mercenaries, from Western Europe, Russia, Scandinavia, and the tribes on their northern borders. Nevertheless, the professional skill of that army was to ensure the survival of Byzantium for almost another four hundred years.

The Crusades

The appeal, in 1095, by the Emperor Alexius to the Pope for assistance in clearing Anatolia of Turks, probably in the hope of attracting a few thousand mercenaries, was to set in train a series of Western European expeditions to the Eastern Mediterranean; the Crusades. Although there were other campaigns waged under the title Crusade, against the Slavs, the Moors, and the Cathars, we are concerned here only with the campaigns in Asia Minor and Palestine. For not least among the many skills which Western Europeans acquired in the East, was a quantum leap in various branches of the military art.

The First Crusade

The First Crusade, from 1096 to 1099, which ended in the capture of Jerusalem, started inauspiciously. The main contingents from Normandy, England, France, Flanders, Germany, and Norman Sicily, grouped under no less than ten leaders, made up an indisciplined army of about 50,000 which at times was no better than a rabble. Its organisation, or rather lack of it, was a reflection of the state of the military art in Western Europe at the time. Although religious fervour and a wish to free the 'Holy Land' from Muslim rule motivated many of the Crusaders, it is also likely that the possibility of carrying out new fiefdoms was not too far beneath the surface in the aspirations of a significant number of those who marched under the banner of Christ.

From the beginning, there was friction within the army, and distrust of the Byzantines, which was returned. The Crusaders were unenthusiastic at being used to restore lost Byzantine territories, and, in return, the Emperor had no interest in the recapture of Jerusalem. This mutual divergence of views was to have adverse effects on this and most subsequent Crusades. The First Crusade nearly came to grief twice through lack of a supply system. Whilst besieging Antioch the Crusaders nearly starved, only being saved by the unexpected arrival of small English and Pisan fleets, which captured two ports and brought provisions. After capturing the city, the Crusaders were besieged in their turn and, cut off from their ports, almost starved a second time. However, inspired by the discovery of a holy relic, they sortied and defeated the besieging army.

In the following year, a much reduced army advanced south along the coast to Jaffa. They appeared to have learned the logistic lessons of the preceding years campaigning. There was far more co-operation between national contingents. This time they had the benefit of the Pisan fleet sailing parallel to their route to provide logistic support close at hand. That is, until they turned inland to Jerusalem. Here they were too small in numbers to blockade the city completely, so the defenders, who more numerous, could not be starved into submission. In addition, the governor of Jerusalem had taken the precaution of driving the flocks of goats and sheep and the herds of cattle from the countryside into the city, as well as laying in large stocks of food. He sent an urgent request to the Caliph of Egypt for assistance. The Crusaders were desperately short of water at this time, because the governor had also poisoned most of the wells outside the city. There was no food to be had locally, and their supply line to Jaffa, 30 miles away as the crow flies, was far too long for them to control continuously. For logistical and tactical reasons, time was not on the side of the Crusaders. Whether it was these imperatives, or the urgings of an ancient Christian hermit who lived near the Mount of Olives, that persuaded the Crusaders to mount an assault as soon as possible, without siege weapons, is not clear. Perhaps their belief in the hermit's pronouncement that, armed with faith in God, they would be victorious was enough to persuade them that they had nothing to lose by making the attempt. Unfortunately, faith alone was no substitute for the right equipment, and although the Crusaders' headlong attack overran the outer defences very quickly, they were unable to scale the inner walls. They lacked sufficient scaling ladders to get enough men on top to swamp the defenders, and had insufficient fire power, in the form of missile throwers, to keep the defenders' heads down. After enduring three hours under a hail of arrows and stones, the Crusaders withdrew.

Their gloom at this reverse was lightened by the arrival of the English and Genoese fleets at Jaffa, loaded with food and war material. But convoying it to Jerusalem was a time consuming operation, expensive in manpower and animals, and the stocks were enough to last only a short time. More serious was the problem of finding enough stout timber to build assault towers to roll up to the walls. Eventually, the nearest suitable timber was found in wooded hills near Nablus, fifty miles north of Jerusalem. Transporting it to the scene of operations was yet another drain on manpower and animals. The painfully slow procession of Muslim prisoners and pack animals dragging the huge baulks over the rough terrain would have been a tempting target for an ambush. Feeding prisoners, packmules, cavalry horses and soldiers over the hundred mile round trip would have added yet another logistic problem to be solved. Over the next two months, three large towers and a quantity of scaling ladders were constructed. By now it was midsummer, and the burning hot Khamsin wind blew, whipping up the dust and covering everything with grit. The Crusaders had to send parties as far as the River Jordan for water, but they seldom brought back enough to meet every need. Animals began to die, and everybody suffered from thirst.

In early July, information was received that a large Egyptian army was marching to the relief of the city. The Crusaders were in a desperate position, weakened by starvation and disease, the small army of about 15,000 men could not hope to defeat the Egyptians, and continue the siege. The work of finishing the assault towers was speeded up. When completed, they were rolled out from where they had been built, out of sight of the defenders of Jerusalem, who were taken completely by surprise and horrified when they saw them rolling towards them.

As an aside, from the vantage point of 890 years later, the governor and defenders of Jerusalem appear to have been singularly inept and supine soldiers. Had an aggressive patrol programme been instituted, they would not have been so ignorant of events just outside their walls. Having a superiority in numbers, the governor could have spared men for sorties which might have succeeded in delaying the work, or bringing it to a halt completely. The energy and courage displayed by the Crusaders, perhaps made desperate by their situation, was almost fanatical. The outer wall of the city had to be breached and a ditch at the foot of the main wall filled in before the towers could be heaved up to the main wall at their assault positions. Under a hail of missiles, the necessary enginering work was done mainly during the night of 13 July and by the night of the 14th, one tower was in position. An assault was attempted, but it was thrown back. On the next day, a second tower was pushed into position and the knights manning it managed to gain a lodgement on the walls of the city. Reinforcements swarmed up scaling ladders and the tower. By that night the city was in the hands of the Crusaders.

The Second Crusade

The Second Crusade, consisting of a German army led by Emperor Conrad III of Germany and a French army under King Louis VII of France, was launched to recover Edessa from the Muslims. It was a logistic disaster. At first all went well, until Conrad's army, first to arrive in Byzantine territory, stirred up the local inhabitants by pillaging. Louis's army, which followed the same route, behaved better and had little trouble, except that the Germans had consumed most of the food and forage and so frightened the peasants that they hid what little food they had left. Relations between the two armies was not improved when the French arrived at Constantinople and found that the Germans refused to sell any of the food that they had collected. About the only matter on which they agreed was their dislike and distrust of the Byzantines. The hostility between the French and German armies led to Conrad making the disastrous decision to march across Anatolia on a different route from Louis. Splitting forces was bad enough, but Conrad compounded the error by dividing his own army in two, planning to take one group through Central Anatolia, and ordering the other to march along the coast road. By the time Conrad's group reached Dorylaeum they had consumed all their food. Here they found a strong Turkish army waiting for them. The exhausted, starving German army was destroyed; only Conrad and a few followers escaped. The other German group progressed well, until they struck inland to cut a corner off their journey and were routed by the Turks at Laodicea, most of the survivors dying of starvation on their way south to the coast.

The first part of Louis's march along the coast went without incident. However, he too turned inland and, like the Germans, also suffered heavy casualties at the hands of the Turks at Laodicea. Desperately short of food, Louis and his knights marched south towards the coast through mountainous terrain and in bitter winter weather. On arrival at Attalia on the coast, they discovered, to their dismay, that the inhabitants too were short of food and strongly resented the presence of the Crusaders, a situation which quickly attracted the Turks, who set about besieging the city. Louis was forced to leave. He and his cavalry travelled by sea in two successive lifts, leaving his infantry to make their own way to Antioch overland. A few exceedingly embittered foot-soldiers survived this example of crass leadership and administration and eventually staggered into Antioch, having escaped the ravages of both the Turks and hunger. The last phase of this Crusade was no exception to the logistic and tactical ineptitude that had gone before. Louis, Conrad, who had joined him, and Baldwin of Jerusalem, decided, against advice, to beseige Damascus. They not only set their siege lines opposite the strongest part of the city's defences, but sited their camp in an area where there was no water nearby. Not surprisingly the siege failed.

The Third Crusade

The Third Crusade, forty years later, following the disastrous defeat of the Christian army at Hattin and the capture of Jerusalem, by the redoubtable Saladin, was a far better managed affair, led by three kings. Two were the ablest and most experienced soldiers in Europe; King Richard I of England and the Emperor Frederick I of Germany. The third, King Philip II of France, was not an inspiring leader. Frederick was the first on the scene, successfully marching through Anatolia, routing the Turks where most of his predecessors had failed. After capturing Iconium, disaster struck the German army. Frederick was drowned, and his son, lacking his father's tactical and logistical ability, lost most of his men to the Turks and those twin scourges of so many medieval European armies, hunger and disease.

A year later, after spending the winter quarrelling in Sicily, first Philip and then Richard, arrived at Acre, which had been under siege by the Christian armies for nearly two years. Within twenty-four hours, Richard had put new heart into the Christian army, having assumed command of the whole force on arrival. Although he fell ill soon afterwards and was forced to command from his tent, such was the power of his personality that siege operations were conducted with considerably more energy than under his predecessor Philip. Saladin's attempts at lifting the siege were beaten off, and the city finally surrendered. Philip went back to France, leaving Richard in sole charge of subsequent operations. He immediately started the advance to Jerusalem, marching along the coast, keeping contact with his fleet guarding his right flank. His planning and logistics were far superior to the haphazard arrangements which were commonplace in most Western armies at the time. He kept his marches short to preserve the strength of his soldiers in the blinding August heat. He even arranged for a laundry organisation to keep clothes clean. After defeating Saladin at Arsuf, losing 700 to Saladin's 7,000, he halted for a time at Jaffa, before pressing on towards Jerusalem in the winter rains. His men suffered miserably, and quickly recognising his mistake, he marched back to the coast at Ascalon.

In the following spring, Richard set out again, but Saladin retired before him, destroying crops and grazing, and poisoning wells. Because of the lack of fodder for his horses and water for all, Richard eventually halted at Beit-Nuba and reluctantly concluded that he could not risk his army by besieging Jerusalem. Even if he had captured the city, it is highly unlikely that it could have been held by the Christian army after Richard's return to England; a move that was becoming increasingly pressing, because of his brother John's treasonable negotiations with the King of France. Before he finally withdrew from Beit-Nuba, Richard improved his logistic situation by capturing a large resupply caravan, after a night reconnaissance patrol which he led personally. On withdrawing to Acre, he learned that Saladin had mounted a lightning attack on Jaffa, taking the city by surprise. Richard reacted with a speed worthy of a German panzer grenadier divisional commander of the Second World War. Despatching most of his army overland, he took a small force by sea to Acre. At the sight of his ships, the Christians in the city siezed their arms and attacked Saladin's men. At this stage, a priest jumped down from the city wall, and swam out to Richard's ship, which was painted red with a dragon's head prow, and so easily recognised. He told the king that Saladin would soon overwhelm the Christians again. Although he had only a few knights and a few hundred infantrymen with him, Richard ordered his sailors to beach their boats and, wading ashore at the head of his men, stormed into the city. Saladin's men were routed.

Richard's conduct of his last battle in Palestine was typical of this great soldier. Saladin, hoping to catch Richard before his main army arrived, and with only a small force of fifty-four knights and two thousand infantry, planned a surprise attack on Jaffa at first light after a night approach march. Fortunately, his force was spotted by a soldier who gave the alarm. Richard drew up his own small force behind the medieval equivalent of a low-wire entanglement constructed out of tent pegs. He ordered his men at arms to form a shield wall, interspersed with long-bowmen and cross-bowmen, and had spears driven into the ground like *punji* stakes. Like a square at Waterloo, Richard's men beat off repeated charges by Saladin's cavalry. By evening Saladin and his men had had enough, and pulled back, convinced that Richard was invincible.

The Lessons

The Crusades, which provided examples of the best and the worst in the military art of Western Europe, were important for the military education of Western soldiers. Several tactical and military engineering lessons were learned, but space precludes discussion of them all here.

One of the most lasting was the importance of logistics, an art that had almost disappeared in the West with the fall of Rome. Western European armies had, for centuries, lived off the countryside and when they had consumed everything, they dispersed or starved. Campaigns were usually short because the length of obligatory feudal service was limited by the amount of time that barons and their retainers could, or were willing to, spend away from their fiefs. Sieges were occasionally protracted and, in a few cases, campaigns would be carried on by small armies of mercenaries, whose lack of numbers reduced the problem of maintaining them. In the face of Turkish scorched earth tactics, most Western armies, lacking knowledge of the terrain and climate, ill-disciplined and without an organised wagon train, disintegrated.[19] In the long drawn out campaigns in Western Asia, with long marches and operations in barren desert or mountain, the generals had to re-learn the logistical lessons that Alexander had learned from his father fourteen centuries before the Crusades; plan properly, or die. In the First and Second Crusades, more men and animals died of starvation than from any other cause. Richard demonstrated that good logistic planning could change the picture completely. He established a logistic base in Cyprus and sea lines of communication, which he used to advantage on his march from Acre to Ascalon. His refusal to embark upon a lengthy seige of Jerusalem, despite the urgings of the medieval equivalent of the 'G Snobs' among the more senior and influential of his followers, is a mark of a general who understands the logistic problem. He was a fearless fighter, a brilliant tactician and a canny logistician.

* * *

Time Passes: A Napoleonic Folly

As the centuries passed, the logistic imperatives remained largely unchanged by strategic and tactical modifications, the advent of gunpowder and the coming of the railways. The main problem facing an army for the greater part of any campaign was still not how to fight the enemy but how to exist in the field. It was to solve this problem that staffs and staff work were invented.[20] In the time of Frederick the Great, by Tempelhoff's reckoning, an army of 100,000 men would be accompanied by 48,000 horses. Dry fodder was so bulky that it could only be transported readily by water. Campaigning did not normally begin until the green grass grew. There were long intervals in campaigns when nothing happened. The greater part of Frederick's instructions to his generals were concerned, not with battles or the higher reaches of strategy, but with the routine of feeding, moving, and encamping the army. Although Napoleon was able to take advantage of the better road system that was beginning to be constructed in Europe by the end of the eighteenth century, and an increasing population density and thus a greater ability to support armies, he still held to the methods of his predecessors, a combination of magazines to stock supplies, and foraging. Clausewitz tells us that armies abandoned tents during the wars of the French Revolution to cut the number of baggage animals, but as these were replaced by cavalry or more guns, drawn by horses, the forage requirement was not reduced and the speed of advance did not increase.[21] Fifteen miles a day was regarded as a normal rate of advance in Clausewitz's day, reducing to an average of ten over a long period in order to allow time for rest days on which repairs and maintenance could be carried out. The penalty for abandoning tents was loss of manpower, because of an increased sickness rate. Although, as Clausewitz records, this did not slow the tempo of operations, it increased the logistic problem, because of the need to set up larger sick quarters (which themselves had to be supplied), and to expand the reinforcement system.

Napoleon for all his genius at organisation, failed the test when faced with the greatest logistic challenge of his career; the campaign in Russia. He crossed the Niemen with 301,000 men, and subsequently detached 13,500 men at Smolensk 52 days later, so that 287,500 should have been left. But his actual strength was 182,000, which means he had lost 105,500. Only two engagements had taken place, which would have caused 10,000 battle casualties at most. So the losses from sickness and stragglers on an advance of 350 miles must have come to some 95,000 men, or about one-third of the army. By the time Napoleon reached Moscow, his total losses were 198,000 men. It was summer, the roads were in good condition, albeit crowded by the enormous mass of troops. The advance was not particularly fast by the standards of the day, so there should have been time for stragglers to catch up.

Napoleon was taking a gamble. He knew that his logistic system would not carry him to Moscow and maintain him there, but, like Hitler, he hoped to defeat the Russians, and dictate peace-terms, before logistics imposed on the strategy. Unfortunately for him, the Russians traded space for time, and their army, although in retreat, was by no means in flight, and certainly not destroyed. For lack of logistic preparation, Napoleon's subsequent retreat was a disaster. The pursuing Russian army did little better, they left the Kaluga area with

120,000 men and arrived in Vilna with 30,000. Few were lost in the fighting. The one logistic problem neither had to face was ammunition supply. The rate of useage was still low, and was to remain so for another hundred years.

*   *   *

The War Between the States

The American Civil War is of considerable interest to the student of the military art in a number of ways. To the contemporary observer there were four particularly significant pointers to the future, all with logistic connotations. The first was its context. Two determined adversaries, with space in which to manoeuvre, reasonably competent generals, large populations from which to recruit armies, and the means to equip them, all creating the conditions for a long war. Battles may be lost by one side or the other, but the war will end only when one side perceives the impossibility of sustaining its war-fighting capability in terms either of material, or of the will of its soldiers and population— in some cases, both. The logistic lack of preparedness of both the Union and the Confederacy contributed to the length of the war. Each was able to trade space for time while they armed. Had one side been in a position to equip a large army on the outbreak of war, and to maintain it, the advantage so gained might have enabled that side to win the war more quickly.

The second pointer, which follows from the first, is that after the industrial revolution, fighting between mass armies recruited from large populations, even armed with the relatively crude firearms of the mid-nineteenth century, will result in heavy casualties in men, horses and equipment. If the arrangements to collect, evacuate and care for the wounded, including the supply of drugs, nursing staffs and doctors, do not take account of this, the medical services will be swamped, with an adverse effect on morale. Systems to replace all these casualties take time to set up. Without pre-war logistic planning, the flow of replacements forward will be held up until the necessary organisation is put in train. In the days of the Civil War this would have included a number of measures, for example: the training, equipping and movement of fresh manpower; a remount procedure, breaking-in new horses and mules, and the provision of the necessary harness; the manufacture of the whole range of war material, from large cannon to the smallest spare part, and the means of delivery into the hands of the soldier. Now, as then, delays will be further exacerbated if the armaments and equipment industry is slow to gear itself up to meet the vastly increased demand; even more so if such an industry does not exist at all and has to be created from the ground up.

Third: the importance of a strategy which takes account of logistics, not merely one's own, but the adversary's. Lee and Jackson were the masters of the operational art. But the war was won by the logistic capability of the North, able to arm and sustain its armies, and eventually to maintain Grant in his strategy of relentless pressure on Lee. Grant 'fixed' Lee so he could not detach troops by rail to reinforce the Confederates facing Sherman in Tennessee and Georgia, and later in the Carolinas. Sherman was left in overwhelming strength to demolish the South's vital railway communications, supply and manufacturing centre of Atlanta, before cutting loose from his supply base and advancing on a front 50 to 60 miles wide, feeding his army by foraging; destroying and confiscating all resources and property that might be of any military value to the South. Spread over a wide swathe of countryside, with about a twentieth of his army committed to foraging, and with an increasing number of stragglers looting, he was in no position to fight anything other than skirmishes, nor did he have to. Sherman's virtually unopposed march through Georgia from Atlanta to Savannah, so beloved of the apostles of the 'indirect approach', and held by some to have decided the outcome of the war, was made possible by, and was an adjunct to, the main campaign in Virginia. Without Grant's unrelenting pressure on the Army of Northern Virginia from May 1864 to April 1865, Lee could have concentrated against Sherman, and perhaps defeated him.

Sherman's less famous march, from Savannah, Georgia to Goldsboro, North Carolina was a far more arduous affair. He marched his army of 60,000 men a distance of 450 miles in fifty days, of which ten were allocated to rest. Although he encountered little resistance from the understrength Confederates under Johnston, his advance was slowed by heavy rains. He was able to make good use of the Union command of the sea to shorten his supply line. He switched his supply base from Savannah 250 miles north to the port of Wilmington, and subsequently a further 100 miles to New Bern harbour. A railway ran inland from each, cutting his axis of advance. Johnston's attempts at concentrating and reinforcing his army by rail, using troops from Tennessee, were frustrated because he was competing for space on the lines that were also supplying Lee.

Which brings us to the fourth pointer; in this, the first major war in which railways played a significant part, the commanders on both sides discovered that although the use of railways speeded up the movement of troops and supplies, the lines did not always run in the direction that the commanders would have wished. Soldiers could not fight from the wagons, and once they de-trained, their speed of movement was at a foot pace. Likewise, supplies had to be transported from the railhead to the consumer. How much could be lifted forward, and the time delay from railhead to soldier, depended on a number of factors, including the distance to be covered, the road system, or lack of it, and the quantity and lift capacity of wagons and availability of prime movers—horses. McClellan's Army of the Potomac in the Richmond Peninsula campaign of 1862 had intended to use the Richmond and York River Railroad as the line of communication for the advance on Richmond. Supplies were landed at the White House on the York River and taken by rail to the point where they were transferred to wagon to supply the army. To begin with the operations of the Army roughly followed the line of the railway, so the railhead was close up behind them. As the Confederates reacted, particularly after Lee took command, and summoned Jackson up with his troops from the Shenandoah Valley, McClellan found himself operating off to one side of his chosen axis astride the railway. His troops were at times six or more miles from the railhead, a modest distance. The Army of the Potomac numbered 105,000 men, and 25,000 animals. Six hundred tons of ammunition, food, forage, medical and other supplies had to be forwarded daily from White House to the front. After a short rail journey, supplies were unloaded, without benefit of mechanical handling equipment, on to wagons for onward movement. The roads were few, mere tracks, often running with water acting as channels draining the swampy forest that covered a good part of tidewater Virginia in 1862. When McClellan realised that far from capturing Richmond, he was being outmanoeuvred by Lee and Jackson, and in particular his logistics base at White House was threatened, he decided to shift his base to Harrisons Landing on the James River. He was faced with the problem of moving something in the order of fifty to sixty days rations, about 25,000 tons, to the new location. To his credit, he succeeded but only because the Union Navy had total command of the sea, and the supplies could be taken by water.

The inflexibility of a large army tied to the railway for its supplies is again illustrated by McClellan's situation after the battle of Antietam, when urged by President Lincoln to advance on Lee's lines of communication. If Lee were to disregard this menace, and cut in between McClellan and Washington, Lincoln suggested that the Army

FIG. 2.4   Union logistic base for the Peninsula campaign of 1862 in Virginia
(*Hulton Picture Company*).

of the Potomac could turn around and attack Lee in the rear.[22] Lincoln
had failed to realise that Lee had so disposed himself to take advantage
of such a move, and had further taken the precaution of organising a
secondary line of supply; McClellan had not. Depending on a single
railway, the Manassas Rail Road running south-west from Alexandria,
for his supplies, he could not switch his large army on to a new axis as
easily as his President imagined. Some idea of the measure of

FIG. 2.5   One of the earliest examples of mechanical handling equipment, 35 years after the American Civil War. Steam road transport used by the British in the South African War, 1899–1901 (*Imperial War Museum*).

McClellan's problem can be gauged by the size of his supply trains. In November 1862, the Army of the Potomac was accompanied by 4,818 wagons and ambulances, 8,693 transport horses and 12,483 mules. The supply train of each corps took up eight miles of road, the supply trains of the whole, six corps and one cavalry division, occupied over fifty miles of road.[23] A European general in the same period, faced with this problem could usually resort to marching his corps on separate routes, concentrating when required. The pre-1861 United States occupied an area the size of Europe with a population the size of mid-nineteenth century England. Roads were few, usually no more than tracks, and, even in Northern Virginia, the chances of finding a number of roads running parallel to each other in the desired direction was slight.

In different circumstances, earlier that year, Jackson (like Alexander and Marius centuries before), was able to speed up his rate of advance when moving to destroy the Union supply depot at Manassas, by leaving his baggage and supply wagons behind. Only ammunition and ambulance wagons accompanied his corps. His men carried three days' cooked rations on them, thus dispensing with the need to light fires and risk giving away their presence, and spending time and effort gathering fuel. He marched 62 miles in two days; not for nothing did his men call themselves 'Jackson's foot cavalry'.[24] Hooker, commanding the Army of the Potomac in April 1863, achieved a very fast move by the standards of the time on his march to Chancellorsville to place himself in Lee's rear, in an attempt to bottle him up in Fredericksburg. In three days, three corps, totalling 70,000 men had marched an average of 46 miles over bad roads, forded two chest deep rivers, and built four pontoon bridges. He took only a small number of wagons with him. His soldiers carried sixty rounds of ammunition, and eight days' rations.[25] Some small arms ammunition was carried on pack mules. However, this move, and others during this war with few or no wagons, and sometimes cut off from the line of communication, would have been nugatory if ammunition expenditure had been higher. Even so, some of Hooker's infantry did run out of ammunition.[26]

Frequently, however, the railway layout dictated the axes of advance and retreat, the siting of defensive positions and the locations of battles. One example must suffice. Johnston's strategy and the tactical manner in which he carried it out, as he withdrew in front of Sherman's advance from Chattanooga to Atlanta, was dominated by the railway from Atlanta, which was his lifeline. Although he fought a series of masterly withdrawal battles, he was like a diver on the end of a long air line. He had to react to any threat to cut it. Every time Sherman hooked round one of his blocking positions, Johnston was forced to withdraw to counter the move. Eventually, Hood was brought in to replace Johnston; much to Sherman's publicly expressed relief. Johnston was a canny soldier, whereas Hood, although an almost legendary fighting general, was not overly intelligent and tended towards hot-headedness. However, once Hood was forced back into Atlanta, hot-head or no, he had to react to Sherman's attempts to cut his remaining rail link to the South. When it was cut, Hood abandoned the city.

Whether all those who observed the war, either at first hand, or by studying reports, articles and books, read these pointers correctly is another matter. There is evidence that the Europeans, and the Germans in particular, did not absorb all the evidence. The American historian Jay Luvaas in two papers[27,28] offers some explanations. According to Captain Scheibert, an observer from the Prussian Army, European soldiers, unimpressed by the shambles of the first battle of Bull Run, lost interest in the war quite early on, no doubt imagining that they had nothing to learn from what they perceived as the undisciplined, armed mobs, which at that stage, lacking training, they were. Eventually, the soldiers of both sides were to become as good as any in the world. However, Schiebert, an intelligent and energetic officer, did not lose interest and published a number of accounts on his return to Prussia. He was particularly impressed by the support given to the Union Army by the Union Navy, not only tactically with fire support, but logistically, thereby enabling the Union Army to solve formidable supply problems. His report on how the Union Army railway repair battalions (an American innovation), kept the railways working so efficiently, inspired the Prussians to create a similar Field Railway Section in 1866. He probably saw more fighting than any of the other foreign observers, and his studies were wide ranging, and not confined to the effect of rifled artillery on masonry and iron, on which he had been sent to America to report.

European Reactions

In Germany

The appearance of Schiebert's main work on the American Civil War,[29] in 1874, touched off a train of writing and comment in Germany. There was general agreement with his views, his superiors being particularly impressed by the significance of Northern industry, the role of sea-power, and the new technology.

However, by this time, the Germans had been involved in two major wars of their own, both highly successful from their point of view; the Austro-Prussian war of 1866, and the Franco-Prussian war of 1870. Both were short, the former lasted five weeks, and the latter seven and a half months. Considerable preparation had preceded both campaigns, so different from the American experience. Schiebert had failed to point to any lessons of the Civil War that would benefit the German Army, which in its turn came to the conclusion that they need look no further back than 1866, when, as they saw it, the needle gun, and Moltke's strategy, had revolutionised warfare.[30] Furthermore, the problem that increasingly obsessed the German General Staff, was how to cope with a two front war, highly likely in the future because of the manner in which the major powers in Europe were forming alliances. The recipe for success, they perceived, was thorough preparation, swift mobilisation to beat the enemy to the 'draw', and relentless prosecution of the campaign to break the enemy's will in a series of decisive battles. They had, after all, done just this twice within a period of five years. They saw little to learn from a war which had started with no preparation, and dragged on for four years with dozens of bloody but indecisive engagements. By 1880, the American Civil War was no longer studied in the German War Academy. The energies of the Historical Section of the German General Staff were engaged on producing a multi-volume history of Frederick the Great's campaigns. These, and Napoleon's and, of course, Moltke's, were studied at length by German officers. The battlefields were close at hand, and accessible for staff rides, which were an important ingredient in the education of every German officer who aspired to high rank.

In Belgium

The Germans were not alone in ignoring the American experience. Brialmont, a Belgian engineer and general, paid lip service to the defensive power of trenchworks during the American Civil War in his book on fortifications, devoting most of the contents to analysis of the campaigns of Condé, Turenne, and Frederick the Great. In one chapter, 'The Instances of Fortified Fields in Battle', he does not mention one Civil War battle. His examples were taken from the campaigns of Napoleon or earlier.[31] His recommended system of defence relied on a liberal distribution of forts over the countryside. He was the creator of the Belgian forts of Antwerp, Liege and Namur, which fell quickly in the first few days of war in 1914. The trench systems which soon appeared on the Western Front, and elsewhere, proved more difficult to overcome.

In Britain

The British, along with most others, were dazzled by the Prussian victory over the French, and study of the American Civil War was dropped from the Staff College curriculum. Only with the arrival of Colonel Henderson on the scene, towards the end of the century, was interest rekindled. To begin with, the thrust of Henderson's writing drew parallels between the American Civil War, fought mainly by unprofessional volunteers with a leavening of regulars, and the likely British experience in a future war. He intended his works to provide a practical guide to tactics for the Volunteers, the forerunners of the Territorial Army, so that in the event of war, they would at least be mentally prepared to face an army of better trained continental conscripts. His best known book, *Stonewall Jackson*, continues with this theme, although much wider in scope, and embracing generalship, strategy, campaign history, a treatise on the art of war, in addition to being a biography of Jackson. It remains, to this day, one of the best books on the Civil War. It was widely studied in the British Army, and the consequent resurgence of interest in the Civil War which both it and Henderson's lectures engendered, were to have a perceptible influence on military thought in Britain. There was a snag, Henderson's writings concentrate on the war in Virginia to the exclusion of the campaigns in the West, and on the period leading up to Jackson's death in May 1863. Grant and Sherman get only passing mention, even when the former, although General-in-Chief of Union Armies in all theatres of war, accompanied Meade's Army of the Potomac and directed its efforts for a year, in the very theatre in which Henderson's book is set. Although Henderson advised officers of all ranks to study Grant's campaigns in the Wilderness as they provided a clue to the fighting of the future, particularly as a lesson in how the ability to manoeuvre had turned Lee's entrenchments, the British Army paid more attention to the first half of the American Civil War, the period before the armies started entrenching to offset the increasing firepower of contemporary weapons; the period before the year of grinding battles of attrition that led to Lee's surrender. In any case, the doctrine of the traditional offensive, which played down the employment of trenches, so brilliantly demonstrated by the Prussians, was favoured by the military theorists of the day, and the British were no exception. The short war, fought with great intensity, was the war of the future.

*   *   *

The Austro-Prussian and Franco-Prussian Wars

Before turning to the war which was to overturn so many of the theories held by most armies pre-1914, it is worth glancing at the two wars which so entranced military thinkers, almost to the exclusion of the far longer Civil War which preceded the later of the two by only six years; the Austro-Prussian and Franco-Prussian wars, to see if they contain any logistic pointers to the future. The logistic aspects have already been well covered in van Creveld's superb book, *Supplying War*, and whilst it is not the intention to cover all the same ground, it may be fruitful to look at two particular aspects, the effect of railways on the campaigns, and ammunition expenditure rates.

Both, and particularly the Franco-Prussian war, have been called 'Railway Wars', which conjures up a mental picture of the armies, with their supplies, riding swiftly into battle, fighting, and riding on. But as

FIG. 2.6   As old as antiquity, ox wagon (*IWM*).

we have already seen in North America, railways have a number of shortcomings in war. Soldiers cannot fight from the train; once they detrain, their movement is at a foot pace. The lines, which take a long time to build, may not run in the direction the general would like. Once the railhead is reached, which may be miles from the area of operations, supplies must be transferred to wagons, in those days drawn by horses or mules which consumed forage, and might take days to reach the army, particularly if it was advancing away from the railhead. What the railways were able to provide was a swift means of mobilisation. Napoleon took four months to raise and equip an army in Southern France and move into Italy. In 1866, against the Austrians, the Prussians mobilised 280,000 men and deployed them into the frontier area in under six weeks. There were not enough lines, nor did they run to destinations to fit Moltke's plan, but because it was still quicker to move men by train, he took a risk, which ended in the Prussian Army being split between the westernmost railhead at Zeitz, and the easternmost at Neisse, a distance of 290 miles. Fortunately, the Austrians did not take advantage of this, and through their passive strategy and bad generalship, rather than the brilliance of Moltke, lost the war. In 1870, the Germans deployed 400,000 men in 11 days. By then there were nine lines available to the Germans to move their troops to the French frontier, compared with the three and a half available for use against Austria. As the railway networks within Germany, after 1866, were built with an eye to their usefulness in war, and the French were the likely enemy, the lines ran to where the commanders wished to go, within Germany. Once in France, however, it was a different matter. The French railways did not always run in the direction desired by the Prussians, sometimes they did and sometimes not. This had a considerable effect on the Prussian supply and reinforcement capability. The French railways were just as efficient (according to van Creveld, they were better than the Germans'),[32] but their mobilisation plan was not. The lethargy of the French commanders completed their downfall. Moltke's overall direction was better, he made fewer mistakes. Tactically, the Germans were no better than the French, except perhaps in their use of their mobile, quickfiring, breechloading artillery well forward to neutralise the superiority of the Chassepot rifle. So, although railways speeded up the mobilisation and initial moves of armies, once operations began, the pace at which troops moved, and their method of supply from the railhead was no different from the armies of the past.

The war of 1870 was similar to the wars of the past in another aspect. Despite the greater sophistication of the weaponry, it was still easier to supply the troops with ammunition than to keep them fed. Ammunition formed less than 1 per cent of all supplies. Prussian infantry regiments carried 200 rounds of small arms ammunition per rifle, split between the men and the wagon trains accompanying the regiment (in modern parlance, first line transport). In six months, only fifty-six rounds per rifle were expended, just over half that carried on the man. At the battle of Sedan, the Prussian artillery deployed 606 guns, firing a total of 33,134 rounds, an average of just over fifty-four rounds per gun.[33] To put this in perspective, in one of the night battles in the Falklands campaign in 1982, 30 British guns fired an average of 450 rounds per gun (similar to the daily expenditure in artillery barrages in the First World War), a total of 13,500 rounds, well over a third of the number fired by the whole Prussian army over the same period of time.

*   *   *

August 1914 and A Very Different War

The next war in Europe was to be very different. The German planners considered that, as always, the supply of ammunition would be as nothing compared with food and fodder.[34] This view was also held by the Russians, whose gloomy forecast was that moving fodder for the fifty divisions of cavalry, totalling nearly a million horses, thought necessary in a country so poorly served by roads, would throw such a strain on the railway system as to inhibit the moves of reserves, slow down any offensive and result in the breakdown of the railway system.[35] To begin with, it seemed as if they were right, but although to the end of the war fodder was the major item on the logistic shopping list in terms of tonnage, ammunition resupply soon became more critical.

The Price of A Gamble

In the summer of 1914, the German armies, totalling about 1,485,000 men, were mobilised and deployed on the frontiers of Belgium and France in seventeen days. The Germans had made sparse arrangements to feed the horses, ordering the cavalry commanders to live off the country. As they wheeled through Belgium and Northern France in August, even though some of the grain had conveniently been harvested and was there for the taking, much of it was still green, and the time and effort expended in foraging over a wide area slowed the rate of advance. So critical did the fodder situation become, through lack of proper logistic planning, that, in some cases, their cavalry and artillery horses died early in the campaign and many more were too weak to move fast. The condition of the cavalry horses was not improved by the troopers riding them most of the time on the march. In contrast, the British cavalrymen rested their horses by spending as much time dismounted, leading their horses on foot, as astride them. The German troops, as had been proved so often before, were easier to feed. They lived off the land—in some cases, quite well; and as they advanced, the country they traversed became richer. However, by the time of the battle of the Marne, the German heavy artillery, which was the one arm in which they had a distinct tactical advantage over the French, was no longer able to keep up. The German cavalry horses became so weak that the reconnaissance capability of the advancing armies was severely reduced. In short, the cavalry generally became more of a hindrance than a help. The German planners had taken an enormous gamble. Only the fact that the war had started after the harvest, something they could not possibly have foreseen, saved them from logistic disaster.

Miscalculations Over Ammunition Supply

Although there was no excuse for such off-the-cuff arrangements for food and fodder, after all the problem was as old as warfare itself, there was no precedent for the even more serious matter of ammunition supply. The Germans, like everybody else, had underestimated the rate at which ammunition would be consumed, and underrated the problem of resupplying ammunition to a fast moving army, using a mix of horse-drawn transport and, for the first time in war, trucks powered by the internal combustion engine. Before the war, they had calculated that the consumption of small arms ammunition would be twelve times that of 1870, whereas artillery ammunition would be fired only four times as fast. Based on this, they assumed that the reserves carried by each corps would have to be replenished once only during the campaign. As the troops advanced, they opened the distance from the railheads, and although new railheads were opened up in the wake of the advance, the ammunition had already been dropped off in depots further back. By the battle of the Marne, in which ammunition was expended faster than in the advance, the German armies were at the furthest point from their railheads, and actually beyond the point where it was possible to support a high rate of consumption not only of ammunition, but also of spare parts for guns and other equipment. Although there is no evidence to show that the battle was lost by the Germans because of logistic failures, had they won on the Marne, it would have proved impossible to supply their armies, and the advance would have ground to a halt.[36]

Flawed Planning and Ever-Increasing Problems of Supply

All combatants found that they used their stocks of ammunition about ten times faster than pre-war estimates; particularly artillery ammunition. Home production had to be vastly increased to cope. In the British Army, shortages of ammunition led to the shell scandal of 1915. The blame was laid at the door of the government in power, although it was, of course, the result of flawed planning well before the war, which resulted in the British taking part in a campaign on the mainland of Europe, for which they were not logistically prepared.

As the war in the West became trenchbound, for lack of a means to break the dead-lock, the armies, still relying on the horse for the majority of their transport, quickly consumed all the local fodder, and had to resort to bringing it up over great distances; in the case of the British Army, across the Channel from Britain, although it has to be said that the British led the field in the use of mechanical transport and that their use of horse-drawn wagons decreased as the war progressed. Added to this were engineer stores, such as barbed wire, pickets on which to string the wire, sandbags, duckboards, miles of telephone cable, and timber and girders to revet and roof trenches and dugouts.

FIG. 2.7 First World War, Western Front. Taking water pipes up to the trench system by light railway, near Mametz July 1916, during the Battle of the Somme (*IWM*).

Wells had to be dug to provide water for the millions of men and animals, and piped to distribution points. A ready supply of spares and complete replacements for guns, small arms, the growing fleets of vehicles and aircraft, and by 1916, tanks; and equipment of all types was essential. It was usually no longer possible to make do with captured weapons and equipment, as was the case fifty years before when the Confederate Army could supplement its own inadequate armaments industry at the expense of the Union Army.[37] By the twentieth century, the ammunition and spares used by one side would rarely fit the weapons and equipment of the other. As weapons became more complicated, it took longer to train a man to use them. The sighting arrangements, and fuzing system on artillery pieces could not, for example, be assimilated quickly by artillerymen on the opposing side, let alone the infantry who overran the position.

The Cost of an Artillery War

But by far the most important commodity was ammunition, particularly shells. The mortar and artillery programmes which prepared the way for the assaulting infantryman, supported him on his objective, and pounded enemy assaults and gun areas, consumed

FIG. 2.8   First World War, Western Front. British Royal Engineers building
standard gauge railway at Hesdon. The track advanced a mile a day. Once
the logistic infrastructure for mass armies is in place, it takes time and effort to
move (*IWM*).

bombs and shells voraciously. Even after the arrival of the tank,
artillery and mortar fire was by far the most effective way of dominating
ground, particularly if the terrain or ranges were such that direct fire
weapons could not engage. Despite the myths associated with the
machine gun, artillery and mortar fire caused by far the greater number
of military casualties in the First World War, and in most wars since.[38]
It took weeks, and sometimes months, to stock up for a big offensive.
The huge piles of shells and bombs were difficult to hide and could be
seen on air photographs, signalling the intention of the commander to
the enemy. Once ammunition dumps had been established, the effort
required to move them was equally prodigious. Changing the sector in
which a major push was to be mounted, meant a postponement while
the move which, in its turn, would be seen by the enemy air
reconnaissance, took place.

Once an assault had gone in, and if it penetrated the enemy defences
to an appreciable distance, the leading troops would be out of the range
of their own guns. These, with their ammunition, would have to be
brought forward over ground peppered with shell holes, and covered
with churned-up mud. Without tracked load carriers, which appeared

FIG. 2.9   First World War, Western Front. Smashed German trenches and dugouts near Boesinghe. British working party resting in the foreground—to bring supplies across this was difficult (*IWM*).

FIG. 2.10   First World War, Western Front. Australian mule-drawn transport in difficulties—Potize Farm October 1917 (*IWM*).

FIG. 2.11   First World War, Western Front. Man-handling an 18 pounder
out of mud, Poelcappelle (*IWM*).

only in the British Army, and no other, and then only in the last few
months of the war, the redeployment depended upon horses pulling
guns and limbers, and pack mules, floundering through the morass.
For this reason, attacks were plodding, with long pauses between
phases in order to drag up supplies. As the attack lost momentum, the
enemy falling back on his own logistic dumps and supply system,
operating over largely intact roads and railways, could react, and bite
off salients, often pushing the attacker back.

It was the enormous logistic problem, and the lack of radios to
command large bodies of troops, that gave the First World War on the
Western Front its ponderous look, until Haig's great offensive from
July to November 1918. It was not, as many authors have maintained,
the stupidity of the generals on both sides.

1917 and the Arrival of the AEF

The entry of the United States into the war created a special problem
for the Allies as it soon became obvious that they were not only quite
without any proper system of supply but lacked the guns, tanks and
vehicles that were an inescapable part of war on the Western Front.
The French and British made good these deficiencies, at considerable

FIG. 2.12   First World War, Western Front, Battle of Arras. Re-aligning the trail of an 18 pounder. The ammunition piled on the left is a modest stock, representing a fraction of the requirement for a sustained battle. Moving even this amount for several batteries, over the terrain in the previous pictures is a major undertaking (*IWM*).

cost to themselves. The Americans had not even got draught horses for their new-found artillery and the British gun teams in France were reduced from six horses to four to help meet the requirement. But it was the inadequacy of the American logistic system which was to create the greatest difficulties for the American Expeditionary Force (AEF). In some units in the Argonne, the troops were approaching starvation point before things were put right. It was in no small part due to the Herculean efforts of Brigadier General George Marshall (later to achieve such fame in the Second World War as Chairman of the American Chiefs of Staff) that AEF was finally put on to a sound logistic footing. How, the reader may well be asking himself, was it possible for this almost incredible lack of logistic foresight to have occurred? Quite simply, the answer lay in a political exchange between the British Prime Minister and the President of the United States. Lloyd George, devastated by the loss of infantry on the Western Front, appealed wildly to the President for infantry in the largest numbers he could provide. Thanks to lack of any proper system of liaison between the two armies, it was infantry of which the AEF was chiefly composed. In these days of sophisticated joint-staff planning and high level co-operation between nations in every aspect of military affairs, that such a logistic nightmare should have been created seems almost beyond belief—but so it was—the logistic principles of Foresight and Co-operation had been ignored and the price had to be paid.

March 1918: Ludendorff's Great Spring Offensive

Much is made by some authors of the German offensive of March 1918, particularly the command and control arrangements and the tactics. It is held up as a model in contrast with the admittedly inflexible British system in 1916; ignoring the factors that forced the British to fight in that way at that period in the war. However, in Spring 1918, provided the Allies, kept their nerve, which they did, particularly Haig, the offensive was doomed before the German stormtroopers crossed their start lines. They had few tanks, the majority of even those which they had had been captured from the British, and therefore no spares. In common with their opponents they had no radios, and were consequently beset by all the command problems that had plagued every offensive on the Western Front so far: the difficulty of passing

FIG. 2.13 First World War, Western Front. Without tracked vehicles and unable to operate away from roads—British transport (*IWM*).

information back to the commander; the inability to give fresh orders to meet a changing situation, to reinforce success, and to concentrate follow-up forces for the decisive blow. The Germans were faced with exactly the same logistic conundrum as all other attackers in this theatre of operations, with the added complication that they were advancing first over ground which they had devastated implementing the 'scorched earth' policy during their deliberate withdrawal to the Hindenburg line, and then over the old Somme battlefields. Without tracked transport, able to operate away from the devastated roads, they lacked the means to re-supply their armies at the rate required to maintain momentum. The men could, and did, live off the British supply dumps. But spares, guns, and ammunition could only be provided from their own resources, being left further and further behind. The British, falling back on their own supplies, were getting stronger daily. As the defences firmed up, after the initial shock, a full blooded, co-ordinated assault by the three German armies acting in concert was needed to smash through, and regain momentum. Although there is no documentary evidence that logistics were the overriding factor in Ludendorff's decision to call off the offensive, after an advance of about 40 miles at its furthest point, it is clear that, despite the new flexible tactics, the Germans were technically unable to support such swift progress.

1918: The Hundred Days

It was left to the British to demonstrate how an offensive should be carried out. In the battles of The Hundred Days, starting in August and finishing in November 1918, including breaching the formidable Hindenburg line, the British armies advanced between 60 and 80 miles, capturing more prisoners than the French and American armies combined. Learning the lessons of the past four years, obsolete tanks pulled sledges loaded with supplies, specially designed supply tanks carried supplies in their hulls, and gun tanks moved artillery pieces; all played a vital part in maintaining the momentum of Haig's advance. Even so, had the Germans not sued for an Armistice, a pause would have been necessary—the British armies were outrunning their logistics.[39] However, the penny had dropped, at least in the British Army. Fuller's brilliantly imaginative tank programme for 1919 called for 7,700 fighting tanks and 3,282 administrative tanks.

*   *   *

FIG. 2.14 First World War, Western Front. 'It was left to the British to demonstrate how an offensive should be carried out'. Supply tank at Bucquoy, August 1918 (*IWM*).

FIG. 2.15 First World War, Western Front. Gun-carrying tank (*IWM*).

FIG. 2.16 First World War, Western Front. The price of logistic unpreparedness. British teams reduced from 6 horses to 4 to make up shortages in the United States Army. British ammunition limbers crossing the Canal du Nord 1918 (*IWM*).

At last, with the advent of the vehicle powered by the internal combustion engine, armies had the ability to supply themselves well away from ports and railheads.[40] Before examining how armies made use of this new flexibility in a war of vastly greater scope than that of 1914–18, it is worth glancing at one sideshow in a remote corner, where conditions favoured mobile operations; and where the logistic perception of a junior officer was to have an effect out of all proportion to the size and skill of the force at his disposal; the place, Arabia, then part of the Ottoman Empire, and the force, the Arabs who had rebelled against their colonial masters. The Turks garrisoned Medina in present day Saudi Arabia, at the extremity of the Hejaz railway, 600 miles from Amman. Faced with the prospect of a fruitless assault on the strongly held town, the British Colonel T. E. Lawrence, advised the Emir Faisal leading the Arab forces in rebellion against the Turks, to turn their attention to the Turkish lifeline, and destroy the railway. So successful was this tactic, that 25,000 Turkish troops were pinned down to blockhouses and posts along the railway, and the garrison at Medina totally neutralised. There were to be more, and greater operations of this kind in the Second World War and others that followed.

Conclusion

The First World War was a watershed in military logistics. No longer was it true to say that supply was easier when armies kept on the move, because when they stopped they quickly exhausted food and fodder, fuel for the prime movers and fighting machines, animals and men. From 1914, the reverse applied, the reason; the huge expenditure of ammunition, and the consequent expansion of transport to lift it forward to the consumers; the most voracious being the artillery. A moving army, even with the arrival of the motorised vehicle, was now much more difficult to supply. The resources of industrialised nations could manufacture the massive quantities of material required for modern war in a surprisingly short time. The major problem was maintaining the flow of supplies forward, and this was greatly aggravated when the customers were advancing.

3

Three Campaigns in a Global War: North Africa 1942–43, Italy 1943–45, Burma 1942–45

'During the last world war eighty per cent of our problems were of a logistical nature.'
Attributed to Field Marshal Montgomery

The Second World War of 1939 to 1945 was global, which its predecessor, the Great War of 1914–18, to give it the name by which it was known until followed by a greater, was not. With the exception of minor campaigns in the German African colonies, some inconclusive battles between the German and British fleets in the North Sea, and the U-boat campaign in the North Atlantic, the fighting in the First World War took place in Western and Eastern Europe, albeit involving huge armies in these two theatres, and in Northern Italy, the Dardanelles, the Balkans, and the Near and Middle East. Most of the principal theatres of operations would have been almost as familiar to a soldier of Napoleon's army as they were to the men who found themselves fighting there in the early twentieth century. In the Second World War, the scale and extent of the war was enormous, at its height involving simultaneous campaigns in Russia, North West Europe, the Balkans, Italy, Greece, the Adriatic, South East Asia, the Pacific, and China; earlier campaigns in Norway, France and the Low Countries, Greece, Persia and Iraq, Egypt, Libya and Tunisia, and Sicily having been concluded. There were a number of 'firsts' in the Second World War, some of which had been given a dress rehearsal, or preview, in the previous contest, others were entirely new either in concept, scope, or

51

both. Most significant; the joint, unified Allied command over armies, air forces and navies, reaching down from government to the equivalent of corps and lower. Because so many campaigns started with an amphibious phase, some an ocean away from the home base, the logistic problems were daunting, but gave rise to ingenious solutions, of which the artificial harbours and under-sea fuel pipelines for the Normandy invasion, and the fleet trains and underway replenishment groups, that accompanied the amphibious task forces and carrier battle-groups in the Pacific, are but two examples. As well as ships, craft, and all the means of transport familiar to soldiers of the First World War, men, equipment and supplies were carried into battle in ever increasing numbers on both sides, by gliders and aircraft, imposing yet greater strain on the logistic staffs; often to keep them supplied with the wherewithal to fight and live deep behind enemy lines.

The Role of the Railways

There were, of course, some well tried and tested methods of transport that were as vital in this war as in the past. Railways, for the reason given in the previous chapter, were, and still are, the most efficient way of moving loads on land. To this day the Soviet Army relies heavily on railways for the movement of troops and materiel.[1] But in the 1939–45 War, with the coming of age of air power, railways were subjected to more pressure than ever before. Aircraft were able to reach out beyond the immediate battle area, cross the sea, and interdict rail networks. Britain's rail system had been virtually immune from the pin-prick air raids of the First World War, but in the Second it was a different story. In the autumn and winter of 1940–41, German air raids produced considerable congestion on the railways in Britain. A principal limiting factor in the British war effort during this period, was the inability of the railways to clear the ports. Shipping was held up, and imports severely reduced. The situation was exacerbated by the totally different pattern of traffic, both at the ports, and on the internal transport system, from that for which the railway layout had been designed.[2] Before the Allied invasion of Normandy in June 1944, considerable effort was put into air interdiction of the key junctions on the rail system in France and Belgium, in order to slow down the movement of German formations to meet the Allied threat.[3] Once the invasion started, resistance groups added to the chaos, by sabotaging the rolling stock and lines likely to be used by divisions being switched to reinforce formations attempting to contain the Allied beachheads. Some divisions were held up for days, travelling by road, for lack of flatcars to carry their armoured fighting vehicles, and because the lines were blocked. Travel by rail, in daylight could be a hazardous affair for German troops throughout most of the campaign in north-west Europe; the Allies controlled the skies, their rocket-firing, fighter-ground-attack aircraft were able to roam well behind the German lines, shooting up trains, and destroying track and rolling stock. Because of the air threat, the German railheads had to be sited behind the Loire and Seine, some 125 and 100 miles away from the Allied lodgement area in Normandy.[4]

As we saw in the last chapter, the key to unshackling from the tyranny of the railroads lay in the vehicle powered by the internal combustion engine, and by 1939 the era of the mass mechanised army had almost arrived, but for some, not totally. The German Army started that war with 103 divisions of which only 16 were armoured or mechanised. The remainder marched, and although there were 942 vehicles on the establishment of each infantry division, the bulk of supplies were carried by 1,200 horse-drawn wagons in each division. In this context it is interesting that for operation SEALION, the invasion of Britain, the German army required 4,500 horses to be lifted in the first wave of landing barges.[5] All these motor and horse-drawn vehicles were organic to the divisions for use in the operational area. For movement of supplies in the communication zone, behind corps, there were only three motor transport regiments for the whole army, with a total capacity of 19,500 tons. As an aside, the Allies in North West Europe in 1944, had motor transport with a capacity of 69,400 tons to support 47 divisions, and were still short of lift.[6] Although the Germans were to vastly increase the number of mechanised and armoured divisions and vehicles to service them as the war progressed, they used horse-drawn transport to the very end, which at times was to prove a grave disadvantage, because, as Van Creveld points out:

> 'Instead of being thinly spread over the entire army, Germany's military motor vehicles were concentrated among a small number of units. In effect, this meant that there were two separate forces, one fast and mobile and the other slow and plodding . . . it was imperative to exercise the strictest control over the movements of the infantry formations in order to prevent them from obstructing the supply convoys of the all-important armoured spearheads. It was a nice problem of selecting roads, calculating the time it would take to move along them, and maintaining traffic discipline—in short logistics.'[7]

Few people today realise how dependent the German Army was upon horse-drawn transport. Hitler's failure to build up the necessary capacity to provide the transport essential for mobile warfare was one of the principal reasons for the failure of the German invasion of the Soviet Union (Operation Barbarossa). Not only did the Panzer Groups far outstrip their supporting infantry in the initial thrust into the Russian heartland but, when winter came, something like 1,000 horses a day were lost and had to be replaced. The problems of providing the necessary forage under such conditions are hard to grasp, particularly when you consider the enormous distances involved and the paucity of the available railways. It has not been possible to discuss Operation Barbarossa in this book, for it is a study in itself, but if ever there was a campaign in which the logistic factor overshadowed almost all else, that was it.

In contrast, the British, although possessing a far smaller and less well prepared army in other respects, sent an expeditionary force to France in 1939 that was totally mechanised. Unfortunately, almost all

FIG. 3.1 'The British sent an expeditionary force to France that was totally mechanised'. 1939 photograph of 18 pounder gun and tractor (*IWM*).

the British vehicles were abandoned after the retreat to the Channel Ports in May 1940, and those that escaped destruction in battle, or by the British before they withdrew, fell into the hands of the Germans.

North Africa

A means of augmenting, and in some cases speeding up, movement by rail was, and still is, the use of a sea flank, to shorten the total distance supplies have to be transported by train. This is particularly valuable if the railway is single line for much of its length, or there are choke points at intervals along its route. In this context alone it is interesting to examine the North African campaign in Algeria and Tunisia. However, the campaign is also of interest for other reasons, all of which impinge on logistics; it was the first joint operation carried out by the British and Americans, their first large-scale amphibious operation, and their first airborne operation at more than company strength; in all these areas it was to prove a testing ground for later operations on a considerably vaster scale. When the time came for the Allied convoys to sail from their respective ports in North America and Britain, it was significant that since June 1941 (six months before the United States came into the war), the British had had a movements organisation in Washington, and since September 1941, branches at three ports on each coast. This organisation was responsible not only for shipments of supplies and equipment to the United Kingdom, but to all other theatres of war in which British or Empire troops were involved. In 1942, 2,717,733 deadweight tons of freight were shipped from North America, rising to 3,832,264 deadweight tons in 1943, peaking at 4,302,154 deadweight tons in 1944, and falling only slightly to 4,246,196 deadweight tons in 1945.[8] So, from the start, the movements organisation was integrated at the highest level. The Allied Force Headquarters (AFHQ) came into existence in August 1942, three months before the landings in North Africa. It was decided that the integrated staff sections should be headed by the most experienced officer of either nationality available, and that it should be organised on the United States staff system. Under AFHQ for the operation were the 1st British Army and the United States II Corps.

At that time, Morocco, Algeria, and Tunisia were French colonies, but were not occupied by the Germans. The terrain in which the campaign took place consists of a coastal strip, mountainous country inland, and beyond that, desert. The main roads were metalled but with soft verges, and very slippery in wet weather. The secondary roads were little more than dirt tracks. Hundreds of water courses were crossed by small bridges. In places where these were not strong enough to carry the heavier vehicles, a detour and ford had to be found.

The Assault

Three assault areas were selected and allocated as follows: Casablanca to be the responsibility of American Forces mounted from the

United States direct and designated the Western Task Force; Oran to be assaulted by US forces mounted from the United Kingdom and designated the Centre Task Force; and the assault on Algiers by a combined British/United States task force designated the Eastern Task Force. Airborne operations were planned for Tunis, Sousse, and other key airfields in Tunisia, but for lack of aircraft only a battalion at a time, and only after most of the parachute battalions had arrived by sea following the amphibious assault. In the event, most of the objectives for these airborne operations were subsequently changed in the light of events immediately after the seaborne landings. The planning for the operation was complicated by one special factor upon which much depended: the degree to which the French would resist the landings. Intelligence reports indicated that there was a reasonable chance that resistance would be light. Indeed, it was possible they might welcome the Anglo/American forces. But there was no certainty, and the Allies had to plan on the assumption that the landings would be opposed. To reduce the possibility of resistance, the leading troops to come ashore, were to be American, even on beaches allocated to the British. It was felt that the French, still smarting after the destruction of their ships at Oran in 1940 by the British, might allow feelings of outrage rather than common sense to dictate their actions if they encountered British troops in the first assault waves ashore.

The British logistic staffs had allowed for sufficient supplies to maintain all the troops in the assault for seven days. The first follow-up convoy contained fourteen days' maintenance for all the troops in the theatre, including all those planned to arrive before the second follow-up convoy docked. The first follow-up convoy would also bring fourteen days' reserves to be landed at Bougie and Algiers, and seven days reserves to be landed at Philippeville and Bone. By D + 90 it was planned to have 45 days' reserves for the total force ashore. The troops would land with sufficient rations to last two days in their mess-tins. Thereafter they would be fed on the recently introduced 14 man composite ration. Planning for fuel was equally detailed. A major problem which exercised the logistic staffs during the planning for the operation was the shortage of motor transport (MT) ships. Progressively more and more vehicles were shut out of the first and subsequent convoys. Without vehicles ashore to move supplies, they would remain in the docks or at the railheads. The situation became so bad that the Deputy Director Supplies and Transport 1st Army told the operational staffs that it would be impossible to maintain the force at a greater distance than 100 miles east of Bone until the convoy on D + 32 brought more transport.[9] He was subsequently proved to be right.

FIG. 3.2 'The British Army was still using the old fashioned petrol tins'. Petrol filling depot, Maison Cantoniere, North Africa, February 1943 (*IWM*).

Fortunately there was only light opposition to the seaborne landings, because many basic mistakes were made which slowed down the disembarkation of American vehicles, such as difficulties in finding the drivers in some of the ships, missing ignition keys, and flat batteries. In the ships carrying British vehicles there was no problem with finding keys, because the drivers had been ordered to wire them to the steering wheel. However, this led to many vehicle toolboxes being pilfered, which had an adverse effect on vehicle maintenance for months. At Y Beach, at Oran, an unexpected sand-bar off the beach caused a number of vehicles to drown. The chaos at Y Beach was exacerbated when the heavy swell prompted the Senior Naval Officer to order all craft to use the nearby port of Arzeu. Unfortunately, for lack of a proper transport organisation, and of transport, the docks quickly became congested, and for a while all craft had to be diverted back to the beaches. It is worth glancing at the offload figures achieved on the three Centre Task Force beaches, X, Y and Z, because they show that only an elementary stage had been achieved in landing techniques and considerably more needed to be done in a number of areas, from staff work to the development of suitable ships and craft, before undertaking an assault against serious opposition. In six days Z Beach achieved an offload of 11,245 deadweight tons, Y Beach achieved 1,204 deadweight tons over the same period, while X Beach managed only 429 deadweight tons, albeit in four days; the total offload rate over the three beaches averaging 2,182.09 tons per day. On the first six days of the Normandy campaign, before the artificial Mulberry harbours at Port en Bessin, and Courseulles were functioning, an average of 5,871 deadweight tons were landed over the three British beaches, a testament to the progress made in the eighteen months between the two operations.[10]

The landings on the three eastern beaches, code named, Apples, Beer, and Charlie, with the aim of seizing the port of Algiers, undamaged if possible, were successful. Within eighteen hours of the first craft touching down, the fighting was over, and Algiers was entered at dawn the next morning. Again, it was fortunate that the French had been disinclined to offer much resistance, because the combat team tasked to assault Beer Beach, actually landed at Apples Beach. The first man to arrive on Beer Beach was the officer responsible for movement control, not usually in the first wave of craft! He had landed miles away, and, having called in at Apples Beach to get his bearings, walked to Beer Beach; followed three hours later by his assistant and the beach group who had done likewise. The confusion on this beach was made worse by a request to give 'absolute priority to the offload of artillery and anti-tank guns'. This delayed the unloading of all ships, without speeding up the landing of 'the absolute priority equipments'; the usual consequence of tinkering with the unloading sequence at the last minute. Fortunately, the only opposition on this beach was a large crowd of enthusiastic spectators, whose misdirected efforts at assistance hindered the task of developing and improving beach exits.

The Germans React

The German reaction to the landings was, as always, rapid. The first manifestation was the bombing of Allied shipping in Algiers bay, soon after they had sailed in early on D+1. The Headquarters ship of the Eastern Task Force was one of the few that entered the port that day, because worsening weather kept the majority of shipping out in the bay. Landing craft were unable to reach them because of the sea state, so unloading was delayed until the following day when the weather moderated. By now it was critical to get aviation fuel to the fighters which had flown into Maison Blanche airfield from Gibraltar; without it, there would be no fighter cover over Algiers bay and harbour. Eventually 100 tons of fuel were delivered by the afternoon of D + 2.[11] German countermoves were not limited to air attacks. The Allies had hoped that with the impending surrender of all French Forces in North Africa becoming increasingly likely, the whole of French North Africa from Casablanca to Tunis would come under Allied control. They hoped in vain. As the British 8th Army, fighting a thousand miles to the east, could have told the Allied Force Headquarters, if they had asked, that however empty of Germans and peaceful the scene appeared to be, if they were touched in an area important to them, their response was swift and violent. They immediately flew troops into Tunis and Bizerta in an attempt to forestall the French defecting to the Allies.[12] This move on the part of the Germans transformed the campaign from virtually a picnic to a tough six month long contest in the rain, mud, and mountains of Tunisia.

Opening the Ports

To counter the Germans, it was decided to move the British 78th Division east into Tunisia with all speed, starting on 11 November (D + 3). This had an immediate effect on the unloading of supplies at Algiers. Two platoons of transport vehicles already working in the docks, were re-allocated to 78th Division to assist with their move. The only replacements available were French commercial chain driven, charcoal burning trucks. They continually broke down, and were highly dangerous working among stacks of fuel and ammunition because they showered red hot sparks indiscriminately. More serious was the limitation imposed on the maintenance and reinforcement of 78th Division by the distance from Algiers and the single railway line that ran east into Tunisia. Plans had already been made to sieze the port of Bougie, 150 miles east of Algiers on 11 November. But this was not nearly far enough to the east to take the pressure off the railway. So General Anderson, commanding British 1st Army, who was responsible for this phase of the operation, decided to open the port of Bone. On 12 November, a combined assault by British commandos and US Rangers, landing from two destroyers, and a British parachute battalion, dropping on the airfield, took Bone without any trouble, forestalling a German parachute operation planned for the same day.

The opening of Bone, and subsequently Philippeville, made a vital

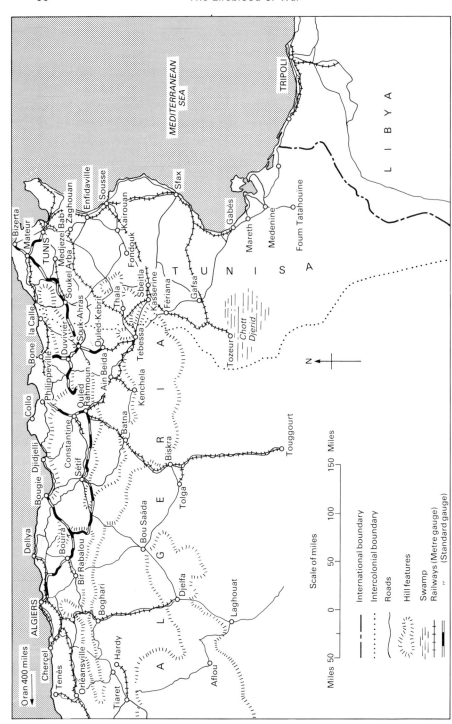

MAP I   North Africa 1942–43.

difference to the future support of the campaign in Tunisia by relieving the single railway from Algiers of thousands of tons of supplies daily. To begin with, and until fighters were deployed forward to the airfields at Bone, and Djidjelli (40 miles from Bougie), the Germans were able to bomb the ports at Bougie and Bone with impunity. In two days, they succeeded in sinking five allied ships at Bougie and slowing down unloading at both. The forward basing of fighters had to await the landing of aviation fuel and ammunition, and at Bone, pierced steel planking and engineer work, in addition to resurface the runway.

Operations Ashore: The Race is Lost

However, despite all their efforts, the Allies failed in the race to build up sufficient force in Tunisia to eject the Germans while they were still weak in numbers. Although elements of British 78th Division, British 1st Parachute Brigade, and US II Corps, all under British V Corps, got within sight of Tunis, they came up against increasing German resistance, as the latter brought a stream of reinforcements to Tunis and Bizerta by air. This German deployment was neither prevented nor interfered with by the French troops in Tunisia. The Germans, able to reinforce their airforce from Sicily, Sardinia and Italy, based fighters and tactical bombers at Tunis, Bizerta, and at some forward strips. They brought over the FW 190 fighter, superior to any Allied fighter at the time, except the Spitfire Mark IX and the Mustang Mark II. Their aircraft operated in support of their own ground troops, in stark contrast to the Allied ground troops, who, fighting at the extreme range of their own air cover, were hard pressed to hold their positions with inadequate air support. All the lessons learned in the Western Desert about army/air force co-operation were ignored from Allied Force Headquarters downwards, and were painfully relearned. V Corps was stopped, pushed back, and soon found themselves fighting a defensive battle.

Some Reasons

Among the reasons for failure were insufficient ground and air forces, inadequate transport,[13] and bad weather. One of the main causes was the problem of supporting a very rapid advance over a long line of communication. Units constantly outran the ability of the logisticians to supply them. Tunis is 600 miles from Algiers, the British base, and nearly 1,000 miles from Oran, the American base. It is worth looking at the lines of communication in some detail. As in the Western Desert, and later in Italy, the advance was made with one flank resting on the coast, with the advantage this gave to the side that controlled the sea. The coastal sea route was set up from Algiers to Bone, with intermediate ports at Bougie and Philippeville. A single standard gauge railway ran eastwards from Algiers through Sétif, Ouled Rahmoun (a few miles south-east of Constantine), Duvivier and Souk Ahras into northern Tunisia, with branch lines leading in from the ports at Bougie, Philippeville and Bone. This standard gauge line was supplemented by a metre gauge line running south-east from Ouled Rahmoun through Tebessa into Southern Tunisia. Tebessa was also connected by metre gauge with the main line at Ouled Kebrit, south of Souk Ahras. The only other metre gauge line of any importance was that running east from Bone to La Calle.

A single main road ran for most of its length, roughly parallel to the standard gauge railway and also to the metre gauge lines to Tebessa from Ouled Rahmoun and Ouled Kebrit. This road, which, on average, was about 50 miles from the coast, had access roads to the ports. The coast road from Algiers, through Bougie, Djidjelli and Philippeville was totally unsuitable as an alternative to the main road. The mountainous section west of Bougie was bad enough, but there was a thirty mile stretch between Bougie and Philippeville consisting of continuous hair-pin bends and numerous tunnels. This made it totally impossible for two-way military traffic, and nearly so for one-way heavy vehicles.

The Impact of Geography on Logistics

Both the railway and main road climbed from sea-level east of Algiers to over 4,000 feet at Sétif, and after travelling over the plateau to Constantine, ran through the mountains for at least half the way into Tunisia, until descending to the Tunisian plain. The main airfields east of Algiers were in the Constantine area, which was the advanced logistic base for 1st Army. Except for these airfields, Tebessa and another east of Bone, there were no suitable strips for air supply using the aircraft of the period, until the Plain of Tunis was reached. The terrrain was far too mountainous for airfield construction. Geography dictated the single sea route, single rail route, single road route, and a lack of airstrips in the area where most of the fighting was to take place. Similarly, geography restricted the forward basing of Allied fighters. The Germans near their bases in Tunis and Bizerta, holding the plain, with numerous airstrips, were in a very strong position both tactically and logistically.

Geography also limited the capability of the ports. Algiers was the only suitable base for the British 1st Army, because of its size and relative freedom from air and submarine attack. It was also large enough to be used as a holding base for American supplies. The restricted capacity and length of the rail and road line of communication from Algiers to the east made it imperative to establish forward ports to supply British and United States forces. Bougie was unsuitable, it was small, and its railway led straight on to the single line between Algiers and Sétif, whose capacity was already being fully used. Philippeville was also very small, and the depth of water alongside the wharves restricted the draught of ships to 21 feet. So, unless ships from America and Britain were specially lightly loaded, shipping using Philippeville was restricted to coasters loaded locally at Algiers, Oran, and Casablanca. Philippeville did however have good rail communications with Constantine, which did not seriously conflict with the main eastward flow to the front. Bone was a good, medium sized port, near to the front line, with good rail communications south to join the main line at Duvivier. From here the rail was restricted, but it was immaterial whether the traffic originated from Bone or ports to the west. However, both Bone and Philippeville were vulnerable to air attack from airfields in Tunisia or across the Mediterranean.

Problems of Rail Capacity

Apart from geography, there was insufficient rolling stock to make full use of the limited capacity of the railway line. Much of it was in a bad state of repair. The shortages were aggravated as more and more American units became involved in the battle, and their supplies were hauled from bases as far away as Casablanca, 1,235 miles from Constantine. Big distances made great demands on locomotives and vastly increased the turnround time of scarce wagons. In addition, there were problems of coal shortages and a lack of trained operators. Locomotives, wagons, coal, and railway units were to take weeks to reach North Africa from Britain and the United States, even though called forward as soon as the problem had been recognised. Fortunately, two months before the first landing, the British transportation staffs had asked the Americans to demand 250 locomotives and 5,000 wagons in order that production in the States could be geared up. They had worked on the assumption that half the total locomotives in

French North Africa would have been sabotaged beyond repair. Their fears were groundless in that respect, but the state of the railways was far worse in terms of serviceability than the intelligence reports had suggested. Thanks to keen foresight, the transportation staffs had taken the precaution of having some coal brought in early to Algiers, and a further 8,000 tons on each fourteen day convoy which was to prove invaluable. In the early days of the campaign, German fighters strafed the trains running on the narrow gauge lines from Bone to La Calle and Ouled Rahmoun to Tebessa. This led to British Railway Operating companies of the Royal Engineers taking over the running of trains on these lines, as well as on some other sectors.

The Impact of Port and Rail Restrictions on Operations

In the first two months of the campaign, the capacities of the ports and railways were to impose limitations on the conduct of operations by 1st Army. Algiers had berths for 18 motor-transport or stores ships available for military use, but its capacity was limited to about 3,500 tons per day because of a shortage of trucks, cranes, and wagons to clear the port. The port had much greater potential, but there was little hope of improvement in the near future. Bougie was clearing 1,200 tons a day, but could get little of this forward because of the rail bottleneck. Philippeville was clearing 1,100 tons a day. It had a potential of at least double this figure, but finding enough shipping of the right draught was the limiting factor. Bone, with half its berths out of action through bomb damage, and frequent interruptions from air raids, was handling only 2,500 tons a day. Three months later, it was clearing between 4,000 and 5,000 tons a day.

Rail capacity east of Algiers during the first two months of the campaign was limited to seven or eight trains a day. Of these, five with a load of 250 tons each (1,250 tons total), could be loaded with supplies. The balance were used for moving troops and tracked vehicles. Forward of Duvivier the limit was also 1,250 tons a day, and this was, therefore, the maximum that could be delivered to corps railheads in Tunisia from Bone and the other ports. The narrow gauge from Ouled Rahmoun to Tebessa was capable of carrying between 750 and 1,000 tons a day, and could be fed by road and normal gauge railway from Philippeville. Road, narrow gauge railway, and coastal water transport, such as tank landing craft and local craft, could take another 500 tons a day from Bone to La Calle and beyond.[14] The totals lifted forward were short of requirement by 250 tons a day, even though the

II US Corps was well below strength until well into January 1943 and equivalent to little more than one division. Throughout this period, and well into 1943, the capacity of the ports far outstripped that of roads and railways to shift supplies forward, by about a factor of two-and-a-half times. The shortfall of fuel and artillery ammunition were acute at times, and the build-up forward, particularly of American formations, was delayed accordingly.

Problems of Command and Control

The original intention had been that the push into Tunisia should be an entirely British show, with the American forces garrisoning Algeria. However, as V Corps became more hard pressed by the Germans, who attacked aggressively and with great skill, they demanded more units to hold the wide frontage, and air support to assist. The response was to move more American ground and air forces into Eastern Algeria and Tunisia. At first these consisted of individual units, particularly artillery, but later complete combat teams (the equivalent of British brigades). The movement and supply of the United States elements, who came under command of British 1st Army, posed a considerable problem, which the United States liaison staff at 1st Army were not organised to solve. An *ad hoc* arrangement was set up on the orders of the US Deputy C-in-C to the Supreme Commander, but this was not up to the task either. The confusion was increased by 1st Army Headquarters being split three ways, with Main Headquarters at Constantine, Rear Headquarters at Maison Carrée, ten miles outside Algiers, and the movements staff remaining in Algiers, where they were in a better position to supervise the railways and shipping. 1st Army movement was, therefore, controlled from three places at once, with indifferent communications. The situation was aggravated further by Allied Force Headquarters (AFHQ) being split four ways. The US Deputy C-in-C was based in Algiers, but not near Rear Headquarters 1st Army. The command post, including General Eisenhower, the Supreme Commander, was in Gibraltar. The main body, including the Chief Administrative Officer, the British Major General Humfrey Gale, of whom more later, was in London. The British General Headquarters contingent for AFHQ was at Maison Carrée with Rear Headquarters 1st Army. Operations and logistics had now become an Allied matter, but the Allied headquarters whose responsibility these were, was in no position to do anything constructive about either, particularly the latter.

While the operational staff of 1st Army at Constantine was immersed in the details of the battle in Tunisia, its administrative staff at Maison Carrée was equally immersed in the problems of Allied logistics. The tasks were inevitably contradictory at times, and the operational staffs ordered moves which were not under the proper control of the logisticians. The same applied to supplies. No sooner was order beginning to appear, than 1st Army suffered reverses in Tunisia, which led to demands for reinforcements, ammunition, and fuel, particularly aviation fuel. The climax was reached when orders came from 1st Army that absolute priority was to be given to 25-pounder gun ammunition, and that until further notice nothing else was to be discharged from ships, moved or unloaded from wagons. The situation off Algiers on D-day was repeated on a vastly greater scale. Ships not unloading 25-pounder ammunition remained full, wagons in transit were uncoupled and left, the whole line of communication became slowly paralysed. Senior officers descended unannounced on ports and railway yards, demanding the reason why a ship or wagon not carrying 25-pounder ammunition was being unloaded or moved. A railway transport officer at Duvivier was ordered to rejoin his regiment for disobeying the absolute priority order. Chaos reigned which affected not only the British, but also the American ground and air forces in the forward area.

Control Restored

Fortunately, a firm hand was about to grasp the logistics helm. Major General Gale, Eisenhower's Chief Administrative Officer, arrived in Algiers in early December, and although AFHQ were not planned to take overall command untl 1 January 1943, Gale saw that the crisis was too serious to be ignored, stepped in and ordered that his staff take action to put matters right.

Immediately they ordered that every wagon was to be unloaded when it reached the railhead, irrespective of its contents and for whom the load was intended. Every ship was to be unloaded likewise and without regard for the priority of its cargo. No wagons were to be loaded at the base for four days, and all loaded wagons were to be sent to their destination railhead as soon as possible. It was expected that the four day embargo would have to be extended, but, in the event, it proved unnecessary thanks to the hard work of all the staffs concerned. The logistic staff of AFHQ, under the direction of Gale, had taken control not a moment too soon. This breakdown in logistics was not the sole contributor to the failure to take Tunisia 'on the run', indeed by the time the crisis came to a head, it was already too late. Tunisia could only have been taken quickly had a number of events gone differently, among them: perhaps bolder use of airborne and commando forces to sieze the key airfields and deny them to the Germans; slower reaction by the Germans; better weather; quicker and more positive action by the French. The breakdown demonstrated that considerable logistical reorganisation was required for the large scale offensive that would now be necessary to dislodge the Germans.

*   *   *

In January and February, the Allied fighting units held the line in the appalling weather in the mountains. The Allied airforces operating from weatherbound strips in the mountainous country could not compete with the Germans using dry airfields on the Plain of Tunis. Some reverses were suffered, and the better formations, such as the British 1st Parachute Brigade and 1st Guards Brigade, found themselves being rushed to plug gaps, or shore up their weaker brethren. Meanwhile, the reorganisation and redeployment of the Allied forces in North Africa went ahead. It was clear that the final assault on Tunis would be a combined effort by Allied forces in North Africa and 8th Army who were approaching from Tripolitania. Headquarters 18th Army Group was set up to command 1st and 8th Armies. But it was realised, that with entirely independent bases and lines of communications, one stretching back to Algiers, the other to Tripoli and beyond, the Army Group headquarters could not hope to be responsible for the logistics of both armies, and therefore it was not attempted. This account follows suit, and is restricted to the logistics of the Allied Forces in Algeria and Tunisia.

Stabilising Measures and a Near Disaster

As well as reorganisation, a certain amount of 'logistic education' was also put in train by Gale to promote the principle of economy. He wanted to cut down on wasteful overbidding and pilfering, both of which were eating into the reserves he was trying to build up for the forthcoming offensive. He and his staff were highly successful, but they found some appalling cases of waste. He also found that merging the American and British staff system had its frustrating moments.[15]

By February, not only had work been carried out to improve some of the roads, but the American locomotives and wagons ordered before the campaign had started to arrive at Oran. Their move forward into

Eastern Algeria, eased the load on the overworked and poorly maintained French rolling stock. British and American railway operating units took over complete sections of the lines, and British railway construction units were responsible for much of the repair and refurbishment of the tracks, and for laying some new track. They also had to repair bridges. Towards the end of 1942, the Germans had mounted a series of raids to destroy the bridges on the metre gauge line south and east of Tebessa. The technique was for the raiding party to land by moonlight in a light aircraft near the chosen target, disperse the Arab guards, blow the bridge, and take off. Attempts by small parties of German paratroops dropped near several bridges on the main line east of Algiers, were beaten off by police and local guards. Although it was not realised at the time, these raids were probably in preparation for their push up the Kasserine pass. When the push came, it was a near disaster. The Germans broke through the United States II Corps, and almost reached the key supply centre of Tebessa. This failure had been caused, in part at least, by the way in which formations and nationalities had been deployed piecemeal by General Anderson, the 1st Army commander.

Reorganisation

The outcome, after the push had been halted, was, however, an improvement in two key aspects. The commander of the US II Corps was replaced by the dynamic Patton, and 18 Army Group tidied up the patchwork troop deployment, concentrating British 1st Army in northern Tunisia, and the United States II Corps in southern Tunisia. The new deployment allowed the logistic chain to be simplified; the British Line of Communication now ran from Algiers and Bone to Souk Ahras and thence eastwards; while the American Line of Communication ran from Oran and Philippeville through Constantine and Tebessa.

A New Spoke in the Logistic Wheel: The Build-Up for HUSKY

In early January 1943, the logistic situation had been aggravated by the decision of the Combined Chiefs of Staff at their meeting at Casablanca, presided over by Roosevelt and Churchill, to mount the invasion of Sicily (codename HUSKY), as quickly as possible after the end of the Tunisian campaign. The Allied armies in North Africa, both 1st, 8th and the Americans would provide the majority of the force for

HUSKY, and these, augmented by formations from Britain and the United States, would mount from ports and airfields in Algeria and Tunisia. Late June was chosen as the period in which D-day for HUSKY would be selected, provided that the Tunisian campaign was finished by the end of April. Experience gained in the North African campaign showed the need to start planning for a major combined operation at least four months ahead; planning for HUSKY should start at once. Furthermore, the shipping of stores, supplies, equipment, and additional formations to North Africa in preparation for HUSKY would have to be done while the Tunisian campaign was still being fought. AFHQ was tasked with overall co-ordination of the planning for HUSKY, an additional burden for the logisticians. But, in material terms, the principal effect was the congestion in the ports as the HUSKY equipment and stores started flooding in, while the logistic staffs were wrestling with the problem of trying to achieve the fastest possible building up of formations and supplies for the final battles in Tunisia.

The ships carrying the transport and equipment of British formations for the Tunisian campaign were unloaded at Algiers, Bone or Philippeville, as many as possible to the latter two to reduce the distance from the Front. But the bigger, faster ships carrying the troops could not go east of Algiers because of the German air threat. To relieve the strain on the railways, and because there were insufficient troop-carrying trucks, the troops were sent forward in four small, fast assault ships, which became known as the 'moonlight ferry', because they steamed most of the dangerous part of the route in darkness. By the end of March, they had moved 45,000 men without a single casualty. Most of the wheeled vehicles were driven from the port to the area where they married up with their units, but tracked vehicles travelled on rail flat cars to save track life. By the end of March, British 1st Army had been built up to two British Corps, V which had been in Tunisia from the outset, and IX. At the same time the United States II Corps was built up to full strength with three divisions.

Preparations for the Final Push

By March 1943, the improved road and rail communications allowed the full offload capacity of Bone and Philippeville to be moved forward. By the middle of April, there were over 100,000 tons of British and American reserves on the ground for the final push on Tunis and Bizerta, and these had been accumulated in seven weeks during which 'the daily maintenance demand had averaged between 5,500 and 6,000 tons a day.[16] This was a considerable achievement when it is remembered that in early April, 18 Army Group switched its American II Corps from the area south-east of Tebessa, north to the Bone-Bizerta axis, on the left of British 1st Army. The Americans were no longer needed in the south because Montgomery had now closed up to Fondouk and Kairouan. This not only necessitated the move of the United States II Corps across 1st Army's main supply route, but also a change of Line of Communication for the Corps. Instead of running from Constantine through Tebessa and forward, it ran direct from the port of Bone, but because some supplies still came on their old route to Constantine, these were taken by rail via Bone and thence forward.

During April, the lift using the sea flank was further increased. Locally requisitioned vessels from 10 to 60 tons capacity, operated by British Army crews, sailed from La Calle to the roadhead at Tabarka. They lifted 1,300 tons of supplies, including POL and ammunition, helping to relieve the transport on a bad stretch of road. The logistic build-up for the final battle was completed in time. The only major worry with which the logistic staffs had to contend, was a shortfall of 400,000 gallons of petrol, oil and lubricants delivered at railheads in the last week. At the same time consumption had increased by 600,000 gallons because of intensified air operations. The French railway stock was starting to crack under the strain. Eventually, a special train carrying aviation fuel was sent forward to Souk el Arba where it was met by queues of RAF and USAAF trucks from airfields all over Tunisia.

THE ADVANCE INTO ITALY

The Allies entered Tunis and Bizerta on 7 May 1943, bringing to an end the North African campaign. Their quarter of a million prisoners included 150,000 Germans, many more than were captured at Stalingrad. The next items on the agenda for those logisticians who until then had been fully occupied with events in North Africa, were the campaigns in Sicily and Italy. Space does not allow a detailed examination of these. But because the North African campaign had some logistical parallels with the Italian campaign, it is worth a passing glance at the latter. In Italy, as in North Africa, geography played a major part in the pattern of logistics. The Apennines severely restrict communications between the east and west coasts, and between the southern half of Italy and the Po valley. To begin with, the railways worked efficiently, but the familiar problem of worn out and defective locomotives soon reared its head. This was aggravated by the comprehensive destruction wrought by the Germans in the course of their slow withdrawal north; with extensive damage to railway bridges and tunnels. Only the west coast ports were damaged, mainly Naples, Civitavecchia, Leghorn and Genoa. However, congestion at all ports was experienced when the railways could not cope with clearing the offloaded stocks. As in North Africa, there was a major distraction caused by mounting another operation from an area in which a campaign was already underway. In the case of Italy, the other operation was DRAGOON, the invasion of southern France by an American and a French army.

The Dividend of Experience

Supply to the airforces was again to add to the logistic burden. But in Italy, in addition to the supply of tactical airforces, the logisticians had to cope with the stores, ammunition and fuel requirements of the Mediterranean Allied Strategic Air Force (MASAF), on the Foggia airfields. The MASAF was not in Italy to support the Allied Armies, but to bomb targets as far afield as southern Germany and Romania. They imposed a great strain on the logistic assets of 8th Army, requiring almost the same supply tonnage as the whole of that Army. Montgomery severely criticised the theatre logistic plan for Italy; a major factor in the failure of the Allies to capture Rome in 1943. This arose because there was no coherent Allied strategy for this campaign; hence the impossibility of formulating a proper, high level logistical plan. The situation was exacerbated when landing craft, and troops were withdrawn for the Normandy landings. However, despite the difficulties, the logistic staffs, with the North African and desert experience behind them, were able to cope, as they demonstrated when required to move two corps of 8th Army across the Apennines in August 1944. In fifteen days, five infantry divisions, two armoured divisions, one armoured brigade, two tank brigades, one independent brigade, one army group Royal Artillery, and two corps headquarters with corps troops, totalling about 80,000 vehicles, were moved over two mountain roads, each of which was mainly one-way.

The Role of the Sea Flanks

As in North Africa, the sea flanks played an important part in the Italian campaign, logistically as well as tactically. But there were more

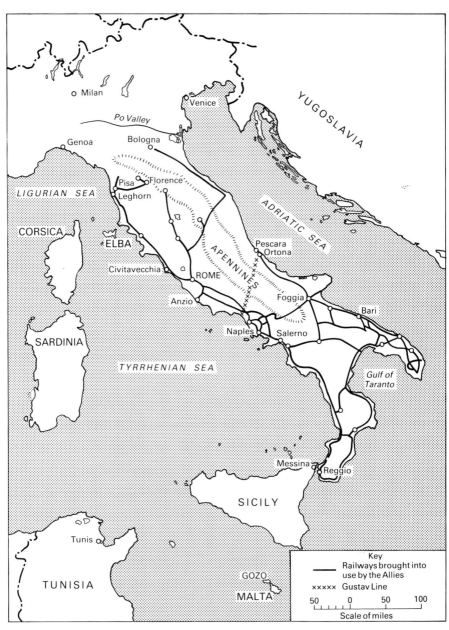

MAP II　Italy 1943–45.

small ports in Italy, and better, purpose-built shipping was now available. There was no need for a regular road line of communication between Naples and Bari and the 5th and 8th Armies forward of these ports. Coastal shipping with a vastly greater carrying capacity was

FIG. 3.3   DUKWs ferrying guns, stores and troops ashore. Anzio, January 1944 (*IWM*).

used, as was the railway. Although, on one occasion, the bridges on a section of the east coast line were washed away, necessitating truck companies ferrying 2,500 tons a day across a sixteen mile gap. As the Allies advanced, the damage to the railways referred to earlier, was increasingly extensive, so that by summer 1944, for example, 8th Army was 200 miles in advance of its railhead. During the Anzio battle, a ferry service by 40 landing ships (tank) (LST), and a mix of 1,700 3-ton and 10-ton trucks ran from Naples to the beachhead. Every day, 300 trucks were loaded into LSTs, 50 to each ship. The loads carried in the trucks was divided 60 per cent ammunition and 20 per cent supplies and POL. The trucks were driven straight off the ships at Anzio, unloaded, and returned empty in the LSTs.[17]

The Armies also reverted to a form of transport, that would have been familiar to armies of antiquity; pack mules. In bad weather in the mountains, they were the only form of transport to cope. Pack transport companies were hastily formed and trained to augment the few that existed. To begin with, their efficiency was greatly impaired by mistakes made by the novice drivers and officers. The art of pack mule driving and maintenance was not a skill that could be acquired in a few weeks training. Such bad habits as loading mules too early before starting the march, failure to offload at halts of more than half an hour, overloading, and unbalanced loading caused sore backs. To compound the problem there was a world shortage of mules.

Attacking the Enemy's Supply Lines

The Allies also attempted to interdict the German supply lines by air attack. For example by the end of March 1944, the Tactical Air Forces were causing an average of 25 cuts a day in the enemy's railways. By May this figure had risen to 71 a day. However valuable these, and attacks on marshalling yards, locomotive repair sheds and motor transport convoys were in the short term in assisting the Allied offensive (codename DIADEM) which finally breached the Gustav Line south of Rome, there were significant portents for the future in the assessment made by Air Marshal Slessor's reports on the results. Slessor, the C-in-C RAF Mediterranean and Middle East, having described how the almost unremitting interdiction was maintained, says:

'On the whole, it is probable that the Germans suffered no serious shortages during the static phase.' (*i.e. before DIADEM*).

After commenting on the serious effect the Italian winter weather had on flying operations, he continues thus:

'But apart from that, I personally underrated the unsurpassed capacity of the Hun's Q staff to keep him supplied in apparently impossible conditions. Since March 24, every single railway behind the enemy front has been cut and kept cut in several places between the front and the Pisa-Rimini line, and at the same time we have delivered a number of really heavy blows at the great marshalling yards, with their loco sheds and repair facilities, in the north. At the same time, in the month of February, we know we destroyed between eight and nine hundred MT vehicles, and in March probably more than half that number . . . We have not yet succeeded in making him pull out, and I don't think we will by air action alone: what we have done, I think, is to make it impossible for him to resist successfully a determined and sustained offensive by the ground forces.'

In June 1944, Slessor crystallised his views in an Appreciation on Air Power given to the American Generals Marshall and Arnold when they visited him:

'It may clear the issue to mention first the things that air-power cannot be expected to do in a land campaign of this nature:

(a) It cannot by itself defeat a highly organised and disciplined army, even when that army is virtually without air support of its own . . .

(b) It cannot by itself enforce a withdrawal by drying up the flow of essential supplies. The German's efficient Q organisation, his policy of living off the country regardless of the interests of the inhabitants, and his extreme frugality and hardiness, result in an unsurpassed capacity to maintain his stocks in apparently impossible circumstances at the essential minimum in circumstances where he is not being forced to expend ammunition, fuel, vehicles, engineer stores etc. at a high rate.

(c) It cannot entirely prevent the movement of strategic reserves to the battlefront, of tactical reserves from one part of the front to another, or of forward troops to fresh positions in rear.

(d) *In short, it cannot absolutely isolate the battlefield from enemy supply or reinforcement.*'[18] (Author's italics)

The battles in Normandy, which were then reaching their height, were to show both the enormous dividends to be gained by the correct application of air power on the enemy lines of communication, and the limitations pointed out by Slessor. His 'wise words', as Terraine has called them, could have been heeded with advantage by the possessors of overwhelming air superiority fighting two other wars, Korea and Vietnam, respectively six and twenty years later.

*　　　*　　　*

THE WAR IN SOUTH-EAST ASIA: BURMA

If the war in the Mediterranean was difficult logistically, that in South-East Asia was infinitely more so. Indeed it is hard to find any other theatre of the war which posed so many logistic conundrums or where supply played such a dominating part in deciding the outcome, on both sides. Before discussing the campaign, it is necessary to look at the overall strategic picture of the war against Japan, jumping ahead of the narrative to do so, because the decisions, and in one case indecision, of the Combined Chiefs of Staff on the part of the British were to play in the strategy to defeat Japan, were to impinge on logistics.

At the May 1943 TRIDENT conference in Washington, the Combined Chiefs of Staff instructed the Combined Joint Planning

Staffs to prepare an appreciation leading up to a plan for the defeat of Japan, including an estimate of the forces required for its implementation. From the start, the plan produced by the staffs covered the whole field of the Japanese war, a battlefield stretching from the Aleutians to Australia, from the Andamans to Honolulu. The plan that emerged, although altered in detail, was to form the basis of the strategy to the end of the war. It envisaged the advance of the main American forces across the Pacific through the Gilberts, Marshalls and Carolines, and then, either north or south of the Philippines to Formosa and Japan. A co-ordinated British advance from the West was to take place via Burma and Malaya. However, at a number of stages in the planning, major alterations to this strategy were mooted. In discussing the subject of planning at the highest, that is Combined Chiefs of Staff, level, it must be borne in mind that, although we now know that the war in Japan ended, because of the use of the atomic bomb, in August 1945, this was by no means the anticipated finishing date. Indeed at the QUADRANT conference in August 1943, the date set for the invasion of Japan was the summer of 1946 at the earliest, the summer of 1947 being more probable. The war ended before two vast amphibious operations, and two potentially protracted land campaigns, Malaya and mainland Japan, could be carried out.

The Strategic Debate: A Conflict of Views

In the initial planning there was a difference of opinion between the British and the Americans on the scale of support to the Chinese forces. While the British appreciated the need to keep the Chinese in the war in order to tie down large numbers of Japanese troops, there was disagreement on the practicability of organising, training and equipping the Chinese in time for them to play a major part before the war ended. The Americans, however, pressed the British to adopt a strategy that would include opening a land line of communication to China, because clearly there was no chance of using ports on the Chinese mainland in the timescale envisaged for the prosecution of the war against Japan. To open the old Burma Road would require the capture of Rangoon, the clearance of most of Burma, re-opening rail and river communications from Rangoon to Lashio, and rebuilding the road from Lashio to Kunming which had been blown at various points by the Chinese to deny it to the Japanese. The alternative was to build a road and a pipeline from Ledo, at the end of the Bengal-Assam railway, to Myitkyina, and on to join the old Burma Road at Paoshan. The

British did not view either course of action with much enthusiasm. Both would tie up large forces in some of the most difficult campaigning country in the world, and even if the battle was won, the enormous construction effort to open the land route would, in the British view, be largely wasted, because it would be too late to affect the outcome. The British favoured by-passing Burma, and going straight for Singapore.

This major divergence of views turned on differing perceptions of logistic difficulties and how to overcome them. The Americans, with enormous resources and boundless enthusiasm and confidence, were not deterred by the huge logistic effort their strategy entailed. The British agreed that there should be improvements made to the lines of communication to support the forces facing the Japanese in Assam and North Burma, and to provide for transport to the airfields in Assam from where they could be air-lifted to China; but they still preferred the fastest possible advance to the strategic objective, in their eyes, Singapore. As late as August 1943, at the Quebec conference, QUADRANT, the British strategy of by-passing Burma was still an option. However, a new factor appeared on the scene, the selection of suitable airfields from which the American Very Long Range bomber, the B29 Super Fortress, could bomb the Japanese mainland. This factor, although not decisive in itself, was nevertheless to have a bearing on the ultimate strategy adopted. Although the bomber was not yet in production, it was due to come into service in early 1944; the Marianas, the only islands in the Pacific suitable for its effective operation against Japan, were not likely to have been captured, and airfields constructed until the end of 1944. In casting around for an alternative which would allow the B29s to be deployed earlier, the planners hit upon the idea of basing them in India, with forward bases in China, where they would refuel and bomb up before flying on to hit their targets in Japan. This led to the need to develop further the base airfields in Bengal; the construction of fuel pipelines from Calcutta to Ledo, and onto Kunming when North Burma was cleared; and, in the interim, a massive increase in the airlift of fuel, bombs, spares, and ammunition from Bengal to the Kweilin area in China, where the 12th Air Force USAAF, 'Chennault's Flying Tigers', was already operating. As in other theatres of war, the British were to relearn the lesson of what Terraine calls 'the disciplines of coalition strategy', which were to override their preferences. In other words, the senior partner in the coalition, in this case the Americans, was going to nudge the junior partner, the British, down strategic paths which they might otherwise have avoided.[19] Furthermore, the Americans would exercise the prerogative of those who pay the piper, they would also call the tune. However, although the strategic plan was never radically changed, and the Burma option went ahead in the form originally envisaged, the uncertainties at the highest planning levels were to have logistic implications, mainly decisions on resource allocations to the South-East Asia theatre of operations.

At the SEXTANT conference in Cairo in November and December 1943, a strategic red herring appeared on the planning scene in the war against Japan, which was to militate further against firm direction on the course of future operations, and hence resource allocation. The staffs considered that because of the higher priority of the war against Germany, the British co-ordinated advance on Burma, still in the plan, would not take place in time to synchronise with the American advance across the Pacific. This led to the formulation of the 'Pacific Strategy', under which the British Main Fleet would operate with the Americans in the Pacific (this eventually partially came about when a British Carrier Battle Group transferred to the Pacific in 1945). In addition, while conducting a holding operation to contain the Japanese in South-East Asia, a force of six British divisions with appropriate air support was to be transferred to Australia to support the American main thrust across the Pacific.

There were a number of arguments in favour of continuing with plans to invade Burma and eventually Malaya: in Assam and Burma the Japanese were already being engaged on a scale bigger than that in any other theatre; any diminution of effort in this area would be perceived by the Chinese as withdrawal of support and might lead them to make a separate peace; the rice, oil, tin and rubber from Burma and Malaya would be valuable assets to regain; and finally, entirely a British dimension, and one not subscribed to by the Americans, the recapture of former British possessions by British forces was of paramount importance. The major factor in favour of the 'Pacific Plan', was the prospect of exchanging a protracted slog, involving large forces and complicated logistics, through the inhospitable terrain of Burma against a very tough enemy on ground of his own choosing, for the flexibility of the island-hopping air-sea war in the Pacific, which maximised the Allied advantages of naval and air supremacy. At the Cairo conference, the Combined Chiefs of Staff made no decision other than to: approve the Pacific Plan in principle as a basis for further investigation and preparations subject to final approval of the combined Chiefs of Staff. Although the decision was deferred, preparations to implement either the Pacific or the South-East Asia strategy had to continue. The delay continued for another eleven months, until September 1944, and was to lead to a series of administrative problems, culminating in the risk that if a decision was not taken, the necessary logistic preparations for either course would not be made in time.[20]

The nub of the problem was that the two strategies were mutually exclusive and the logistic support for one could not apply, except in a limited way to the other; and time and assets were short; time to build up the base, Australia or India; and assets, particularly specialised shipping, landing craft, and equipment. In Australia, port facilities were good but the distances were enormous. Communications were complicated by the differing rail gauges of the State railways, and accommodation for troops and storage spaces would have to be provided and built by British resources, since the small population of Australia was already fully mobilised, and there were already considerable American forces based there. As we shall see shortly, India had problems of a different kind. In early 1944, the Minister of War Transport represented to the British Joint Chiefs of Staff that even after the defeat of Germany, then set for October 1944, there would be insufficient shipping released to implement the Pacific Plan because of the great distance to Australia and the long turn-round. Not until the OCTAGON conference in September 1944, was Mountbatten given the orders by the Combined Chiefs of Staff to go ahead with the South-East Asia plan. By which time, the British were following up the retreating Japanese on the western borders of Burma. The timing of the decision is interesting, just before Operation MARKET GARDEN, which Montgomery confidently predicted would lead to the end of the war in Europe in 1944.

Assam and Burma: The Impact of Geography

We must now return to the campaign in Assam and Burma, which was being fought for over two years whilst the Joint Combined Planning Staffs were planning and their Chiefs deliberating.

The main base for this campaign was India. Except to provide large numbers of volunteer soldiers for the Indian Army in the First World War, that conflict had passed India by. To begin with, it had looked as though the pattern would be more or less repeated in the Second World War. Formations stationed in India, both British and Indian were shipped to the Middle East Theatre (Egypt and Iraq), and a departure from the previous war, Malaya. A good part of the logistic demands for formations shipped from India to the Middle East, were met by that theatre, whose lines of communication stretched back to Britain, round the Cape of Good Hope, but did not include India. The same applied to troops from India stationed in Malaya. Most stocks, particularly the heaviest item, ammunition, were shipped direct from Britain and, until the fighting started, consumption was low. With minor exceptions, India only fitted into the logistic framework when supplying troops stationed on the North West Frontier and the understrength division in Burma; and here again, consumption was low.

Historically, the threat to India had always been perceived as coming from the North-West. The railways were orientated to cater for this. Before the Second World War, no thought had been given to India as a base for operations elsewhere, least of all towards the East. Early in the war, bases and depots had been built to serve Bombay and the North-West Frontier. But there was no such infrastructure to supply military activity on the eastern frontier.

The onset of the war with Japan saw a fundamental change. As a consequence of India becoming the base for South East Asia Command (SEAC), fighting the campaign against the Japanese in Assam, Burma, and the Far East, the logistic system had to be completely re-orientated and vastly expanded. Geography, as ever, was crucial and it is necessary to examine the terrain and climate in Eastern Assam and Burma in some detail, and the communications in India, if the problems facing the Allies, particularly logistical, are to be properly understood.

Eastern Assam and Burma

Just south of the great Brahmaputra river, which flows in a generally south-westerly direction through Assam, lie the Naga hills, with Kohima as the administrative centre of the area. South again is Manipur State, whose capital is Imphal, and further south still, lie the Chin hills. Between the Brahmaputra valley and the River Chindwin is a wide mountainous belt rising to 13,000 feet. Imphal is situated on a large plain, 40 miles from North to South and 20 miles from East to West, surrounded by high hills. In the monsoon, May to September, most of the plain becomes a swamp. The hills west of the road running from Kohima to Imphal and to the south, are high and form a natural barrier to military operations. East of this road, the terrain is lower, and more open. The scale of the country is remarkable. The hills are high, and most are covered with dense jungle, the valleys are deep. Even tracked vehicles were roadbound until engineer work was carried out. Until jeep tracks were made, loads could only be carried on mules, or by men; and movement was very slow. As an example, the Chindits, Major General Orde Wingate's deep penetration force, marching across the grain of the country, including some not very protracted fighting, took five weeks to cover 140 miles in 1943.

North Burma is formed by the Irrawaddy basin, and its tributary the Chindwin. To the west lie the Chin and Naga hills; in the north, in the region of Myitkyina, the terrain is mountainous; and more mountains lie to the East, forming the watershed between the Irrawaddy and Salween rivers. There are scarcely any roads. The mountain ranges, densely covered with jungle, run from North to South, with swift rivers flowing in deep ravines. Sometimes the valleys open out into thickly wooded plains, dotted with low hills. South of Mandalay and Shwebo the country is arid, with sparse vegetation. East of the Irrawaddy, from below its junction with the Chindwin, and west of the Mandalay–Rangoon road, as far as Tharrawaddy, lies the Pegu Yomas range, rising to 3,000 feet. South Burma, from the lower Salween to Malaya, is tropical rain forest country. In the Arakan, the features run from North to West and South to East. The flat river valleys are intersected by *chaungs* (streams) and rice paddy. The valleys are passable to vehicles in dry weather if the banks round the paddy are flattened. But in the heavy monsoon rains, the muddy fields are impassable to wheels or tracks. The *chaungs* flood, overflowing their banks, and as they are fringed with mangrove swamps, ferrying in craft is the only practicable way of crossing. The steep, razor-backed hills are covered with dense forest.

Because the lie of the land in Burma runs from North to South, the communications follow the same direction. Waterways were the chief means of transport. Before the war, steamers ran up as far as Bhamo and to Homalin on the Chindwin. A railway ran up the centre of the country from Rangoon to Mandalay, where it branched off to Lashio, Myitkyina, and Ye-U. Lines also ran from Rangoon to Bassein and Prome, and to South Burma. Two motor roads ran from Rangoon to Mandalay; one alongside the railway, and another on the eastern bank of the Irrawaddy. Another ran from Mandalay to Lashio, and north to join the Burma Road, through which the Allies had sent supplies to the Chinese, until the Japanese reached it; and about which, as we have seen, the Americans were so exercised. From Mandalay, an all weather road led to Myitkyina, and unmetalled roads to Sumprabum and Mogaung. Apart from these two, there were only tracks in North

Burma. There were no rail connections between Burma and India, and only one under-developed road. Since 1887, plans for improving this road had been mooted, but nothing was done until the late autumn of 1941. By the time the Japanese invaded, the road from Manipur Road (Dimapur) to Imphal had been widened to take two-way traffic. The section from Imphal to Tamur (65 miles) was only a bridle track, and Tamur to Kalewa (120 miles), only a cart track. In the Arakan, the railway ran only as far as Chittagong.

Calcutta became the main base for the campaign in Assam and Burma, but when the British Forces evacuated Rangoon in early 1942, all sea lines of communication were cut. The only method of entry was overland through Assam. Furthermore, communications to, and in, Assam, which hitherto had been a backwater, were rudimentary, and totally unsuitable for the supply needs of General Slim's British 14th Army fighting in Assam and Burma, and Stilwell's Chinese/American Task Force in North Burma.

Although Calcutta remained the main base for most of the campaign,[21] the west coast ports of Karachi and Bombay played a major part, particularly for troop movement, and for some stores. To a lesser extent, the ports of Madras, Cochin, and Vizgapatam were also used; both as a back-up to Calcutta and because they were the closest to the extensive training and staging areas in Southern India. However, the total capacity of all the ports in India was no greater than that of Southampton.[22] The distances involved were enormous. From Delhi to Myitkyina in North Burma, is the same distance as from London to Helsinki; Karachi to Calcutta, Leon in Northern Spain to Gdansk; Karachi to North-West Assam, Leon to Finland. It was commonplace for troops to take a week to complete a rail journey from one side of India to the other. The total mileage of railway track in India in 1942 was the same as for the railways in Britain (a country a tenth the size), but with only one-third the number of freight wagons. The most important road in India, the Grand Trunk Road (immortalised by Kipling), ran 1,500 miles from the North West Frontier to Calcutta. It was joined between Allahabad and Delhi by the road from Bombay. These roads were open in all but the worst weather. The road from Madras to Calcutta was a different proposition altogether. It crossed many large rivers, which in the monsoon were swollen by floodwater, cutting off substantial sections. Fortunately, it ran parallel and close to the railway, and the rail bridges were all-weather. To keep the overland route open to vehicles, a rail link was instituted on each of the most troublesome sections. Convoys of vehicles were loaded at the nearest station one side of the flood, ferried across on rail flat cars, and offloaded at a convenient station on the other side. As this was sometimes necessary several times in one journey, the delays were considerable.

There was no road into Assam from Calcutta. Wheeled vehicles had to be taken by rail 235 miles to Siliguri, before joining the road to Assam. This road crossed the Brahmaputra at the Jogighopa ferry, and split at Jorhat. One road ran south-east to Manipur, the base for 14th Army, and on to Kohima, Imphal and Burma. The other ran north-east to Ledo, the American base supporting the Chinese. From Ledo, as we have heard, stores were flown at a height of 25,000 feet over the eastern end of the Himalayan range, known as the 'Hump', a remarkable feat in unpressurised Dakotas and Liberators, lacking the power to climb above the often appalling weather. A road was eventually constructed from Ledo into China, but it took two years to build, over some of the most inhospitable country in the world.

Road and Rail Links

The railway running north from Calcutta to Siliguri, was broad gauge (5 foot 6 inches). About 200 miles north of Calcutta it was joined by a metre gauge system. One branch serving Assam ran north of the Brahmaputra to Amingaon, where wagons were transported across on a rail ferry to Pandu. From here, the metre gauge ran to Manipur and Ledo. Another branch served East Bengal (now Bangla Desh). This also had to cross the Brahmaputra by wagon ferry, before dividing. One line ran south-east to Chittagong, the base for the Arakan front; the other north-east to Manipur. The metre gauge was used not only for stores and troop movement, but also for vehicles such as tanks and engineer plant, to reduce their road journey to the minimum. Because of geography, the routes for most overland journeys from Calcutta to the road and railheads described at least three sides of a square, and one major ferry crossing. Trains taken across rivers on ferries had to be broken up before embarkation, and remarshalled on the far bank. The ferry from Amingaon was capable of handling only 125 railway wagons a day. Furthermore, every ounce of stores, bound for any destination on the metre gauge lines had to be transhipped from broad to metre gauge wagons, an enormously time-consuming process before the days of mechanical handling equipment (fork-lift trucks and pallets). Many of the loads sent forward were heavy and unwieldy: Bailey bridging, tugs and river craft, boxed locomotives for the Burma railways,

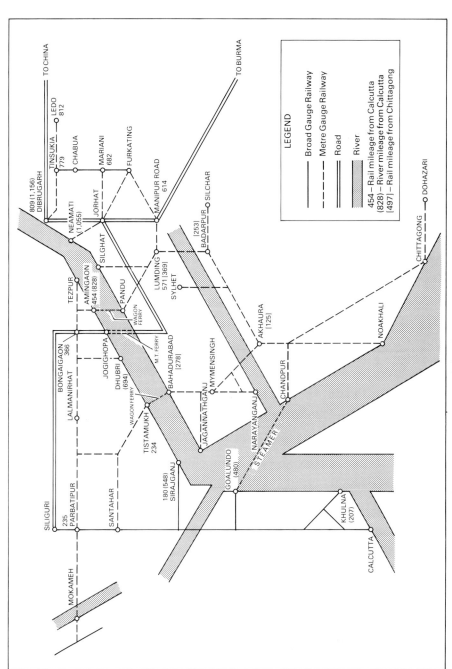

FIG. 3.1 Diagrammatic Layout of the Assam Lines of Communication 1943–45.

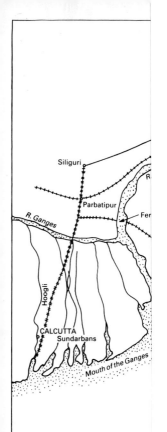

Siliguri

R.

Parbatipur

Fer

R. Ganges

Hoogli

CALCUTTA
Sundarbans

Mouth of the Ganges

BAY

OF

BENGAL

Scale
Miles 25   0   25   50

KEY

—·— International Bounda

+++++ Railways (Double tra

+++++ Railways (Single tracl

— — — Roads, under constru
motorable in fair wea

········· Pack tracks } Only sh
Footpaths

⊚ Airfield

○ Airstrip

——— Motorable Roads

FIG. 3.4   The Ledo Road, Burma (*IWM*).

bulldozers and heavy plant for the Ledo road. Cranes at the railway yards and at the river ports were either too small, too few, or non-existent. As if this was not enough, there were also problems with some of the railway staff. In May 1942, the Manipur Road station received an Air Raid Warning Red. The staff promptly deserted. This and other incidents led to the formation of Defence of India units manned by volunteers from the railway staffs, serving under military law, but stationed in their own districts.

Waterways and Pipelines

To relieve the pressure on the rail and road links, an inland waterway line of communication was set up using huge rafts, known locally as 'flats', with a capacity of 600 tons, and towed by a pair of tugs. The route ran north through the Sundarbans, the vast maze of waterways formed by the mouths of the Ganges, and after about 500 miles, branched off into the Brahmaputra, ending at Dibrugarh, 1,136 river miles, and 809 rail miles, from Calcutta. Chittagong could also be supplied by water, and this allowed the greater part of the effort put into developing the railways to be devoted to those serving the Assam front.[23] To begin with, however, there was a shortage of craft. In 1941, twenty-seven large river steamers and forty-nine flats had been sent to Iraq to work the Euphrates from Basra. These were released in 1943 when the war situation in the Middle East improved. Lack of trained skippers, crews and dock operators also delayed the full exploitation of the water transport system. This situation was alleviated, to some extent, when the crews of the Irrawaddy steamers arrived in India, overland from Burma, but without their craft.

To back up the small number of fuel tank wagons, five pipelines were eventually built by the Americans and the British. Laying them, let alone maintaining them in the mountains and jungle, was a remarkable feat of engineering, probably unsurpassed in any other campaign in the Second World War. They were completed between April and June 1945, but sections were in operation a year before, and as northern Burma was cleared of Japanese the extensions were constructed. The first section from Calcutta to Tinsukia in northern Assam (575 air miles, 779 rail miles), was working by August 1944. The longest ran from Calcutta to Kunming in China to serve the air effort described earlier, although by the time it was completed, the B29s were able to operate from the Marianas, and had been doing so since the end of October 1944.

Thus, the Line of Communication was a combination of rail, road, water, pipeline, and air. It had to serve seven groups of customers. In addition to the 14th Army in Burma, the Americans building the Ledo road, and the Chinese/American Task Force operating in North Burma; there was the United States Air Force flying stores to China over the 'Hump'; the tea gardens which had to be kept supplied with fertilisers, tea chests and other stores; the civil population of Assam; and coal for the railways, river steamers and the Armed Forces.

The Weather

Then there was the weather. In the cold weather, the climate is perfect. In April and May temperatures rise so that at noon, the heat strikes like an open oven, with high humidity. The south-west monsoon arrives in Rangoon about the middle of May and envelopes the whole of Assam and Burma by the end of the month, except for the dry zone in the lower Irrawaddy valley, of which Meiktila is the centre. Disease flourished. In the year 1943–44 the British suffered 250,000 cases of malaria and dysentery alone. Only the dry zone of Burma was free from malaria. General Slim, being the truly great commander that he was, had no illusions about the importance of the fight against disease—both as a casualty producer in a remote theatre of war where every fighting man was precious and as an insidious influence on morale in a climate which demanded much of the staying power of the soldier. In consequence, he moved his medical support well forward and had special arrangements made to ensure that the fullest use was made of the new drugs to fight disease and to nurse the sick within the combat zone, rather than have a steady stream of sickness casualties backloaded to India.

A Momentous Decision

When Admiral Mountbatten the Supreme Allied Commander SEAC took over in autumn 1943, he decreed that there was to be no interruption to the campaign caused by monsoon conditions. The Japanese considered this impossible, and the pressure maintained on them when they thought that the weather would bring a respite was a major factor in bringing the campaign to a successful conclusion. Mountbatten's order, which was to have a decisive effect upon the outcome of the campaign, threw a considerable responsibility on the logisticians because a drop in tonnages being delivered forward was not acceptable. Indeed, it should be realised that had the logisticians failed, nothing could have saved the 14th Army. That they succeeded so brilliantly, as we shall see, was a tremendous tribute to their skill and to the rugged determination of the British and Indian troops to fight on in such conditions, often on half-rations. The monsoon regularly caused the water level in the Brahmaputra to rise up to 37 feet high, making the small river ports (ghats) unusable; breaches in road and rail communications happened every week; vehicles moving off the road drowned; and stores disappeared from view under the floodwater at dumps and railheads. These difficulties had to be, and were overcome. Work was put in hand to double the broad gauge track the whole distance from Calcutta to Parbatipur, the northerly of the two junctions with the metre gauge system. The transhipment and marshalling facilities at key points along the system were extended, and constructed where they did not already exist. The river ghats were enlarged. These and other measures were so successful that whereas in November 1943 an average of 2,800 tons a day was moved forward against a target figure of 3,700 tons a day, by September 1944 the tonnages achieved were 6,537 tons a day against a target of 5,900 tons a day; and by March 1945 the average tons a day being lifted was 8,973 against a target of 6,900 tons a day.[24] Here again, Slim's remarkable qualities as the whole soldier, in whose calculations the logistical factor was never far from the front of his mind, emerged. It was he who saw the opportunities offered by the seizure of a sizeable stretch of the Chindwin to create an additional means of producing lift—by creating a fleet of boats and rafts from the limitless timber available. The 500 tons a day he aimed for may have seemed modest in relation to the overall requirement but in that campaign, every ton counted. Furthermore, he was already looking ahead to the formidable problems posed by the Irrawaddy and foresaw how invaluable a fleet of river craft would be, no matter how rudimentary. In addition, numerous much larger vessels were salvaged from the bottom of the Chindwin, victims of the first Burma campaign or of Allied air attack. In this way, the Inland Water Transport organisation of the 14th Army made a substantial contribution to the success of its operations against an enemy whose logistic difficulties were driving his troops to the edge of starvation and beyond.

*   *   *

The Campaign

However, all these improvements to the logistic system were a long way off when, in May 1942, the exhausted, malaria-ridden soldiers of what was then known as Burma Corps, arrived in Assam by the track from Kalewa to Imphal. Fortunately, with the onset of the monsoon, the Japanese did not follow-up hard. They had their own logistic problems. By remaining in Burma, with their bases in the malaria free zone, and using the natural communications in the country, and eating the bountiful rice harvests, they would live perfectly comfortably. Any attempt on their part to invade India with a force of sufficient size to have a chance of succeeding, would require a major upgrading of their lines of communication forward of the Chindwin river. Furthermore, their supply lines for spares, ammunition, and equipment ran all the way back to Japan. Unless, and until the Japanese made a radical reappraisal of their strategic priorities, with a reassignment of the necessary assets to support them, an improvement of the order required to support a major offensive was highly unlikely. Put simply, they had overreached themselves. They faced the classic logistic dilemma, if they advanced they outran their supplies, and, unless they could resupply themselves at their opponent's expense, they became progressively weaker. The British falling back on their own bases, became progressively stronger. Provided they did not take council of their fears, as they had in Malaya and Singapore, where they had given ground and surrendered to an enemy who was weaker both numerically and logistically, the Japanese would not prevail. Strategically the Japanese were on the defensive, but mounted a series of attacks to secure a better defensive position from which to hold Burma. The Allied aim was offensive, to retake Burma, and force the road through to China. In this case they would be moving away from their bases, and have to improve their supply lines. But first they had to build up their strength, while holding off the Japanese attacks, like a badly hurt boxer keeping an aggressive opponent at bay, while he recovers sufficiently to go over to the attack.

The British Build-Up

In general terms, therefore, the British forces in Assam and Arakan, remained on the defensive from May 1942 to May 1944. Although there were offensive operations, they were of a comparatively minor character. Active operations virtually ceased during the monsoon of 1942/43. This static situation naturally made the supply of the force easier, and allowed time for the improvements in the logistic system discussed already. Another feature of the earlier part of the campaign had been the tendency of units threatened with being cut off by the Japanese infiltration tactic, to withdraw to keep open their logistic life-line. The means to keep open this life-line, air supply, was not available to begin with, but when it arrived it was to change the tactical and logistic picture so radically that it has been deemed the single most important reason for eventual victory.

Manipur Road became the logistic base for the Army in Assam long before it was ready to take on this task. It was responsible for maintaining 30,000 troops at a distance of 100 miles. The railhead, it was planned, would handle 1,000 tons a day, rising to 2,000 tons. But the rail extensions had not yet reached the supply depots, and to begin with all supplies had a six to seven mile journey by road, throwing an unwelcome additional strain on the already overworked transport. At the beginning of May, there were only six general transport companies at Manipur Road, each with 100 task vehicles and 22 spares. The drivers were inexperienced, the road difficult and dangerous. In the 40 miles from Manipur Road to Kohima, the road climbed 4,000 feet, round hairpin bends, with a steep cliff up on one side, and another cliff down on the other. The gradients were heavy, the road edges soft. From Kohima it climbed another 1,500 feet. One way traffic was quickly instituted.

FIG. 3.5   Mud—Burma (*IWM*).

Food was difficult to obtain locally, because the Hindus of Manipur State objected to the killing of cattle, and drove them away to prevent them from being taken to feed the army. Eventually, in a reversion to the logistic methods of earlier wars, sheep and goats were kept at Imphal, where there was plenty of rice straw available for feedstuff, and 18,000 acres of vegetables were cultivated. Pigs and goats were kept in locations quite well forward of Imphal.

Despite these self-help measures, which took time to implement, the difficulties of supply were enormous. In Assam, to maintain a division 1,500 strong deployed forward, required 36,700 men, of whom 5,000 were in the transport and supplies branch. The Arakan was no better, 50 per cent of the tonnage which left Chittagong for the forward areas was absorbed by the line of communication personnel and services before the corps area was reached.

Long Range Penetration

In March 1943 Brigadier Wingate's first long range penetration operation into Burma, at brigade strength, was a portent of things to come both tactically and logistically. The force had been fully supplied by air drop. The operation itself was a costly failure except in the very important matter of convincing the British that the Japanese could be defeated in the jungle, and that the jungle itself was not an impenetrable 'green hell' to well trained troops.[25] However, the boldness of the plan and use of air supply by the Chindits had so impressed Churchill, and General Arnold, the Chief of the United States Air Staff, that Wingate was given vastly greater resources for a second deep penetration by the Chindits the following year, including a reinforced division of six infantry brigades and a complete air group of USAAF transport aircraft, gliders, and fighter bombers. These would not only carry his division into battle, but supply it as well. The air group also had light aircraft for casualty evacuation, a great help to morale; in his first operation, Wingate had had to leave badly wounded men behind. His second, was to be in support of theatre-wide plans.

*   *   *

The Allied Plan

The Japanese and Allies faced each other in three areas on the general line of the Indian/Burmese frontier. In the North Stilwell's Chinese/American Task Force faced the crack 18th Japanese Division. Slim's 14th Army was deployed with 4 Corps based on the Imphal plain, faced by the Japanese 15th Army; and, in the Arakan, 15 Corps faced a Japanese corps. The Allies planned four interrelated operations for the period up to the start of the monsoon in May 1944. In the North, Stilwell was to advance to capture Myitkyina and Mogaung, with the aim of extending the Ledo Road into China. Wingate was to dominate the area within forty miles of Indaw, thus sitting astride the Japanese lines of communication to their forces confronting Stilwell. In the centre, 4 Corps, in contact with the Japanese between the Imphal plain and the River Chindwin, was to advance to the Chindwin, and cross it if the opportunity presented itself. In the South, in the Arakan, 15 Corps was to advance to the Maungdaw–Buthidang Road. Keeping the

Japanese busy in Assam and Arakan, would assist Stilwell in taking his objectives.

Japanese Plans

The Japanese were planning too. Mindful that their overall aim in the region was to secure the best terrain from which to defend Burma, General Kawabe, the Japanese commander, saw that he could achieve this if he shortened his long and vulnerable main defence line on the Chindwin on the central front by advancing to capture the Imphal plain and Kohima. He would then control the few approaches from India through the mountains. In his eyes he would also be better placed logistically. The large rice crop in Assam would feed his army, and he could supply himself from the British dumps and bases at Manipur Road, Kohima, and Imphal. The British, denied these bases would be forced back to India. At the same time he would be astride Stilwell's lines of communication, forcing him to withdraw from the northern front. Finally, by capturing the airfields in Assam, he would stop the airlift over the 'Hump'. As a deception, Kawabe planned to advance in the south, in the Arakan, in February, threatening Chittagong and Calcutta, in sufficient strength to force Slim to reinforce the Arakan from the central front, 300 miles away, thus weakening 4 Corps, on whom the main attack would fall. In the Arakan, he also planned on living off his enemy. So on neither front did the Japanese plans have any solid logistic foundation. They relied almost totally on capturing British stocks, and until they did, on both fronts they would be extending their own lines of communication in difficult country, and in addition on the central front, across a large river, the Chindwin.

The Value of Timely Intelligence

Allied intelligence assessments gave Slim forewarning of the Japanese intentions, and he amended his own plans accordingly. Deeming the central front the most vital, he decided to withdraw 4 Corps to the Imphal plain and there receive the Japanese attack in the best position for defence. Logistically it would give him an advantage, his lines of communication from his railheads, airfields, bases and supply depots to forward troops would be shortened. He ordered 15 Corps, in the Arakan, to hold its ground, warning the corps commander that not only would he not be reinforced, but, in addition, he was to stand by to send reinforcements north to Imphal; once the southern Japanese offensive died away. Stilwell and Wingate were to proceed as before.

The Japanese Offensive in the Arakan February 1943

On 4 February the Japanese offensive in the Arakan started. They cut the lines of communication of 7th Indian Division, and surrounded the administrative area. However, neither withdrew. Administrative areas had by now formulated a defensive tactic which involved setting up a perimeter defence, known as an Admin Box, and dominating the surrounding area by patrolling. All administrative personnel, including clerks, and coolies, were armed and trained to shoot. The Admin Box put up such a stout resistance, that the Japanese utterly failed to supply themselves at their enemy's expense. It was air supply that made this stand possible. Men knew that if they stayed and fought, they would be supplied with food and ammunition. During the 17-day siege 3,000 tons of stores were dropped. Acting on intelligence, and anticipating the attack, ten days supplies for 40,000 men had been accumulated near the airfields, and aircraft warned for the task. It cost the Japanese nearly 8,000 men, and by the time the starving survivors retreated, the myth that they could live for long periods on a few handfuls of rice and local resources had been exploded.

*   *   *

Wingate's Second Operation

Meanwhile the Allied plans went ahead. Wingate's part in these was to capture and dominate the whole of the Indaw-Katha area down to the 24th Parallel, which he would hold until relieved by the Chinese under Stilwell and by 14th Army. It is worth covering these operations in sufficient detail to see how they fitted into the overall Allied plan as it actually unfolded; they were to point up a number of lessons, not least, one of logistic priorities.

The penetration took place in three phases. First, an approach march by 16th Infantry Brigade. Second, the fly-in of 77th Indian and 111th Indian Infantry Brigades to three landing zones, nicknamed Broadway, Piccadilly and Chowringhee. Third, a follow-up air-lift by 14th Infantry and 3rd West African Brigades. The brigades were to establish strongholds, based on an airstrip through which they would be supplied. From the strongholds, 'floater' columns would operate to harass the Japanese lines of communication, and at the same time prevent them attacking the stronghold. Once these conditions were fulfilled, the strongholds would become a spear wound in the enemy's side, through which his life-blood would flow. At least that was the theory.

The Fly-In

The first phase went well. The first lift of the second phase was to consist of 80 gliders carrying in the first wave of 77 Brigade to Piccadilly and Broadway on 5 March 1944. At the last moment it was discovered that Piccadilly was covered with large felled trees; by the enemy it was thought at the time. But in fact they were part of normal logging operations. The number of gliders was reduced to 60, and 77 Brigade started their lift to Broadway. Despite some exciting moments and a few casualties, by dusk that evening the strip was ready to accept Dakotas. Two flew in that night, the second with a full load of 6,000 lb. That night the sequence was repeated at Chowringhee, and Dakotas were being accepted with troops and stores within 24 hours. Wingate then decided to switch the main effort to Broadway, and evacuate Chowringhee, which was close to a motor road and an airfield. By mid March 1944, three brigades were behind the Japanese lines, well placed to disrupt the lines of communications of four enemy divisions. Wingate ordered a new block set up, codename Aberdeen. Gliders flew in with engineer plant to construct a Dakota strip. A follow-up lift of 360 Dakota sorties over six nights was planned to complete the move of the Chindit division. At this juncture, the Japanese offensive against 4 Corps south of Imphal started, slightly earlier than anticipated. All the units of 4 Corps were back in their planned positions, but only just. As the attack gathered momentum, 14th Army needed all available supply dropping aircraft to maintain the hard pressed 4 Corps. The number of Dakotas available to the Chindits was cut to 25, and the airlift of the two follow-up brigades took 20 days.

Choking the Japanese Lines of Supply

By early April 77 Brigade had set up a very successful block, nicknamed White City; firmly astride the road and rail communications of the Japanese 18th Division facing Stilwell. Lentaigne, now commanding the Chindits, after Wingate's death in an air crash, closed down Aberdeen, and reinforced White City. Although the Chindits dominated the area of the Japanese lines of communication, Stilwell was so inactive, that the Japanese 18th Division had no need to call on their third line ammunition and supplies. At the same time it was clear that the Chindits were a logistic embarrassment to 14th Army. The Japanese having cut in behind 4 Corps at Imphal, attacking with fanatical courage, maintained the siege for more than two months. But as in the Arakan a month earlier, the defenders by standing firm, denied the Japanese the supplies they so desperately needed. 4 Corps was supplied entirely by air. Five-hundred-and-forty tons a day were flown in to the airstrips. The main problem was not food, but ammunition, and other stores with which to fight the battle. Again, as in the Arakan, the Japanese could not support their offensive logistically, and the emaciated survivors drifted back across the Chindwin. Although the monsoon was about to break, Mountbatten, as was noted earlier, and with Slim's full support, decided to continue operations. 4 Corps was ordered to follow up the retreating Japanese. Greatly weakened by losses in battle and from starvation resulting from inadequate logistics, the Japanese now found 14th Army on their heels.

Air Supply: A Conflict of Priorities

Meanwhile the Chindits were ordered to evacuate all existing blocks, and operate in support of Stilwell. A new block, Blackpool, was set up nearer Stilwell. But by now surprise had been lost, the monsoon had begun, and night drops were too hazardous. The Japanese brought up anti-aircraft guns as well as artillery and soon day supply in the breaks in the monsoon downpour became far too risky. Blackpool, running low on ammunition and supplies, was evacuated on 25 May. Men too severely wounded to be carried on mules, the only means of casualty evacuation, were shot by their own side. Eventually the severely depleted Chindits captured Mogaung, and linked up with Stilwell. In August, soon after the capture of Mogaung and Myitkyina, the Chindits were withdrawn. Many were weakened by the strain of operating in such harsh terrain, with minimum support, and after medical examinations, a large proportion of the force was declared unfit for action until after a period of rest and recuperation. Although a limited success, the second Wingate operation was extremely wasteful of five well trained brigades, the sixth was used in a conventional role. The air effort to keep such a large force supplied especially when in contact with the enemy, and consuming ammunition, was out of all proportion to the effect it was

FIG. 3.6   Mules—Burma (*IWM*).

having on the battle. When the Japanese attacked in the centre, Slim
was faced by a logistic choice: maintain air supply to the Chindits at the
originally planned level, at the expense of aircraft to supply 4 Corps in
their crucial battle to keep the Japanese out of the Imphal plain; or vice
versa It could hardly have taken much cerebration to arrive at the
solution he did.

*   *   *

The 14th Army Advances

We must now return to the main battle. The 14th Army was on the
threshold of the campaign that would eventually carry them to
Rangoon and beyond. As they followed up the retreating Japanese,
they opened the distance from their bases, and soon found that the
replenishment of ammunition entailed a round trip of 100 miles, a
journey that could take 24 hours because of the state of the roads, and
in particular, landslides blocking the route. To cater for this, mobile
ammunition points were set up, consisting of trucks loaded with small
arms ammunition, anti-tank shells, and some other natures; but, for

lack of sufficient trucks, not artillery ammunition. Fuel, artillery ammunition, and rations were dumped as far forward as possible, and units came back to collect as required. Fuel usage was higher than normal in an advance of this nature, because guns were ferried forward, rather than towed; this being found easier.

As the advance gathered momentum,[26] and the army drew further and further from its bases on the Imphal plain, it became necessary to set up the North Burma line of communication which will be described in full at this stage, although, plainly, each section could only be set up after it had been cleared of the enemy. It was a combination of road, water, and rail: from Manipur Road, 320 miles by road to Kalewa on the west bank of the Chindwin; thence by river, 240 miles to Myingyan; and the 430 miles to Rangoon, by road or rail. A total of 990 miles, more than twice the distance over which the Germans supplied their thrust on Moscow in 1941; and only marginally less than the lines of communication of Rommel's Deutsche Afrika Korps in the desert, and of Hoth's Army Group B advancing on Stalingrad. And these figures discount the distances and difficulties involved in a line of communication that ran from Britain and the United States to Calcutta, and from Calcutta to Manipur Road. But even a recitation of the distances do not convey the complete picture in the Burma campaign. The weather and terrain as always had a dramatic effect on logistics as well as tactics. For example the turn-round time from Manipur Road to Kelawa, a total journey of 640 miles, took 7 days in dry weather; in the monsoon it took 14–16. Air supply played an increasingly important part in covering these distances; by April 1945, out of 14th Army's daily requirement of 2,090 tons of supplies of all kinds, an average of 88 per cent (1,845 tons) were delivered by air. The economic range of the Dakota was 250 miles, after which the payload decreased in proportion to the distance flown. So, if possible, supplies were air-landed rather than air-dropped,[27] and, as a rule of thumb, only troops out of economic truck range of an airfield, or operating off the axis, were supplied by air-drop. In January 1945, the aim of 15 Corps in the Arakan campaign was to capture sites suitable for the construction of airfields from which to maintain the remainder of 14th Army, now consisting of two corps, 4 and 33, in the re-conquest of Burma. While 33 Corps cleared the Yenan-gyaung oilfields, and then advanced parallel with the Irrawaddy, 4 Corps consisting of about 70,000 men, 250 tracked and 8,000 wheeled vehicles, thrust down the Mandalay–Toungoo–Rangoon road.

Fig. 3.7   Air re-supply by C-47 Dakota, Burma (*IWM*).

On to Rangoon: A Triumph of Air Supply

On 4 April, with 300 miles to go to Rangoon, logistic imperatives began to drive strategy. The American Dakotas which provided the bulk of the airlift, were due to be withdrawn to China in June. Much of the road network was of fair weather standard only, and the monsoon was due in early May. It became necessary to take Rangoon at all costs before the monsoon. It was decided that a combined sea and airborne operation should be mounted by 15 Corps from the Arakan to capture the port. On 3 May the assaulting troops from 15 Corps captured Rangoon, while the leading division of 4 Corps, 17 Indian Division, was still 30 miles from the city held up by demolitions, mines, and mud. 4 Corps, in its 300 mile dash for Rangoon, had been supplied entirely by air, which, taking into account the support by air of the other two corps, consititued the biggest air supply operation in any theatre in the Second World War.[28] On no occasion was the advance delayed for lack of ammunition and stores for the battle. Forward troops were on reduced rations, because of the need to carry the maximum number of days food in trucks between airfields, to dispense with the need for air dropping. In the last stage of the advance, and until Rangoon was restored to a working port, thanks to a combination of the monsoon arriving two weeks early, rendering all airfields south of Meiktila unusable, and an increased expenditure of ammunition and fuel, all troops were on half rations for 34 days. The inability to use the airfields meant that for a period 4 Corps lived on a supply drop of 175 tons a day, instead of 450 tons.

*   *   *

Victory: The Pay-Off for a Rigorous Application of Logistic Principles

It is not the intention to continue this account of the Burma campaign after the capture of Rangoon, except to say that the logistic problems did not disappear with the opening of the port. The lack of aircraft, now removed for tasks elsewhere; lack of all weather airfields nearer than 300 miles, and even these were often unserviceable because of the early monsoon; and the loss of supplies on air-drops for lack of airfields, led to considerable shortages. In 4 Corps rations were at less than half scale, and even then there was little spare tonnage for fuel and ammunition. Fortunately only one of the divisions in the Corps was actively engaged, and that at low intensity. Despite a huge air lift capacity, air superiority, and all the other advantages enjoyed by the Allies, they had driven the campaign in Burma to its successful conclusion only by the most rigorous application of logistic principles. It must also be said that 14th Army was fortunate in its commander, General Slim, thought by many to be the most successful fighting general produced by the British Army since Wellington. For three and a half years his army fought the longest continuous campaign against by far the largest body of enemy in the war against Japan. In doing so he inflicted upon the Japanese the greatest defeat in a land battle they had ever suffered. More Japanese troops died in Burma than in the whole Pacific campaign. 14th Army was one of the most remarkable armies ever seen for the variety of races which its soldiers represented: providing rations acceptable to the plethora of different religions and castes among the Indian troops alone was a logistic triumph in itself. But this represents only a fraction of the many logistic achievements of Slim's Army.

*   *   *

CONCLUSIONS

When the Second World War came to an end after the dropping of the atomic bomb on Nagasaki on 9 August 1945, the logisticians could congratulate themselves on their achievement, without which Victory could never have been attained, but they could not rest on their laurels. While the operational staffs could perhaps unwind a little, the logisticians had, among other things, to provide fuel and food to populations, as well as the occupying troops; move large bodies of men back to bases, and finally to their home countries; ship stores home, or dispose of them. The Allied logisticians triumphed over difficulties by the determined application of the principles of Foresight, Economy, Flexibility, Simplicity, and Co-operation. Had they not done so, the undeniably greater logistic potential of the Allies over the Axis forces, in terms of lift and supply, could not have been brought to bear so effectively.

Unlike the Germans or the Russians, the Americans and the British, in their campaigns against all the Axis powers, had to cope with the complexities of combined operations, joint command, long vulnerable sea lines of communication, and all the problems associated with beach and port operating. Twice only, the campaigns in Tunisia, and in Egypt and Tripolitania, were the Italians and the Germans to face similar problems, with far shorter, direct sea lines of communication across the Mediterranean. Although these were subject to Allied air and sea interdiction,[29] the Germans, too, in their turn, were able, for appreciable periods, to deny the use of the Mediterranean to the Allies, thanks to airfields in Crete, Sicily and Italy. Furthermore, in German eyes these campaigns on the North African littoral were sideshows, and at a pinch could be abandoned without jeopardising the eventual outcome overall, whereas to the British at least, they were crucial to the conduct of the war. However, the cost to Hitler in terms of the loss of manpower he suffered rather than surrender in North Africa was by no means negligible.

The Japanese were in a different position altogether from their Axis allies; driven into expanding south into the Pacific and south-west into Southeast Asia, as a result of being on the horns of a logistic dilemma, expressed by Paul Kennedy thus:

> 'Seen from Tokyo's viewpoint, however, the decision to expand southward was utterly logical. The West's embargo on trade with Japan and freezing of its assets in July 1941 (following Tokyo's seizure of French Indochina) made both the army and the navy acutely aware that unless they gave into American political demands (*i.e.; wind up the campaign in China*—Author's emphasis) or attempted to seize the

oil and raw materials supplies of Southeast Asia, they would be economically ruined within a matter of months. From July 1941, therefore, a northern war against Russia became virtually impossible and southern operations virtually inevitable—but since the Americans were judged hardly likely to stand by while Japan helped itself to Borneo, Malaya, and the Dutch East Indies, their military installations in the western Pacific—and their fleet base at Pearl Harbour—also needed to be eliminated. Simply to keep up the momentum of their "China incident", the Japanese generals now found it necessary to support large-scale operations thousands of miles from home against targets they had scarcely heard of.'[30]

The Japanese thus extended themselves strategically and logistically for ammunition, equipment and other warlike stores, although not fuel and food. However once they had staked out their claims, they were in essence on the defensive, and to apply the necessary 'overwhelming force', the Allies, and the Americans in particular, had to haul their men, beans, bullets and fuel at least as far from the home base as did the Japanese, and maintain the pressure against a fanatical enemy until he was, in Churchill's words, 'ground to a powder'.

Logistically, as in every other way, the Second World War was by far the most testing war in history. The combatants had learned considerably in the five years following the remark by the then Major General Paget in 1940:

'It has become the habit of the British Army in recent years to assume that what the General Staff considers to be politically or operationally desirable, is administratively possible. No greater or more dangerous fallacy could exist.'[31]

Because of advances in technology, notably in specialised shipping and craft, transport aircraft, and motor vehicles (both tracked and wheeled), and always provided there were enough of these assets, supplies could be carried forward to keep up with the tempo of operations in the Second World War in a manner that had been unattainable in the First. Technology had not yet progressed to the stage where equipment was so complex and expensive that cost was a limitation on the numbers that could be produced. The quantity of tanks, guns, and aircraft that a nation could produce were a factor of the state of its industry, coupled with its access to raw materials. Experience had shown that industrialised nations, even when submitted to intensive bombing, could manufacture enough to keep abreast of the expenditure of supplies (the most important being ammunition), and replace losses in equipment. In this respect, the United States, who had by far the greatest industrial base, and were never bombed, outstripped all others. The rate of attrition of supplies was never a problem for the United States, nor its allies. Neither was the fighting power of the Germans diminished by their huge expenditure of ammunition and equipment to the point where they could not continue the war. Indeed, at the war's end, production was still rising. Without material assistance from anyone else, they were able to conduct a dogged, often brilliant, defensive strategy for two-and-a-half years. As the Allied strategic bomber offensive was less successful in bringing the Axis powers to their knees than had been hoped, similarly, air interdiction of land lines of communication was not in itself sufficient to cut the flow of supplies to the point where the enemy was unable to resist.

The logistic legacy of the Second World War was not only an unsurpassed expertise in the matter of supplying far-flung enterprises, particularly in the case of the Allies, but a lesson for all participants in the art of the administratively possible. We shall see how long the lesson was remembered in some quarters.

PART TWO

4

Unpreparedness and Speedy Recovery: Korea 1950–53

'There is no one but yourself to keep your back door open. You can live without food, but you cannot last long without ammunition.'
Lieutenant General Walker commanding 8th US Army in Korea.[1]

'The history of war proves that nine out of ten times an army has been destroyed because its supply lines have been cut off. . . We shall land at Inchon, and I shall crush them.'
Douglas MacArthur.[2]

Years after the Korean war had ended, a T-34 tank stood on a street corner of the town of Taejon in South-West Korea. On its turret was painted '*Knocked out 20 July 1950 under the supervision of Maj. Gen. W. F. Dean*'. For a divisional commander to take part in a tank hunting party is unusual. That he felt it necessary to do so, in order to restore the confidence of his men in their equipment and themselves was symptomatic of the state of unpreparedness of the United States Army on the outbreak of the Korean War.

Unarmed and Unready

The North Korean Army invaded South Korea at 4 a.m. on 25 June 1950, striking without warning in the half light before sunrise, gaining complete tactical surprise. The intelligence agencies of the United States had failed to forecast the attack. Although some information had been received in Washington that hinted at the strong possibility of moves by the North Koreans in June, incorrect evaluation and dissemination resulted in it failing to reach people who might have taken some action. Although there had been border incursions, and talk of a North Korean invasion was frequent at intelligence briefings at United States Far East Command Headquarters in Japan, the United States was far more concerned with communist activities in the rest of the world, principally South-East Asia, and especially Indochina. Because the intelligence picture of a North Korean troop build-up did not fit the preconceived ideas being held by the United States Government and its military advisers, it was discounted, with, as so often happens in this type of situation, plenty of rationalisation. The reasons ranged from the belief that the South Koreans were prone to cry wolf, to the assessment that the North Koreans would continue to employ guerrilla and psychological warfare together with political pressure, rather than overt use of military forces.[3] Ultimately, it was academic that there was an intelligence failure, because the United States had no plans to counter an invasion. The only contingency plan was to evacuate American nationals from South Korea.[4]

The Republic of Korea (ROK) Armed Forces were in no state to hold an invasion by over seven well trained and equipped North Korean divisions, including 150 T-34 tanks, and supported by a small tactical air force. The South Koreans had no tanks, no medium artillery, no heavy mortars, no anti-tank guns, no fighter or bomber aircraft. Ten old F-51 Mustang aircraft had been delivered that month, but no South Korean pilot was yet qualified to fly combat missions. The ROK Army supply of artillery and mortar ammunition would be exhausted within a few days. As a final piece of self-delusion, the United States military did not recognise the inferiority of the ROK Armed Forces and, right up to the day of the invasion, believed that if the North Koreans attacked they would easily be repulsed by the ROK Army. This view was shared by no less a person than the Chief of the United States Korean Military Assistance Group (USKMAG).

The political and military discussions that eventually reversed the United States policy not to keep a foot-hold in Korea, following a personal reconnaissance and report by General MacArthur, the Commander-in-Chief Far East, need not concern us. Eventually, permission was given to deploy ground forces from the United States occupation troops in Japan, as well as the naval and air forces already sent to cover the evacuation of Americans from Seoul and Inchon.

The four divisions that formed the United States Eighth Army of occupation in Japan in 1950, were understrength, undertrained, and unfit.[5] Their mental and physical state of mind is summed up in the official history:

> '. . . the command was flabby and soft, still hampered by an infectious lassitude, unready to respond swiftly and decisively to a full-scale military emergency.[6]

The logistic situation was as serious. Out of the 226 recoilless rifles (RCL, anti-tank guns) on Eighth Army's establishment, they had only 21. Of the 18,000 jeeps and 4 × 4 trucks, 10,000 were unserviceable, and of 13,800 6 × 6 trucks only 4,441 were in running order.[7] Supplies at hand in the Far East at the beginning of the war were sufficient only to sustain troops in peacetime activities for sixty days. Levels in various supply classes ranged from 45 to 180 days, with the majority falling into the 45 to 60 day range. Supplies in the pipeline amounted to only a trickle. While large quantities of equipment from de-activated units were available, most of this material was unserviceable, and repair operations could do little more than supply the current needs of the occupation forces. A significant portion of the repairable equipment had to be taken back from the Japanese Ministry of International Trade and Industry, to which the United States Government had given large stocks of surplus property as a stimulus to the Japanese economy. Rectifying this situation was made all the more difficult by the repeated assumption by American policy makers that the Korean War would end in six months. The attitude of mind of many officials in the United States to this state of affairs can be summed up by the remark ascribed to a Pentagon budget expert, when asked how long the war would last and how much it would cost. 'Oh about two or three months or so. It's hard to talk about cost at this stage but I would say that it would be approximately the expense of one or two military exercises. We'll use up some left-over World War II ammunition and supplies.' Although the source for this statement cannot be found, and it may be apocryphal, it is nevertheless accurate in one respect: the age and state of repair of the ammunition and equipment, with which the first American troops went into battle in Korea. This lack of preparedness, and unwillingness to set matters right with the minimum delay, lay in the assumptions by military planning staffs after 1945, that the next war would be a repeat of the Second World War. Build-up would be slow, with large-scale overseas deployments beginning two years after mobilisation day. To put it crudely, because the Korean war did not fit the preconceived idea of what the next conflict would be like, it was not recognised as being 'the next war'.

The Terrain

The country in which the Americans and their United Nations allies were to fight for the next three years was unfamiliar to most Western armies. A British soldier described it:

> '. . . it presented a hostile environment for military operations. It was known in antiquity as "Chosun", which translated means "land of the morning calm', and quickly became known as "frozen Chosun" by the many Commonwealth gunners who fought there. The winters were prolonged and very severe. Temperatures were frequently over 40 degrees F below freezing, and accompanied by Siberian winds. Torrential monsoon rains, mainly in late June to August, often resulted in the Imjin river rising 40 feet in a night. In the summer, temperatures crept up to 105 degrees F and more, and the humidity was high.'[8]

There were few roads or tracks. The terrain was hilly, many rising over 1,000 metres, mainly rocky and bare higher up, the lower slopes were covered with shrubs and small trees. In summer the luxuriant growth on the steep hillsides impeded the sweating soldiers as they toiled up, often under heavy load. Paddy fields dotted the wider valleys. The sides of the narrower defiles were often precipitous. Malarial mosquitoes and rats, which spread many other diseases abounded. Locally grown products could not be eaten raw because of the extensive use of human faeces as a fertiliser. In the shimmering heat of the summer the whole countryside stank.

The Enemy

The enemy, at first the North Korean People's Army (NKPA), and later the Chinese Communist Forces (CCF), were tough, fanatically brave and masters of camouflage and fieldcraft. They attacked relentlessly in human waves, usually at night, screaming and blowing bugles. In defence, they dug extensive fieldworks, concealing and providing overhead cover for guns and mortars to an extent which astonished Western armies fighting in Korea, but would not have surprised the French in Indochina, faced by equally industrious human moles.

First Clash: Task Force Smith

The first American soldiers to encounter the North Korean Army consisted of two rifle companies and part of Headquarters Company, 1st Battalion, 21st Infantry Regiment, 24th Infantry Division, under their battalion commander Lieutenant Colonel Smith, reinforced by two 4.2-in heavy mortars, and two 75 mm RCLs. On 1 July 1950, this understrength battalion, designated. Task Force Smith, flew from Japan to Pusan; their orders: to advance to contact with the enemy, and there delay him for as long as possible. The Task Force totalled about 440 men. Each man had 120 rounds of rifle ammunition, and two days supply of C rations. One other battalion, and the divisional headquarters of the 24th Infantry Division, also transported by air, formed the advanced guard of the remainder of the division which followed by sea. Major General Dean, the divisional commander, assumed command of all United States Army Forces in Korea, until superseded by Lieutenant General Walker, commanding the United States Eighth Army.

As the Task Force moved forward, by train and truck, they were treated to the sight of over-enthusiastic Australian and American aircraft strafing South Korean ammunition and fuel dumps, trains, and columns of troops, causing enormous damage and killing several hundred South Koreans, soldiers and civilians alike. On 5 July, the troops of Task Force Smith started digging in on their positions north of Osan, a location chosen by Smith himself. They had been joined by a battery of six 105 mm howitzers, with 73 vehicles and 108 men, under the command of Lieutenant Colonel Perry. In the battery position, about one mile in rear of the infantry, there were 1,200 rounds of ammunition (200 rounds per gun, a meagre supply with which to start a battle, with no prospect of re-supply). More serious, there were only six rounds of High Explosive Anti-Tank (HEAT), which represented one third of all the HEAT ammunition available in Japan. A high explosive HE shell from a 105 mm gun has a very small chance of stopping a tank as well armoured as a T-34, even if it scores a direct hit. Anti-tank mines would have been useful, but there were none.

It had been raining all night. At about 7 a.m., still in rain, North Korean tanks could clearly be seen advancing along the road towards the Task Force position. A fire mission was called for from the 105 mm battery, but the tanks kept coming. When the leading tanks approached to within 700 yards of the Americans, they were engaged by the 75 mm RCLs, but although hits were seen, the tanks did not stop. As they rumbled on, they came under fire from the 2.36-inch bazooka anti-tank launcher teams. These did not stop them either. One officer fired 22 rounds at about 15 yards range against the rear of the tanks where their armour is weakest, but to no effect. Finally, the two lead tanks were stopped by a single 105 mm howitzer sited forward of the battery position, firing HEAT ammunition. However, the six rounds of HEAT were soon expended, and a third tank knocked out

the forward gun. Within an hour, 33 tanks had passed through the
Task Force position, in two waves. The first wave cut the telephone
wire from the infantry to the guns. The radios were wet and functioning
badly, and by 11 a.m. ceased working altogether.

The tanks approached the battery, with hatches closed, but
fortunately did not leave the road to overrun the position. The 105 mm
howitzers fired at ranges of 150–300 yards as the tanks went by, but the
shells had little effect. Three bazooka teams from the battery gamely
took on the tanks, but caused no damage. Finally one tank was
immobilised when a 105 mm shell hit its track. By the time the second
wave of tanks approached the battery, most of the gunners were badly
shaken and started to run off the position, leaving only officers and
non-commissioned officers to man the guns. Again, except for disabling
another tank by blowing off its tracks, the HE rounds had little effect on
the tanks. However, this time infantry were riding on some of the tanks,
and the HE shells were very effective in blowing off and killing or
wounding most of them. By 10.15 a.m. the last of the tanks had passed
the battery position. Later it was discovered that they were from the
107th Tank Regiment of the 105th Armoured Division, in support of
the North Korean 4th Infantry Division. By good leadership, Perry
persuaded most of his gunners to return to the battery position. The
battery had destroyed or immobilised four tanks out of the 33, which
was quite creditable considering how little HEAT ammunition they
had, and the ineffectiveness of the bazooka. The tanks had destroyed
one gun, and damaged another, killed or wounded twenty infantrymen, and destroyed all the marked vehicles behind the infantry
position. Only Perry and one other were wounded in the battery
position.

About an hour later, a column about six miles long, consisting of
trucks and marching infantry, led by three tanks approached the Task
Force position. Later it was confirmed that they were the 16th and 18th
Regiments of the 4th Infantry Division. When they closed to within
1,000 yards, the Americans opened fire with mortars and machine
guns, causing considerable damage and casualties. Artillery fire would
have been more effective, but there was no communication with the
guns, and Smith assumed that the battery had been destroyed. After
attempting a frontal attack, the North Koreans began working round
the flanks. Smith decided that with ammunition running low, he had no
option but to withdraw.

A withdrawal, in daylight, in contact is a very difficult operation at
the best of times, and this occasion was no exception. Task Force Smith

suffered its heaviest casualties as it withdrew. Without artillery support to keep the enemy from harassing the troops as they moved back, the withdrawal became a shambles. When Smith arrived at the battery position, he was astonished to find so few casualties and all but one of the guns in working order. The battery, on being ordered to withdraw, abandoned their guns, although the vehicles left further down the road were undamaged. Some of the infantry took off their boots and abandoned their weapons, in order to run faster. Initially, 185, out of the 440 infantrymen in the Task Force, and most of the artillerymen got back to the American lines. A few others trickled in over the following days.

The Price of Complacency

In company with the remainder of Eighth Army, Task Force Smith was not mentally or physically prepared for battle, and for that responsibility lies with the battalion commander, and on up to MacArthur the Commander-in-Chief. Walker had instituted a training programme for the Eighth Army in Japan in the summer of 1949, in an attempt to shake the troops out of the comfortable ways they had acquired on occupation duty. When the Korean War started, most units had carried out battalion training, although some had failed their tests. Higher level training had not been carried out. Nor was the Task Force logistically prepared. Not only was much of their equipment obsolete, but no arrangements had been made to resupply small arms and artillery ammunition. It takes a brave, well-trained, and motivated soldier to stick it out against armour, without armoured support of his own. If his anti-tank weapons consistently fail him, he will rapidly see little point in remaining to hold the position. The responsibility for ordering the Force to carry out such an impossible task, out on a limb, with so little support, lies with the commanders in Korea at the time. The responsibility for allowing the US Army's equipment to reach such a parlous state stretches back to the department of the Army, and Congress itself.

As the American troops fought a series of delaying actions, in a rapidly deteriorating situation, it became apparent to MacArthur that Eighth Army would have to take over running the war in Korea. Accordingly, Walker was appointed ground force commander; but without being relieved of his responsibilities in Japan. Thus Walker now found himself coping with a war on one land mass, including all the ramifications of logistical support, while administering occupation forces several hundred miles away across the sea of Japan. This state of affairs lasted for about seven weeks, until a special Logistical Command Japan was set up which relieved Walker's Eighth Army Rear Headquarters of the responsibility. Fortunately Walker was a tenacious, uncomplaining, and competent soldier, able to make the best of the less than perfect weapon with which he had to fight the opening round of the war. This was fortunate because the organisation of the logistic base through which all his reinforcements and supplies had to come was far from perfect. The port of Pusan was excellent, but the railways could not keep pace with the flow of men and supplies pouring in as fast as they could be outloaded from Japan. Consequently some troops moved to the front with only their personal weapons and equipment.

Withdrawal to Pusan

It was during one of the delaying actions, at Taejon, that General Dean, commanding 24th Infantry Division, led the tank hunting party mentioned earlier. He had been asked by Walker to impose the maximum delay on the North Korean advance on the main axis Seoul-Pusan. Walker had in mind withdrawing to a defensive position behind the Naktong River, around Pusan; and holding there while he built up Eighth Army sufficiently to take the offensive. Taejon, the sixth largest city in South Korea at the time, lay 100 miles south of Seoul and 130 miles north-west of Pusan. Eight days before, the 24th Division had received the first consignment of the new 3.5-inch anti-tank rocket launcher. The rockets had been in production only fifteen days before the war started. It is a measure of the speed with which the Americans could react that, within five days of MacArthur's request for the new launchers, the first batch was airlifted to Korea, accompanied by instructors. On 20 July, the second day of the battle, a number of North Korean tanks entered the city, without infantry support. The 3.5-inch bazookas, used in battle for the first time, accounted for 8 tanks; one of them by General Dean's team. His reason for personally bringing a tank to bay, was a calculated attempt to persuade his troops, shaken by reverses and stories of the invulnerability of the T-34 than 'an unescorted tank in a city defended by infantry with 3.5-inch bazookas should be a dead duck.' It was a gallant effort. But he might have been better employed commanding his division, and in particular trying to find out what was happening in the rest of his divisional area. He did not know that his infantry, who he thought were still holding the main positions overlooking the river to the west of the city, had been driven, or drifted, off. Instead of falling back into the city, where they might have been rallied, and used to assist in the withdrawal, they had wandered off to the South into the mountains. Poor radio communications have been blamed for this, but if communications are bad, it is the job of the commander, and his staff, to find out what the situation is by personal reconnaissance. But according to some accounts, Dean was badly served by his staff, and divisional headquarters was in disarray.[9] Eventually, the North Koreans cut in behind the division, and in the chaos of the withdrawal, Dean was cut off and taken prisoner.

Also chaotic was the withdrawal of 25th Infantry Division in the first days of August, following a switch in their axis of withdrawal ordered by Walker to take them from the north-east corner of the evolving Pusan perimeter, to the south-west corner around Masan. This involved a 150 mile journey first by single road and then by rail. Both the road and railway were the main supply artery to the front, and the route took the division across the route of other formations, also on the move. The move by road was bad enough, at the railhead it was worse:

> 'Congestion in the rail yards was almost indescribable. Units seeking transportation commandeered locomotives, cars [rail wagons] jammed the tracks, native refugees crowded into cars [rail wagons], and general chaos threatened. The ROK 17th Regiment, moving south-west at this time . . . further complicated the traffic problem.'[10]

The Perimeter Established and the Enemy Halted

By 4 August, US Eighth Army and the ROK Army was back behind the Naktong River, and had established the Pusan perimeter; a rectangular area about 100 miles from North to South, and about 50 miles from East to West. Each held about half the line, with Eighth Army on the left, and the South Koreans on the right. Although the North Koreans made several attempts to pierce the perimeter and drive on Pusan, the line held, but not without some close calls. Walker, during a speech to the staff of the 25th Infantry Division, said that the Eighth Army would retreat no more, and that in effect every man would 'stand or die'. Stopping the North Koreans was a major milestone in the war. It was a classic example of how an army withdrawing to a natural defensive position, shortening its own overland lines of communication and supply, and falling back on a port through which it receives stocks supplies, grows stronger. Conversely the advancing army finds its lines of communication and supply becoming more tenuous, thus weakening in fighting power.[11] As Eighth Army, until now made up of three badly mauled divisions, was preparing to fall back behind the Naktong, reinforcements were arriving from the United States and Hawaii, in the nick of time. The North Koreans suffered heavy casualties in men and materiel in the advance and in their attempts to break through the perimeter in August and September. Although American air interdiction of the North Korean lines of communication was not particularly successful, it was a long overland haul from Wonsan, where most Russian supplies came in by sea from Vladivostok, to the Pusan perimeter.

Build-Up

Holding the port of Pusan was the key to the success of the defence of the perimeter. It was only about fifteen miles behind the crucial Naktons and Masan sectors of the perimeter. During the period 2–31 July, a total of 309,314 tons of supplies and equipment were unloaded at Pusan, a daily average of 10,666 tons. During the final half of the month 230 ships arrived and 214 departed.[12] The airlift of critical supplies reduced as sealift began to meet demand. Railways also played a vital part. A 'Red Ball Express', using express trains, was organised to transport urgently needed items, which ran from Yokohama to Sasebo in a little over thirty hours. Here supplies were loaded aboard ships, which arrived at Pusan the following morning, under two and a half days after the supplies had left Yokohama. From Pusan two main rail routes ran to the railheads behind the battle front. In July, 350 mixed trains ran to the front, carrying freight and men, and 71 troop only trains. The trains returning included 38 hospital trains carrying 2,581 sick and wounded, and 158 wagons loaded with personal belongings stripped off men by their commanding officers in an effort to trim loads to the essentials needed in battle.[13] The Korean railways had been built by the Japanese, an important factor when it came to repair and replacement. Spares and replacements, including locomotives and rolling stock, could be air or sealifted from Japan.

The Red Ball Express was so successful (on 25 August it delivered 949 tons) that it eliminated the need for nearly all the airlift of supplies from Japan to Korea. It was not only far cheaper, but more reliable. However, this put the Air Force nose so out of joint, that the Commander Far East Air Force complained to the Army, that they were not using the Air Force's 200 ton daily capacity. After some negotiation, a formula was agreed whereby the Red Ball Express would

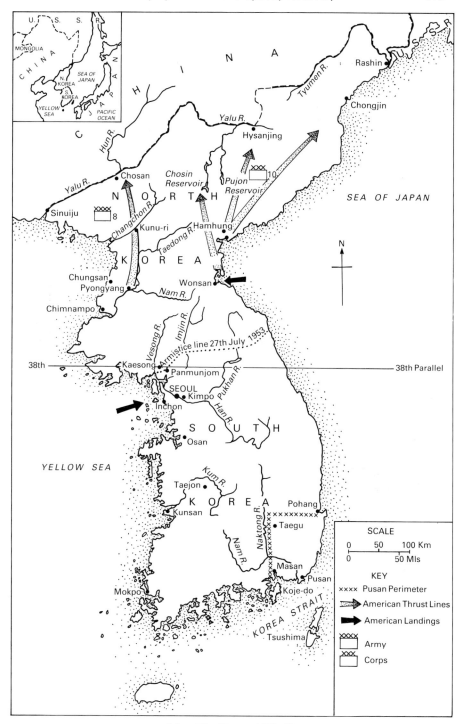

MAP IV   Korea 1950–53.

take the cargo which could not be loaded in aircraft, the rest would go by air.[14] An Army that has such lavish movement resources, that the agencies squabble over who shall have the privilege of taking the goods forward, is lucky indeed!

Reinforcement: The First United Nations Contingents Arrive

The first United Nations troops, other than Americans, arrived in Korea on 25 August, the British 27th Infantry Brigade from Hong Kong. The British 27th Infantry Brigade was short of administrative backing throughout its time in Korea, particularly critical was second line transport, which was only intermittently supplied by the Americans. However, the British 29th Infantry Brigade, which arrived

Fig. 4.1   Korea. Replenishing a British Centurion tank with ammunition— time-consuming and physical (*IWM*).

later, was superbly supported and included a tailor-made organisation, the British Commonwealth Korea Base. The British and Common- wealth Brigades, and eventually the Commonwealth Division, were to establish a reputation for steadiness, efficiency and fighting qualities throughout the Korean war. In this respect, it was equalled, but never surpassed, by only one United States formation, the 1st Marine Division.

As South Korea was not a member of the United Nations, the ROK forces were designated 'allies', a nice distinction. Fortunately, the Americans were in such overwhelming preponderance, that all United Nations Forces were put under United States command, thereby avoiding command by committee, which has since bedevilled all United Nations operations. This arrangement also had enormous logistic benefits. The ROK forces used American equipment exclusively. Eventually, many, although not all, of the United Nations contingents were provided with United States equipment, and weapons. Even those, like the British, who retained their own weapons, guns and tanks, eventually wore many items of American clothing. The majority of contingents used the ubiquitous jeep and other American trucks. This standardisation simplified the supply problem.

MacArthur Intervenes: Inchon

Despite heavy losses, the North Koreans persevered with their attacks in an attempt to break through to Pusan. In mid September the Eighth Army and the ROK Army were still heavily engaged at nearly all points of the perimeter. After two weeks of the heaviest fighting of the war, the line had held, but only just. However, a dramatic change in the situation was about to occur.

When the war was barely a week old, General MacArthur instructed his chief of staff, Major General Almond, to begin planning for an amphibious operation to hit the North Korean communication centre at Seoul. For MacArthur to think in terms of an amphibious landing in rear of the enemy to win the Korean War, was only natural.[15] Most of his Second World War campaigns in the South-West Pacific had started with an amphibious hook, by-passing enemy-held islands, or coastlines. The Americans possessed two priceless strategic cards; command of the sea, and the means to project military power from the sea in the form of amphibious ships and craft. Used correctly, applying the two great and enduring principles of war, taking advantage of one's own strengths and the enemy's weaknesses, and surprise, amphibious operations enable mobility and manoeuvre to be applied at the operational level of warfare, unlocking stalemate. All through July and August, despite other distractions, planning and discussion took place at MacArthur's headquarters on an amphibious landing behind the enemy lines. The planners refined the options to two beachheads: Inchon, 18 miles from Seoul; and Kunsan, 100 miles south of Inchon. MacArthur favoured Inchon, the Navy and the Marines preferred Kunsan. The lack of suitable beaches at Inchon, the large tidal range, and navigational problems made it a far less attractive prospect from a Naval point of view.[16]

MacArthur held firm for a landing at Inchon, despite the advice of the Navy. He considered that the North Koreans had neglected their rear and were 'dangling on a thin logistical rope that could be quickly cut in the Seoul area, that the enemy had committed practically all his forces against Eighth Army in the south and had no trained reserves and little power of recuperation'. Precisely because it was so difficult to land at Inchon, the enemy would believe that no one would be foolish enough to attempt such a move. He also considered that the quick capture of Seoul would be a psychological as well as a strategic victory. In his words: 'the anvil on which the hammer of Walker's Eighth Army from the south would crush the North Koreans'.

A landing at Kunsan would not sever the North Korean supply line, and succeed in destroying their army.[17] As a landing never took place at Kunsan, it is difficult to disprove MacArthur's contention that such a move would not bring about the cutting of the North Korean line of communication. However, a glance at a map shows that the distance from Kunsan to Taejon, the nearest road and rail centre on the North Korean lines of communication to Kunsan, is 50 miles as the crow flies, and nearer 70 miles along the twisting road. Taejon itself was only marginally further from the North Korean Army's positions, than from Kunsan. It was conceivable that the North Koreans could have moved troops to contest the seizure of Taejon, once the landing at Kunsan had been made, and bottled up the landing force in a second perimeter. Inchon being further away, would take longer to reinforce. In the event, it took thirteen days for the landing force to secure Seoul, only eighteen miles from the beaches.

MacArthur got his way. The landing was set for 15 September 1950. The force assigned to the operation was the newly formed X Corps, commanded by Almond until then MacArthur's chief of staff, and consisting of the 1st Marine Division and 7th Infantry Division. The landings at Inchon were a complete success, and Seoul was captured on 28 September. Until the link-up with Eighth Army, the Inchon operation was supported exclusively by ship-borne supply, much of which had come straight from the United States, thereby avoiding double handling in Japan or Pusan. Herculean efforts which had been made in the United States to meet MacArthur's logistic requirements made this amphibious landing possible.

The Eighth Army Breaks Out—Link-Up

Eighth Army began its attack all along the Pusan Perimeter on 16 September, aiming to fix the enemy to prevent him moving forces to meet the threat to his rear. Walker had logistic problems. His most serious shortage was artillery ammunition.[18] Even for the break-out, he had imposed a ration of fifty rounds per-gun per-day for important attacks, and twenty-five rounds for secondary attacks, until a ship-load of 105 mm shells arrived just in time for their use in the offensive. To begin with there was hard fighting, as the North Koreans resisted strongly. But from 19 September the effect of the Inchon landing and the battles round Seoul became apparent when the North Koreans started withdrawing from around the Pusan Perimeter, and moving north. By 23 September, they had withdrawn completely, and were in full retreat. MacArthur's choice had been vindicated. Eighth Army and the ROK Army advanced on eight axes. The leading troops of US I Corps linked up with X Corps at Osan on 27 September 1950, exactly twelve weeks after Task Force Smith's battle with the advancing North Koreans.

To Sieze a Port: Wonsan

After the junction of Eighth Army and X Corps, it would have appeared logical to place the latter under Walker. Apparently Walker thought so too, because shortly before the link-up, he sent a signal to MacArthur asking to be kept informed of X Corp's movements and plans so that he could plan for the junction. It then emerged that MacArthur had plans for another amphibious hook by X Corps, this time on the East coast at Wonsan, while Eighth Army continued with the main advance in the West. This plan was almost entirely driven by logistical arguments on the part of MacArthur in support of his plan to advance on a broad front to the borders of North Korea. He reasoned that he had to seize a port through which he could supply his forces operating on the eastern side of Korea. Two corridors ran to Wonsan from the west coast: one from Seoul, one from Pyongyang, the North Korean capital. A railway and a road ran along each corridor. North of the Pyongyang corridor there were no satisfactory lateral communications. Therefore, any operations in the rugged mountains of the interior of North Korea stretching to Manchuria, would be extremely difficult to sustain. Because the main logistic base for the war in Korea was Japan, it was as simple to ship supplies to Wonsan direct as to Inchon, thus reducing the overland distance. In arriving at this conclusion MacArthur took into consideration the state of communications from the Pusan Perimeter to the 38th Parallel. Air interdiction and North Korean demolitions had destroyed nearly all the road and rail bridges north of the Pusan Perimeter. The communication system in North Korea was in a similar state.

MacArthur had a second reason for the Wonsan landing, subsidiary to logistics, but nevertheless important. By driving west from Wonsan, X Corps could take Pyongyang from the north, while Eighth Army advanced from the south.

There were flaws in MacArthur's operational and logistic concepts, some of which were spotted by Walker. To delay the advance while X Corps reloaded in the ships, would allow the remaining North Korean forces to escape. Furthermore, the ROK Army, advancing up the East coast, might capture Wonsan before X Corps landed. Walker believed that X Corps should take Wonsan by advancing along the corridor from Seoul. When this had been achieved, their logistic support could be switched to that port and Hungnam, further north. He was supported by the Commander Naval Forces Far East who considered that X Corps could march to Wonsan in shorter time than it would take to reload, steam round, and land. Walker was proved right in his forecast that his Army would arrive at Pyongyang before X Corps could move west, and that the ROK I Corps would take Wonsan before the amphibious landing. However, MacArthur persisted with his plan to land X Corps at Wonsan, and for them to operate independently. He confirmed it by drawing the boundary between X Corps and Eighth Army to run north from the Pyongyang corridor to the Yalu River, along the watershed of the Taebaek Range.

Conceptual Flaws Create Logistical Problems

The decision to continue with the Wonsan landing by X Corps, despite the capture of the port by ROK I Corps on 10 October, was to have logistic repercussions on Eighth Army. For the first half of October, nearly all the facilities of Inchon port were busy mounting out the 1st Marine Division, and unable to offload ships for Eighth Army. Supplies had therefore to continue to come all the way from Pusan. Levels of stocks were at times reduced to one day's worth of supply.

Each day, armoured units operated in the battle zone, without knowing whether there would be fuel available to continue the following day. This situation continued until after mid-November. Eighth Army needed 4,000 tons of supplies a day for offensive operations, and this level of supply was not achieved until 20 November. Walker was forced to advance into North Korea with I Corps only, leaving IX Corps behind, until the logistical situation improved. As the army advanced, the age-old problem of stretched lines of communication and supply manifested itself. The key to the logistical problem lay, as so often before, with the railway. But despite prodigious efforts by the engineers re-building the bridges over the numerous rivers and replacing track, in general the railhead lagged about 200 miles behind the advancing Eighth Army front throughout October 1950.[19]

The distance from railhead to the front threw a considerable strain on the truck companies moving supplies forward along the rough roads. The longer the trucks ran over these roads, the more they became unserviceable, and as spares were in short supply, a breakdown of the logistic system looked likely. By the end of October a pipeline for aviation fuel was laid from Inchon to Kimpo airfield east of Seoul, which eased the strain on road transport. Eighth Army had captured Pyongyang before Inchon was available for its logistic support. As soon as Pyongyang fell, supplies began to be airlifted from Japan and Kimpo. Most of the loads consisted of ammunition; on one day, 28 October, 1,037 tons of ammunition was carried from Kimpo to Pyongyang.

A Dangerous Complacency

At the end of October, there was a general feeling among most American senior commanders that although the logistic situation was precarious, this was beginning to matter less and less for, in their opinion, the Korean War was all but over. Plans were in hand to backload troops to Japan, the United States, and Europe. General Walker sought permission to divert to Japan all ammunition ships arriving in Korea, because he considered there was enough ammunition in Korea to meet foreseeable requirements. MacArthur approved, and his chief logistician cancelled further sailings of ammunition ships from the United States. Meanwhile MacArthur having ordered a general advance on all available axes to the Yalu River, the ROK II Corps reached Chosan on the Yalu on 26 October, and ROK I Corps pushed to Chongjin, in the north-east corner of Korea, 60 miles from the Russian border. X Corps having landed administratively at Wonsan and Hungnam between 26 and 31 October, advanced to the Yalu at Hyesanjin. Although the Chinese Army had attacked the advancing Eighth Army at the end of October, by early November, they had withdrawn, and apparently faded out of the picture.

Soldierly Precautions

X Corps, with the exception of 1st Marine Division, had rushed forward to the Yalu in a precipitate manner. Major General Smith, commanding the Marines, had objected to the X Corps plans for the dispersal of his division over a wide area, and much to General Almond's dissatisfaction, the Marines had taken a long time to move; at times averaging about a mile a day. Smith also argued that he should not advance to the Chosin Reservoir with winter so close. Almond became more amenable to Smith's representations about leaving his Division concentrated, after Eighth Army's contact with the Chinese Army, and the appearance of Chinese on his own front, in early November. However, when this was followed by reports that the Chinese were withdrawing, Almond reiterated the order to close up to the border. Smith still advanced slowly, concentrating his attention on improving the road behind him, and securing his exposed line of communication back to Hungnam with outposts on the high ground overlooking the route. He was particularly concerned about his left flank, exposed by the gap between his Division and Eighth Army.[20] He improved his base at Hagaru-ri, including building an airstrip which would take C-47s. By 23 November, despite Almond's irritation, Smith had established a firm base for further operations in the frigid barren wastes around the Chosin Reservoir. The winter had already arrived two weeks before, bringing snow and sub-zero temperatures. Smith's careful preparation, and soldierly precautions, would ensure the survival of his Division.

... And a Faulty Assessment

Almond had been making plans to advance to destroy North Korean and Chinese forces in the Chosin Reservoir area, and threaten or cut the Chinese line of communication in the Eighth Army zone. The absence of enemy contact on Eighth Army's front led to optimism in MacArthur's headquarters that air attacks had succeeded in cutting the flow of supplies to the Chinese Army. He felt that if they tried to stop the advance of Walker's troops, they would be at a disadvantage. He told the Joint Chiefs of Staff in Washington that: 'the Chinese had embarked on their Korean venture in some cases with only three days' rations, and that constant contest with UN ground forces had undoubtedly depleted the enemy's ammunition reserves.'[21] And Major General Willoughby, MacArthur's chief of intelligence, did not consider the Chinese high command would make any appreciable effort to alleviate the supply shortage of their forces, . . . 'as the Chinese have always been, by Western standards, notoriously poor providers for their soldiers.'

This assessment was probably based upon experience in the Second World War, when the performance of Chinese troops, including their commanders' staff work and administration, had consistently been inferior to the Japanese, and thus by inference, to the Americans.

The Chinese Re-Enter and the Eighth Army Withdraws

Hopes of victory, which seemed so close on 24 November, waned when the Chinese Army re-entered the scene on 25 November, starting by crushing ROK II Corps, and following up with attacks on the remainder of Eighth Army, the ROK Army, and X Corps. As Eighth Army withdrew towards Seoul, X Corps was ordered to pull back to a perimeter round Hungnam, and eventually to re-embark and abandon North Korea. The 1st Marine Division was cut off at the Chosin Reservoir, but thanks to Smith's preparations, and the fighting qualities of his marines he was able to battle his way out of the trap. Asked if he was withdrawing by correspondents, he replied, 'Gentlemen, we are not retreating. We are merely advancing in another direction'. The Marines' performance was by far the most creditable of any American formation that winter. It had its basis in good logistic planning, the leadership of Smith, and, it must be said, in a soldierly pride and spirit, lacking in the majority of the United States Army at the time.

Ridgway

By Christmas 1950, Eighth Army and the ROK Army were back on the general line of the 38th Parallel. As they fled south in near panic, they abandoned 8,000–10,000 tons of supplies in Pyongyang, and destroyed another 2,000 tons that could not be saved at Chinnampo.

They had a new commander, Lieutenant General Ridgway; Walker having died as a result of a traffic accident. X Corps and ROK I Corps had completed their withdrawal from Hungnam, and come under command of Eighth Army. Largely because neither the Chinese nor North Korean forces attempted any serious disruption of the operation, the withdrawal from Hungnam was a model of organisation. In all 105,000 troops, 98,000 Korean civilians, 17,500 vehicles, and 350,000 tons of bulk cargo were evacuated, in 193 shiploads.

Given *carte blanche* to employ the Army as he thought best, Ridgway set about restoring morale, which was about to suffer yet another blow when the Chinese mounted an offensive at the New Year.

The 1st United States Marine Division, which included the 41st British Commando Royal Marines, and the British and Commonwealth Brigades were among the only, if not the only, formations whose morale was not sagging after the events of the previous weeks and months.

Ridgway, a great commander and soldier's general, went on an immediate tour of the battlefield to see for himself the state of morale. He knew that he would never get a feel for the situation second-hand. Eighth Army's fighting spirit and its pride in itself must be restored before it returned to the offensive. Everywhere he went he found a loss of confidence and lack of spirit. (He makes it plain that the Xth Corps, which included the 1st Marine Division had not re-joined the Army at this stage). Leaders at every level were unresponsive, surly, and slow to answer his questions.

He could not help contrasting this to the way a young British subaltern:

'trotted down off a knoll to greet me when he spotted the insignia on my jeep. He saluted smartly and identified himself'.

Ridgway knew that the British Brigade had only a few men to cover a wide front, and that a Chinese attack was expected hourly. He asked the subaltern how he found the situation:

'"Quite all right sir," he replied quickly. Then he added with a pleasant smile, "It *is* a bit drafty up here".'

Ridgway's comment in his book is:

'Drafty was the word for it, with gaps in the line wide enough to march an army through.'

Ridgway set about putting matters right. As well as insisting on proper standards, and sacking those commanders who did not come up to scratch, he made changes that soldiers, particularly in the bitter winter weather, could appreciate. He ordered that hot meals were to be sent forward as far as possible. He took to carrying a supply of gloves with him, to hand to soldiers who had lost or torn theirs.[22]

For the next six months, as offensive was followed by counter-offensive, the United Nations[23] line moved to and fro, as far south as Osan, and back, just north of the 38th Parallel. From the end of June 1951, despite violent but sporadic fighting, except for small gains and losses of ground, the line remained static while Armistice negotiations dragged on for two years. Ridgway has given logistics as one of his reasons for not wishing to pursue the Chinese further north, and close up to the Yalu again, when it appeared they were on the run, and short of supplies in June 1951. He was sure that the Eighth Army could have driven the Chinese back however, 'it would have greatly shortened the enemy supply lines and greatly lengthened our own'.[24]

Positions Stabilise and the Logistical Situation Eases

Once the positions stabilised, supply for the United Nations forces became easier, although there were still problems. The logistical effort in Korea depended on the railways, and on any given day in 1951, there were likely to be more than thirty trains despatched from Pusan, about three-quarters of them carrying supplies to forward railheads. Each train consisted of twenty to forty wagons, carrying about 500 tons of freight an average distance of 100 miles. About twenty-five to thirty miles behind each division was a supply point which held a three to five day stock of supplies. Behind this was a back-up point which also held three to five days' stocks. Further back again was a regulating point holding two days' stocks on rail wagons. Movement forward from supply points to divisional dumps was under divisional control by truck or train. The problem facing the Military Railway Service was twofold, a shortage of rail wagons, and one third of these sitting idle, sometimes for weeks at various points between Pusan and the railheads. The establishment of intermediate depots between Pusan and the frontline would have alleviated this situation, but this was never done.

More reliance on road transport would have helped, but was difficult to implement. The road network in Korea was poor, and remained so despite engineer effort. Also, considerably less trucks were allocated to Eighth Army than were warranted by experience in the Second World War. More trucks would have cost more in terms of fuel and maintenance; rail transport was more economical. However, truck convoys were used, sometimes as an 'informal distribution system' calling at the depots in and near Pusan, by-passing the regular distribution system, in an effort to obtain supplies more quickly. These expeditions led to hoarding and waste.

Forward of the roadhead, often well behind the front line, supplies were carried by Korean porters. Using an A-frame, each was expected to carry fifty pounds ten miles daily. There were few helicopters available before 1953, and these could lift only light loads. Some air-drops were carried out, mostly by aircraft based in Japan, since there were few airfields in Korea, and this proved very expensive. Pack animals would have solved some of the problems of supplying forward units, but there were few available in Korea, and expense, again, precluded their importation.

This inflexible logistic system, with overdependence on railways, was adequate for the situation over the period of stalemate after mid-1951. But in the opinion of General Taylor, who took command in early 1953, although Eighth Army 'achieved a tactical mobility which allowed it to shift its reserves readily to meet threatened points along the immediate front, it depended for its mobility upon an elaborate supply system which would have been most difficult to displace if our forces had been required to move rapidly forward over considerable distances into enemy territory'. So it is perhaps fortunate that the aims of the United States government with regard to Korea, did not include an advance from the general line reached in mid-1951; Eighth Army's logistic system may not have been able to cope.

*   *   *

Operation STRANGLE

It is instructive to look at United Nations efforts to disrupt the Chinese supply system over this same period of two years between July 1951 and the signing of the Armistice. Starting in August 1951, the Fifth US Air Force under General Everest concentrated its efforts on the interdiction of railways, bridges, roads, marshalling yards, and supply points, in an attempt to slow down the flow of Chinese and North Korean troops and equipment.[25] The rail interdiction programme was given the codename STRANGLE; whether the selection of this particular title was a conscious decision or not, it was an unfortunate choice being identical to the codename used for the 1944 rail interdiction operation in Italy, about which Slessor had expressed doubts.[26] By October, American intelligence reported that the lines

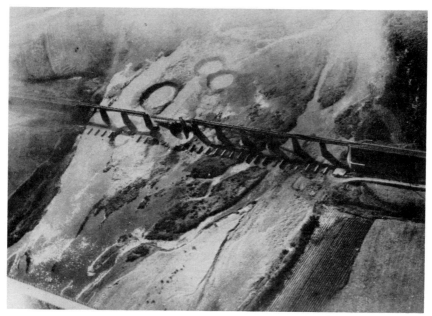

Fig. 4.2   Bridge in North Korea after an air strike (*IWM*).

were being destroyed faster than the Communist forces could repair them. At first the main bombing effort had been directed to the rail bridges, but the Communists became adept at repairing or bypassing the damage. They stockpiled spare bridge sections by the key bridges to speed up the repair. The Americans retaliated by switching to cutting the railway at several points along its length, which had the effect of slowing down repairs. The United States and British Navies also assisted in railway cutting operations, using carrier-born aircraft, commando raids, and gunfire, the latter mainly on the East coast where for many miles the line ran close to the sea. As the effort was stepped up, it took the Communist forces as much as three days to repair breaks in the rail system that had previously taken only one.

Despite this, rail traffic continued to move, and the line of communication was not cut. The Communists managed to bring forward winter clothing to the troops, even though it had to be carried by porters. Interdiction made supply more difficult but not impossible. The ingenuity of the Communists was one reason for the failure of Operation STRANGLE to live up to its name. For example at an important rail bridge north-east of Pyongyang, pilots kept reporting the bridge out of service for lack of two spans. Only after a night photograph was taken, was it discovered that the Communists fitted removable spans each night, allowing the bridge to be used throughout the hours of darkness.

The Resourceful Enemy

Communist resourcefulness was not the only reason for STRAN-GLE's partial success. In a period of static defence, the consumption of ammunition and supplies was low enough for the Communists not merely to support their troops adequately, but also to stockpile supplies and build up their troop strength. By early January 1952, General Ridgway assessed that unless the Communists were forced to expend their supplies at a faster rate, by a change in the battle situation, they would be in a position to mount and sustain a major offensive. Rail cutting operations were accordingly stepped up, to include putting out of action ever longer stretches of line. To begin with, this took the Communists by surprise and lines were sometimes out of action for as much as ten to fourteen days at a time. However, the Communists countered by moving flak guns to the threatened areas, shooting down ever increasing numbers of attacking aircraft. Communist manpower was also mobilised to meet the threat. The North Koreans had three brigades of 7,700 men each, engaged exclusively on railway repair. At every major station 50 men were positioned to carry out the skilled work, and 10 man teams were spaced at four mile intervals along the track. When a rail walker reported a break, these teams rushed to the scene. Unskilled local labour was moved in at once to refill holes and repair the road-bed. At night the experts laid sleepers and rails. American intelligence estimated that up to half a million troops and civilians were engaged on rail repair work. In this way 'the Communists have constantly been able to repair a given stretch of track on a vital line in twelve hours or less. On occasions repair crews were found repairing fresh cuts while strikes were still being made', reported naval pilots.[27] The Communists also hid their trains during daylight in the numerous tunnels in the mountainous country. Wagons containing the important supplies, such as fuel and ammunition, were located in the centre part of the train. Attempts by United Nations airmen to skip bombs into the mouths of tunnels, merely blocked the tunnel entrance. Unskilled local labour could clear the debris in daylight, and the trains steamed on as soon as it was dark. As spring 1952 approached STRANGLE was becoming less and less cost-effective. Even an operation known as SATURATE, which consisted of concentrating on a particular stretch of road-bed around-the-clock proved disappointing. The Communists repaired the section in six days, meanwhile, during SATURATE, other parts of the network were left free from attack. Muscle power and simple tools were frustrating all the efforts of air power, summed up in a sentence from the United States Air Force historical study: 'to continue the rail attacks would be, in effect, to pit skilled pilots, equipped with modern expensive aircraft, against unskilled oriental coolie laborers armed with pick and shovel.'[28] This extract also unconsciously reveals a lack of understanding of, and contempt for, the Asian peasant; a sentiment that was to persist into the next war in which the United States was to be involved in Asia, with dire consequences. It must be said that the United Nations air forces were unable to bomb at night and in bad weather, during which repairs could be effected and trains moved. By the end of April 1950, the interdiction campaign had reached stalemate. In May the realisation of this led to a significant change in the air interdiction methods employed by the United Nations.

However, all the efforts had not been completely wasted, a report from Eighth Army to Ridgway in mid-March included the paragraph:

> 'The air interdiction program has not been able to prevent the enemy from accumulating supplies at the front in a static situation. It has, however, been a major factor in preventing the enemy from attaining equality or superiority in artillery and other weapons employed at the front. Thus it has also decreased the offensive and defensive capability of the enemy.'[29]

The new tactics involved fighter-bombers striking at the Communist supplies, equipment and troops massed behind their lines, while medium bombers devoted their attention to airfields, railway systems, and supply and communication centres. In addition attacks were mounted on hydro-electric systems in the north of North Korea, which resulted in a two week power black out of the whole country, and only gradual restoration for weeks afterwards. This was followed by further attacks on industrial and strategic targets, which continued up to the end of the war, aimed at putting pressure on the Communist side in the Armistice negotiations, as well as reducing the war-fighting capability of the North Koreans. The ending of the rail interdiction programme released more aircraft for close air support of ground troops, particularly heartening during the bitter battles of winter 1952 and spring 1953. These battles usually started with massed Chinese attacks, followed by United Nations counter-attacks, often resulting in hand-to-hand fighting, as features with names like Porkchop, Old Baldy, Spud Hill, Reno, Vegas, and the Hook changed hands, or were held in desperate fights. Despite the air effort against the Communist supply system, they were still able to stockpile enough in the forward areas to sustain themselves for thirty to forty-five days.

THE LESSONS

In the last months of the war the Communist forces were stronger than ever both in numerical and logistic terms. In one ten day period in July 1953, they expended 197,550 artillery rounds, and in the whole month fired more shells than in any other month of the war. Even after the huge losses in June and July, there were over a million well fed and clothed Chinese and North Korean soldiers in Korea. Throughout the war the Communist lines of communication had been bombed and shelled, but the vast pool of human labour, deception, and subterfuge had enabled enough supplies to arrive at the front to maintain their forces and to build up reserves. They were considerably aided by the static nature of the campaign in the last two years, a result of the United Nations understandable unwillingness to pay the cost in blood and treasure to mount a major offensive aimed at breakthrough and a war of maneouvre. Had such an offensive taken place, most of the logistic cards would have been held by the United Nations, because of their command of the sea and air. Although, as alluded to earlier, the inflexible United Nations logistic system, caused mainly by parsimony, would have been a considerable hindrance.

Two Critical Periods

Logistically, the two critical periods in the war, from an American/ South Korean point of view, were: first, during the retreat to, and battle for, the Pusan Perimeter; and second, during the advance to the Yalu. In the first period, the situation was saved by the ability of the Americans to react quickly, using their huge resources of air and sea transport to move large quantities of supplies to Pusan. Regarding the second with the advantage of hindsight, had MacArthur not insisted on the Wonsan landing, thus both delaying Walker's advance north of Seoul, and limiting it initially to one corps, it is conceivable that Eighth Army would have been better balanced and able to withstand the Chinese offensive. However, the operational concept was also at fault. Instead of a broad-front advance to the Yalu to hold ground of no significance whatsoever, it would have been better to remain concentrated, and thus poised to strike at the Chinese once they had showed their hand. Indeed by his piecemeal deployment, MacArthur was inviting attack. However, this can only be being wise after the event. What is clear is that had the occupation divisions in Japan been properly equipped, trained, and logistically supported, they would have been better able to hold, and even defeat, the invading North Koreans in the opening phase of the War. Training is only one of the ingredients that go to make up a state of readiness for war. Logistics play as important a part, covering a wide range of requirements: the availability of modern weapons, equipment, and their state of repair; readily available spares and efficient repair facilities; adequate stocks of fuel and ammunition; a well tested supply system; movement resources capable of operating over a wide variety of terrain, and able to lift the tonnages needed to sustain the force engaged in battle. It takes longer to provide all these than to train any army, and involves much planning, foresight, and expense. Although the United States was logistically unprepared for the Korean War, its enormous industrial capacity, energy, and optimism, a legacy of the Second World War, enabled it to close the gap. The gap would have been closed quicker had the United States not spent the years between 1945 and 1950 preparing to fight the last war rather than the next. However, she was not the first to fall into this trap, and very likely not the last.

Use of the Sea Flank

The Korean War also demonstrated the advantages that accrue to the side that commands the sea, and has the ability to project its power ashore by amphibious operations, in a situation where there is a sea flank, in this case two. Such power not only enables its possesser to unlock stalemate, and return to manoeuvre warfare, but to use the greater carrying capacity of ships to shorten land lines of communication.

Strangulation Rather Than Interdiction

The war in Korea showed yet again, for those who chose to see it, that sitting astride the enemy's logistic windpipe with a strong force is a surer way to guarantee denying his supply than bombing or shelling. This was convincingly demonstrated at Inchon because the Americans possessed the ability to manoeuvre round the enemy, through the imaginative use of power projected from the sea. Where the conditions for such operations do not exist, and in the search for other means, it is tempting to fall back on the use of air power because it is less expensive, remote, and the effort can be switched on and off. It is likely to be less than effective. If in addition there is an under-estimation of the effectiveness of the opponents' 'primitive' logistic system, combined with an unwillingness, or inability, for whatever reason, political or military, to take the battle to him, so that he is not forced to consume supplies faster than he can replace them, air interdiction is unlikely to cut his supply system completely. Putting it crudely, if your opponent is allowed to 'call the shots', because he is able, for geographic, or political reasons, to dictate the tempo of operations, he will also be able to cut his operational coat according to the amount of logistic cloth he has available.

A Final Comment and an Unheeded Warning

Seeking a final comment on the logistic aspects of a war fought against an Asian nation, one could find few more apposite than the view expressed in the fourth volume of the United States Army Official History of the Korean War published in 1966:

> 'Lacking construction equipment, Chiang Kai-shek had used hand labor to construct the airfields for US planes in World War II and successfully completed the huge task. In Korea the Chinese again demonstrated how manpower could be used in quantity to take the place of machines. Although this process might be uneconomical and wasteful in principle, it was effective as an expedient and as a countermeasure In this case superior technology, far from leading to an easy victory, produced no victory at all . . . It would be unfortunate if the hard-won lessons learned in the Korean War, both on the battlefield and in the negotiations should be ignored or forgotten because of the absence of victory.'[30]

By 1966 the United States would again be pitting itself against an Asian nation.

5

Insufficiency and Super-Abundance: Indo-China and Vietnam 1946–75

On 7 May 1954 the exhausted survivors of the French garrison of the main, central camp at Dien Bien Phu surrendered to the forces of the Vietnamese Independence League (the Vietminh) after a siege lasting three months. Over the preceding days, successive waves of attacks had overrun the mutually supporting strongholds sited to provide an interlocking system of defence round the central position. In a landscape reminiscent of the Third Battle of Ypres, both sides fought, often waist deep in waterlogged trench systems, battered by artillery fire. Mining operations by the Vietminh collapsed the French trenches, and in one case blew up a complete strongpoint. The wounded of both sides lay in mud and filth in the field hospitals, without drugs, many dying of gangrene. The stench of hundreds of decaying bodies pervaded the air. Some of the finest fighting units in the French Army had been completely destroyed, their officers and soldiers, dead, wounded or taken prisoner. When the battle started, the garrison had consisted of twelve infantry battalions, including élite parachute and Foreign Legion battalions, the equivalent of two battalions (in British terms, regiments) of artillery, and ten light tanks. In the course of the battle, five more parachute battalions and three complete Airborne Surgical Teams were dropped to reinforce the garrison, and 1,530 volunteers were parachuted in as individual replacements for specialists who had become casualties. The last group of 94 volunteers dropped one day

133

before the central position fell. Only seventy men from the whole garrison found their way back to the French forces in Laos. Round one in the Vietnamese struggle for independence was over. General Giap had won a crushing victory, and part of his country. The French had lost the whole of Indo-China[1] to a man who ten years before had led a platoon of ragged guerrillas in the jungles just south of the Chinese/ Vietnamese border; a man, who despite his boast to Le Clerc in 1945, 'I have been to a military academy—that of the bush and guerrilla war against the Japanese', had little experience, but learned fast.[2]

Giap was born in 1912, and his early years were influenced by his father's loathing of the French. In 1924 he entered the Lycée National at Hue, a recognition of his intellect. At 14, he was exiled to China for revolutionary activity, where he first met Ho Chi Minh (see below). At sixteen he returned to Hue as an underground member of the Tan Viet party, who were almost, but not quite, communists. His part in an abortive uprising earned him a spell in jail. Here he met the girl who was to become his first wife. In 1932, the French allowed him to take the Baccalaureate at Hue, and enter Hanoi university, where he gained a Bachelor of Law degree. An avid reader of military history and communist theory, in his day, he was considered one of the most brilliant students at the university.

After qualifying he supported himself financially by teaching at a private high school. A former pupil remembers how he could draw on the blackboard every battle plan of Napoleon in the minutest detail, and was known as 'the general'. By this time Giap had joined the communist party, and when it was outlawed by the French in 1940, he was forced to flee to China to escape imprisonment. His immediate family were not so fortunate. His wife and daughter, his father, two sisters, brother-in-law, and sister-in-law all died in prison, or were executed by the French before 1943.

In early June 1940, Giap again met Ho Chi Minh, who despatched him to the Chinese Communist headquarters in Yenan to study politics and military techniques. But before he arrived, his orders were changed. Ho Chi Minh, realising that the defeat of the French army in France would change the situation in Indo-China, told Giap and other Vietnamese communists in China to return to Vietnam. Here he set up his first 'self-defence unit', ambushing a few French patrols, assassinating reactionary Vietnamese officials, and spreading propaganda.

In December 1944, Giap was ordered to form the first of the Vietnam Propaganda and Liberation Units, the forerunners of the People's Army of North Vietnam, the North Vietnamese Regular Army. This combination of a military and political force was a feature of the North Vietnamese Army. With these units, Giap began his career as a leader of organised military forces, and played a leading part in the almost bloodless seizure of power throughout North Vietnam in August 1945. It must be emphasised that his military experience at this stage was miniscule, less than most platoon commanders in Western armies in 1945. Therefore, despite profound study of the great masters of military strategy, including Napoleon and Lawrence of Arabia, it is remarkable that he could have propelled himself to the equivalent of a four star general in the short time he did. It is a tribute to his power of intellect, ruthlessness, and above all ability to learn, albeit painfully and at great expense in terms of his soldiers' lives. The strategy for the war he was to fight was hammered out with Ho Chi Minh and Truong Chinh. The latter was the Vietnamese communist party's leading theoretician, and converted Giap to communism in 1937.

Ho Chi Minh was a founder member of the French communist party in 1920, and went on to form the Vietnam Revolutionary Youth League among a group of Vietnamese exiles living in Canton. From the training school for cadres established by Ho Chi Minh in Canton, graduates returned to Vietnam to organise cells in their home districts. In 1930 the first attempt at overthrowing French colonial rule in Vietnam was suppressed with great brutality. In 1941, in a cave in a remote part of north-eastern Vietnam, Ho Chi Minh founded the Vietnamese Independence League (Viet Nam Doc Lap Dong Minh Hoi or Vietminh), aimed at attracting all who opposed the French and the Japanese, the latter having taken control of Indo-China following the fall of France. After a spell in a Chinese prison, Ho Chi Minh was released to take charge of all Vietnamese exiles in China. In March 1945, the United States Army Air Force contacted him to ask him to provide intelligence and assist in rescuing downed Allied pilots in return for communications equipment, medical supplies and small arms. This initial contact was expanded towards the end of the war with Japan, to include co-operation between the Vietminh and the United States Office of Strategic Services (OSS), the forerunner of the CIA and special forces. This OSS/Vietminh co-operation, which on the whole was not a success, was to lead to French assertions that had the United States not armed the Vietminh, the guerrilla war would have been easier to contain; not easy to prove, but an ironic twist in the light of the subsequent involvement of the United States in Indo-China.

Space does not permit a complete review of the French/Vietminh war; eight years. But as the title of this chapter implies, it was a war in which logistics decided the outcome. Giap defeated an army led by experienced and well trained generals, and well supplied with equipment by the most powerful nation in the world. Nor was the quality of the soldiers at the disposal of the French generals, the instruments through which they implemented their plans, a factor in their defeat. The French Expeditionary Force was composed entirely of volunteers, Foreign Légionnaires, parachute battalions, marines, colonial battalions,[3] Africans, and last, but not least, Vietnamese units led by Frenchmen. Admittedly, the 100,000 strong Vietnamese National Army, not to be confused with Vietnamese units in the French Expeditionary Force, was of little use because of desertion, recruiting problems, and poor leadership. In 1947, the early part of the war, the French had about 115,000 troops in all of Indo-China. They were well equipped, the soldiers were well-trained and experienced. Their leaders had been tested in battle. However, there was a serious weakness, one that was to make a significant contribution to eventual defeat. France, weakened economically and psychologically by her defeat by the Germans in 1940, rotten at the core, plagued by a seemingly endless procession of governments, never supported the war wholeheartedly. Her political leaders lacked the will, and this manifested itself in an unwillingness to provide enough troops and money.

The Vietminh were numerically superior in North Vietnam, in Round One the vital area, although the size of their forces was never exactly known, then, or until the end of the Fourth Round in 1975. But they probably had about 50,000 in Main Force Units and some 30–50,000 in Regional Forces and guerrillas.[4] Despite their numerical superiority, the Vietminh, from Giap to the newest guerrilla, were inexperienced and under-equipped. They had no artillery, no air force, no armour, no signals organisation and, above all, no logistic system. The largest unit was a battalion of about 1,000 men. The Vietminh were untrained in operations of over battalion size, as were their commanders in handling more than one unit. They had four great advantages. They were fighting for their own independence, and had the majority of the populace on their side. This, combined with excellent propaganda and indoctrination gave the Vietminh high morale. Second, the large size of the area and the unwillingness of the French government to supply sufficient troops made control of the countryside very difficult. If the French tried to control the whole country, they would be spread in penny packets and defeated in detail. If they concentrated round the key areas, they abandoned the countryside to the Vietminh. Third, they had a base area adjacent to China, the

Viet Bac. Here they had a training area, a potential logistic base and a safe zone for the Vietminh government. Fourth, the terrain and climate favoured guerrilla operations and defence. The Vietminh knew the country and were acclimatised. It is worth digressing for a moment to look briefly at the geography and the physical and climatic features of the country, not only do these have an effect on tactics, but also on logistics.

The War Zone

Indo-China (and in none of the Rounds was the fighting confined only to North and South Vietnam), is larger than Burma. The juxtaposition of Vietnam (where most of the fighting took place), with Laos, Cambodia and China endowed the Vietminh with priceless advantages. In Round One, Giap could draw French troops away from Vietnam by threatening Laos and Cambodia. In Rounds Two and Three, the inability and unwillingness of these two countries to deny the North Vietnamese use of their territory, handed Giap base sanctuaries and two lines of communication, along which the Viet Cong and the North Vietnamese operating in South Vietnam could receive huge quantities of supplies—the Ho Chi Minh trail running down the Eastern side of Laos and northern Cambodia, and the lesser known Sihanouk Route from the Cambodian port of Sihanoukville, where eastern bloc ships unloaded supplies, which were then transported via Phnom Penh to extensive base areas just inside Cambodia. The proximity of China on Vietnam's northern border was even more important, and particularly when the communists arrived late in 1949. China is a mortal enemy of Vietnam, as she has been through most of history, but in the period 1949 to 1975, China was perfectly happy to support the Vietminh, and later, the North Vietnamese, if it meant weakening the West, and in particular, the hated Americans. The Soviets took a similar view, with the added incentive that a strong, independent, pro-Russian Vietnam would act as a very effective distraction to the Chinese.

Geography

Vietnam is about 850 miles from North to South, and varies in width from 50 to 300 miles. Its shape has been described by Giap: 'stretching like an immense "S" along the edge of the Pacific, it includes Bac Bo or North Vietnam, which with the Red River Delta, is a region rich in

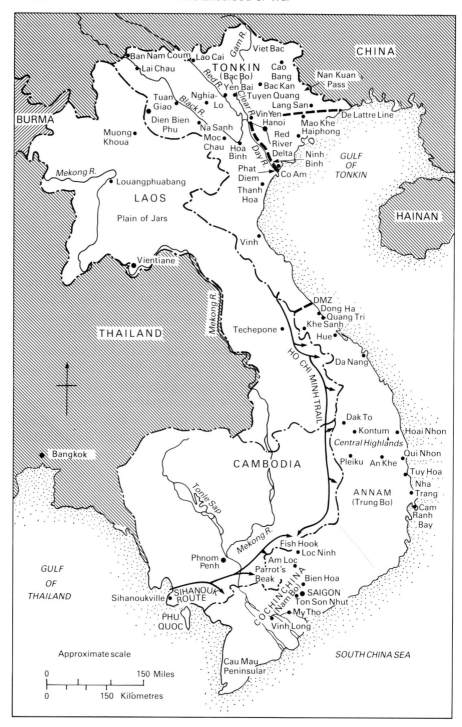

MAP V   Indo-China 1947–75.

agricultural and industrial possibilities: Nam Bo or South Vietnam, a vast alluvial plain furrowed by the arms of the Mekong and especially favourable to agriculture, and Trung Bo, or Central Vietnam, a long narrow belt of land joining them.'[5] More than one half of Vietnam consists of heavily forested hills and mountains. The Annamite chain of mountains runs from China along the western edge of, and for two-thirds the length of, Vietnam. Not high by European standards, these mountains are steep and covered with dense jungle. In many areas, the mountains contained numerous, large limestone caves, big enough to store supplies, and hide headquarters and equipment. The two huge river deltas are connected by a narrow coastal plain. The plains in the river deltas are heavily populated, and subject to natural flooding, the Mekong delta more so than the Red River, or Tonkin, delta. The Mekong delta is criss-crossed by streams, rivers and canals, forcing all vehicles to follow dikes, dams and the few roads. From mid-May to mid-October vast areas of the Mekong delta are under water. In the monsoon, the Red River and its tributaries actually flow above ground level in some places because of the huge earth banks, or bunds, built to contain them in the flood time. This constituted a weakness, which in Round Two the Americans decided not to exploit. Although views are divided on the matter, the balance of opinion is that despite the banks being up to forty feet thick in places, they could have been breached by iron bombs, causing extensive flooding of the key agricultural and industrial areas in the delta.

Climate

The climate is sub-tropical, with high humidity throughout the year. The South-West Monsoon starts about mid-May and ends about mid-October. The North-East Monsoon starts about mid-September, ending towards the end of December. Of the two, the South-West Monsoon has by far the greater impact on operations. The North-East Monsoon affects only coastal areas in the centre of the country, with drizzle, fog (known to the French as *Crachin*, spit), and rain. Most, although not all, Vietminh and North Vietnamese/Viet Cong major operations took place in the dry season, early January to mid-May; among the exceptions, Dien Bien Phu.

Terrain

Over 80 per cent of the country is covered by forest. The triple canopy jungle provided cover for defensive positions, movement, supply lines and depots; cover which the Vietminh, the Viet Cong and the North Vietnamese Army used to their advantage. Bamboo, shrubs, and grass, even in the more open areas, provided numerous excellent ambush positions and impeded movement. The Ca Mau Peninsula, at the southern tip of the country, is an expanse of stagnant marshes and low-lying mangrove forests, impassable except by small boats, and the hide-out of guerrillas for most of Rounds One, Two, Three and Four. Diseases flourished: principally, malaria, dengue, cholera, hepatitis and typhoid. Between 1950 and 1954, about 25 per cent of French Union Troops were debilitated by schistosomiasis and leptospirosis.

Communications

Vietnam had a number of ports, although as will be explained later, not all were fully developed. In Round One, the most important was the Haiphong port complex, supplying the French. In Round Three the dependence of North Vietnam on one port complex was a major military weakness, ready for exploitation by an enemy. The road system was underdeveloped, mostly tracks. The few main roads were cut by demolished bridges, in the mountains by landslides, and everywhere overgrown and potholed. There was one railway line, built by the French, running from Saigon to Hanoi, and on into China. Unsurfaced roads quickly became quagmires in the rains. Floods following rain in the low-lying areas prevented cross-country movement by wheeled vehicles, and even tracked vehicles became road-bound. Typhoons endangered shipping at exposed anchorages, snapped ship-to-shore fuel lines, and halted unloading. The dry season brings clouds of dust churned up by helicopters, vehicles, engineer plant, and aircraft. This permeates everywhere, most significantly engine intakes and the moving parts of equipment, clogging and causing damage.

*   *   *

The Early Pattern of the Wars

This is not the place to discuss the years leading up to the start of Round One, the French/Vietminh war. Until December 1946, the Vietminh had openly maintained large self-defence forces in Hanoi and the major cities and towns, and had campaigned on a political rather than the military front. Suffice it to say that after the breakdown of political negotiations, because the French were not prepared to grant the Vietnamese full independence, the French drove the Vietminh out of the cities and villages into the mountains and jungles. The French held the populated lowlands, while the Vietminh withdrew to the Viet Bac. The French sought to defeat the Vietminh quickly, before war-weariness at home, the weak economy, and world public opinion forced them to give up. At the outset the war was one of colonial re-conquest. It therefore damaged the French in the eyes of their own allies, principally the Americans, who were suspicious of colonialism. The war became respectable, indeed even 'sanctified' to use Fall's expression,[6] when the North Koreans invaded South Korea, and the French battle with a Communist enemy could be portrayed as part of an Asia-wide strategy: defeating Communism from Korea to Malaya, where the British were combating Chinese Communist guerrillas. This change of perception, which the French politicians did not hesitate to exploit, invoking the bogeyman of a communist dominated South-East Asia down to Australia, led to a huge influx of American equipment. It did not alter more key factors such as terrain and geography, particularly the ability of the Vietminh to train and find sanctuary in China from 1949 onwards. From 1953, the cease fire in Korea allowed the whole Asian communist war effort to concentrate on the struggle in Indo-China.

The Vietminh wanted a long war to exploit the French weaknesses, and to give themselves time to build up and equip their forces. In choosing this strategy the Vietminh were opting to follow a classic principle of war, perhaps, with surprise, one of two key principles: take advantage of your own strengths and the enemy's weaknesses while negating your own weaknesses and the enemy strengths. From 1947, therefore, the Vietminh tried to avoid major actions involving their Main Force units, while Regional and guerrilla units harassed the French. The French strategy, on the other hand was always aimed at bringing about one big battle which would dispose of the Vietminh Main Forces once and for all. The main battlefield in Round One was North Vietnam, the Red River delta and the area to the north and west.

Operation LEA: October 1947

It is worth looking at the first attempt by the French to destroy the Vietminh main force in October 1947, because it encapsulates the faults in French strategy and tactics that were to be repeated time and again. The French commander-in-chief, Lieutenant General Valluy was under pressure from the government to achieve a quick result. But even more pressing was the prospect of Nationalist China crumbling, and the arrival of communist forces on Vietnam's northern border. Valluy's aim was to take the Vietminh governmental and military headquarters in the village of Bac Kan in the Viet Bac. The concept for the operation, codeword LEA, was two pincers and a prong. The prong would be provided by Groupement S, two parachute battalions under Lieutenant Colonel Sauvagnac dropping on to Bac Kan, and two villages on the track to Bac Kan; Cho Don, twelve miles away, and Cho Moi, twenty miles away. Quite a dispersion for a force of 1,100 men! Meanwhile Groupement B, under Colonel Beauffre, consisting of three infantry battalions, supported by three armoured and three artillery battalions, one engineering and one transport battalion, would form the northern pincer. Starting at Lang Son, they would advance 140 miles along the road via Cao Bang and Nguyen Binh to link up with the parachute force. The southern pincer, Groupement C, consisted of three infantry battalions, supported by one artillery battalion under Lieutenant Colonel Communal. They were to be lifted in landing craft from Hanoi up the Red River, the Clear River to Tuyen Quang, and on, if possible up the Song Gam River, to assault the Bac Kan area from the south and west. Close air support was provided by all the Spitfire IXs of 4th Fighter Group. The parachute battalions were to jump from American C-47s (Dakotas), and German Junkers 52s (the same types that had delivered the German paratroopers to Crete six years before); the equipment had a distinctly Second World War look, which was fair enough as that war had ended barely two and a half years before. However, the tactics were Second World War too, and this nearly led to disaster.

The parachute drop went exactly to plan and took Giap and Ho Chi Minh, sitting in their headquarters, by surprise. They hid, and then escaped. It was the last time that the French came near to having either of them in their grasp. The next day, the Vietminh, inspired by Ho and Giap, attacked the paratroopers in strength, and by Day Three had them surrounded and battling for their lives. The prong had failed to spear the fish, and was in danger of being destroyed. Group B, the northern pincer, crawled slowly forward. The whole group, the equivalent of a reinforced brigade group, tied to one road by its vehicles, was forced to advance on a section (8–10 men) front. Ambushes, blown brigades, road demolitions, felled trees, resulted in clearing operations every mile or so of the 140 miles. The Vietminh did not stay to fight, but melted away as soon as the infantry, supported by the leading tank, deployed to attack. It took six days to cover

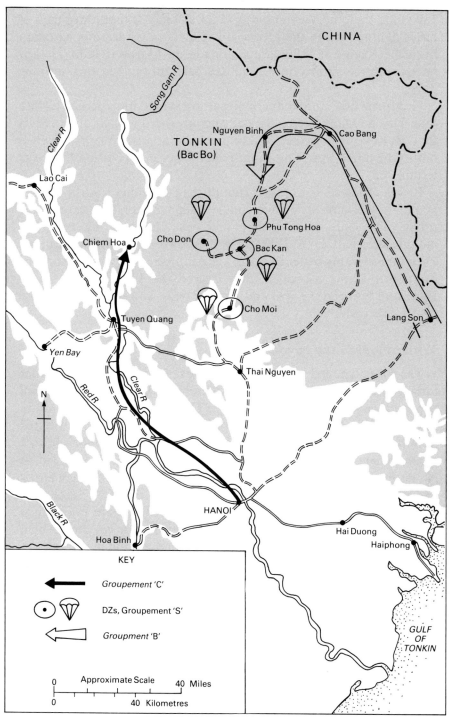

MAP VI   Operation LEA Autumn 1947.

130 miles, then the Vietminh dug in for a stand. It took three days of bitter fighting before the Moroccan soldiers of the leading battalion from the Regiment Infanterie Coloniale du Maroc (RICM), joined hands with the paratroopers who had held out on their own for nine days.

Groupement C, the southern pincer, prevented from getting further than Tuyen Quang in craft, landed and advanced to their objective on foot. However, before they could encircle the area, the Vietminh pulled out to the north-west. One month after it began, operation LEA was terminated.

It was followed by another month-long operation, north-west of Hanoi, in the same style, involving a similar size force, with the same result. The only success that year was achieved by two T'ai mountaineer battalions. Fighting in their own mountains, which they knew considerably better than the Vietminh, and receiving intelligence from their fellow tribesmen, they cleared the Vietminh from their homeland between the Red and Black Rivers, and kept them out for nearly five years.

Withdrawal to the Lowlands

The French pulled back to the lowlands, leaving a string of border forts which achieved nothing but preserved the illusion of French control along the frontier with China. They even kept the garrison in Bac Kan until August 1948. It was a logistic burden and contributed nothing to the conduct of the campaign. Beyond the range of its guns, it controlled nothing. Although the Vietminh guerrillas continued to harass the French in the Tonkin Delta and waged a campaign of terror and propaganda to win over the local population, the Main Force units withdrew into the Viet Bac. Giap realised that the Main Force units would be the principal instrument with which to defeat the French. Although they had done well so far, they had glaring deficiencies in organisation, command, and, above all, logistics. He grouped battalions together into regiments, and eventually divisions. He created a staff system copying the French and American general staff with its four principal divisions.[7] But without an increased logistic capability, these reorganisations would be wasted.

An Army Based on Porterage: The Vietminh

The equipment in the Vietminh units at all levels was a hodge-podge of French, Japanese and American (parachuted in during the Second

World War). There were few spares and little ammunition. He had a handful of captured trucks, but no spares or fitters to maintain them. Giap's solution was to set up factories in the Viet Bac. From producing grenades, rifle ammunition, mines, and a few light machine guns, they progressed to making some 120 mm mortars. However, heavy equipment, such as trucks, and guns of all calibres and types and the ammunition for them, was beyond the capability of this 'cottage industry'. Had the Chinese Communists not arrived on the border in 1949, the campaign in Vietnam would have taken a very different course. The Chinese supplied the bulk of the equipment and ammunition, but only as far as the border. Distribution was Giap's problem, and he solved it by using a resource of which he had, if not an inexhaustible, at least a very large supply; human porters. It has been said that the extent of this effort was never fully understood by the West. This may be so, but given the length of time that the two campaigns lasted, it is difficult to understand why. It was well known that Giap was using porters, and the enormous scale of the effort in human terms, albeit expressed loosely, 'thousands of porters', was a constant ingredient of briefings, certainly in Round Three when the Americans were fighting the war.[8]

Even when the Vietminh had thousands of trucks, a vast army of porters carried supplies to Giap when he defeated the French at Dien Bien Phu, and supplied the Viet Cong and North Vietnamese formations as they closed in on the cities of South Vietnam for the Tet offensive of 1968. Like the animals in Alexander's army, the porters ate what they carried, with two added disadvantages; unlike a horse or a mule, they could not supplement the fodder carried with the arms by grazing, nor could large parties of porters be fed by foraging without antagonising the villagers on whose good will, or at least passivity, they depended, and possibly betraying their presence. On a long trip, the porters ate 90 per cent of what they carried.[9] But despite these disadvantages, the system worked.

First Efforts at Pacification

In late 1949, and early 1950, General Alessandri, put in command of Tonkin by the French Commander-in-Chief, Carpentier, changed the thrust of the French effort in the Delta. Alessandri realised that the notion of a quick decision achieved by enticing the Vietminh on to a piece of ground which they could not afford to lose, fixing them and defeating them in a great, devastating battle was a pipe dream. There was no terrain that the Vietminh would regard as so vital, that it warranted being held at the risk of the destruction of their Main Force units. But there was a commodity that was indispensable: rice; as well as feeding the soldiers and porters, it was the currency in which they were paid. Goods and services provided by the local communities were also reimbursed in rice by the Vietminh. He saw that the French strategy of holding a ring of forts around the Tonkin Delta was a waste of effort, if nothing was done to pacify the area itself, because the Vietminh guerrillas controlled it, the millions of people, and, most important, the huge quantities of rice. If he occupied and pacified the Tonkin Delta, he could undermine the Vietminh logistically. He would deny them reinforcements, taxes, and, most important, rice. If he could starve the Vietminh Main Force, they might have to come out and fight.

Alessandri set about pacifying a small area at a time; a patch first, then several patches; linking up patches, and steadily increasing the spread of patchwork. The French troops held off the Vietminh, while local non-Communist Vietnamese cleared the patch. Giap responded by guerrilla war in the Delta. Peasants by day, and guerrillas by night, the local forces laid ambushes, carried out small attacks, terrorised the local population, eliminated 'traitors', and never stayed to fight it out. Although at first the pacification programme, the first of many in Vietnam, appeared to be working, it failed. First, there were not enough French troops to prevent the Vietminh guerrillas from infiltrating back into a cleared patch; and the French Government refused to supply more. Second, the French made no attempt to win the support, and hearts and minds of the Vietnamese people. To them, the Tonkinese were rice producers, a source of taxes and recruits. The French had nothing to offer them, except continuing as chattels in a French colony. The Vietminh had plenty to offer, in the longer term, independence, but here and now, Vietminh assistance with the harvest, backed by a constant stream of propaganda; and the ultimate persuader, threats, kidnapping, and assassination. Alessandri's strategy came very near to its aim of drawing out the Vietminh Main Force. The reinforcements to the Main Force dried up to a trickle, and rice supplies to the Vietminh outside the Delta were cut in half. Rations were reduced to the extent that in some areas the Vietminh faced starvation. Giap and Ho began to think that a major offensive would have to be mounted in the Delta, despite it having little chance of success; but they hung on in the hope that the situation would improve. They were saved by the event that solved most of their other logistic problems: the Chinese Communists closing up to the northern border of Vietnam.

Ignominious Defeat

The French still hankered after the big set-piece battle in which they could out-gun the Vietminh, but instead, by the end of 1950, they had lost, or evacuated, all the posts along the northern border of Vietnam. In doing so, they handed Giap a logistic prize, huge quantities of food, clothing, and medical supplies, tons of ammunition, thirteen howitzers, 125 mortars, 940 machine guns, 450 trucks, 4,000 new submachine guns, over 8,000 rifles, and thousands of gallons of petrol.[10] The French, besides losing 6,000 men, had handed Giap enough equipment for a complete Vietminh division.[11] 'When the smoke had cleared,' says Fall, 'the French had suffered their greatest colonial defeat since Montcalm died at Quebec.'[12]

Giap Threatens the Delta: The French React Under a New C-in-C

At the end of the year, Giap posed a threat to the Tonkin Delta, by moving his divisions south. Carpentier, his morale sagging after the disasters of the year, contemplated withdrawing to the eighteenth parallel, only sixty miles north of where the border between North and South Vietnam was eventually to be. Giap was indeed considering a quick attack on the Delta, but he realised that his logistic system based on coolies, was not capable of stocking the new supply points required for an offensive by the end of 1950. So he postponed the offensive. The first stage, on 13 January 1951, ended in a defeat for Giap. Despite Chinese assistance, his men were still short of rice, and his army needed recruits. The solution to both problems lay in controlling a substantial area of the Delta. Two other factors led him into an attack on the key French position at Vinh Yen: the arrival of a new dynamic Commander-in-Chief, General de Lattre de Tassigny, and the increasing flow of American equipment to the French. In the end, French airpower, including the use of napalm, and the ability to reinforce by air, and, perhaps, the personal intervention at a critical stage in the battle by de Lattre, swung the contest in his favour; but only just. Giap also missed several chances, and did not grasp the command and control of his divisions firmly enough; he still lacked practice in the co-ordination of a multi-formation battle.

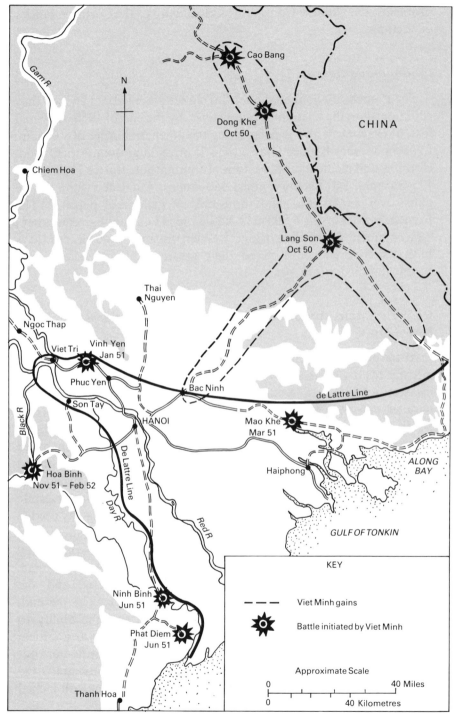

MAP VII Vietminh Offensive Operations October 1950–February 1952.

Defeats for General Giap

Giap's second attempt at securing a foothold in the Delta, at Mao Khe on the northern hinge of the de Lattre Line,[13] also ended in defeat. Logistics had influenced Giap's choice of objective: Mao Khe's proximity to Haiphong, the French supply lifeline, and its closeness to the Viet Bac and China, thus easing his own supply problems. It was held by 400 men. Once again Giap failed to take into account the French ability to reinforce rapidly by air, and the effect of air attack on troops in the open when committed to an assault. However, a major miscalculation was selecting an objective near a major river, which enabled the French to steam destroyers to within range of Giap's troops and subject them to heavy bombardment. Like others before him, including Napoleon, he paid the penalty for ignoring the sea flank.

Despite these two defeats, Giap decided to mount one more offensive before the monsoon broke. Again logistics was the driving force behind this decision: the need for rice and his perception that with American aid the French were growing stronger. His objective, the Day River line, along the south-western face of the de Lattre Line, was aimed at gaining control of the Ninh Binh and Nam Ha provinces. These had three rice crops a year, and were densely populated; the latter important not only as a source of manpower, but so that the Vietminh could be seen to be controlling an increasing percentage of the people. The Day River campaign was the most ambitious attempted by Giap to date. His plan involved four divisions, one (312th), to attack the western tip of the de Lattre Line at Vinh Yen as a diversion. The other three divisions were to mount the main assault across the Day River. Two divisions (304th and 308th), assisted by two independent regiments striking from guerrilla bases within the Delta, were to seize objectives aimed at tying down the French reserves, while the third (320th), struck out for Phat Diem and Ninh Binh in the southern hinge of the de Lattre Line. The use of such a large force which included moving one division right round the Delta, about 10,000 troops and 40,000 porters, was a massive logistic undertaking.

Giap planned to start his offensive just before the South-West monsoon in mid May, so that if it succeeded, the rain would protect him from French air attacks; if it failed, he could withdraw, covered by the bad weather. Unfortunately for Giap, his staff were still too inexperienced for the task of calculating the complex march tables required to move such large bodies of men by night along jungle tracks;

a daytime move would have drawn the attention of the French air force. Giap had planned on procuring rice on the way, but the villagers refused to supply any, this resulted in yet more porters to carry rice from the Viet Bac. Then the monsoon broke early, further delaying logistic preparations, so finally Giap started his offensive on 29 May, about three weeks into the monsoon period. This worked in Giap's favour, surprising the French, because until then neither side had campaigned during the monsoon.

Initially the offensive was a success, but de Lattre reacted with great speed to move reserves into the battle. The Vietminh found themselves in flooded, open paddy fields under intense artillery bombardment; and the Vietnamese Catholic militia slowed up the 320th Division until the French arrived. The Catholic militia also harassed the moves of the independent Vietminh regiments. In consequence, they were unable to operate in conjunction with the assaulting divisions by attacking the rear of the positions in the de Lattre Line. Giap now found himself having to supply three divisions across the Day River. French river craft units (*dinassauts*, an abbreviation of *Division Navale d'Assaut*), assisted by the French air force, cut his line of communication by sinking the boats. The Vietminh advance ground to a halt for lack of ammunition and food. By mid June, Giap had withdrawn his battered divisions back over the Day River. In choosing a plan that resulted in all his lines of communication crossing a major river, he showed that he still failed to understand how the use of air and waterborne power could affect his plans; particularly the ability of the latter to cut off the fighting men from their supplies.

Giap Tries Again

It has been argued that Giap, instead of mounting a series of attacks (three in the first five months of 1951), should have put in a strong co-ordinated offensive by all five divisions simultaneously around the perimeter of the de Lattre Line. It is likely that the answer lies in the logistic limitations of the Vietminh. It has been calculated[14] that it took about one month per attacking Vietminh division to stock its logistic base. So the earliest that a co-ordinated, five division offensive could have been launched was early May 1951. Giap did not consider that he could afford to leave the French to their own devices for that long; particularly with the dynamic de Lattre in command.

After the monsoon, Giap tried again; this time not against the de Lattre Line, but against the town of Nghia-Lo, the capital of the T'ai people, strong supporters of the French. The town was sixty-five miles outside the de Lattre Line. Once again the French dropped parachute battalions in to reinforce the garrison, that and air attacks caused Giap to withdraw. However, he learned an important lesson; he could entice the French out on to ground of his own choosing, by threatening areas, towns, or French allies.

General de Lattre Takes the Offensive

De Lattre now decided to go on to the offensive, and capitalise on the high morale engendered by the series of Vietminh defeats. He chose Hoa Binh as his objective. Besides being the capital of the Muongs, another people whose loyalties lay with the French, the town lay on the lines of communication from the region which supplied most of the rice to the Vietminh army to the Viet Bac. It was also close enough to the de Lattre Line to be supported and supplied. However, there were problems with all three lines of communication from the de Lattre Line to Hoa Binh. The road, *Route Coloniale 6*, had become a jungle track over the years, thanks to the efforts of both the Vietminh and the French Air Force. The bridges were blown, and the road cratered. The jungle came right down to the roadside—good ambush country. The jungle also grew densely along the banks of the Black River, providing first-rate sites for Vietminh rocket-launcher and recoilless guns. The air strip at Hoa Binh could be dominated by artillery, mortars and flak guns from two nearby hills.

The offensive started with three parachute battalions dropping on the Hoa Binh airstrip on 14 November 1951. At first all went well for the French. Giap took about a month to react. Having decided that the attack was the main effort, not just a diversion, he had to establish his own logistic base, a time-consuming business. Perhaps following the example of T. E. Lawrence cutting the Turks' supply line, rather than assault Medina, Giap decided not to attack the strong French force in the town, but their lines of communication, the road, the river, and the airstrip. At the same time, two divisions would infiltrate the Delta from the north and the south to distract the French command from the battle at Hoa Binh. By mid January the Vietminh had succeeded in closing the Black River and the *Route Coloniale 6* lines of supply, and reducing the flow of air supply dramatically, by the use of flak guns along the aircraft approach and departure routes. Worst of all, from the French point of view, de Lattre had been invalided back to France dying of cancer. His deputy General Salan took his place.

Salan Takes Over: Withdrawal from Hoa Binh

Salan decided to re-open *Route Coloniales 6*, and to clear the undergrowth from the roadside. It took twelve infantry battalions and three artillery groups eleven days to clear twenty-five miles of road. At this point Salan decided to withdraw from Hoa Binh which had become a trap. Besides he needed the troops to deal with the two Vietminh divisions who had successfully infiltrated the Delta. He succeeded in evacuating the Hoa Binh garrison in a conventional, phased operation; withdrawing units through each other, from one defensive position to the next. On the first day, Giap was taken by surprise, enabling the French and 1,000 Muong civilians to get back over the Black River during the night unmolested. He struck the next morning and a savage running fight ensued. Last back in to the safety of the de Lattre Line was a battalion of the Foreign Legion. The French artillery had expended over 30,000 rounds in three days, and the French Air Force had provided continuous close air support. The French lost 5,000 men, and the Vietminh at least as many. The Hoa Binh battle was a pointer to the future, which the French chose to ignore. Despite having been clearly shown that they had little offensive capability outside the Delta, very largely for logistic reasons, they persisted in what Fall has called, 'their search for the big set-piece battle in which they could outmanoeuvre and outgun the enemy.'[15]

Hoa Binh had also underlined the difficulties faced by Giap when he was forced to react to a swiftly changing tactical situation, such as the well executed and sudden French withdrawal; of which he had no warning, because the local inhabitants, the Muongs, were hostile. He was hampered by lack of good radios, and the Vietminh propensity to plan in great detail and rehearse. But most of all, he was encumbered by a logistic system that could not respond to a change of axis at short notice.

*   *   *

De Lattre's Approach to the United States

Despite his considerable achievements, particularly in restoring French morale, de Lattre's first and only offensive had failed. He was more successful in achieving another aim: to increase the volume and pace of delivery of American military material. To this end, in September and October 1951, he visited the United States. He realised that his mission would be greatly assisted if he could convince the American leaders and population that the Korean and Indo-China Wars

were all part of the same conflict: against 'Red colonialism'; and that
the West in general, and America in particular had as much to lose in
Indo-China as in Korea. At the Pentagon he was specific in his warnings
of the outcome if Indo-China was lost, and, although he did not refer to it
as such, he used the terminology of what was to become the 'domino
theory'.[16] De Lattre outlined his supply difficulties, for example during
the Day River campaign there were at times less than 6,000 artillery
shells in the whole of Indo-China. Lack of reserve ammunition had
prevented any counter-attacks for eight days. Lack of airlift had reduced
parachute operations. The French Hellcat piston-engine fighter-
bombers were 'finished', and should be replaced by F-86 jets.

The Price of Poor Administration

The Americans conceded that deliveries in the summer of 1951,
particularly of military vehicles, had been slow; less than half the jeeps,
and about a third of the 6 × 6 trucks. American domestic problems such
as strikes; and lack of production capacity, machine tools, materials,
and the necessary skills in producing new equipment had contributed
to the problem. Nevertheless, the French were also partly to blame for
the parlous state of their equipment. Lack of maintenance was just as
much a reason for the Hellcats being 'finished', as battle damage and
wear and tear. Delivery of supplies in Vietnam could only be by armed
convoy, by water or by road. This resulted in a high level of stocks
being held in forward areas to compensate for the long re-supply cycle.
Poor maintenance had been a constant theme in reports from the
American Military Assistance Advisory Group (MAAG) which had
been in Saigon since September 1950. French aircraft fitters came in for
considerable criticism for 'lack of appreciation of safety precautions,
lack of respect for preventative maintenance . . . the standard French
procedure of drinking while working . . . insufficient maintenance was
draining spare parts . . . Under these conditions no amount of logistical
support supplied . . . will greatly reduce the difficulties now being
experienced by the French Air Force in maintaining sufficient aircraft
at operational level.'[17] The French logistic system was similarly
chaotic. For example they had no stock control system and did not
know what they had received or despatched forward.

America Steps Up Supplies

However, the Americans promised to speed things up, and were as
good as their word. Between October 1951 and February 1952, the

French received over 130,000 tons of equipment including 53 million rounds of ammunition, 8,000 vehicles, 650 combat vehicles, 200 aircraft, 3,500 radio sets, and 14,000 automatic weapons. Part of the difficulty in supplying the French was the enormously long line of communication stretching back from Haiphong and Saigon across the Pacific to the United States. The MAAG suggested to the French that they manufacture simple items in Vietnam. There was ample manpower, wood and coal in-country. With simple American machine tools, the Vietnamese could make cartridge clips, tinned rations, tyres and tubes, webbing equipment, camouflage nets and small arms ammunition, and probably at a lower cost, because Vietnamese workers were paid less than their counterparts in America. The French were unenthusiastic, partly because they did not wish to lose control of the distribution of military equipment, which might find its way into the hands of the Vietminh. But their main concern seems to have been to ensure the continued dependence of the Indo-Chinese on France. In the end nothing was done to set up a local military equipment industry. However, Giap was right to be concerned about United States aid to the French, and to accord it a high priority among the factors to be taken into account in deciding on the timing of his offensives. Contemporary observers attribute the narrow French victories in the first half of 1951 to the arrival of American equipment and weapons; although there was at least one occasion when only the personal intervention of the Commander of the USMAAG produced the supplies to the hard-pressed French in time to avert defeat.[18]

*   *   *

Giap Re-Organises and Re-Equips

By the time the monsoon ended in September 1952, Giap had increased the number of his main force units to six infantry divisions, four independent infantry regiments, and six independent infantry battalions. The Chinese had equipped all these units with plenty of machine guns and mortars. Giap also formed a heavy division which provided support to the infantry formations. For this purpose the division was equipped with 120 mm mortars, 105 mm howitzers, and anti-aircraft guns of 20 mm and 40 mm calibre. His main force units totalled about 120,000 men. Regional troop strength was about 75,000 and guerrillas about 200,000. The French, including the air force and navy, numbered about 90,000 men. The Vietnamese National Army was about 100,000 strong, but of very little use. Giap could use his entire main force of 120,000 men for offensive action, whereas the French, hampered by having to deal with guerrillas in their rear, and with large numbers tied to defending the de Lattre Line, could find only about 50,000 men for an attack.

He Strikes Again

Giap had learnt from his reverses the previous year, and from the Hoa Binh battle. Most important, he must not attempt to attack the de Lattre Line, where the French enjoyed all of the advantages. He must exploit the French weaknesses: their inability to logistically support a large force more than a few miles outside the de Lattre Line; the political compulsion to defend friendly tribes such as the T'ais and the Muongs, and supporters, such as the Catholics; as the distance away from the Delta increased, so the effectiveness of their offensive air support diminished; and, finally, of all their soldiers deployed throughout Vietnam, they could spare less than half for an offensive. With these points in mind, Giap selected as his first objective the string of forts along the Fan Si Pan range of low mountains between the Red and Black Rivers. The tribal capital of the T'ais at Nghia Lo was the key post along the ridge. To the south of the Black River the French had another string of forts. The French had to react to any move by Giap in this area. As soon as they discovered the direction of his offensive, they dropped a colonial parachute battalion to cover the withdrawal of the scattered detachments manning the forts to the Black River. In the ensuing battle, Nghia Lo was overrun, and although the parachute battalion fought with great bravery and skill, it was destroyed. Fortunately for the French posts on the south side of the Black River, the Vietminh offensive began to run out of steam, because Giap's logistic system could not keep pace with his advance. He halted, then bypassed the forts, to overrun the small garrison of a place called Dien Bien Phu.

The French Strike Back: Operation LORRAINE

After reinforcing the forts bypassed by Giap, the French struck out for his supply base in the Viet Bac, using about 30,000 men, all the mobile forces they had available. They hoped to force him to withdraw by threatening to cut his logistic line of communication. The French plan was complicated, and involved a number of inter-connecting moves; overland, by river, and by parachute. Twelve days after the operation (code named LORRAINE) started, the parachute force of three battalions was dropped on to dropping zones across the river from the objective, Phu Doan. The river craft arrived on cue and began to ferry the parachute soldiers across to seize the undefended objective. The leading tanks of the overland element arrived two hours later. All had gone amazingly well, so far. After a thorough search, the French found a moderate amount of equipment, but not sufficient to justify an operation by the equivalent of two divisions.[19] Salan now ordered a task force consisting of five battalions with strong armoured and artillery support to push on, still hoping that he could capture a big supply depot and force Giap to withdraw.

Giap had correctly discerned the French intentions at an early stage in Operation LORRAINE. He assessed that the main striking force was road-bound, and that its very size presented a logistic problem to the French; this would limit the depth to which the French could drive into the Viet Bac and that they would be unable to reach two key logistic bases; Thai Nguyen and Yen Bai. He would therefore not react by withdrawing. He wished to stay in the T'ai country for political reasons, and to use it as a base for operations in Laos. He gave orders to his reserve, two regiments, to stop the French advance from reaching the two bases, at all costs.

Withdrawal and Failure: Logistics Dictate the Outcome

The French task force advanced, with light opposition, to a road junction about fifteen miles from Yen Bai, left a battle group of armour and infantry on the junction as a block, and pushed on, finally reaching Phu Yen Binh, 40 miles from Phu Doan, and almost 100 miles north of the de Lattre Line. At this stage, Salan ordered the whole LORRAINE force to withdraw to the de Lattre Line. In bypassing Yen Bai, the French were admitting to themselves that they did not have the strength and resources to take the town, and that Operation LORRAINE was therefore a failure. Only by taking Yen Bai could they have forced Giap to withdraw, by not doing so, they as good as told him that the whole operation was a feint which would not require him to change his plans. Once again it was the imperatives of logistics which played a large part in the French decision. The supply of 30,000 men accompanied by a large number of vehicles, tied up almost the whole air transport force in Indo-China (about 100 C-47 Dakotas); and consequently other areas, particularly the forts south of the Black River, were starved of re-supply. To take Yen Bai would have required

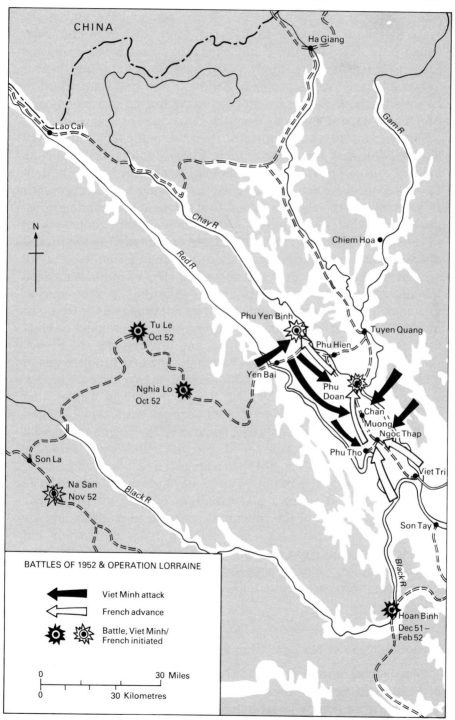

CHINA

Ha Giang

Lao Cai

Gam R

Chay R

Red R

Chiem Hoa

N

Phu Yen Binh

Tuyen Quang

Tu Le
Oct 52

Phu Hien

Yen Bai

Phu
Doan

Nghia Lo
Oct 52

Chan
Muong

Ngoc Thap

Phu Tho

Viet Tri

Son La

Na San
Nov 52

Black R

Son Tay

Black R

BATTLES OF 1952 & OPERATION LORRAINE

Viet Minh attack

French advance

Battle, Viet Minh/
French initiated

Hoan Binh
Dec 51 –
Feb 52

0   30 Miles

0   30 Kilometres

MAP VIII   Operation LORRAINE 1952.

more than the five battalion task force, and to have moved the remainder of the Operation LORRAINE force north from Phu Doan would have been difficult, if not impossible, besides increasing the range over which air re-supply would have to operate, thus further aggravating the logistic problem. Besides, Salan could not afford to have such a large slice of his mobile reserve tied up in a bloody and prolonged battle so far away from the Delta and the T'ai country.

The withdrawal was to show just what this battle might have been like. The bloodiest part occurred in the Chan-Muong valley, involving a heavy convoy protected by two mobile groups. The Vietminh Main Force Regiment 36 cunningly isolated the two mile long string of soft-skinned vehicles travelling in the centre of the column, by pinning down the leading infantry, and preventing the armour at the rear moving up to assist, by disabling a tank, which blocked the road. As the French did not have a single armoured bulldozer in Indo-China, recovery of armoured vehicles under fire was impossible. The Vietminh massacred the drivers and logistic troops, before blowing up the vehicles. Fortunately, the French commanders were not caught in the trap, and quickly set about extracting the force. After bitter hand-to-hand fighting, with the help of air support and artillery fire, the French succeeded in clearing the road of Vietminh. The next problem was to clear the hills on either side to enable the column to move on. The task was given to 2nd Battalion 2nd Regiment Foreign Legion and *Battalion de Marche Indochinoise* (BMI), a tough battle-wise battalion of Frenchmen, Cambodians, and Vietnamese. The Legionnaires, with less distance to go, made good progress, and soon held the commanding hillsides. The BMI had a tougher time, after being pinned down three times, the battalion fixed bayonets and charged. The Vietminh had had enough, and withdrew, but not for long. They snapped at the heels of the column as it moved to establish a block where they could draw breath after eighteen hours of marching and fighting. Eventually, over a month after Operation LORRAINE was launched, the last French troops were back behind the de Lattre Line. It had cost the French about 1,200 men.

*   *   *

A Bloody Nose at Na San: Giap Withdraws

Giap, having refused to abandon his plans, proceeded to capture one of the Black River forts. His next attempt, to seize Na San, was a failure. Operating in unfriendly T'ai country, his intelligence was scant, and he was under the impression that Na San was held by five understrength battalions, whereas it contained ten well dug in full strength battalions, with artillery and air support. He left 1,000 dead in front of Na San when he finally called off the attack; and the offensive had cost him a total of 7,000 casualties. After this set-back, he reverted to the strategy of drawing the French into distant areas which, for political, or other reasons, they had to defend. Bypassing the remaining Black River forts, he headed for Laos. Although he encountered only light opposition, he was forced for logistic reasons to halt short of his objective. His problem on this occasion, the need to conscript T'ais to supplement his Vietnamese porters. The T'ais either hid in the jungle to avoid the press, or threw away their loads when they could and vanished. Giap withdrew to north-west Vietnam.

Into Laos: A Logistic Triumph

His defeat at Na San taught him that he needed to draw the French further away from the Tonkin Delta if he was to stretch their logistic resources to the point where they could not sustain operations. He chose Laos. It had a number of attractive features: the politicians in France would be perturbed that the war was being carried into the most loyal Indo-Chinese colony; the French forces in Laos were weak, reinforcing and supporting them from the Delta was extremely difficult; and the monsoon, a month away, would cover him if he had to withdraw. For him it was a 'can win, can't lose' operation; he might gain an easy victory, but if he did not, the unsettling effect that his ability to invade Laos would have on the French, Laotians and Vietnamese would far outweigh any lack of military success. To improve his logistic ability, he stocked a forward base to cut the distance his porters would have to carry supplies, he persuaded the communists in Laos to stock rice along his planned invasion routes, and he dispensed with the need for the unreliable T'ais by bringing porters from other areas.

Giap advanced on three axes, a division to each. Within three weeks, the French had abandoned all the small posts in the path of Giap's three-pronged advance, and he had surrounded the Laotian capital of Louang Phrabang, a large French garrison at Jars Camp, on the Plain of Jars, and a small unit at Muong Khoua. At first the French had indicated their wish to abandon Louang Phrabang, but the Laotian King refused to budge. To avoid losing face, the French flew in three battalions of Legionnaires and Moroccans, artillery and defence stores.

Again logistics decided the outcome. Giap was unable to recruit porters from the Laotians, who were lazy and loathed the Vietnamese. Because the onset of the monsoon would exacerbate his logistic difficulties, and, for lack of cover against the rain, jeopardise the health of his troops, he withdrew to Vietnam in early May. He left elements of one division to keep the French occupied, to recruit Laotian guides, and to stockpile rice. Had he been able to capture Na San, which he had planned for his logistic forward base for the invasion of Laos, it is likely that he would have had fewer logistic problems; it was not so far to the east as Moo Chau which he was eventually forced into using for this purpose. Nevertheless, not only was his invasion a strategic success,

FIG. 5.1   French Air Force C-47 unloading Vietnamese soldiers in Laos for operations in the Plain of Jars 1952 (*Keystone*).

but also a considerable logistic achievement. His regiments covered about twenty miles a day on the mountain tracks of Laos. To keep up with and support them, 200,000 porters marched over the same tortuous paths. In the face of this astonishing rate of advance, the French dithered, and what Montgomery would have called 'wet henned about', unable to make up their minds what to hold in Laos, and what to abandon.

The French Bait Their Trap

The campaign of winter 1952 and spring 1953, including the invasion of Laos, confirmed to Giap that his strategy, referred to earlier, was correct. The French, however, came to different conclusions. They rightly perceived that Giap now had the capability to mount a serious invasion of Laos, and reasoned that the best way to counter this was to establish a strong base astride Giap's invasion routes. From their experience at Na Sang, Louang Prabang and Jars Camp, they deduced that a fortified camp could be supplied by air deep inside enemy territory, and be made sufficiently strong to hold off any Vietminh attack. They believed that Giap would attack this camp, as he had at Na San, particularly if it was across his logistic line of communication. With careful siting, such a camp might be the bait which would draw the Vietminh into the great set-piece battle, where their Main Force divisions would smash themselves to pieces on the rocks of the defence, while the French Air Force pounded them from the air. They found the camp, but before they were ready for the set-piece battle. It was in a small mountain valley, which in English is 'seat of the border county administration', in Vietnamese, Dien Bien Phu. It led to their defeat and the loss of Indo-China.

*   *   *

Navarre Relieves Salan and Giap Re-Arms

In May 1953, General Navarre relieved Salan as Commander-in-Chief Indo-China. He found himself faced with a situation that held few prospects of an honourable solution, let alone a French victory. Giap now had an offensive capability of eight or nine divisions. Vietminh morale was high, staffs were well versed in co-ordinating the activities of two or more formations, and the Main Force divisions had American equipment, some of superior quality to the French, thanks to the Chinese who had captured large quantities from American and South Korean forces in Korea. Of particular importance, Giap acquired further supplies of artillery, heavy mortars and anti-aircraft guns. Although not fully appreciated by the French at the time, Giap had spent the early part of 1953 improving his logistic capability. Roads in the Viet Bac were improved, and the Chinese had provided 600 trucks, the majority with Chinese drivers. The force of porters was expanded until it numbered hundreds of thousands.

In addition to his Main Force troops, Giap had at his disposal about

75,000 Regional troops, and between 150,000 to 350,000 Local Force militia, the latter mainly untrained and unequipped men, women and children. However, the Regional troops and militia were an indispensable force multiplier to the Vietminh. They controlled the majority of the villages in the Tonkin Delta, assisted by independent Main Force regiments and battalions, some of which operated within the de Lattre Line. This, and the threat of a Main Force offensive, tied down about 100,000 French troops to defensive tasks, out of 175,000 in Indo-China. The balance, available for mobile operations was the equivalent of about three divisions, made up of seven mobile groups and eight parachute battalions. Giap could discount the Vietnamese National Army of 150,000 men. Its low morale and lack of motivation made it totally ineffective; as was shown in May 1953, when the training school for potential leaders at Nam Dinh was attacked by three companies of Vietminh. All 600 trainees and the complete weapons holding of the school were captured, without the loss of a single Vietminh soldier.

The French Re-Equip

The Vietminh were not alone in getting help from outside. By early 1953, the 137,000 tons of American equipment delivered to the French included 900 armoured fighting vehicles, 15,000 other vehicles, 99,000 small arms and automatic weapons, and about 900 radios. The French air force had taken delivery of 160 F-6F and F-8F fighters, 41 B-26 light bombers, and 28 C-47 (Dakota) transports. The USMAAG, were at a loss to understand why the French did not use this equipment to mount an all-out offensive against the Vietminh to deliver a knock-out blow. They not only failed to appreciate the military mathematics of comparable strengths imposed on the French by Giap's strategy and tactics, but still laboured under the delusion that the French supply was superior to that of the Vietminh. The USMAAG only saw the large numbers of trucks, aircraft, and craft available to the French. But their logistic system was largely road-bound and therefore vulnerable to attack. Whereas the thousands of porters supplying the Vietminh divisions could move unimpeded by the need for roads, and usually undetected by the French. Although the Vietminh logistic system lacked the flexibility conferred on the French by the use of air power, provided the distance was right, overall their supply system was more flexible and better suited to the terrain.

Navarre's Search for a Politically Honourable Solution

Navarre found that there had been no plan for operations in Indo-China since de Lattre's departure eighteen months before. The French merely reacted to the Vietminh moves. Navarre set about drawing up a comprehensive plan to achieve what he perceived as his mission, to create the necessary conditions in Indo-China to gain a politically honourable solution. Having reviewed the options open to Giap, he assessed that the one posing the greatest threat would be another invasion of Laos, because it would be the most difficult to counter; the distance from the Delta and the consequent logistic problems being the major factor. Space does not permit a full review of Navarre's plan to fulfil his mission, but in summary, except for spoiling attacks to disrupt Giap's moves, he aimed to avoid a major battle with the Vietminh until the 1954–55 campaigning season. He would launch an offensive in Annam and the Central Highlands where tactically and logistically conditions were more favourable to the French. By accelerating the training of the Vietnamese National Army, and stepping up the pacification programme in the Delta, and provided that the French Army in Europe could send reinforcements equivalent to two divisions, he would build up his striking force to a total of six or seven mobile divisions. With this force, equal or slightly stronger than the Vietminh force available for offensives, he would seek a major battle in Northern Vietnam. In his view, victory was on the cards, but if only stalemate ensued, it would provide the basis for an honourable negotiated settlement.

The spoiling attacks which took place between July and September were tolerably successful; the last of them pre-empting a major offensive by Giap. The operation in Annam between Hue and Quang Tri was less so. However, during this period the French carried out a highly successful withdrawal from Na San. A clever deception plan took the Vietminh by surprise, and the whole garrison of 12,000 men were pulled out by air. This was to convince Navarre that fortified airstrips could be held, and then withdrawn at will.

Meanwhile Navarre had been to Paris in July 1953, to present his plan to the Government, in the course of which he asked if he was required to defend Laos, because clearly his task would be immeasurably easier if he could ignore any moves Giap made in that direction.

Cowardice and Duplicity in High Places

Before flying to Paris, Navarre left a contingency plan with his staff that provided for the reoccupation of Dien Bien Phu to sit astride

Giap's lines of communication, in the event of him making a move towards Laos. However, Navarre forbade any implementation of the plan until he had resolved the matter of his responsibility for the defence of Laos. Unfortunately, the National Defence Committee of the French Government would not give Navarre a straight answer, leaving him with the impression that he still had responsibility for Laos. The Committee, presided over by the President, and including the Premier, several senior ministers, and the Chiefs of Staff, hesitated to declare their hand, which was that they had no intention of honouring their obligation to defend Laos as a member of the French Union. Their cowardice was coloured by the knowledge that almost everything said in the Committee was invariably leaked to the press, and they did not wish the Laotians to discover the intention to dump them if push came to shove. For lack of clear direction, Navarre signalled back to his deputy in Indo-China the order to implement the contingency plan to reoccupy Dien Bien Phu if Giap started an offensive towards Laos. In October 1953, the French politicians gave further proof of their duplicity by entering into a treaty with the Laotian Government, which by inference declared that France intended to defend Laos. This further confirmed Navarre's belief that he was required to protect that country. The French Government finally came off the fence on 4 December 1953, when they sent a directive to Navarre telling him that he was not responsible for the defence of Northern Laos; two weeks after he had initiated the battle of Dien Bien Phu.

*   *   *

DIEN BIEN PHU

At the end of October 1953, French intelligence detected that Giap had started to move his divisions out of the Viet Bac towards Laos. On 2 November, Navarre ordered General Cogny, the commander of Northern Command, to implement the contingency plan, and seize Dien Bien Phu with a force of six parachute battalions no later than 1 December. Both Cogny and two senior air force officers protested. Apart from presenting a number of tactical objections, Cogny stated that the operation would need almost all the combat and air support aircraft in his command. The commander of the air transport fleet reported that he could not guarantee the flow of supplies into Dien Bien Phu because of poor weather and heavy flak over the village. He was supported by the air commander in northern Vietnam, adding that the average distance from the Delta airfields to Dien Bien Phu was

200 miles, which would limit the time close air support aircraft could spend over the target to a few minutes, and even this would be expensive in spares because of engine wear, and fuel. The picture was muddled further because Cogny understood that Dien Bien Phu was to be seized as a 'mooring point' from which guerrillas and mobile units could interdict the Vietminh supply line; although he did not say so, rather in the manner of the strongholds set up by the Chindits in Burma. This was not Navarre's intention at all. He envisaged a fortified airstrip, a hedgehog (*hérrison*) actually sitting astride the Vietminh supply line.

Navarre's motives for continuing to order the operation in the face of Cogny's and the airmen's objections are difficult to unravel, and it has been suggested were strongly influenced by his notions of the honour of the French Army. However, if he felt obliged to defend Laos, and chose the hedgehog concept, then Dien Bien Phu was unquestionably the best place. Giap himself in an appreciation of the situation written beforehand said:

> 'Dien Bien Phu is a large plain 18 kilometres long and six to eight kilometres wide in the mountain zone of the North-West. It is the biggest and richest of the four plains in this hilly region close to the Vietnam-Laos frontier. It is situated at the junction of important roads running to the North-East towards Lai Chau, to the South-East towards Tuan Giao, Son La, Na San; to the West toward Louang Phrabang, and to the South towards Sam Neua. In the theatre of operation of Bac Lo (Tonkin) and upper Laos, Dien Bien Phu is a strategic position of first importance, capable of becoming an infantry base and air base of extreme efficiency in their scheme of aggression in South East Asia.'[20]

There were two major disadvantages to locating a base at Dien Bien Phu. First, and absolutely crucially, it was dependent entirely on air supply and reinforcement, and the distances over which this would have to be delivered have already been discussed. Second, although Navarre thought that the commanding heights around the valley bottom were 10 to 12 kilometres from the airstrip, actually there was a hill line 700 metres above the valley floor, and only 5,500 metres from the centre of the position. A secondary hill line about 100 metres above the valley floor lay within 2,000 metres of the centre of the position. Once two hills, codenamed Gabrielle and Beatrice were taken, the Vietminh would have an uninterrupted view of all the French positions and the airstrip. Despite these disadvantages, Navarre pressed ahead, advised by his intelligence staff that there was little risk, based on the assessment that Giap could not possibly support a large force at Dien Bien Phu. Furthermore, they said that because of the terrain, Giap could not bring large amounts of artillery

to bear on the base, neither was his logistic system capable of keeping
his guns fed with shells.

The Garrison Drops In

On 20 November 1953, as the Dakotas carrying 6th Battalion
Colonial Parachutists (6 BPC) and 2nd Battalion, 1st Regiment
Chasseurs Parachutists (2/1RCP), were approaching the DZs at Dien
Bien Phu, an emissary from the National Defence Committee was in
Navarre's office telling him that he would get no further reinforcements
from Europe; he would have to do as best he could with what he had
already. He then asked Navarre if the French should start negotiating
with the Vietminh now, or wait for a more favourable military
situation. Navarre suggested that negotiations should be delayed until
spring by which time the situation should have improved.

The landings of the leading battalions went well, despite the usual
chaos of parachute assaults. However, both battalions were battle
experienced and led by formidable commanding officers, which was
just as well, because the Vietminh were in greater strength than the
French had bargained for. That afternoon 1 BPC dropped to reinforce
6 BPC, and together they attacked the village of Dien Bien Phu held by
a battalion of 148th Vietminh Regiment, an artillery battalion, a
mortar company, and an infantry company from another battalion.
Because 2/1 RPC had a scattered drop and lost most of its radios, it was
not able to put in the cut-offs in time to prevent most of the Vietminh
escaping, but they left about ninety dead in the village. The next day 1st
Foreign Legion Parachute Battalion (1 BEP), 8 BPC, an artillery
battalion, heavy equipment, and Brigadier General Gilles, the
parachute force commander dropped on to the Dien Bien Phu DZs. On
the third day the final parachute battalion of the assault force, 5th
Vietnamese Parachute Battalion (5 BPVN) dropped.[21]

A Change of Command as Giap Reacts

Giap reacted to the French move by ordering three divisions to move
to Dien Bien Phu, and another division plus the 148th Regiment to
attack the French fort at Lai Chau, forty miles north of Dien Bien Phu.
Despite being warned of this by intercept of the Vietminh radio
network, Navarre, believing that Giap could not logistically support
four divisions on operations, convinced himself that the threat to Dien
Bien Phu consisted of only one division. So when he visited the airstrip

for the first time, he deduced that the camp would be an ideal base for mobile defence using light tanks flown in parts and re-assembled on the spot. Navarre and Cogny decided to replace Gilles, who had a heart condition, with a thrusting cavalryman, Castries. What is interesting is that Cogny, who, unlike Navarre, believed that Giap was moving on Dien Bien Phu with four divisions, should have supported the appointment of the dashing Castries, when he knew perfectly well that once the Vietminh invested the camp there would be no more forays, the garrison would be under siege. Indeed, he issued orders which reflected this view.

Navarre's Directive

Navarre produced a directive which included his acceptance of a battle being fought in North-West Vietnam, centred on Dien Bien Phu, which he ordered to be 'held at all costs'. In doing so he clearly continued to hold to the opinion that for logistic reasons only one Vietminh division would invest Dien Bien Phu, which would constitute no greater threat to the garrison than at Na San earlier in the year. He would not, therefore, be departing from his strategy of avoiding a decisive battle in the North in that campaigning season. As he saw it, he was merely defending Laos with his hedgehog, while going ahead with his plan for the major offensive, Operation ATLANTE, between Nha Trang and Da Nang in Annam.

Lethargy and Logistic Weakness

A curious lethargy seems to have overcome the French command in Indo-China in the interval between the seizure of Dien Bien Phu, and the start of Giap's offensive, a period of three months. In December the French made two sorties from Dien Bien Phu. The first, an attempt to link-up with the remnants of the Lai Chau garrison, as it withdrew in the face of 316 Vietminh Division, was beaten back with heavy losses. The second, to meet a force moving north to Dien Bien Phu from Laos, succeeded but only because it met no opposition. Both had been efforts to show that Dien Bien Phu could be used as a base for offensive operations. Actually they showed the opposite. The country with its limestone cliffs and dense jungle made movement extremely difficult, and the enemy was too strong. The French did not possess the equipment, principally fleets of helicopters,[22] which would have given them the necessary mobility to overcome the terrrain difficulties.

Therefore, any idea of disrupting Giap's logistic installations and lines of communication from Dien Bien Phu was a fantasy. On 29 December, Navarre spotted this, and ordered Cogny to prepare a plan to withdraw the garrison. Cogny did not deliver the plan until three weeks later, by which time the Vietminh had surrounded Dien Bien Phu in great strength. Cogny suggested that the withdrawal plan be shelved, and Navarre, who had only been lukewarm about withdrawing, agreed. If Dien Bien Phu was to be held against heavy artillery fire and massed infantry attacks, military prudence demanded that certain steps be taken to make the position as strong as possible. A combination of the lethargy referred to earlier, and logistic weakness resulted in incomplete and inadequate preparations.

Inadequate Preparation for the Defence

To build a position that can withstand prolonged pounding by artillery requires copious supplies of construction materials. Wood taken from every building in the valley provided only about 5 per cent of the shoring required. Parties sent to the surrounding hills to cut wood, were driven back by the Vietminh. The French airlift was already stretched supplying the daily consumption of the garrison, and had no spare capacity to fly in the tons of sandbags, concrete, steel and wooden beams; let alone the plant, bulldozers, diggers, and concrete mixers that would have been needed to build a really strong position. Forced by lack of materials to dig, and without sufficient revetting, the light, friable soil only allowed shallow positions to be constructed. The earth soon broke up into dust under artillery fire, making further digging impossible. The high water table softened the soil, causing many of the bunkers to collapse, and flooded others. The monsoon rains, arriving in April, earlier than usual, flooded out whole areas of the defensive positions.

Because the trees in the valley had to be cut for construction of bunkers, and what brush remained was soon gathered as fuel for cooking fires, the French positions were quickly stripped bare of natural camouflage. The movement of hundreds of men around, within, and between positions, soon wore a web of paths, which combined with the freshly turned earth of the bunkers and gun pits, enabled the Vietminh on the surrounding hills to pin-point every position. This state of affairs reveals a lack of grip by commanders from Castries downwards. There seems to have been no attempt made to dig dummy positions, institute track discipline, fly in camouflage nets, or ban the use of brush for cooking fires. By 1954 most armies had equipped their soldiers with small, portable stoves using smokeless, solid fuel blocks, to avoid the time consuming and revealing business of cooking on wood fires. Camouflage nets are cheap to make and could have been produced in Indo-China. Although they are bulky, they are also light, and considerable numbers can be dropped in bundles from large formations of aircraft, at low level, without need for parachutes. This method of delivery is quick, dispensing with the need to keep aircraft on the ground, taking up valuable space on a limited airstrip while they are unloaded.

Although the French defensive plan, like any other, called for counter-attacks to eject penetrations by attackers, few plans were made, and none rehearsed. Valuable airlift had been allocated to lifting in light tanks, a sensible move in view of the Vietminh superiority of numbers, but lack of armour. But no training was done in infantry/tank co-operation. This lackadaisical approach extended to the preparations for the artillery fire plan. There were insufficient guns, poor co-ordination, and the open, uncamouflaged gun pits became death traps for the crews.

There was time to replace the unreliable T'ai battalions and the eleven companies of the T'ai Mobile Group at Dien Bien Phu with troops whose morale, training and steadfastness could be relied upon to sustain them in the tough days ahead. It was not done.

Most of these deficiencies in planning and preparation flowed from French underestimation of the Vietminh and Giap. They believed that the heaviest artillery they would have to face would be mortars and a few 75 mm howitzers, for which there would be little ammunition. As the Vietminh attacks came in they would be broken up by artillery fire and air attack. Any guns or mortars that revealed their positions by firing, would be quickly neutralised by air attacks and counter-battery fire. Consequently, there was, in French eyes, nothing unduly to worry about.

While the French had been making desultory preparations, the Vietminh had, by the end of January 1954, concentrated three infantry divisions with supporting artillery, anti-aircraft units, and logistic support units around Dien Bien Phu. The staff work and logistic planning to complete such a move, and maintain a force of this size was a major achievement, and an indication of the level of professional expertise attained by the staffs of the Vietminh Main Force formations and units.

Meanwhile Navarre was pre-occupied with operation ATLANTE in

Annam, planned as his major offensive in 1954. Here the Vietminh were weaker than in the North, and the climate allowed operations at a different time than in Tonkin or Cochin China. Navarre's objective was the elimination of the Vietminh Military Region V, which stretched in a semi-circle, 200 miles long, from Da Nang on the coast through Kontum in the Central Highlands to Nha Trang on the coast. So important was the region in his eyes, that he decided to subordinate Operation ATLANTE to the conduct of the whole Indo-China campaign.

It was an important area, containing two and a half million people, producing vast quantities of rice and fish. Transferring it to the control of the National Vietnamese government would be a major boost to morale. Besides the political benefits, the Vietminh forces in the area totalled some 30,000 men. Although less formidable than Giap's North Vietnamese formations, they were rapidly improving and would pose a serious threat in 1954 or 1955, which would tie up at least five or six French mobile groups. There was far more to be gained, in his view, by offensive action in Annam than by defensive operations in Tonkin.

Navarre's operational concept for ATLANTE consisted of three phases. In phase one, involving 30 battalions, an amphibious operation at Tuy Hoa would be launched in concert with an advance out of Nha Trang to clear the coast to the north, and hold Route 19 from Qui Nhon to An Khe. Phases two and three never took place, but would have included a pincer movement from Da Nang in the north and Pleiku in the west. The second phase would have required 39 battalions, and the third phase 53.

Navarre has been criticised for mounting this operation and tying up troops and logistic support in a region of far less importance than the Tonkin Delta or Dien Bien Phu. However four of the six mobile groups in Annam consisted of troops from Central Vietnam who could not be employed outside their home area. The families of South Vietnamese soldiers lived in the army camps, or in adjacent villages. If the unit moved, families would be left unprotected, and without financial support. This always ended in mass desertions of troops returning to look after their dependants. Employing soldiers in their home areas had some advantages: they knew the country, spoke the local dialect, and were motivated to protect their homes and families; caring little about defending another part of the country. This limitation on the use of South Vietnamese troops was to bedevil operations until the end of Round Four in 1975.

It is also easy to be wise with the advantage of hindsight; in

December 1953, when Navarre gave the orders which were to set ATLANTE in motion, he was not to know that Dien Bien Phu was to be a disastrous debacle. Navarre's problem was that even if he succeeded in Military Region V, this would not win the war. Indeed Giap would not have to surrender the initiative by having to divert Main Force troops from a more important area. But he could, and did increase guerrilla activity to ensure that Navarre was tied down as much as possible.

The first phase of ATLANTE quickly became bogged down in the face of Vietminh harrassing and delaying tactics. This was the first operation by the Vietnamese National Army, and they proved to be utterly incapable, deserting in droves, mutinying, and looting. Giap struck back while Navarre was pre-occupied with the coastal region, taking Dak To and Kontum in the Central Highlands. Navarre's counter moves proved fruitless, and he abandoned Kontum to the Vietminh.

Not content with this, Giap managed to keep Navarre off balance by offensives in central and southern Laos, and the Central Highlands. He even moved 308th Division away from Dien Bien Phu, about 25 miles to Muong Khoua, where they destroyed the garrison, a French battalion. These moves were aimed at forcing Navarre to deploy his mobile reserve as widely as possible, where they would then be a drain on his precious air supply assets, thus hindering the logistic build up at Dien Bien Phu.

Logistics the Key

Navarre and Giap were well aware that the key to Dien Bien Phu was winning the logistic battle. Each realised that as well as building up stocks and supplying his own force, he had to reduce the flow of supplies reaching his opponent.

Giap's Supply System: A Triumph of Organisation

Giap's supply system at Dien Bien Phu depended on porters and trucks. The trucks carried the heavier items: artillery, most of the ammunition, and the larger spares. The porters mainly carried rice, about 76 per cent of which came from Thanh Hoa province, south of the de Lattre Line. This rice was carried by 260,000 porters walking up the Song Ma river valley from Thanh Hoa to the forward base at Tuan Giao 35 miles from Dien Bien Phu; a journey of 350 to 400 overland miles. The Vietminh had about 800 Russian and 200 American trucks, all of two-and-a-half ton capacity. The latter had been captured from the French, or given by the Chinese who had taken them in Korea. The Vietminh lines of communication to Dien Bien Phu from China ran from four crossing points on the Vietnamese/Chinese border, to Tuan Giao forward base. The primary line of communication ran from Cao Bang and the Nan Kuan Pass, joined at Tuy en Quang, crossed the Red River at Yen Bai, and thence to Tuan Giao. A secondary line of

FIG. 5.2   North Vietnamese women porters. A propaganda photograph taken by AFP in 1970. Porters would not be armed. But the use of bicycles by porters supporting Giap's troops was widespread from the earliest days
(*Popper*).

communication ran down the Red River from Lao Cai, joining the primary route at Yen Bai. Another secondary line of communication crossed the border at Ban Nam Coum, passed through Lai Chau and on to Tuan Giao. The Vietminh truck companies were each responsible for a section of road, the length of a particular section was determined by carefully selected choke-points, such as bridges, or passes which were likely to be blocked by the French. Loads were always transferred at these points. If the choke point was blocked, so that trucks could not drive up alongside each other, the porters who were prepositioned to transfer the load to the collecting truck were on hand already; it was just more difficult for them. Despite the problems of several transfers of load at points along the route, there were plenty of coolies, and the drivers came to know their section of road so well that they could drive on a dark night without lights. All the roads were rudimentary—by Western standards, little more than cart tracks.

To improve the mule track, which crossed nearly 100 small and big streams, and wound up and down steep gradients from Tuan Giao to Dien Bien Phu, to take trucks, involved a complete rebuild. The task took 10,000 coolies, two Main Force engineer regiments, one infantry regiment, and 7,000 army recruits. Once built, this, and all other roads, had to be kept open in the face of French air interdiction. As soon as the attacking French aircraft had pulled away from a bomb run, gangs of peasants equipped with hand tools, and the ubiquitous small wicker basket of the Asian labourer, would descend on the damaged section to fill in craters, or create a by-pass. After a while, the Vietminh identified about forty key points to which the French air force returned time and again. Coolies were permanently stationed at these places, and the road was rarely out of service for more than twenty-four hours. The Vietminh turned the primary line of communication into a flak corridor by siting anti-aircraft guns along its length, concentrating them at the key points here, and on the secondary supply routes. Finally, as much of the road as possible was camouflaged, by interlacing the branches of trees overhead, to form a tunnel, so that detection from the air, either visually or on a photograph, was nigh impossible, before the days of thermal-image technology. The Vietminh logistic system was able to keep a force of 49,000 troops at Dien Bien Phu supplied, as well as about 40,000 to 50,000 logistic troops along the lines of communication. It was a triumph of organisation, discipline and motivation which resisted all the French efforts to disrupt it.

French Interdiction Fails

The French effort failed for a number of reasons. First, and fundamental, as Slessor had pointed out in Italy ten years before, an air interdiction campaign cannot prevent an enemy moving supplies forward. Only if he is forced to expend supplies, the vital ones being ammunition and fuel, faster than he is receiving them, will he become logistically bankrupt. The French did not have the tactical initiative at

Fɪɢ. 5.3   '. . . gangs of peasants equipped with hand tools', women repair
bomb damage. Although this is a propaganda photograph taken by TASS in
1966, the methods used apply equally to 1954 and earlier (*TASS*).

Dien Bien Phu, and were not therefore in a position to force the
Vietminh to expend supplies at a faster rate than they could afford.

   To attack the Vietminh lines of communication, and to provide close
air support to their forces in Dien Bien Phu and in the remainder of
Northern Indo-China, the French had a puny, obsolescent striking air
force: thirty-two fighters, forty-five fighter-bombers, between thirty
and forty-seven B-26 medium bombers, six C-119 (flying box-car)
transports converted to drop napalm, and five anti-submarine
bombers each of which could carry a four ton bombload. These figures
are totals, and even the best maintained air force in the world does not
have a 100 per cent serviceability rate all the time, least of all when it has

to cope with battle damage. The French kept about 75 per cent operational at any one time, which, despite the remarks made earlier about French repair standards, is quite creditable, considering that the maintenance force was one-third under-strength, and in the last stage of the war had to be augmented with American technicians.

Finally, the flak corridor along the Vietminh line of communication forced French aircraft to attack at a higher altitude, and divert a proportion of aircraft to flak suppression, limiting the numbers on interdiction, and close air support of ground forces.

But Giap Succeeds

The Vietminh were more successful in their efforts to disrupt the French line of communication to Dien Bien Phu. In their favour was the inadequacy of the French air transport fleet. The figures of transport aircraft possessed by the French in Indo-China vary, but not by much, and Davidson comes to the conclusion that a maximum of seventy-five to one hundred aircraft were available to support Dien Bien Phu, giving a serviceability figure of between fifty-six to seventy-five.[23] Sources disagree on the proportion of C-119s to C-47s. However, it is clear that there were still a considerable number of C-47s in use. The C-47, the great parachuting and air supply work-horse of the Second World War was obsolete, even by the standards of 1954 and, unlike the C-119, did not have a tail-gate. With only a side door, the C-47 was slower to load and unload on the ground, and therefore had a longer turnround time. When it came to parachuting supplies, the C-47's disparity was even more marked, it was restricted to far smaller and lighter loads. This was to be significant in the days to come at Dien Bien Phu.

The shortage of suitable air transports was aggravated by the shortage of airfields in the Delta from which the aircraft could operate. Only around Hanoi, at the maximum radius of operation, were there any suitable airfields. Other low-lying, and therefore flat, areas were so wet that building airfields required a ton of crushed rock per square yard, which had to be allowed time to settle. The French had neither the engineer resources nor the time to build airfields at this stage. A further hindrance to air support operations was the lack of accurate weather forecasting and navigational aids. This, combined with inaccurate French maps, made night and bad weather flying over mountains, whose heights and positions were sometimes incorrectly plotted, hazardous.

Giap was absolutely clear from the outset where the French logistic 'Achilles Heel' was situated. On 6–7 March Vietminh guerrillas infiltrated the two major French bases of Gia Lam and Cat Bi, and, ignoring other aircraft, destroyed seventy-eight transports. By mid-March, the Vietminh had so cratered the runway at Dien Bien Phu by artillery fire, that the French were forced to deliver supplies by parachute. Besides preventing fighters being forward-based close to the troops they were supporting, Vietminh artillery put paid to air casualty evacuation. The last aircraft to land at Dien Bien Phu was a casevac C-47, during the early hours of 28 March 1954. As it was about to take off the next morning with twenty-five casualties, having been delayed until daybreak by an oil leak in one engine, it was destroyed by Vietminh artillery fire. The crew, including a nurse, Genevieve de Galard-Tarraubes, stayed in Dien Bien Phu until the end.

Parachuting supplies is wasteful at the best of times. But instead of dropping from the normal height of between 500 and 1,000 feet, the French were forced by Vietminh flak to drop from 2,500 feet, then from 6,000 feet, and finally from 8,500 feet. Dispersion increased with the height of drop. During the battle of Dien Bien Phu, the French dropped an average of 120 tons of supplies a day. The defenders never recovered more than 100 tons a day, and even that is a surprisingly high figure, comparing well with other operations supplied by parachute.[24] Some fell into enemy hands, including 105 mm howitzer ammunition which fitted their guns. However, far more significant, is the calculation by United States Army logistic experts that the French garrison needed a minimum of 200 tons a day to maintain combat effectiveness.[25] So even if every ton of supplies had landed on the DZ, it would not have been sufficient. Finally, most French vehicles were soon destroyed by Vietminh artillery and mortar fire, so supplies had to be collected and distributed by men on foot, a time consuming and exhausting task. Eventually, the centralised logistic system at Dien Bien Phu broke down, and supplies were consumed at the strongpoint where they landed, which was not necessarily where they were needed.

The Battle

The Vietminh got their supplies through, the French did not. It is now time to round off the story of Dien Bien Phu by briefly relating the course of events which led to the French surrender.

Castries's defensive layout consisted of a main central position around the airstrip and village of Dien Bien Phu; divided into four mutually supporting defensive areas, Huguette, Dominique, Elaine, and Claudine. These were manned by a total of five infantry battalions, a 105 mm artillery battalion, and the four 155 mm guns on which the French were relying to win the counter-battery fire fight. Castries's reserve and counter-attack force was also situated here, consisting of 1 BEP and 8 BPC, supported by seven light tanks. Three forward positions, each manned by a battalion, were sited about two kilometres out from the main position, in the direction from which the French had correctly discerned the Vietminh would launch their first major attack: to the North-West, Anne-Marie; North, Gabrielle; and North-East, Beatrice. Seven kilometres to the south of the main position, Castries located a strong post, Isabelle, held by two infantry battalions, two 105 mm batteries, and three light tanks. Castries's reason for siting so many of his guns in Isabelle was to provide artillery support for the main position, but his reasoning was flawed, because enemy attacking the exposed positions of Gabrielle and Beatrice were out of range of over half of his artillery. He had also hoped to use Isabelle as an anchor position from which to mount counter-attacks, but again it was too far away; something he might have discovered had he made proper counter-attack plans, and rehearsed them.

In addition to the airstrip at Dien Bien Phu, the French constructed a secondary strip just north of Isabelle. It was never used. Six Hellcat fighters and six observation aircraft were forward-based on the main strip, and it was capable of accepting C-47s and C-119s; until the Vietminh artillery closed it.

The Concept of the Defence

Castries had a textbook defence plan: counter-battery fire on the enemy artillery to weaken his supporting fire, artillery and mortar fire missions on the enemy as they formed up for the attack, continuing and intensifying as they assaulted and started breaching minefields and barbed wire. All the while, the defenders would remain under cover to protect them from the enemy bombardment supporting the attack. As the enemy closed up to the bunkers, and their own artillery lifted, the defenders, hitherto crouching under cover, would man their machine guns and small arms, to pour streams of bullets into the thinned ranks of any enemy who had survived a pasting by artillery and mortars. Any enemy that succeeded in penetrating French positions would be hit with artillery fire, followed up by a swift counter-attack while they were still re-organising.

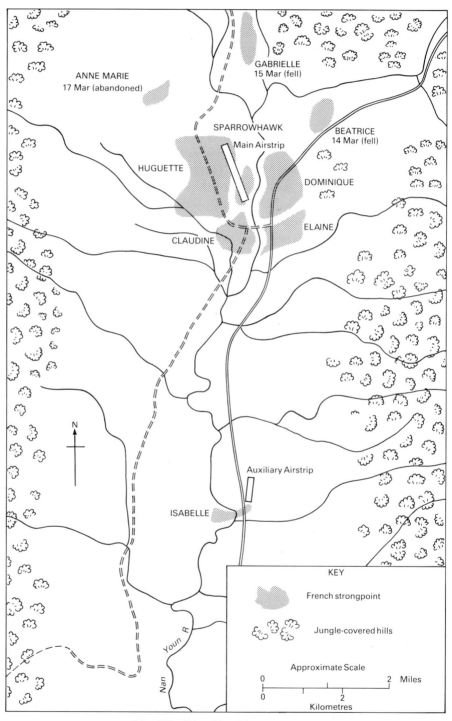

MAP IX   Dien Bien Phu March 1954.

Its Flaws

There is nothing wrong with this recipe for defence, provided all the ingredients are to hand. A number were missing on this occasion. For reasons which have already been given, the French bunkers did not have enough overhead cover. So the defenders were pulverised, by the Vietminh artillery and mortar fire; which caused many casualties and dazed many of the survivors, reducing their effectiveness when the attackers closed in. Furthermore, without adequate overhead protection, the French could not resort to the time-honoured practice of bringing down their own artillery and mortar fire right on top of their own positions, to catch the attackers as they milled about looking for bunker entrances, in the time consuming business of fighting through and clearing a position. Next, the layout and dispositions that Castries had chosen, particularly the wide dispersal of his guns, did not always allow him to concentrate fire where it was needed, nor mount counter-attacks quickly enough to hit the enemy while they were still off balance. Finally, the French counter-battery fire was ineffective, because the Vietminh had not sited their guns in groups, behind hills, in the conventional manner. They had dug them in on forward slopes, contravening all the principles taught in every other army in the world, in single gun emplacements or earth casemates. These could often be reached from the back of the hill by means of a tunnel. But in almost all cases, the gun could be pulled back from the firing point if it came under fire or air attack. The positions were well camouflaged by under-growth, bushes and trees, which had been left undisturbed. Groups of guns were defended by anti-aircraft positions similarly sited and camouflaged. Guns so positioned could be directly aimed at their targets. Only an army with a vast pool of labour could afford to construct what Navarre later called a 'human ant hill' and 'make a shambles of all the estimates of our own artillerymen. It was the major surprise of the battle'.[26]

Beatrice

It was a surprise that was not revealed in its entirety until 13 March 1954, when at night-fall, after an hour of fire directed at the emplacements before last light, Beatrice, held by 3rd Battalion, 13th Demi-Brigade of the Legion, was hit by two regiments of 312 Division. By day-break, after a desperate fight, during which the commanding officer and his entire command post staff were killed at an early stage,

Beatrice was in Vietminh hands. The French had lost 400 out of the 500 man garrison, all the officers were dead, wounded, or taken prisoner; 312 Division lost 600 dead and 1,200 wounded. The French counter-attack was beaten off. That day, 5 BPVN were dropped on to the DZs within the perimeter. The aircraft all escaped the flak, but the Vietnamese paratroopers took casualties on the DZs from artillery and mortar fire.

Gabrielle

That night it was Gabrielle's turn. Held by 5th Battalion, 7th Algerian Rifles, it was the only strongpoint with a second line of defence, and proved a harder nut to crack. For a while it seemed that the French had contained the attack by two regiments of 308 Division, who dug in on the edge of the position. After a furious bombardment of the French strongpoint, the Vietminh resumed the attack, pushing back the two forward Algerian companies, who had taken heavy casualties and lost all their officers. At this point, a shellburst killed or wounded the battalion commander, his deputy, and all the battalion staff, destroying the radios communicating with the companies and with Castries. Two Algerian companies fought on, clinging to the southern half of the position. Before dawn, Castries ordered Langlais, who commanded all the parachute battalions, and was in command of the reserve and of the main position, to mount a combined tank/infantry counter-attack. Langlais ordered one company of 1 BEP, his own former battalion, to spear-head the counter-attack supported by the tanks. He chose 5 BPVN as the main force. This was a major error. After an unpleasant drop the previous day, the battalion had spent most of the night digging in on Elaine. To get to the forming-up position for the counter-attack, they were required to move in darkness across the whole of the central position, a mass of bunkers, minefields, and wire, with which they were totally unfamiliar. Finally, they were far less experienced than the other two reserve battalions.

As the counter-attack force was advancing it was hit by a heavy mortar and artillery concentration, and small arms fire from a battalion of infantry dug into their left front. The 1st BEP company and the tanks, moved on out of the fire zone. Most of 5 BPVN did what the majority of inexperienced troops do the first time under fire, they went to ground. They were pinned down and took heavy casualties. By themselves, the tanks and company of 1 BEP could not maintain the momentum, and the counter-attack ground to a halt south of

Gabrielle. Here they were joined by the remnants of the Algerian Rifles who had withdrawn from Gabrielle. Together this force clawed its way back, lashed by fire, and eventually regained the main position. On Gabrielle and in the counter-attack the French lost about 1,000 men, dead, wounded and taken prisoner. Giap lost between 1,000 and 2,000 dead, and about twice that number wounded.

The Beginning of the End

The loss of Beatrice and Gabrielle spelled the end for the French garrison of Dien Bien Phu, for now the Vietminh possessed most of the ground which would give them an uninterrupted view over the whole position. The last piece fell into their hands on 17 March, when the 3rd T'ai Battalion abandoned Anne Marie under the cover of thick fog, and either joined the Vietminh or headed home. They had been subjected to weeks of Vietminh propaganda, and had seen the fall of Beatrice and Gabrielle. It is hard to blame them, it was not their style of warfare. The blame should be placed with Navarre, Cogny, and Castries, who failing to replace them when they had the opportunity, instead placed them in a vital outpost. Anne-Marie was abandoned, and the few T'ais, and the Frenchmen who had remained, were absorbed into the Huguette strongpoint.

By 16 March the French artillerymen in Dien Bien Phu knew that they were outnumbered and outgunned. The coming days would prove that the air force would not be able to provide much help. Locating the Vietminh guns under the cover of the foliage was difficult enough. To attack, the fighter bombers had to fly directly at the gun position, so presenting a good target to the flak guns sited in the vicinity. Losses were heavy. Once the monsoon started, the heavy, wet foliage was almost impervious to napalm. The French air force was incapable of the sustained offensive required to destroy the ring of Vietminh guns. Colonel Piroth, Castries's artillery commander, ridden with guilt at the failure of his command, and aware how flawed his advice had been, committed suicide the night after the fall of Gabrielle.

Ammunition: A Fatal Lack of Foresight

Between 17 and 30 March there was a lull in the fighting, which was probably just as well for the French who had started with an estimated six days' worth of ammunition at Dien Bien Phu, and expended most of it by the second day. This has not been the first, nor will it be the last, example in this book, of underestimation of ammunition expenditure by commanders and staffs. But any commander with three months to prepare before he is besieged, who lays in only six days stocks of ammunition deserves to be censured in the strongest terms. Navarre and Cogny are also to blame. It is a measure of the deficiencies in the French logistic system that this was allowed to occur. Air resupply built up the stocks again, but careful ammunition conservation was necessary thereafter.

*   *   *

The Vietminh used the period to dig over 100 kilometres of trenches, encircling the main position, and isolating Isabelle. Elaine, Dominique and Huguette were next on Giap's agenda. Castries withdrew to his bunker and according to some accounts effectively relinquished command, although he remained as the channel through which orders and information passed back and forth between the garrison and Hanoi. Langlais took over the day to day running of the battle, assisted some allege, by a 'mafia' of parachute and Foreign Legion officers, of whom the foremost was Bigeard, commanding 6 BPC. Cogny, now aware of Castries's shortcomings, and in an agony of guilt over his part in the bungled concept that he could see was leading to disaster, contemplated parachuting into Dien Bien Phu to take command. He was rightly dissuaded by his staff.

Bigeard's Attack

All was not gloom at Dien Bien Phu during this time. Bigeard was ordered by Castries to destroy some nests of flak guns to the west of Dien Bien Phu. This was probably at the insistence of Cogny, or Nicot the air commander at Hanoi. Bigeard selected the cream of the garrison for this enterprise, 6 and 8 BPC, 1 BEP, and a Foreign Legion Infantry battalion, supported by all the tanks and artillery in the main position, and air support. The attack was a brilliant success, seventeen flak guns were destroyed, 350 Vietminh killed, and ten captured; for the loss of twenty French dead and ninety wounded. Surprise, one of the two working principles of war, was the key to success. The Vietminh believing that the garrison was totally demoralised, were caught napping. However, although the sortie was no doubt good for morale, the loss was a drop in the ocean to the Vietminh. They had a total of eighty 37 mm and one hundred 0.50 inch flak guns around Dien Bien Phu.

Giap's Phase Two

Phase Two of Giap's offensive started on 30 March and lasted until 30 April. First he aimed to capture the strongpoints on five small hills in Elaine and Dominique, to the east of the main position. This part of the battle lasted until 5 April. Giap did not completely succeed in taking all his objectives, thanks to the self-sacrifice and spirit of the defenders under the inspiring leadership of men such as Langlais and Bigeard. The battle ebbed and flowed, as the French fiercely counter-attacked every Vietminh penetration. At the end of this phase, French radio intercept heard Giap ordering his rear bases to speed up the flow of reinforcements to make good his losses. For the French there was a small reinforcement in the form of 2nd Battalion 1st RCP. They were dropped at night, using the whole camp as a DZ. There were surprisingly few casualties. Giap ordered renewed sapper operations to reduce the distance his assault troops would have to be exposed to French fire.

From 5 April to 1 May, the battle took on a First World War texture with waterlogged trenches in all directions, wire, mud, sap and counter-sap operations. Attacks and counter-attacks were brisk and bloody, biting off small areas of ground, which changed hands, often several times. The French succeeded in taking back part of Elaine lost to Giap at the beginning of April. Giap's attempts to retake it were thrown back with huge losses. Cracks began to appear in the Vietminh morale, which is not surprising. By mid April the Vietminh losses at Dien Bien Phu had reached between 16,000 and 19,000 men, the equivalent of the rifle strength of the three Vietminh infantry divisions taking part in the battle. Like the defenders, the besiegers lived in the mud and filth of flooded trenches. Perhaps the most serious cause of low morale was the virtual absence of any medical service. To care for 50,000 troops besieging Dien Bien Phu, the Vietminh had one surgeon and six assistant doctors. Infection and gangrene must have taken a huge toll in the unsanitary aid stations, and it is likely that more men died after evacuation than on the battlefield. Giap responded with orders to shoot men who refused to attack, pep talks, and moved the equivalent of two fresh regiments to join him from other areas.

Giap now turned his attention to Huguette, on the west side of the main position. By 22 April, half of the area had been overrun. This reduced the size of the camp to about a two kilometre square. Vietminh flak covered the whole area, and many of the supplies and men dropped into the garrison fell into enemy hands. By now, 2 BEP, the last formed unit to join the main camp, had parachuted in. It was during this period, with the DZ swept by fire, and fewer and fewer vehicles to move loads, that the French logistic system within the camp broke down. Since 30 March strongpoint Isabelle had been cut off from the main camp and on its own. The situation here was a miniature version of the main camp, except that if anything, conditions were more severe. Isabelle was sited in a swamp, had worse flooding, and containing a smaller DZ, lost a greater proportion of supplies to the enemy. The fighting followed the same pattern; the encircling enemy trenches, sapping and counter-sap operations, attacks, counter-attacks, over-whelming Vietminh artillery and mortar fire; and mud, excrement, rotting corpses and the pervasive stench of death. The position was held initially by 3rd Battalion, 3rd Foreign Legion Infantry Regiment and 2nd Battalion, 1st Algerian Rifle Regiment, two 105 mm batteries, and three light tanks. Langlais reinforced it by sending the remnants of the Algerians from Gabrielle, and T'ais from Anne-Marie. By the end of May the 1,700 man garrison hung on grimly, despite having exhausted its supply of food, and nearly all its artillery ammunition.

The Final Moments

The final phase of the battle began on 1 May, with attacks on Elaine, Dominique and Huguette. For six days the fighting raged, as Giap squeezed the garrison. Even when a huge sap under one of the positions of Elaine was filled with 3,000 pounds of TNT and blown, devastating the bunkers, the handful of French survivors fought on. One cannot help being filled with admiration for the courage of the soldiers on both sides. The French, in particular, whatever the faults of their commanders, put up a heroic performance that ranks with those of the Germans at Cassino or the British at Khohima. Finally bunker by bunker, the Vietminh overcame and by 5.30 p.m. on 7 May 1954, it was all over in the main position, and a few hours later at Isabelle.

*   *   *

Conclusions

The French lost the war because they lacked the means to apply the overwhelming force necessary for the first step to victory, crushing the Vietminh. Whether they had the will, or were capable of formulating and carrying through the policies necessary to proceed further along the path after this first step, is a matter for conjecture. What mattered is that they lost, fighting the type of battle thought by them to be the key to eventual success. Whereas Giap was able to bring overwhelming force to bear at the vital place, thanks to his logistical arrangements; the French, despite the means at their disposal, totally failed. If manpower and military hardware constitute the vehicle which applies the necessary force to win a war, logistics are the power plant and fuel which drive it. In the end, both the French 'vehicle' and its power plant were found wanting, with one exception; the courage of her soldiers, of many races. Total French casualties in Indo-China were 140,992, including 75,867 dead or missing.[27] The Americans, who were to suffer 25,000 fewer dead in the same area over a longer period, possessed both the vehicle and the power plant. How did they use it?

HELICOPTER WAR

Eleven Years Pass: The Scene Changes

Eleven years passed between the Geneva Conference, which ended Round One, and established South and North Vietnam, divided by the 17th Parallel, and the deployment of American forces in South Vietnam in other than an advisory role. The early part of those years saw the reorganisation of the North Vietnamese Army (NVA), as the Main Force regulars became, and the Army of the Republic of South Vietnam (ARVN). Among other measures, including training, Giap attempted a thorough restructuring of his logistic system. He was successful in some areas, but not in others. By replacing the mix of French, Japanese, Chinese and American equipment by Chinese and Soviet equipment, he reduced the problem of providing a wide range of spares and ammunition for an array of differing weapons and other hardware; as well as easing the training load. He increased his establishment of trucks and drivers. He rebuilt roads, railways, and the ports of Haiphong, Hong Gay, and Ben Thuy. He was not so successful at reorganising his battlefield support system. It was still ponderous, and would remain so for the greater part of Round Two. This was largely a function of the type of war that Giap was forced to fight by United States air striking power and mobility. In this situation, a conventional logistic system in the battle area would have been vulnerable to attack and disruption. Giap could, and did, stockpile supplies, but pushing them forward to the consumers, in amounts sufficient to support large concentrations of troops engaged in battle, was beyond his capability. The same limitation applied if he wished to switch the direction of effort, or regroup rapidly. His stockpiles might be in the wrong place, and need reconstituting in another location. This accounts very largely for the episodic nature of his offensives right up to the early 1970s; attacks were followed by pauses, often long in duration, while stocks were built up for the next move.

While the NVA was being reorganised, a debate was in progress in North Vietnam over the correct strategy to adopt for the conquest of South Vietnam. The outcome was to have a profound effect on NVA logistics over the years to come. One faction, led by Le Duan, a southerner, argued for large-scale military action in South Vietnam. Giap and others supported a long-drawn out guerrilla campaign. In 1959 Ho Chi Minh came down on the side of the southerners, deciding that the campaign would take the form of an armed revolt supported by North Vietnam. About 4,500 South Vietnamese communists who had moved north after the partition in 1954, infiltrated back to form the nucleus of the Viet Cong (Viet Cong, or VC, derived from Viet Con Son, meaning Vietnamese Communist) battalions and regiments. In response to this, a transport group was formed by the NVA to provide logistic support to the Viet Cong; their line of communication through Laos, the Ho Chi Minh Trail.

In South Vietnam, the ARVN had also been re-equipping, and training. For about a year this had been a joint French/United States task. The Americans had been reluctant to see a complete French withdrawal from South Vietnam, particularly as the ARVN was neither trained nor organised to meet an attack by the NVA. They suggested a number of ways in which the French could retain substantial forces in the country, without offending Diem, the President of South Vietnam; including the artifice of keeping them there under the terms of the South East Asia Treaty Organisation (SEATO), which would make the French subordinate to the SEATO commander. But a number of factors frustrated the American hopes; among them, Diem's desire to get rid of the French, in any capacity, as speedily as possible. This coincided with the French wish to be shot of Vietnam in general, and Diem in particular, for what they saw as his treachery and irresponsibility, and concentrate their energies on the growing insurrection in Algeria.

The French Depart

The bitterness felt by the French at their defeat and the brash attitude of the inexperienced Americans, manifested itself particularly strongly when it came to allocating the American equipment supplied to the French Army during the last four years of Round One. The terms of the aid scheme under which the equipment had been provided, stipulated that it was all to revert to the Americans at the conclusion of the war. However the small USMAAG had been unable to keep track of which items the French had bought, and which had been furnished under the scheme. The French were determined to keep the best and removed it, sometimes refusing to allow the American inspection teams to examine depots or ports, and erasing assistance scheme markings. At the same time, they dumped huge quantities of unserviceable equipment on the ARVN. As the French had removed most of the spares, it could not be repaired until more spares had been shipped over from the USA. The ARVN was unable to cope with such a massive logistic burden. Formed from the remnants of the ineffectual Vietnamese National Army, which had little logistic capability, the ARVN was overwhelmed with a deluge of equipment, most of which was fit only for the scrap heap. The strain on the creaking logistic services was aggravated by Diem and his army commander's reluctance to part with a single item.[28] To save an investment estimated at $500 million, the Americans found themselves being sucked inexorably into advising on the management of the ARVN logistics.

The ARVN: A Pattern of Corruption, Incompetence and Poor Leadership

Space does not permit a full review of the years leading up to full American involvement in Vietnam. Suffice to say that they faced daunting problems in attempting to assist with the formation and training of an army which was riddled with corruption at every level from the generals down. Political considerations were invariably uppermost in Diem's mind when selecting his senior officers, and many in their turn responded to this cynical approach by supplementing their income by dealing on the drug and black markets, running prostitutes, embezzling public funds and, in remoter areas, setting up as warlords and collecting taxes. Taking their cue from their superiors, junior officers resorted to extortion and robbery against the local population in outlying districts. Motivation was lacking at all levels in the South Vietnamese population. Students called up for service on mobilization, volunteered for service in the Navy, not from any wish to serve at sea, but to avoid the Army. In any case the Navy hardly ever put to sea; there was no incentive, even for the most venal, since a bonus in the form of 'sea pay' was received by everybody in the Navy, irrespective of whether or not they did time at sea.

Training under these conditions was often a farce. The commandant of the ARVN basic training school, through which all recruits for the Army, for both regular and reserve units passed, was described by the United States Army Attaché in Saigon, as 'a pompous, fat, stupid man . . . who will do anything to increase his personal fortune.' He was reported to be financing a brothel run by his mistress. His brother generals were scandalised; not by his business involvement with whores, that was commonplace, but because he flaunted his relationship with the madam. It was not surprising, therefore, that at a lower level, standards that Vietnamese officers had learned in Army schools in the United States, were instantly dropped when they arrived back in South Vietnam.[29]

The difficulties in equipping and training the ARVN were aggravated by differences in opinion on its role, and hence its organisation. The problem was that there were two types of adversary: a potential enemy, the NVA increasingly organised on conventional lines; and an actual enemy, the Viet Cong, at that time a guerrilla force. General Williams, the commander of the USMAAG, was of the opinion that countering insurgency was not the primary business of the ARVN. The outcome was that although Williams denied that the ARVN divisions were carbon copies of their American counterparts, they were actually very alike in organisation. Although the divisions were designed to be superior in firepower to the NVA formations, they were intended to fight in jungle, swamp, and mountains. Thus Williams maintained that the soldiers in the divisions had the same foot mobility as a guerrilla. This was a delusion, because although the riflemen could move on foot away from roads, their guns, mortars, the ammunition for these, and their general logistic back-up could not do so; the divisions were therefore road-bound. This divisional organisation, and the advice on which it was based, were symptomatic of a serious deficiency; the lack of any Counter Insurgency doctrine in the United States Army in the 1950s. When eventually the ARVN, contrary to Williams's advice, deployed against the Viet Cong, they were able, despite ponderous and bungled operations, to deal them some heavy blows and severely dented their organisation and morale. It was at this point, with the Viet Cong organisation seriously weakened in some areas, that Ho Chi Minh issued the directive, referred to earlier, on the future course of the war. Despite this being one of a number of key policy decisions in the course of the thirty year long war in Indo-China, the insurgency was still containable. By March 1960 the armed strength of the Viet Cong in the whole country was only between three and four thousand.[30] The insurgency was not contained because the ARVN was incompetent, corrupt, badly led, lacked motivation, had been penetrated by Viet Cong agents and had low morale. Like most armies, the ARVN was the mirror image of the society from which it came; in this case the corrupt Diem régime which was ill-equipped morally and politically to cope with a burgeoning social revolution throughout the country.

*   *   *

1961: The First American Helicopter Units Are Committed

By late 1961, there was every prospect of Viet Cong victory in South Vietnam. At this point President Kennedy made the decision to commit US helicopter companies to South Vietnam. He had jibbed at the introduction of US ground troops, and had settled for the helicopter-only option. It was a decision which was to lead eventually to the commitment of United States ground troops to the war. To begin with, the introduction of the helicopters on the battlefield took the Viet Cong by surprise, and for several months the ARVN inflicted a series of heavy defeats on them. These operations were at the lowest end of the scale of airmobile operations. The helicopters were used as 'battle taxis', there were no heavy lift helicopters to move guns and logistic loads, and no armed helicopters to give fire support. Reactions to intelligence were slow and the intelligence itself often flawed. The American advisers spent much time training the South Vietnamese troops in command and control of heliborne operations, the co-ordination of fire support and the bread and butter skills of airmobile soldiering. The ARVN soldiers were hesitant and lacked drive, but once again Giap was caught on the hop, as he had been by French parachute operations, by a weapon of which he had no personal experience. This state of affairs did not last for long. The Viet Cong soon learned how vulnerable the helicopters were to ground fire, particularly if unsupported by armed helicopters. Instead of running, they fired at the troop carrying helicopters, ambushed the landing zones, or retired to mountainous and jungle areas outside the operational radius of the obsolescent H-21 helicopters. Nevertheless, the battle seemed to be going the ARVN's way for a while. The USMAAG, now renamed the United States Military Assistance Command Vietnam (USMACV), began to feel optimistic about the

FIG. 5.4   Early days of United States helicopter support for the ARVN. Unloading rice and other supplies at base camp. United

outcome of the war. But, under the surface the situation was deteriorating rapidly; there were three reasons.

The Situation Deteriorates

First, the ARVN exemplified the saying that there are no bad soldiers, only bad officers. The hardy Vietnamese peasants made good soldiers, fighting well in the French Army and in the Vietminh and Viet Cong. On the whole, for reasons that have already been explained, their officers were appalling. Despite encouraging reports on the performance of the ARVN, sent to Washington by Harkins, the commander USMACV, most of these did not reflect the actual situation on the ground. For example, the battle of Ap Bac, which took place on 2 January 1963, was reported back to Washington as a success. Whereas the United States Army adviser attached to the ARVN 7th Infantry Division, who had mounted the operation, reported a dismal failure. The village of Ap Bac, 40 miles south-west of Saigon, was held for a day by 350 Viet Cong guerrillas equipped with small arms and one 60 mm mortar, against a force four times its size, consisting of one ARVN battalion, two Civil Guard battalions, a parachute battalion, and a company of infantry mounted in M-113 armoured personnel carriers, supported by mortars, artillery and ground attack aircraft (ARVN infantry and marine battalions were small by British standards, usually about 350 at maximum strength). The ARVN attacks were faltering, the leaders cowardly, from the Divisional commander down. Eventually, having held off the ARVN all day, the guerrillas slipped away under the cover of darkness. Throughout this disgraceful episode, the American adviser, an exceptionally brave and forceful officer, tried to get the ARVN divisional commander to mount an attack, in vain. The following morning, 7th Division shelled the empty village, and followed this up with a half-hearted probing attack. The ARVN soldiers never penetrated the village, and for days Harkins believed, and announced to the press, that the guerrillas were surrounded. This pusillanimous showing was typical of many ARVN operations. Diem did nothing to help. Indeed, wishing to preserve the ARVN intact as the principal bulwark against a coup, he constantly exhorted his commanders to avoid casualties.

Second, the Strategic Hamlet scheme, which herded villagers into areas where they would, in theory, be immune from Viet Cong intimidation, proved to be largely a wasted effort. The Viet Cong easily infiltrated the hamlets, welcomed by the majority of the inhabitants who deeply resented being forcibly re-located away from their ancestral homes. The civil guards either locked themselves away in their watch tower, were disarmed, or were members of the Viet Cong already. Apart from the destruction of the hamlets, whose occupants, with Viet Cong help, promptly moved back to their old areas, the scheme had another, unforeseen effect. It greatly assisted in the arming of the Viet Cong. By January 1963, the Americans had supplied more than 130,000 small arms, machine guns, mortars, and recoilless guns to the Civil Guards and Self-Defence Corps militia. By mid 1963 this figure had risen to quarter of a million weapons distributed to strategic hamlets and outposts. These constituted convenient weapon stocks for the Viet Cong, who were not slow to take advantage. By January 1963, equipped largely at American expense, the regular and provincial Viet Cong strength had risen to about 23,000, backed by another 100,000 militia; a quantum leap in just three years.

Finally, Diem overreacted to demands by the Buddhist community for more say in the affairs of South Vietnam, which were largely in the hands of the Vietnamese Catholics. Eventually, Diem was overthrown with the connivance of the United States Government, and murdered by a group of officers. Although the people at first greeted Diem's fall with enthusiasm, and the ARVN soldiers were feted in the streets of Saigon; the novelty soon wore off.

American hopes that Diem's fall would signal a turning point in the war were soon dashed. Within a week the Viet Cong launched offensives north of Saigon. In one province alone, twenty-five outposts fell in one month. Within a few days of Diem's death, President Kennedy was also dead. There were now 17,000 American servicemen in South Vietnam. Although, since the start of their involvement, the Americans had taken only 370 casualties, including 120 dead, enough blood and treasure had been poured out, and enough rhetoric expended, to ensure that American prestige was now at stake.

1964 and Crisis

By the end of 1964, the situation in South Vietnam had reached crisis proportions, the Viet Cong main and province forces, 23,000-strong, had grown to 56,000. They were beginning to look like an army, organised into regiments, with combat, engineer and communications support units. The first Viet Cong division to form, the 9th, dealt a deadly blow to two élite ARVN units on 31 December 1964. A marine battalion lost nearly 200 dead, wounded or captured, out of a strength of 326, including 29 officers dead out of a total of 35. One of the new ranger battalions, set up by General Westmoreland, now Commander USMACV, was completely destroyed.

1965: The Americans Committed in Strength

By mid June 1965, the Viet Cong looked to be poised for the fight to the finish. But now they were about to take on the armed might of the United States in direct confrontation. Starting with a marine brigade landed in March 1965, to defend the enclave of Da Nang, the build-up of American troops continued with an airborne brigade from Okinawa to secure Saigon airport, and steadily accelerated to a total of 184,300 by the end of the year.[31]

A New Logistic Situation

The logistic system was required to support a force that rose to a maximum of over half a million at the end of a line of communication between 9,000 and 11,000 miles long, into a country that lacked many of the necessary facilities to support such a huge and sudden upsurge in troop strength. The logistic situation was totally different from that for which the American forces had trained, and had experienced in the Second World War and Korea. There were no clear areas in which logistic installations could be set up, there was no front and no rear in the conventional sense. There were no advances and withdrawals on linear axes, along which the sinews of war could flow. Most operations were mounted from isolated base camps dotted around the country-side. There were few fixed terrain objectives. The conventional pattern of a combat zone and a communications zone did not exist.

The reinforcement was imbalanced, so that the troop strength almost always out-stripped the logistic build-up. Consequently the plans made by 1st Logistical Command were constantly out of date, and there was much *ad hoc* planning. 1st Logistical Command, activated in April 1965, had responsibility for supplying all the United States forces in South Vietnam, except the two United States Marine Divisions and their two air wings, in I Corps, the most northerly corps area; these were a Marine Corps and Navy responsibility. In 1968, after the Viet Cong Tet offensive, when substantial Army reinforcements moved north, 1st Logistical Command expanded their responsibilities to include I Corps area.

Chaos on the Move

The troop build-up in that first year was so rapid that it bore all the hallmarks of an 'off the cuff' operation. The order and counter-order experienced by the 1st Air Cavalry Division, may have been exceptional, but they illustrate the logistic problems encountered in moving a formation without adequate shipping and full briefing to all concerned, to a destination which has not been reconnoitred properly. The division consisting of over 400 aircraft, mainly helicopters, nearly 16,000 men and over 1,600 vehicles was lifted to Vietnam in the carrier, USS Boxer, three Military Sea Transportation Service (MATS) ships, and several Liberty ships. Despite the protestations of senior commanders within the Division, that loading should be tactical, the Division was loaded administratively to save shipping, with men and equipment crammed into ships wherever there was a space. (Tactical loading demands that men and their equipment, tanks, guns, helicopters, vehicles, travel in the same ship, and that unloading can be carried out in a sequence that allows every unit to start fighting the minute it gets ashore). Half way across the Pacific, the commander of the Air Cavalry Squadron (a nine hundred man strong heliborne battalion), received a signal from the divisional task force commander already in Vietnam, telling him to be prepared to fight his way ashore, on the orders of somebody in Heaquarters United States Forces Vietnam. The Squadron's 90 helicopters were in the Boxer and all three MATS ships. All the vehicles and administrative personnel were spread among half a dozen Liberty ships, whose position was unknown to him, and with whom he had no means of communicating. All he had with him was 600 men and their personal weapons. He set to and made what plans he could.

When he called on the Master of the ship, to ask him to break out the scrambling nets so that the men could practice on them, he was informed that not only were there no nets on board, but that he was unaware of the sailing destination. Wherever it was, he was convinced that he would be able to discharge alongside. The commanding officer of the Air Cavalry Squadron finally persuaded the Master that his destination was Vietnam, and his port of unloading, Qui Nhon harbour where there were no facilities for discharging a ship of his size. Fortunately for the Air Cavalry Squadron, there was no opposition on the beach, and never had been. Lighters were used to land the troopers from their ship at her anchorage.[32]

It was to take until the end of 1967 before the ten ports used by US

Forces in Vietnam were fully operational. In 1965, at the most critical time in the troop reinforcement, deep draught ships could wait up to 20 days for a berth, three years later, the average was less than two days.

The Blessings of Total Air Superiority

Despite the many problems encountered by the logisticians, and some close calls in 1965 during the build-up, there are no recorded instances of operations being constrained by lack of logistic resources. Indeed, supplies were lavish, and the section on subsistence in the volume on Logistic Support in the Vietnam Studies proudly reports: 'US Soldiers in Vietnam ate well. Ice cream and eggs to order were not uncommon items at fire support bases. Extensive use of large refrigerators, refrigerator vans, and helicopters permitted the troops in the field to enjoy garrison type rations on an almost routine basis'.

The key to this extraordinary effort lay in the helicopter and the tactical transport aircraft, the most notable being the Army C-7A Caribou and Air Force C-123, augmented by the C-130s of the Air Force. Tactical transport aircraft lifted only slightly less tonnages than all the helicopters, both Army and Marine.[33] Operations which the French would have found impossible to support logistically ten years earlier, were made commonplace by the helicopter and tactical transport aircraft. Neither would have been effective unless the Americans had total air superiority. Ground fire both en route and on landing zones, dropping zones, and airstrips was often a problem, but the air line of communication did not have to contend with the threat of inderdiction by fighters. Aircraft, including helicopters, could therefore fly high to avoid flak, so that there was nowhere in South Vietnam over which the Americans and their allies could not fly.[34]

Road and Rail Movement

Despite the picture of this as a helicopter war, roads and railways also had a part to play. By mid 1966 Westmoreland directed that more use was to be made of roads. For example, in 1968, motor transport moved nearly ten times the tonnages lifted by helicopter. Although the railway system had been seriously disrupted by the Viet Cong, the Americans made considerable efforts to repair it and improve its capacity. Hundreds of thousands of tons of rock and gravel were transported by rail to airfield and port construction sites, and to road improvement locations.[35]

Problems of Adjustment

To begin with there were hiccups, of which the worst was ammunition supply. Again this was a product of the hurried build-up of troop levels, staffed by a headquarters that lacked logistic staff officers, in a country with few facilities. In Vietnam, ammunition was supplied in push packages; as were other commodities.[36] These were standard packages made up some years before and based on the Second World War and Korean War experience. The ammunition packages contained a mix of ammunition designed to meet a pre-determined expenditure rate. Other packages contained spares, food, clothing and so on. Each package was tailored to meet the requirements of a particular unit or formation. As their name implies, these packages were pushed forward to meet the anticipated demand. The disadvantages of this system were that if demand exceeded what had been planned, there were shortages, and if expenditure on some ammunition natures and logistic items was lower than anticipated, there was a likelihood of storage locations being inundated with unwanted supplies. These problems were aggravated in the case of the ammunition push packages in the early days of the American build-up. When 173 Airborne Brigade arrived at Tan Son Nhut airport and immediately started operations, they found that not only were they consuming ammunition faster than the rate for which their packages were designed, but their packages contained obsolete items such as 3.5 inch rockets, and anti-tank ammunition for guns that were no longer in service with the US Army. To correct this, 255 tons of ammunition was flown directly from Okinawa to Tan Son Nhut, using all the available transport aircraft in the theatre for seven days.

From April to July 1965, the ammunition situation was 'chaotic'. Push packages arrived before units, and units were diverted elsewhere from their designated disembarkation points, while ammunition piled up on the beach, or in hired sampans and barges on the Saigon river. The problem was compounded by the delayed arrival of the necessary logistic units to manage the procedures for receiving, storing, issuing, and requisitioning ammunition. Eventually, with the establishment of Headquarters United States Army Vietnam in July 1965, order began to appear.[37]

Air Supply in the Forward Areas

In the early days there was disagreement, mainly within the United States Army, on how far forward the USAF should supply. This came to a head during the 1st Air Cavalry Division's operations to relieve the ARVN base at Plei Me in the highlands around Pleiku, culminating in the battles at the River Drang (Ia Drang), near the Cambodian border. The first head-on confrontation between American troops and the regulars of the NVA. At the outset, the divisional commander, Major General Kinnard, wanted priority call on the USAF to supply direct to his divisional base at An Khe. But Westmoreland decreed that the division would use the normal request system.[38] Shorn of the USAF's logistical support, Kinnard was forced to send his own cargo helicopters and Caribous back to Qui Nhon and Nha Trang, respectively 50 and 130 miles away, at a time when he needed them all to lift forward to Pleiku, where his troops were engaged in battle.

On 25 July, as the 1st Air Cavalry Division's operations gained momentum, Kinnard's Caribous and Chinooks laboured to supply Pleiku, lifting 513 tons from An Khe, Qui Nonh, and Nha Trang. The next day, fuel stocks at Pleiku fell to 7,000 gallons, against a daily consumption rate of 70,000 gallons. On that day (26 July), only 18 out of the 30 Chinooks in the division were able to fly. Clearly, the scale of the airlift had to be enlarged; particularly as on that same day, Westmoreland ordered the division to seek out and destroy the NVA retreating from Plei Me; an order which led to three weeks aggressive airmobile warfare in the Ia Drang valley. The USAF lift started before dawn the following day, but consumption outran supply. Within two days, 1st Air Cavalry Division reported 'zero gallons of Jp-4 (fuel for all aviation turbine engines), on hand to support operations'. However, within three days deliveries reached three-quarters of the daily rate requested, thanks mainly to the impressive lift capacity of the great workhorse, the C-130 which could carry fifteen 500 gallon fuel bladders. At first, fuel deliveries were to Pleiku, but soon the USAF started taking fuel bladders to a four thousand foot long dirt strip at Catecka Tea Plantation, ten miles forward of Plaiku. This strip became the division's helicopter Forward Operating Base (FOB) and refuelling point, thereby drastically reducing the need for the division's Chinooks to be employed moving fuel bladders from Pleiku to the FOB, releasing them for other tasks. 1st Air Cavalry Division reported later that the USAF transport stream into Catecka 'was certainly one of the biggest Godsends of the whole exercise (sic)—otherwise we would have had to grind to a halt for lack of fuel'.[39] The USAF delivered 5,400 tons in support of 1st Air Cavalry Division, a daily average of 186 tons, of which 58 per cent was fuel; an indication of how voraciously the helicopter consumes fuel. The success of that operation did much to

FIG. 5.5   Unloading mortar ammunition from a Huey helicopter, 1st Cavalry Division, Ia Drang Valley, Operation Paul Revere IV (*US Army*).

change the Army's willingness to seek Air Force assistance. The further forward the USAF could supply, the better.

Centralising the Logistic System

The centralised logistic system under 1st Logistical Command in Vietnam has been criticised, notably by General Starry in his monograph, *Mounted Combat in Vietnam*.[40] The burden of the complaint: that logistic units were stripped away from formations, centralised, and lived in base camps. Although the first part of the complaint is fair, the second, implying that logistic units never moved is not. For specific operations, normally brigade size or larger, Forward Support Areas (FSAs), were established adjacent to a forward airstrip capable of accepting C-130s. The FSA was hived off from the 1st Logistical Command, and handled all types of supply. From the FSA, helicopters lifted supplies out to the fire support bases, and battalions and companies operating in the field. By 1966, nearly everywhere in Vietnam was within 25 miles of a C-130 capable strip.[41]

Given the circumstances of this war, it is difficult to see what else could have been done. In a conventional war, logistic units usually form part of almost every formation, from brigade upwards. They operate as part of the formation, and, to provide the necessary service, occupy real estate in the rear of the formation for workshops, supply points, transport parks, fuel dumps, and so forth. They move, using their own transport resources, in order to conform to their customer's moves, following the ebb and flow of battle. In Vietnam, as has already been explained, there were no rear areas behind the customers, the formations and units doing the fighting. Nor, as has already been stated, did operations during the period of American involvement conform to the 'normal' pattern. Units and formations lived in bases from which they sortied, usually for a few days at a time, by helicopter, on foot, or in armoured vehicles; and to which they withdrew on completion of the operation. Their objectives were rarely exactly the same each time. There was no question of logistic units moving with them to 'set up shop'. The drain on transport and defence resources would have been prohibitive. Siting logistic units at the unit or formation base would have enlarged the dependency: mouths to feed, and the need for clothing, spares, equipment, and ammunition for personal weapons; incrasing the resupply bill and the resources to lift the additional items. The presence of logistic units and the real estate to provide working space, would expand the area to protect, placing an extra burden on the occupying unit. Logistic units, if they are so trained, can take, and have taken, responsibility for their own defence, but every hour spent in a trench defending the perimeter, is an hour less to attend to the tasks for which they are in business; support. It was better to leave them centralised, or form FSAs for specific operations. Units which could be based right forward were those whose task it was to maintain and repair the heavier equipment and helicopters. In many cases this was done; on the principle that it is usually easier to move technicians to the heavy equipment than vice versa.

The Strategic and Tactical Background to the Logistic Requirement

What were the strategy and tactics for which the logistical arrangements were tailored? The directive given to Westmoreland set out six tasks:

1. Attrit (sic), by year's end (1966), Viet Cong and North Vietnamese forces at a rate as high as their capability to put men in the field.
2. Increase the percentage of VC and NVA base areas denied the VC from 10–20 per cent to 40–50 per cent.
3. Increase the critical (important) roads and railroads open for use from 30 to 50 per cent.
4. Increase the population in secure areas from 50 per cent to 60 per cent.
5. Pacify the four selected high-priority areas, increasing the pacified population by 235,000.
6. Ensure the defence of all military bases, political population centres, and food-producing areas now under government control.[42]

Whether this was the right strategy is still a subject for argument, often heated, and is likely to remain so for the foreseeable future. Any discussion of even the main strands in the reasoning deployed by those who opposed the strategy, is irrelevant in the context of this book. The point is that at no time did Westmoreland, or his successor, General Abrams, find themselves constrained by United States logistic weakness, nor is it possible to discern any point at which their strategy was shaped by considerations of what was and what was not logistically feasible. Similarly the strategies put forward by those who favoured a different approach were also supportable logistically. Clearly it would be overstating the case to say that the Americans never had any logistic problems at a tactical level, but in contrast to Round

One, logistic shortcomings were not the ball and chain that so inhibited the French, and which were, in the end, the main cause of their military defeat.

THE BATTLE OF KHE SANH

Clearing Away the Mythology

One of the most impressive examples of the use of the logistic resources available to the Americans, including the successful use of air power for strike and supply, was the battle of Khe Sanh. As Davidson says,[43] 'more drivel has been written and televised about the siege of Khe Sanh than about any other episode of Indo-China War II' (his term for Round Three). Most of this drivel eventually homes in on the following misconceptions: that Khe Sanh was a diversion to draw American troops away from Giap's real objectives, the cities in the Tet offensive; or that the siege was a second Dien Bien Phu, and the defenders were doomed. The first myth can quickly be disposed of by saying that there has never been any evidence that it was a diversion, either at the time or in the published statements of the North Vietnamese since. Indeed, the NVA continued to reinforce their units round the base, and construct siege works, long after most of the fighting associated with the Tet offensive was over. If it was a diversion, it was a very expensive one, tying down four NVA divisions (two directly involved, and two in support), a total of 40,000 top rate regulars, to besiege four marine battalions and one ARVN ranger battalion, a total of 6,000 men.

The second misconception was the outcome of a trait discernible from time to time in some sections of the media, the journalistic equivalent of the gibe that generals usually 'fight the last war'; the twist being that the media 'write the last war'. In this case, the selective presentation of evidence to peddle a preconceived notion became so compelling, that the peddlers were taken in by their own advocacy, and failed to notice that the differences between the situations at Dien Bien Phu and Khe Sanh outweighed the similarities. The marines at Khe Sanh were surrounded by a superior force which could bring artillery and mortar fire to bear on every part of the base; and the defenders were totally dependent on air supply. There the similarities ended. The French were beaten because they were outgunned, and even given ideal conditions, i.e.: the ability to land aircraft at Dien Bien Phu, they would have been unable to keep up the pace of the battle logistically. The Vietminh merely hastened the end by denying them the use of the strip,

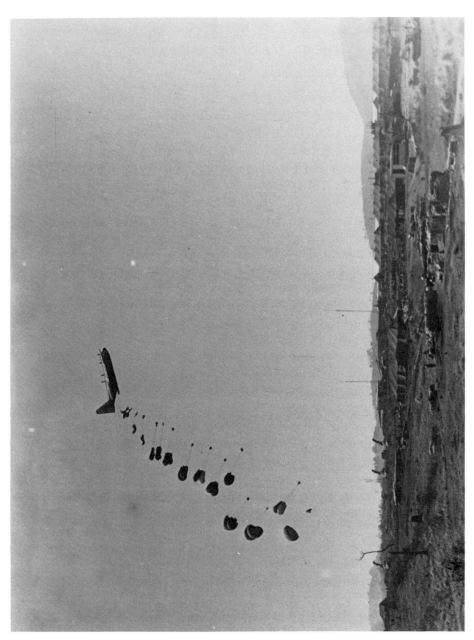

FIG. 5.6   A C-130 drops supplies to Khe Sanh (*United States Marine Corps*).

and forcing them into relying totally on supply by parachute, delivered by an inadequate, largely obsolete, air transport force. At no time did the NVA have fire superiority at Khe Sanh. The Americans had an enormous firepower advantage, from B-52s, ground attack aircraft, 175 mm howitzers and 8 inch guns outside the base, and 105 mm guns and 81 mm mortars inside it. Over 100,000 tons of bombs and 150,000 artillery rounds were delivered by the Americans on to the NVA during the 77 day siege.[44]

More important, the NVA never cut, or seriously inhibited the air supply to Khe Sanh.

Techniques for Re-Supply by Air

The techniques of re-supply by air had come a long way since Dien Bien Phu. When, some six weeks after the battle began, a C-130 was destroyed on the strip by NVA mortar fire, air supply was switched to the use of the Low Altitude Parachute Extraction System (LAPES), the Ground Proximity Extraction System (GPES), parachute dropping, C-123 fixed wing transports and helicopters.

When making a LAPES run, the C-130 flew at five feet over the runway, with tail-gate down. At the extraction point, the pilot threw an electronic switch operating a drogue parachute attached to the roller-mounted cargo pallets in the fuselage of the aircraft. The deploying parachute snatched the cargo out of the rear of the aircraft, and the pallets skidded to a stop on the runway. Marines moved in with fork-lift trucks and quickly gathered in the supplies. With the GPE System, the C-130 followed the same flight profile, but attached to the cargo was a long hook, with which the pilot attempted to catch an arrester wire, similar to the one used on aircraft carriers. If he succeeded, the pallet was pulled out, and stopped dead on the runway. Once the initial problems with this system were overcome, it was so successful that a load containing 30 dozen eggs was extracted without a single egg being cracked. However, only 15 GPE deliveries were made during the siege compared with 52 LAPES. Both systems required good visibility, and the low cloud and *crachin* of the North-East monsoon, precluded their use for much of the time. So the majority of supplies were dropped by parachute. By 1968, techniques for air dropping supplies had improved considerably since Dien Bien Phu, as had the sophistication of navigational aids. At the computed release point the pilot, aided by the Marine Air Traffic Control Unit at Khe Sanh, pulled the C-130 up into a nose up attitude, and 16 parachute bundles, containing 15 tons of supplies were spewed out of the tailgate. Under their parachutes they floated down through the haze. Dropping by instruments, the average error for drops was only 133 metres. If the pilot could see the DZ, it was even less: 95 metres.

Helicopters and C-123s continued to land at Khe Sanh, despite the mortaring and shelling and the shooting down of one C-123 on the approach, killing the four crew and all 44 passengers. The C-123s needed less than half the strip to land and take off, and were invaluable for casualty evacuation and flying in reinforcements. Helicopters could not only land at Khe Sanh, but were also used to supply the hill outposts, cut off from the main base and too small for paradrop of supplies. During the siege, 12,430 tons of supplies were delivered by the Air Force C-123s and C-130s (8,120 tons by paradrop, LAPES and GPES, 4,310 by aircraft landing at the strip). This is not the complete picture for deliveries by transport aircraft, because the USMC C-130s also played a vital part, but their records show the tonnages carried throughout I Corps area, and do not break down the figures to indicate the amounts delivered to individual bases like Khe Sanh. In addition Marine helicopters carried 4,661 tons of supplies, much of which was delivered direct to the outposts from the Logistic Support Area at Dong Ha.

The 'Super Gaggle'

The helicopter deliveries to the hill outposts were a triumph of organisation and an example of the close co-operation that occurs when a service owns its own air force. The air wings of the United States Marine Corps (USMC), unlike some air forces in the past, did not dissipate their strength by conducting a private war which bore no relation to what was happening on the ground. A typical resupply mission would include 12 CH-46 helicopters, each carrying 4,000 lbs of supplies underslung. Flak suppression would be provided by 12 A-4 Skyhawk ground attack jets. Four UH-1E gunships flew 'shot gun' behind the CH-46s. Control was provided by a TA-4 overhead. All aircraft were flown by Marines, and the whole effort was nicknamed the 'Super Gaggle'.

The timing of a 'Super Gaggle' was critical. The TA-4 pilot initiated the run. Having flown over the landing zone and judged the cloud base high enough for the A-4s to provide suppressive fire, he gave the 'go'. An H-hour would be set, and the 'Super Gaggle' began. Twelve A-4s would launch from Chu Lai. Simultaneously between 12 to 16 helicopters would launch from Quan Tri 100 miles to the north. The helicopters would fly to Dong Ha and pick up their loads, which were already laid out in nets. The trick was for all aircraft to arrive over the objective on cue. First the A-4s would hit the enemy flak positions with napalm and iron bombs. More A-4s would follow spraying tear gas. Just before the run-in by the helicopters, two A-4s laid a smoke screen corridor. While the helicopters ran into the landing zone, four A-4s with bombs, rockets and cannon provided flak suppression. Because of visibility and hilly terrain, once the heavily-laden helicopters committed themselves to the run-in, there was usually no chance of turning back if the flak was not completely suppressed. But the crews could comfort themselves that following on their heels were the gunships, ready to pick them up, if they survived being shot down. These tactics were so successful that only two CH-46s were shot down during the run-in on 'Super Gaggle' missions; and their crews were immediately rescued by the escorting gunships. It all sounds more orderly than it looked:

> 'Only those who have experienced the hazards of monsoon flying can fully appreciate the madhouse that often exists when large numbers of aircraft are confined to the restricted space beneath a low-hanging overcast. Coupled with this was that the fluffy looking cloud around Khe Sanh housed mountains which ran up to 3,000 feet . . . Even though the missions were well co-ordinated and executed with a high degree of professionalism, it often appeared that confusion reigned because planes were everywhere. A-4s bore in on the flanks of the approach lanes, blasting enemy gun positions and spewing protective smoke; Ch-46s groped through the haze trying to find the landing zones; the hornet-like UH-1E gunships darted in from the rear in case someone was shot down; the lone TA-4 circled overhead trying to keep his flock from running amuck.'[45]

But madhouse or not, the air supply of Khe Sanh was a far cry from the gallant but desperate efforts of the French Air Force, dropping small quantities from C-119s and creaking C-47s, at ever increasing heights over Dien Bien Phu. American logistic power, coupled with the fighting spirit of the Marines, enabled the defenders of Khe Sanh to hold out until relieved, without losing one outpost; and confound the doom-mongers of the media, and other amateur generals. The Americans suffered 205 killed and 852 wounded at Khe Sanh, winning the battle; the French lost nearly 10,000 men, dead, wounded, and taken prisoner at Dien Bien Phu.

Giap's Oversight?

One unsolved mystery about Khe Sanh remains. Water for the base was largely supplied by the small Rao Quan River which rose in hills held by the NVA north of the base. The NVA could have poisoned the water within the terms of the Geneva Convention, and forced the Marines to fly in water, vastly increasing the logistic problem. Perhaps Giap and the NVA commanders on the ground, simply overlooked the vulnerability of the water supply to the base. This is the opinion of Major General Tompkins, the commander of 3rd Marine Division, who visited the base almost daily. He has also stated that he believed that the base could have been supplied with water.

*   *   *

The Impact of the Tet Offensive

The Tet offensive virtually destroyed the Viet Cong and mauled the NVA, it was a major military defeat for Giap, who had been against the concept from the beginning. The immediate outcome was a drastic scaling-down of operations reverting to an emphasis on guerrilla raids. No large offensives were planned, and operations at battalion level and above were rare. But the Viet Cong and the NVA had unwittingly gained a stunning political victory. Domestic disillusionment in the United States with the war was growing. It was fuelled by predictions of failure by some of the most respected personalities in the American media, who portrayed the Tet battles and the siege of Khe Sanh as defeats. There was growing pressure on the United States Government to disengage. Eventually the new American President, Nixon, announced a new war policy based on four pillars: Vietnamisation; building up and modernising the ARVN, the navy and the air force, so that they could take over all the fighting; negotiations with the North Vietnamese for an honourable peace; pacification of the countryside in South Vietnam; and American troop withdrawal. This played straight into the hands of Giap, who merely had to maintain sufficient activity to keep the coffins going home to the United States, whilst keeping his own casualties to the minimum, until the Americans withdrew. Time was on his side, as it had always been.

Logistic Problems of Vietnamisation

The Vietnamisation programme immediately ran into trouble for logistic reasons. There was no dearth of equipment, the Americans could supply that. But possessing military hardware is only one third of the picture. Not only must an army be trained in its use in battle, but it must also know how to store, maintain, issue, and repair the equipment. The more complex the equipment, the more highly trained must be the fitters and storemen needed, and equally well qualified officers and NCOs to plan and supervise the work, tying together the supply and maintenance framework without which no army can exist. In a word, logisticians. There were some, but never enough, and skilled technicians and logistics staff officers cannot be trained overnight.

Cambodia

In early 1970, the political situation in Cambodia led to combined United States and ARVN forces dealing a major blow to communist plans in the south of South Vietnam. For years the ruler of Cambodia, Prince Sihanouk, had allowed the Vietnamese communists to bring in supplies through the port of Sihanoukville. From here, the Sihanouk Route ran to a complex of logistic bases and troop staging areas just inside the Cambodian/South Vietnam border, which sustained the whole communist war effort in southern South Vietnam. These bases were concentrated in two salients where the Cambodian border bulged into South Vietnam, nicknamed the 'Fish Hook' and the 'Parrot's Beak'. In his efforts to run with the fox and hunt with the hounds, Sihanouk turned a blind eye to American bombing of these bases. In March 1970, the prime minister of Cambodia, Lon Nol, led a successful coup against Sihanouk, who was out of the country. Lon Nol, immediately closed the port of Sihanoukville, and foolishly announced that he would evict the Vietnamese communists from their bases on the Cambodian/Vietnamese border. The Viet Cong and NVA reacted swiftly by advancing on the Cambodian capital Phnom Penh, pushing back the puny Cambodian army. It soon became clear that if the United States did not assist Lon Nol, the Vietnamese communists would soon control the whole of Cambodia, re-opening Sihanoukville, and turning the whole country into a base; outflanking South Vietnam.

Capture of 'The City'; A Heavy Blow to the NVA's Logistics

After about six weeks of indecision, Nixon gave clearance for American troops to be used in a raid on Cambodia; General Abrams having said that he could not guarantee success without American involvement. On 1 May 1970, the Americans with an ARVN airborne brigade attacked the northern salient, the 'Fish Hook', and the ARVN the southern, the 'Parrot's Beak'. Both salients were attacked by enveloping movements, with a combination of armour, infantry, and in the case of the 'Fish Hook', heliborne troops landing in the enemy's rear. Most of the enemy fled, and the big battle did not materialise. What fighting there was ended after the first three days. The Central Office for South Vietnam (COSVN) which was thought to be in the 'Fish Hook', had slipped away in mid-March, perhaps in anticipation of an invasion of Cambodia, but huge quantities of stores and acres of camps, hospitals, and bunkers were discovered. This area had been a sanctuary for years, to which the Viet Cong and NVA withdrew time and time again when things got too hot in South Vietnam. Evidence of re-training camps and political indoctrination centres abounded, with ranges, lecture halls, pamphlets, and other training material. One complex, typical of several others, was discovered by an American air cavalry unit, and dubbed the 'City'. It had 182 storage bunkers each of 1,280 cubic feet capacity, 18 mess halls, a training area, and a small animal farm. It covered approximately three square kilometres, and the storage depot was capable of rapid receipt and issue of large quantities of supplies. From captured documents it was apparent that the 'City' had been in operation for at least two and a half years. The haul of weapons it yielded was enough to equip an NVA regiment.[46]

In one depot, new communications equipment was discovered by another air cavalry unit, an indication of the speed with which the operation had been mounted, forestalling the removal of even high priority radios. In other depots, trucks, and major assemblies and spares for trucks were found. 1st Air Cavalry Division alone unearthed 305 trucks, and evidence of heavy recent use of trucks on the roads showed that these were merely the ones that were not driven away when the attack started. The logistic system in Cambodia was vast, and had the capacity to move thousands of tons of supplies by truck from Sihanoukville, to the depots near the border. A network of roads connected the supply points, and there was evidence of an extensive fuel and repair organisation. The NVA had come a long way since the days of the all-coolie transport system, although porters were still used in vast numbers.

The Americans withdrew at the end of June, and the ARVN forces remained for a little longer. The border bases were razed by plant flown in by the American heavy lift helicopters and C-130s, to hastily constructed strips. The quantity of weapons captured overall was immense, surprising even the Americans.[47] The raid on Cambodia was a success. It did buy time for Lon Nol to build up his forces, and the equipment losses and disruption to the logistic system, including the loss of the use of Sihanoukville, set back the NVA invasion timetable by anything up to two years.[48] The Ho Chi Minh Trail now became the sole line of communication from North Vietnam through Laos to the NVA in South Vietnam.

Disturbing Signs of ARVN Logistic Weakness

Although the ARVN units on the raid had shown up better than expected, there were disturbing signs of weaknesses in a number of areas. They relied heavily on American artillery and air strikes, and without the latter it is doubtful if they would have succeeded. But most revealing of all, poor logistics brought much of their armour to a halt for lack of fuel, spares, and forward repair capability. Useable armoured vehicles were pressed into service to tow the broken down ones, further reducing the availability of 'runners', and often wearing out the tower, producing two break-downs for the price of one.

Lam Son 719

After the success in destroying the Cambodian base areas, Abrams realised that there would be enormous dividends to be gained by a repeat performance on the Ho Chi Minh Trail. Success would mean the severance of the only NVA line of communication to the South. The ground part of the operation would have to be an ARVN only effort, since a recent Senate amendment banning American ground troops from entering Cambodia or Laos without Congressional approval. The North Vietnamese were not slow to sense their vulnerability. The Cambodian operation seemed to indicate that the Americans had at long last moved the goal posts in this game, and might well invade Laos, or even North Vietnam. Perhaps Giap did not believe that Congress would be wet enough to enforce its ban. So he established 70B Corps to take command of the three NVA divisions in Laos, the demilitarised zone (DMZ), and southern North Vietnam. Route 9, which ran from Khe Sanh across the Laotian/South Vietnamese border, led to Tchepone, the logistic hub of the NVA in Laos. The NVA prepared the road inside Laos for ambushes and demolitions, pre-recorded potential helicopter landing zones as artillery targets, and moved much of their supplies out of the area.

An operation, codenamed Lam Son 719, was devised, involving three ARVN divisions advancing to Tchepone astride Route 9; the Americans to clear and hold the section from Khe Sanh to the Laotian

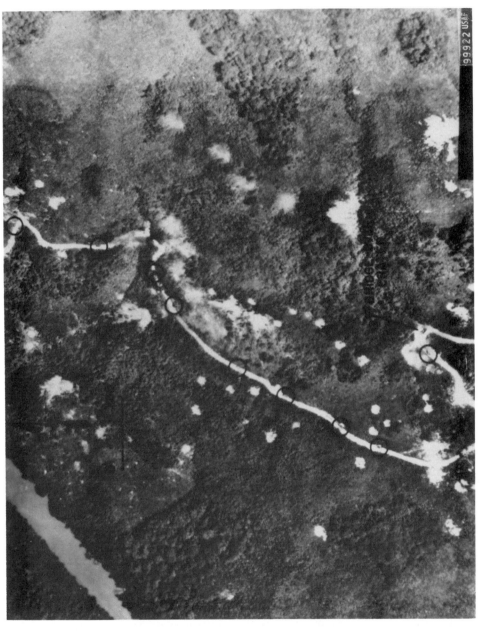

Fig. 5.7 Part of the Ho Chi Minh Trail after bombing by the United States Air Force, destroying 42 NVA trucks and damaging 20

FIG. 5.8 North Vietnamese trucks with branches of foliage to aid camouflage on the Ho Chi Minh Trail (*Popper*).

border. The mission to hold the NVA base areas for ninety days, destroying the installations and supplies. The ban on American ground troops crossing into Laos included the advisers with ARVN units, artillery forward observers, and air controllers. This was to have a drastic effect on the outcome. As it turned out, it was fortunate that the ban on American participation did not extend to helicopters. United States Army Support Command at Da Nang also gave considerable logistic assistance to the ARVN 1st Area Logistic Command (1 ALC), and ARVN FSA at Khe Sanh. In a classic example of 'G snobbishness', although the expression would have meant nothing to him, the ARVN Corps Commander, Lieutenant General Hoang Xuan Lam, did not see fit to tell 1 ALC, who were responsible for all the ARVN logistics, about the operation until just before it began.[49]

The Price of Poor Training

The operation was a disaster. It was Ap Bac writ large. The rotten ARVN command structure collapsed under the strain of a battle for which most of the soldiers were inadequately trained. Without their American advisers, many ARVN commanders at all levels felt lost. For the first time they found themselves adjusting fire, calling in air strikes, and controlling helicopters. Infantry/tank co-operation was poor. Training would have sorted out these deficiencies, but the training standards of the ARVN were little better than they had been in the mid-1950s. It was too late to start learning the tricks of the trade locked in combat with the battle-wise NVA formations. Having advanced about half way to Tchepone, President Thieu of South Vietnam, ordered the Corps commander to halt. He feared heavy casualties before the election which was due soon. In any case, two of the divisions, the airborne and the marines, were his insurance against a coup. It was Diem at Ap Bac over again. Thieu interfered constantly, his final folly to order two battalions to fly forward 65 kilometres to Tchepone as a publicity stunt. They had to be quickly withdrawn a day later to avoid being wiped out by the NVA.

While the ARVN troops waited, all momentum lost, the NVA moved fast to destroy them, eventually assembling over four divisions, with tanks, artillery, and large numbers of flak guns. When the ARVN started to withdraw losses were high, on both sides. The ARVN were ambushed, and helicopters were shot down as they evacuated the troops. The Americans lost 108 helicopters destroyed and 618 damaged. The losses on the NVA side were huge, caused by American B-52s and fighter ground attack aircraft. The Ho Chi Minh Trail was in full operation a week after the ARVN withdrawal.

American Culpability

Apart from the ARVN faults, the Americans must also bear a share of the blame for the failure of Lam Son 719. The intelligence assessments were far too optimistic, despite there being indications that the NVA had been warned in advance of an assault into Laos or the DMZ. Even before the NVA started to move in reinforcements, there were sufficient forces in the area (22,000 men) to provide formidable opposition to the three weak ARVN divisions of doubtful fighting quality. Route 9, which had been assessed as a suitable axis for armour, turned out to be a neglected forty-year old, single lane road with high shoulders on both sides and no manoeuvre room. As units advanced they found the area pockmarked with huge bomb craters, undetected earlier because of the dense grass and bamboo. The armoured vehicles were therefore restricted to the road. It was like the operations mounted by the French all over again.

It is possible that none of the mistakes and deficiencies above would have mattered, but for the greatest error on the part of the Americans and the ARVN: failing to appreciate that, for logistic reasons, the NVA were compelled to fight for their bases in Laos. There is a reason for this misappreciation; never before in Round Two or Three had the NVA/VC fought resolutely to defend their base areas. But in all previous cases, although the base areas had been important, they had not been absolutely vital to continued NVA/VC operations in South Vietnam. The Ho Chi Minh Trail was the only line of communication to Cambodia, southern Laos, and South Vietnam. Had the ARVN succeeded in cutting this life-line, destroying existing stocks, and stopping the flow of supplies for three months, the logistic build-up for the NVA offensive planned for spring 1972 would have been set back to the extent that the offensive would have been unsustainable. ARVN success would have inflicted a crushing defeat to the NVA, and bought time. Time to continue with Vietnamisation, time to keep the communist forces off-balance while the American troop withdrawals continued uninterrupted. Giap could not afford a set-back of these dimensions; logistic imperatives drove him to defend his line of communication and his stocks with all the power he could muster.

Spring 1972: The NVA Offensive

The NVA spring, or Easter offensive of 1972, started on 30 March. They deployed a conventional army of about 120,000 men in fourteen divisions and twenty-six independent regiments supported by masses of tanks and artillery, a force equivalent to twenty divisions. The Viet Cong played almost no part. A massive re-equipping programme had been instituted in the NVA. Russian T-34 and T-52 tanks, surface to air missiles, and 130 mm guns poured into North Vietnam. NVA formations in Laos were recalled, reinforced, re-equipped and retrained before returning to their jumping off positions for the offensive. Giap planned a fast-moving, modern war, using tanks, artillery and infantry. He lacked only air support. His concept was three simultaneous attacks. In the north his objectives were Quang Tri City and Hue, with the aim of expelling all South Vietnamese troops and authorities from the two northern provinces of Vietnam. If this was successful, he would extend the border of North Vietnam as far as Da Nang. In the centre, he planned to cut South Vietnam in two along a line Kontum-Hoai Nhon. In the south, three divisions would advance on an axis Loc Ninh/An Loc to threaten Saigon, while another division attacked in the Mekong Delta to seize rice and terrritory while tying down the ARVN troops, and preventing them reinforcing elsewhere.

The Value of American Support

Although the NVA made substantial territorial gains in the Easter offensive, they attained none of their objectives. On the whole, in contrast to Lam Son 719, the ARVN fought the defensive battle well. The American advisers, staying with their units whatever the outcome, played a vital part in this metamorphosis. The advisers, besides virtually commanding the ARVN units and formations they advised, buttressed the commanders at all levels. Well led, the ARVN could fight as well as anybody. As important, the advisers planned and controlled the awesome power wielded by the American B-52s from Guam and U-Tapao in Thailand, the close support by ground attack jets and the gunships and TOW Cobras (wire guided anti-armour missiles mounted on Cobra gunships). American air power blunted the NVA armoured thrusts and destroyed huge quantities of tanks, guns and equipment, as well as inflicting mass casualties on the NVA. Time and again, assaults withered away in the face of air strikes. In one area, the B-52s bombed an NVA regiment moving in the open. When the dust cleared, the regiment had vanished without trace. United States air power was also critical in supplying the battle, the helicopters and C-130s made resistance possible, and fuelled the ARVN counter-attacks.

Giap's Mistakes

The NVA helped by making mistakes. This was the first time they had fought an armoured battle on this scale. Their command and control was slow, and tactical employment of armour and infantry pedestrian. By fighting on three fronts, and not co-ordinating his attacks, Giap allowed the ARVN to shift troops, and the Americans to move their air power to meet them. He actually had no alternative. His logistic system was still inflexible and inadequate. He could not mass his army on one front because he could not support such a deployment. Had he stockpiled behind one massed thrust, he did not possess the ability to push supplies forward from the stockpiles at the rate (thousands of tons a day), required to feed a high intensity battle being fought by his whole army. Even had he possessed the means, the large concentrations of supplies, and long convoys of trucks required to support massed mobile warfare would have been hit by American air strikes. Because of the time it took to build up for each push, he was forced into the attack-lull-attack-lull pattern that has been noted before in this war. Giap was facing a new operational situation; because he was attacking, using armour, he was forced to expend his supplies at a rate faster than he could replenish. He was attempting the impossible, to conduct mobile warfare with high ammunition and fuel expenditure, and the need to refuel and re-ammunition well forward, by day if necessary, if momentum was to be maintained, in the face of air supremacy. This was totally different from the situation noted by Slessor in Italy, and the American attempts to cut the Ho Chi Minh Trail. In the former the Allies were attacking. In the latter, Giap could trim his operations to take account of his supply situation.

*   *   *

As the Easter offensive ground to a halt, there was much euphoria at the political level in the United States about the success of Vietnamisation. American air power, including the vital logistic and troop lift capability, and the crucial part played by the advisers concealed the cracks that still lay under the surface in the ARVN structure: poor leadership, poor organisation and the lack of mobility. The next time, the ARVN would be on its own.

The Full Weight of United States Air Power Unleashed

In December 1972, after fruitless negotiations for most of the year, the Americans 'bombed the North Vietnamese to the conference table'. At last American air power was allowed to be exercised to the full and hit the North Vietnamese where it would have the most effect, their economy, their industry, their military potential; their logistic base. Haiphong harbour was mined, not for the first time, with the aim of cutting off Soviet supplies. But more important, in place of the restricted attacks of the years before, often miles from Hanoi, the strikes were aimed where they would hurt. Previously there had been extensive strike-free areas particularly around Hanoi and Haiphong and the North Vietnamese had moved their military installations and logistic dumps into there sanctuaries. This time it was to be a maximum effort aimed at all military installations in the Hanoi/Haiphong area, as well as railway yards, bridges, roads, electric power plants and steel works. The Red River dikes, destruction of which would have flooded the area to a depth of eleven feet in some places were not attacked. Improved techniques helped accuracy. In an earlier bombing campaign that year, the railway bridge at Thanh Hoa, on which the United States Navy had lost 97 aircraft between 1965 and 1968, without bringing it down, was destroyed in one run in May 1972 by a 'smart' laser-guided 2,000 lb bomb. After 12 days, the North Vietnamese military potential, its industry and economy were totally destroyed. For the last three days, American aircraft were hardly fired upon, there was no more ammunition, and more important, no more surface-to-air missiles. Nixon had demonstrated, for the first time by any President in this war, the will to win. In doing so he had used one of the two real principles of war, surprise. Few people expected him to defy the American media, who had predicted that a bombing campaign would stiffen resistance, or the cries of condemnation all over the world. The next item on the bombing programme might be the Red River dikes. The Politburo in Hanoi agreed to talk.

Agreement Follows

The resulting agreement included, among other things, the withdrawal of all United States forces from Vietnam. The effect was to suspend operations until the North Vietnamese could prepare for the final denouement in South Vietnam. As a palliative, the United States poured equipment into South Vietnam, but the logistic system and training apparatus in the South Vietnamese forces could not cope with the influx. They had aircraft they could not fly, ships, tanks and other equipment they could not man or maintain. The flaws in the structure of the armed forces were unchanged. The South Vietnamese clung pathetically to the hope that if the North Vietnamese attacked, the Americans would come to their aid. Congress had no intention of allowing any such thing.

1973–4: The NVA Re-Organise and Re-Equip

In 1973 and 1974, the NVA, now under the command of General Van Tien Dung reorganised and re-equipped. Enormous strides were taken in improving the logistic system to support a large, mobile conventional army. The Ho Chi Minh Trail was widened and given a hard surface. A new all-weather road, eight metres wide, was constructed from Khe Sanh to Loc Ninh, down the east side of the Annamite Chain. Altogether 12,000 miles of roads were built by the NVA in the areas they occupied in South Vietnam. A fuel pipeline was built from North Vietnam to Loc Ninh.[50] A comprehensive military telephone system was installed by the NVA in South Vietnam, which involved stringing 20,000 kilometres of lines. The NVA built thirteen new airfields in South Vietnam. In base areas in Cambodia, Laos and

South Vietnam huge depots were built or expanded, including hospitals, training centres, and repair facilities. The realisation by the North Vietnamese that logistics had always been the Achilles heel of the NVA and that a conventional army needs an effective logistical system, was the key to their battlefield success. To this enormously increased logistical capability, the NVA added a major reorganisation, grouping their divisions into four corps. The command system was thus modernised and streamlined. To better their position in preparation for the final campaign, the NVA mounted a series of 'strategic raids' throughout South Vietnam. One of the major aims of these was to widen their logistics corridor east of the Annamites. In addition these raids seized the initiative, regained territory and population lost in the Pacification Programme, caused casualties to the ARVN and lowered its morale, while enhancing the battle worthiness of the NVA.

The Problems Facing the ARVN

The ARVN had enormous problems. The United States Congress drastically cut military assistance to South Vietnam. The first to feel the pinch was the Republic of Vietnam Air Force (RVNAF) which had been trained on American lines to be lavish with fuel, ammunition, and spares. They were suddenly forced to cut their coats according to their cloth, of which there was pitifully little. To save resources, the RVNAF cut training to nothing. Shortage of spares cut the strategic mobility of the ARVN by use of helicopters and transport aircraft by up to 70 per cent. Shortages of spares also resulted in the grounding of aircraft, and the cannibalisation of vehicles for parts. Fuel stocks dwindled, and were not replaced. All types of ammunition were rationed. Hand grenades had to be accounted for, fire plans were curtailed, and rifle ammunition was cut by 50 per cent. The blow to ARVN morale was devastating. Less ammunition meant more casualties. Casualty evacuation was often done by Honda motorbikes, or a string of ambulances with empty petrol tanks, pulled by a truck and even sampans. If a casualty arrived at a hospital alive, he found shortages of bandages, medicines, antibiotics, and intravenous fluids. As the malarial season approached, the supply of insect repellent was exhausted.

The supplies of boots and clothing ran short. Pay did not keep up with inflation. Men deserted at a rate of 15,000 to 20,000 per month to look after their families. Others made arrangements with their commanders to 'moonlight'. The junior commanders made money through graft, and by selling equipment. Their seniors became rich by feeding on the corruption. As the fighting spread, commanders avoided the battlefield. The miasma of defeat spread.[51]

ROUND FOUR

Round Four of the Indo-China war kicked off in earnest on 26 December 1974, with the battle for Don Luan and Phuoc Long province. It ended with the Ho Chi Minh campaign to take Saigon beginning on 26 April 1975. The NVA attacked with the equipment of eighteen divisions, organised into five corps, supported by engineers, artillery, tanks, flak units, and a hastily scraped together tactical air force; a far cry from Giap's ragged platoon in the Viet Bac in 1945. The NVA entered the city on 30 April 1975. They had finally learned that logistics was the key to success, the two years of logistic preparation and build-up had paid off. It was not entirely a walk-over. The 18th ARVN Division, attacked by the entire IVth NVA Corps, lost 30 per cent of its strength destroying 37 NVA tanks, and killing over 5,000 North Vietnamese. Again, they demonstrated that South Vietnamese soldiers could fight, and again, the truth of the saying; 'there are no bad soldiers, only bad officers'.

CONCLUSION

It is not the purpose of this chapter to defend, or otherwise, the French or the American involvement in Indo-China, or become involved in rights and wrongs. Sadly, being 'right' does not always guarantee victory, indeed 'nice guys' often come last. As a professional soldier, the Author is only interested in the military possibilities which are always linked to logistics. The French were never logistically powerful enough to win; the Americans were, but chose the wrong strategy. The French had the supplies and much of the equipment needed to win, much of it from the USA, but lacked the means to deliver it to where it was required, and keep it sustained in battle. The United States had both the equipment and the means to move it. Once shorn of United States support and supplies, the ARVN never had the resources to enable them to win. Despite their logistic power, the Americans played into the North Vietnamese hands by using the tactics for a long war, without the support back home for such a strategy. They failed to maximise their strength, massive air power, and couple this with an invasion of the North, to crush the North Vietnamese in the mid-sixties; as they had demonstrated that they could have with their December bombing campaign in 1972.[52] By not keeping up relentless pressure both in the air and on the ground, they allowed the NVA to dictate the pace of the war, and tailor their operations to their resources and logistic capability. Again, it is not the purpose of this book to suggest that the Americans would have been morally right to have invaded North Vietnam and bombed them to the conference table much earlier, only to suggest how they might have won the war, if it was worth winning in such a way. In the end, they had the worst of all worlds, took more casualties, and lost more prestige by their strategy; losing the war in the process. The scars remain.

6

Into Africa—Sinai to Suez: The Yom Kippur War 1973

'The desert—a tactician's paradise, a quartermaster's nightmare.'
Attributed to a German General

The crossing of the Suez Canal by the Egyptian Army and assault on the Golan Heights by the Syrians on 6 October 1973, took the Israelis by surprise; a classic case of cognitive dissonance.[1] Grave misperceptions over Arab intentions, partly a result of overconfidence, led them into not believing what their intelligence was 'seeing'. The same overconfidence combined with faulty command procedures resulted in the Israeli counter-attack, on 8 October, ending in, what has been called, the worst defeat in the history of the Israeli Army. Labelling it thus is a comment on the extraordinarily high standards in the Israeli Army, and its hitherto unbroken record of smashing victories. Most armies would have called the events of 8 October a set-back; serious, but not catastrophic. Eventually, after winning a tank battle in the Sinai, greater than any since the Second World War,[2] the Israelis crossed the Canal into 'Africa', as they always called the West Bank of the Canal. A bitterly fought defensive battle on the Golan, followed by a rapid follow-up, ended in the Syrians being pushed back so far beyond the original frontier that Damascus itself seemed threatened. This chapter will concentrate on the Sinai campaign, because logistically the Syrian front presented few problems, at least insofar as the Israelis were concerned.[3]

The war is interesting logistically for two reasons, both concern consumption rates; men and supplies. First men; in 19 days of war, the Israelis suffered more than 11,000 battle casualties, including nearly 3,000 dead. It has been calculated that taking population differences into account, this represented a loss rate over 30 times as great as the American loss rate in the Second World War; although Israeli battlefield loss rates for each unit per day were considerably lower than comparable American loss rates. It is no consolation that the Arab loss rates were twice that of the Israelis. A tiny state with a small population cannot afford to lose manpower at this rate for long. The effect on the commercial and social fabric of Israeli society, of having so much human resource tied up in defence is profound enough without the added burden of high casualties.[4,5] Extend the period of conflict, and the drain on a critical national resource, manpower, might become too hard to bear. This has always offered a possible strategy for the Arab states; to fight a long war with the aim of gaining their ends by grinding down the Israeli will to resist—a possibility that the Israelis have not been slow to recognise. Hence their system of rapid mobilisation and their strategy of seeking to take the war to their enemy with the aim of securing speedy victory.

A Questionable Plan

Bearing this in mind, the operation plan adopted by the Israelis for the Sinai theatre after the war of 1967 was questionable. The Bar Lev Line, named after the then Israeli Chief of Staff, was neither a trip-wire nor a heavily fortified system with mutually-supporting positions.[6] By seeking to fight as far forward as possible in the Sinai (on the Syrian border they had no choice), the Israelis were contravening one of the two great principles of war, alluded to earlier: the need to take advantage of your own strengths and your enemy's weaknesses, while negating your own weaknesses and your enemy's strengths. The Egyptians having brilliantly applied the other enduring principle, surprise, by crossing the Canal and staying to fight, the Israelis were forced to supply their forces in the Sinai over a line of communication 200 miles long. Their reservists had even further to go after mobilisation, and therefore took longer to reach the battle area than their normal mobilisation plans envisaged.

In this forward battle, the Israelis were largely denied one of their hitherto decisive weapons, close air support. Long range Egyptian surface-to-air missiles (SAMs) were able to engage Israeli aircraft from the West Bank of the Canal, out of range of Israeli artillery. Shorter range SAMs deployed on the East Bank, behind a screen of SAGGER wire-guided missiles and RPG anti-tank weapons, also took their toll of Israeli aircraft. Against a screen of anti-tank weapons, without close air support and neglecting the use of artillery to neutralise these weapons, the Israelis lost 100 tanks in the first day's counter attack, and about the same number on the second day.[7] Manpower losses were correspondingly high. Their strategy could have condemned them to a war of attrition, had the Egyptians played a stubborn waiting game behind their defences. The reasons for the Israelis selecting such an operational concept are beyond the scope of this book to discuss, as are the ramifications of both the late mobilisation and move forward of reserves in the Sinai. They are well covered in a Staff College Camberley paper on the subject.[8]

The construction of the Bar Lev Line had also resulted in the destruction of an asset which Herzog claims the Israelis would have found useful during the mobilisation period. When they captured Sinai in 1967, a railway ran from Gaza to El Arish. They tore it up to use the sleepers and rails in the Bar Lev Line defences. Had they left the railway line, and extended it with spurs, they could, according to Herzog, have saved much wear and tear on armoured fighting vehicle (AFV) tracks and engines, which, in the absence of rail communications, had perforce to motor the whole way to their battle positions. Some AFVs broke down and blocked the roads, further delaying the arrival of reserve units in Sinai.[9] However, it could be argued that such a railway system would have been vulnerable to Arab commando raids, and its protection a liability that outweighed its usefulness; besides re-imposing the tyranny of the railroad.[10]

The Advantage Switches

However, on 14 October, the operational situation changed dramatically, when the Egyptians advanced beyond the defence line they had established east of the Canal. This attack out of the bridgehead was made despite the opposition of the Egyptian Armed Forces Chief of Staff, General El Shazly. Plans had been prepared for such a move well before the war, despite Shazly's protestations. But he was overruled by General Ismail, the Egyptian War Minister. Shazly says that he was ordered to implement the plan on Sadat's orders to take pressure off the Syrians. According to him, Shazly was made the scapegoat after the war for the disaster that followed, on the grounds that he was hot headed. But he seems far too astute to have believed that the offensive had any chance of success.[11] The boot was now on the other foot. It was the Egyptians who were being ambushed by well sited tanks. In this situation and on the move, their SAGGERS and RPGs were mostly ineffective. Particularly as the Israelis had formulated tactics for dealing with these weapons, using artillery and machine guns to neutralise or destroy them. With few SAMs to cover them, the Egyptian armour was heavily engaged by the Israeli Air Force. This was the battle the Israelis should have aimed to fight in the first place, waiting for the Egyptians to advance into the trap.[12]

The Impact of High Losses and High Expenditure Rates

High losses of tanks, and the rate of expenditure of ammunition and missiles, on both sides, led to the need for rapid re-supply of the protagonists' stocks by the two superpowers. Just how vital this was to the eventual Israeli success is a matter for conjecture, but is an interesting line to pursue in the context of Israeli action as the war unfolded. On 8 October, within two days of the start of the war, the Israeli Government had informed the Americans of their need for equipment and ammunition to replace the losses of the first two days fighting.[13] However, those losses did not deter them from planning to cross the Canal and carry the fight into enemy territory. Herein lies an interesting tale. When Major General Sharon had been GOC Southern Command, before retiring to go into politics, he had prepared a number of places on the Israeli side of the Canal as potential crossing sites. At each of these the embankment, at last 20 metres high and 10 metres thick,[14] was thinned out so that gaps could be bulldozed through to allow the abutments of pontoon bridges to be constructed. A large area behind each of these points had been surfaced with bricks to provide about 700 metres by 150 metres of hardstanding, where engineer equipment could be concentrated. These hardstandings were covered with a thin layer of sand to conceal them from the Egyptians, and surrounded by a sand rampart to provide cover from view and fire.[15,16]

The Israelis' Plan to Cross the Canal

Sharon, back from politicking, and now in command of 143rd (Reserve) Armoured Division, was selected to lead the crossing. His division consisted of three armoured brigades, having exchanged his mechanised brigade for another armoured brigade with 252nd Armoured Division. He was also reinforced by a parachute brigade, in the infantry role. He would be followed by Major General Adan's 162nd (Reserve) Armoured Division. Major General Gonen, now

GOC Southern Command, to whom Sharon had handed over command a few months before, chose the pre-prepared site at Deversoir for the crossing. The plan was approved by General Bar Lev, plucked out of retirement and his job as Minister for Trade and Industry, and sent down to oversee Gonen after the debacle of the 8th October counter-attack.

Deversoir offered three advantages. First, the Great Bitter Lake would protect the left flank of the crossing. Second, there were better opportunities for manoeuvre south of Ismailia than to the north of the town. Finally, this crossing point was near the junction of two Egyptian armies, and air reconnaissance showed that neither the home nor far bank of the Canal was occupied at this point. Two bridges were moved up from their storage sites to a position codenamed Yukon about 15 kilometres from the crossing point. One consisted of a pontoon bridge in nine sections, each of which could be used to ferry tanks before being linked up to form a bridge. The other was a prefabricated span 170 metres long. Before the war, the road to the crossing point had been prepared with minimum grades and sufficient clearance on each side to allow bridges and bridging equipment to be moved to the site. As with other pre-prepared crossing points, the brick surfaced 'yard' was at the end of the access road, just east of the canal.

Operation STRONGHEART

In outline, Sharon's plan for the crossing, codename STRONG-HEART, consisted of diversionary attacks by the bulk of two armoured brigades against the southern flank of the Egyptian Second Army's positions, just north of the Great Bitter Lake; aimed at deceiving them into thinking that the Israeli aim was to roll up the defence line from the South. These attacks would also clear the way to the West Bank of the Canal. This would allow the parachute brigade, who would be following in half-tracks, to cross the Canal and the Sweetwater Canal, which runs parallel a few hundred metres to the West, in rubber boats. Followed by tanks ferried across on pontoon sections, the parachute brigade would stake-out a bridgehead about four kilometres square. The pontoon sections and the prefabricated bridge would be towed by tanks the 20 kilometres from Yukon to the Canal.

Hard Fighting and a Threat of Failure

The operation, starting on the night 15/16 October, was a success, but it came close to failure for two reasons. First, the Israeli bridging

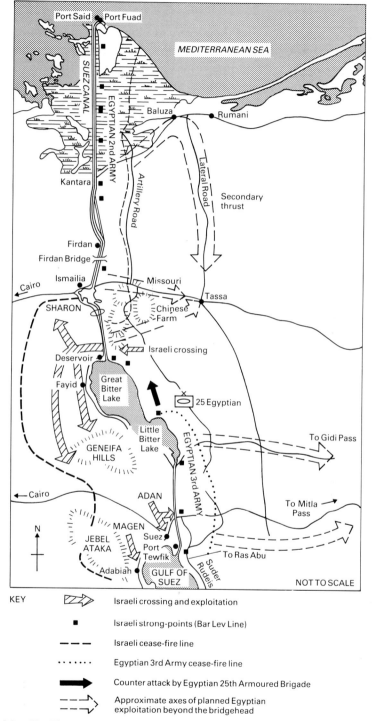

MAP X   The Yom Kippur War. The Israeli Crossing of the Suez Canal.

KEY

▱⇨   Israeli crossing and exploitation

■   Israeli strong-points (Bar Lev Line)

- - -   Israeli cease-fire line

· · · · · · ·   Egyptian 3rd Army cease-fire line

➡   Counter attack by Egyptian 25th Armoured Brigade

- - -⇢   Approximate axes of planned Egyptian exploitation beyond the bridgehead

equipment was bulky, and their pre-war plans had envisaged bringing
it forward to one of the Bar Lev strongholds before assembly. They had
not bargained for a 20 kilometre tow under artillery fire. Second, the
Egyptians had far stronger forces on the right of their Second Army
than the Israelis expected; in the order of two divisions. These troops
resisted stubbornly, and mounted vigorous, but unco-ordinated,
counter-attacks. There is little doubt that if the Egyptians had
recognised the true nature of the Israeli operations, they had sufficient
force on each side of the Canal to crush them. However, the Israeli
diversionary attacks kept the Egyptians deceived for more than 24
hours.[17,18]

Sharon Begins to Cross

To add to the Israeli problem, the delays caused by these two factors
were aggravated by heavy Egyptian artillery fire on the road and road
junctions, which were clogged with traffic, thanks to inadequate traffic
control by the Israelis.[19] However, by dawn on 16 October, the
parachute brigade was across the Canal unopposed; there were no
Egyptian troops opposite the crossing point; and the tanks of one
armoured brigade began to be ferried over. But the bitter fighting
during the night by the armour to clear the way, and hold open the
corridor on the East Bank, had resulted in 300 Israeli dead, and 70 out
of Sharon's 280 tanks destroyed. The Egyptians lost about 150 tanks.
During the morning Sharon suggested that Adan should now follow
him across the Canal, apparently unaware of the precarious situation
behind him. Gonen brusquely rejected Sharon's suggestion. In present
circumstances, the logistical requirements of two divisions fighting
west of the Canal would be beyond the capacity of the ferries and any
airlift arranged as a back-up. Indeed, unless the corridor could be
widened, and kept open, it was doubtful if Sharon, with less than half
his division, could be kept supplied. This led Bar Lev to order that no
more men or tanks would cross the Canal until the situation improved.
At about midday, the Egyptians blocked the two roads to the crossing
point. Sharon was cut off. Nothing loth, he sent out a raid to disrupt the
Egyptian SAM sites, and destroy supply dumps on his side of the
Canal.

The Bridges Move Forward Under Fire

All that day and for most of the night, Adan's division fought to drive
two corridors to the crossing point and move the bridging forward. By

3 a.m. the 17th, the bridges had not moved for 24 hours. The parachute brigade attached to Adan, sent by him to open the route, had been pinned down north of the road, attempting to clear the Egyptians from a group of buildings known to the Israelis as the Chinese Farm.[20] Just when the whole operation looked close to failure, with Sharon isolated, reconnaissance sent forward by Adan reported that the yard at the crossing point was clear of enemy. The Egyptians, their eye taken off the ball by the fighting round Chinese Farm, had omitted to hold the yard. At dawn on the 17th, the pontoon sections arrived in the yard, and Sharon's sappers started building one bridge. The prefabricated bridge would have to wait until the second route was open.

Further attacks by the Egyptians on the corridor ended at about midday on the 17th, when a final attempt was bloodily repulsed and the remnants of an Egyptian brigade withdrew to the high ground to the north to lick their wounds. They still held Chinese Farm, and from here, and the high ground, could sweep the corridor with fire. But at least the way through to the Canal was secure. In the 36 hours of fighting, about 250 tanks had been destroyed, two-thirds of them Egyptian, in an area approximately seven kilometres by three.

At around 11 a.m., Adan was joined at his headquarters by the Defence Minister Dayan, Chief of Staff Elazar, Bar Lev, and later, by Sharon. That Adan was able to fight his division, while distracted by a conference is a tribute to his powers of concentration and ability as a commander, a quality he was shortly to demonstrate again. The senior visitors arrived fully convinced that the crossing operation would have to be called off, but found that suddenly the situation was much brighter. One bridge was almost across, and the other would be arriving at the Canal bank before long. After a short altercation over whether Sharon's or Adan's division would break out of the bridgehead, once both were across complete—decided in Adan's favour—a new distraction thrust itself on the meeting.

Counter-Attack from the South

A dust column to the south, clearly visible to the distinguished group at the conference, was reported by Israeli observation posts as about 100 T-62 tanks. It was the Egyptian 25th Armoured Brigade, heading in the direction of the crossing point along the eastern side of the Great Bitter Lake. Adan was now faced by a battle on two fronts. Excusing himself from the meeting, he dashed away to beat off the new threat. In the path of the Egyptian advance were the remnants of one of Sharon's armoured brigades, still on the East Bank. After some rapid redeployment, Adan reinforced this depleted brigade with two tank battalions from one of his own armoured brigades, to act as a stop, and swung another armoured brigade round to hit the Egyptians in the flank. By 4 p.m., 86 out of the column of 96 Egyptian tanks had been destroyed in less than an hour.[21] Adan led his tanks back to refuel and re-fill with ammunition, before taking his division across the Canal.

Adan Crosses and Moves South

His troubles were not over. At 9.30 p.m., after driving over the pontoon bridge at the head of his division, he pulled his armoured personnel carrier (APC) off to one side to watch the column cross. To his dismay he saw that only two tanks had joined him. Egyptian artillery fire had broken the link between two pontoons. Adan now ordered the ferries to start carrying his tanks, and sent for a bridge-layer tank to fill the gap in the pontoon bridge. By dawn on 18 October, Adan's division had joined Sharon in the bridgehead.

FIG. 6.1   Pontoon bridge across the Suez Canal—Israeli logistic vehicles crossing into Egypt (*Popper*).

All that day, Adan enlarged the bridgehead, to enable his tanks to get out into the open desert beyond the green belt which extends each side of the Sweetwater Canal. Meanwhile a strange convoy was creeping towards the East Bank of the main Canal. Like worker ants moving the body of a large insect, the 170 metre long preconstructed bridge was towed and pushed by ten or more tanks.[22] More tanks, anti-tank guns, and anti-aircraft guns provided protection. By early evening the convoy reached the Canal bank, and just after midnight, the bridge was open to traffic. The Egyptian artillery had the original pontoon bridge registered precisely, and were causing considerable casualties. On 19th October another pontoon bridge was built just north of the preconstructed bridge, and the corridor on the East Bank was widened by Israeli attacks pushing the Egyptians back about 8 kilometres. Starting on 19 October, Adan eventually joined by Magan's 252nd Armoured Division,[23] struck south heading for Suez. Sharon pushed north towards Ismailia.

The purpose of the southbound thrust was to encircle the Egyptian Third Army located in Suez town, Port Tewfik, and then to move on the east side of the Canal going north to the southern end of the Great Bitter Lake. By 22 October, both divisions, having secured the vital ground of the Geneifa Hills (about a third of the way on the axis to Suez), had advanced to within 15–20 kilometres of their objectives, but well to the west of the Canal. At this point Adan considered that, for logistic reasons, he had to clear the route that ran through the green belt between himself and the Canal. To winkle out SAGGERs and RPG-7s concealed in the bushes and undergrowth would require more infantry than he had available. During the night of 22/23 October, he received infantry reinforcements, mostly from the Syrian front which had stabilised, transported by helicopter and bus; but no further armoured fighting vehicles. However, he had captured some Egyptian APCs. Grouping his infantry reinforcements with two battalions he had received earlier, to make up a brigade of five battalions under his deputy commander, he gave them the captured APCs. It is a measure of the flexibility and standard of training of the Israeli army that, having re-grouped units switched from a front 450 kilometres away, and re-equipped them with captured and unfamiliar APCs, they could be pitched straight into battle without undue pause. One ventures to suggest that no other army in the world, save the German Panzer and Panzer Grenadier divisions of the Second World War, could have done likewise. Leaving most of his infantry, and one armoured brigade to clear his chosen line of communication, Adan charged south, with

Magan on his right flank. By nightfall on 24 October, Adan's two brigades had reached the outskirts of Suez. At first light, Magen's leading armoured brigade, down to 17 tanks, reached the shore of the gulf of Suez, at Ras Adabiah, ten kilometres south-west of Suez town. The encirclement of the Egyptian Third Army was now almost complete.

Rebuff at Suez

Adan's attempts to capture Suez were, however, rebuffed. Although two of his armoured brigades fought their way into the centre of town, clearing it was a different matter. This was a far cry from slashing attacks and massed tank charges in the open desert; instead, a grinding house-to-house battle, where a handful could hold up a host, inflicting heavy losses. A battle, moreover, for which the Israeli Army had neither the training nor the experience. Eventually, the Israelis settled for sealing off the town from the desert.

Containment and Cease-Fire

The Israelis now turned their attention to squeezing the Egyptian Third Army until it surrendered. Success would more than compensate for the defeats the Israelis had suffered initially. As the ceasefire was finally imposed before Israeli redeployment had been completed, one can only speculate on the outcome. However, despite the Third Army's position, they still had plentiful stocks of food and ammunition, and water was available from wells in Suez. The Egyptians were also able to organise a supply route across the Gulf of Suez.[24] The Third Army's morale was high as they repulsed repeated Israeli attacks on their northern flank. To bring sufficient pressure to bear on the Third Army, the Israelis ordered Adan back to the East Bank, leaving only two divisions in the salient on the West Bank. The Egyptians sealed off this salient. For the Israelis to concentrate their efforts on attacking Third Army on the East Bank, would have left their troops in the salient thinly spread, inviting attack by the Egyptians, who might have battered through to Suez. It is possible, however, that had the cease-fire not intervened, the Israelis, with their overwhelming air superiority, and greater skill in armoured warfare, could ultimately have succeeded in forcing the Third Army to surrender.

The Value of American Support to Israel

How important was the American supply effort to the Israeli prosecution of the war, and the way in which they fought? Within two days of the start of the war, the Israelis sent civilian Boeing 707, 720 and 747 airliners to the United States to pick up small quantities of urgently needed specialised equipment, such as chaff to confuse radars, and 'smart' bombs to hit pin-point targets. But the capacity of even the 747s was too limited to lift large amounts of bulky and heavy items. The first of these flights left the United States on 9 October. A limited American airlift also began on 9 or 10 October with small quantities of anti-tank and artillery ammunition, Sidewinder and Sparrow air-to-air missiles and chaff. However, shaken by early Arab success, and high ammunition expenditure on the first two days of the war, the Israeli Government came to the conclusion that another week of consumption at that rate and Israel, shorn of supplies, would be overrun. On 12 October the Israeli Ambassador presented a note to the United States Government part of which read: 'the future of the State of Israel is at stake.' On 13 October, President Nixon decided to provide the Israelis with almost everything they wanted, even at the cost of digging into American war reserves. On 14 October, the first aircraft of this lift arrived in Israel. Over a period of 33 days the C-141s and C-5s flew 566 sorties, lifting a total of 22,395 tons. In addition 56 combat aircraft, A-4 Skyhawks and F-4 Phantoms, were delivered from the USAAF in Germany, possibly via, or air-to-air refuelled by tankers from, the carriers of the Sixth Fleet in the Mediterranean.[25]

It has been argued that the Israelis would not have beaten off the Egyptian offensive of 14 October without American re-supply, in particular of TOW wire-guided anti-tank missiles. This is difficult to substantiate. The first aircraft of the main airlift did not arrive in Israel until 14 October, far too late to influence the battle. On the matter of the TOWs, Dupuy[26] who spoke to Adan, Elazar and others, is unable to discover if any were available on 14 October, but has concluded that there may have been a few in Sharon's division. Adan categorically denied having any in his. Whereas Keisewetter, an armoured officer in the Bundeswehr, who visited Israel in November 1973, and spoke to a number of Israeli officers, mentions that TOWs were employed on the Golan front.[27] If there were TOWs, even in small quantities, who trained the operators? TOW has different sighting and control arrangements to SS11 and SS10 with which the Israelis were equipped, but which were so unreliable that they had ceased to use them. A number of Israeli students on courses in the United States were ordered to the US Army Infantry School at Fort Benning to learn how to operate and, as important, maintain, the TOW system. However, by the time these 'instructors' arrived back in Israel, on 24 October, the war was virtually over. It was, in fact, good tactics on the part of the Israelis that defeated the Egyptians, not a handful of allegedly 'war winning weapons'.

Planning for the Israeli counter-offensive across the Canal started well before it was known that there would be a substantial American supply effort. The plan was approved by Gonen on 11 October, the day before the Israeli Ambassador presented the emotional note to the Americans. According to Dupuy,[28] it was discovered after the war that, with the exception of one or two natures of ammunition, the Israelis never actually used up their pre-war stocks. Van Creveld maintains that the shortages at the front were caused by hoarding of up to 50 per cent of stocks of ammunition at various points along the supply pipeline.[29] The Israelis finished the war with more than they began, thanks to American supply. It is doubtful whether the American airlift had any influence on the outcome of any battle in this war. However, it is probably true to state that it affected the way in which the Israelis fought, because they always had at the back of their minds the knowledge that stocks would not run out.

Striking a Logistical Balance

It is evident that, at the operational level, the Israelis usually struck a nice balance between what was logistically possible and what was not, without letting logistics bear down too heavily upon them. Bar Lev stopping further crossings on the first day of the cross-Canal operation, despite pressure from Sharon, and Adan's measures to open up his line of communication while he headed for Suez, are the marks of level-headed generalship. Most logisticians, in most armies, would recoil from the idea of pushing three divisions across a double water obstacle, which involved their line of communication running across the flank of a superior and undefeated army, at the most only 8 kilometres away. It was a nice judgement on the part of the Israelis that they would get away with it. If to some it smacks of 'bash on regardless', it is worth bearing in mind that if logistics is about supply, it is also about movement. In this respect, as in so many others, the Israelis, with their canny preparation of crossing sites and the roads leading to them, and their skill in improvisation when all did not go to plan, showed themselves to be operational masters of the battlefield.

Principal Lessons: A Watershed in the Study of Logistics

However, the war also showed that high attrition rates are a consequence of a confrontation between two sides who both possess modern weapons, and are both determined to win. The exact figures have not been published, but there is general agreement that the Israelis lost between 97 and 102 combat aircraft. The combined losses by the Egyptians and Syrians amounted to around 347 to 387 combat aircraft, and 41 helicopters. All but three of the Israeli aircraft were shot down by SAMs or anti-aircraft fire. The Egyptians and Syrians lost 334 aircraft in air-to-air combat with the Israeli air force. The Egyptians lost 900 AFVs, the Syrians 1,050, and the Israelis 810.[30,31] There is universal agreement that the loss rate, particularly in tanks and aircraft, took everybody by surprise.[32] Throughout history, a clash between mass armies has produced mass casualties in men and materiel. The attrition rate experienced in the Arab-Israeli war of 1973 raises the question of how long a major war between the super-powers and their allies, could be sustained after losses which, in view of the greater numbers that would be engaged, would be higher in absolute terms.

Herzog claims[33] that, in 1973, the tank production of the United States was 30 tanks a month, 360 a year. The Soviets were able to resupply Syria with all tanks lost in the war (1,050). This followed, or was concurrent with, shipments of tanks totalling over 1,000 to Egypt, Iraq, Algeria, Somalia, India and the two Yemens. The Russians, with a mathematical and analytical approach to strategy and the operational art, are likely to be better prepared to meet high attrition rates than the West, whose amouries are not based on the threat, but on what their defence budgets will stand. However, it remains to be seen if the Soviets could maintain their tempo of operations against a determined defence. This will be discussed in a later chapter. But the Arab-Israeli war represents a major watershed in the study of logistics and armed conflict, in that it serves notice that the sophisticated weapon systems which allow operations to be carried out at such a high tempo, are so expensive that supplies are not virtually limitless as they were in earlier wars. The high tempo of itself is a voracious consumer of the very systems which make it possible.

7

War in a Snipe Marsh:
Bangla Desh 1971

'While Bangla Desh might be a paradise for waterfowl, it must be a nightmare for a campaign planner.'[1]

In March 1971, East Bengalis serving in the Pakistan Army in what was then East Pakistan, mutinied and formed the Bangla Desh Liberation Army, with the aim of freeing Bangla Desh from Pakistani domination. The Indian Government recognised that the situation might call for intervention, however, there were a number of factors which argued for delaying any action until mid-November. First, the Indian Armed Forces' expansion and re-equipment programmes, although well underway, needed several more months before completion. Second, because of the internal security situation in West Bengal and in the Mizo Hills in the North-East Frontier Area (NEFA), the Indian Army deployment was unbalanced. Three divisions deployed near the Bangla Desh border were committed on aid to the civil power duties, without their heavy equipment. Additional formations needed to be brought in, and a new operational and logistical infrastructure provided. Third, air bases needed to be developed for operations in Bangla Desh. Fourth, any attempt by India to carry out even limited action in Bangla Desh would invite a riposte by Pakistan in the West; probably an attack on Kashmir. So action by India must be delayed, until reinforcements could be moved in, particularly on the lines of communication in the sensitive Jammu and Kashmir sector. Fifth, the Freedom Fighters in Bangla Desh, the *Mukti Bagini*, were in some disarray after Pakistani Army operations aimed at their elimination. Time would be required to re-fit and re-train the *Mukti Bahini*, if they were to be employed as an adjunct to Indian operations. Sixth, and most important, the monsoon, due in April or May, would make ground and air operations in Bangla Desh almost impossible; and at the same time melt the snow in the mountain passes on the Chinese/Indian border, risking intervention by the Chinese while India was otherwise engaged. The ground in Bangla Desh is not dry enough for mobile operations until mid-November. The passes on the northern border are not blocked by snow until some time later. Therefore India had to bide her time until November 1971, at the earliest.

For a time there were hopes that the *Mukti Bahini*, with support from India, in the form of sanctuaries within her borders, arms, and training, might defeat the Pakistan Army and free Bangla Desh. However, in common with most, if not all, resistance movements faced by a well equipped and ruthless army of occupation, backed by an equally ruthless and determined government, the *Mukti Bahini* had no hope of winning. Guerrilla or resistance movements only succeed when their activities are carried out as an adjunct to, and closely co-ordinated with, the operations of a conventional army. It matters little whether the conventional army is indigenous, or from an ally. History is full of examples: the Peninsular War, the Arab revolt, the French Resistance, the Yugoslav Partisans, the Partisans in Russia. The *Mukti Bahini* were badly led at all levels, and disorganised. Lacking an overall commander, there was no co-ordinated plan. At no time did they come near to ejecting the Pakistan Army. The value of the *Mukti Bahini* lay in creating the conditions which led to brutal Pakistani repression, this in turn enabled the Indians to intervene in Bangla Desh, to the mutual benefit of the Bangla Deshis and the Indians. When the Indian Army eventually moved in, the *Mukti Bahini*'s most valuable service was as guides and intelligence gatherers.[2]

The Aims of Indian Intervention

The political objectives given to the Indian Chiefs of Staff in the event of an intervention in Bangla Desh were:

> To liberate Bangla Desh as quickly as possible.
> To fight a holding action in the West and in the north if attacked.
> To make limited gains in the West, as a bargaining point in case a Pakistani surprise attack succeeded in capturing any part of Indian territory.

When war came, the Indians achieved all three. But this chapter will concentrate on the first, because it is the most interesting from the logistical point of view.

The Operational Area: A Land of Rivers and Swamps

As the quote at the beginning implies, Bangla Desh is an unpromising country in which to campaign. Most of the country consists of an alluvial plain formed by the deposits of three great rivers, the Ganges, the Brahmaputra/Jumana, and the Meghna; and their numerous tributaries. In the monsoon the bigger rivers are so wide, they are more like vast, flowing lakes, in places too wide to see from bank to bank. Even in the dry season they can be up to five miles wide. The countryside is criss-crossed with a maze of small channels or *nullahs*, as they are known on the sub-continent. Even after the monsoon, when the larger rivers are flowing within their banks, an army moving across country is faced with a seemingly endless succession of water obstacles to cross. The soil on the plain, several hundred feet thick, is a mixture of clay, silt and sand. The water table is very high, so while the surface appears hard in the winter after the monsoon rain has drained off, in most places it would not bear the weight of medium tanks. On the map the maze of rivers is as confusing as the way in which they change names. On entering Bangla Desh from Assam, the Brahmaputra becomes the Jamuna. Soon the Brahmaputra reappears, splitting off from the Jamuna to flow to the East of the capital, Dacca. The Jamuna joins the Ganges north-west of Dacca; at which point the Ganges/Jamuna combination becomes the Padma. The Meghna, having joined Brahmaputra south-east of Dacca, flows into the Padma. Dacca is at the southern end of a lozenge shaped island about 150 miles from North to South, and 50 miles from East to West at its widest point, bounded by the Jamuna, Padma and Brahmaputra rivers. Numerous small rivers split away from the main rivers to form a vast delta of mangrove swamp, islands and tidal creeks; the Sundarbans, on some maps, the 'Mouths of the Ganges'. Apart from the hills in the Chittagong district, which rise to 1,200 feet, the only other high ground is the plateau north of Dacca, which varies from 40 to 100 feet in height.

The rivers in Eastern Bengal had played a vital part in the logistic support of the British in the Burma campaign, and little had changed in the intervening twenty-nine years. The transport and communications of Bangla Desh were, and are, shaped by the rivers, which play a major part in the movement of goods and produce. The local population depended on boats and ferries for normal movement. Bullock-carts could be driven across the rivers and *nullahs* at carefully selected fords. Most movement was by bullock-cart, bicycle, and motor-cycle.[3] The railways and roads roughly conform to the line of the major rivers, which run generally north–south. East–West movement, other than on river tributaries, and by ferry, is difficult even in peacetime. In the war, which was about to begin, the transportation of large numbers of men and equipment was made infinitely more arduous because so many of the bridges had been blown by the *Mukti Bahini* during the resistance campaign.[4] These random, and unco-ordinated demolitions were sometimes more of an obstacle to their deliverers than their suppressors, and were proof that the *Mukti Bahini* lacked direction.

*   *   *

The Indians Re-Group

Considerable re-grouping within the Indian Army was necessary before a campaign in Bangla Desh could be undertaken. Eastern Command, which would be responsible for conducting operations, was geared almost completely for mountain operations in the Himalayan border region, or for internal security duties in NEFA. The formations were all mountain divisions, and equipped accordingly; they had no bridging equipment and no armour. Their artillery was mainly pack or light towed pieces, unsuitable against concrete pill-boxes and heavily fortified bunkers which the Pakistan Army had been constructing in Bangla Desh. Most important, Eastern Command did not have the necessary transport for logistic support of operations in riverine terrain. By denuding other fronts, armour, including two regiments of PT-76 Russian amphibious light tanks, and medium and field artillery, was attached to Eastern Command. Bridging resources were built up to allow Eastern Command to lay 10,000 feet of bridging.

A Joint-Service Command

An inter-service joint command was set up in Headquarters Eastern Command, with Air Force and Naval representation; a new departure in India, to judge by the comment: 'Unlike in other wars, the Indian land forces operating in Bangla Desh were not deprived of close air support while the Air Force fought its own battles in the air.'[5] This command arrangement was to pay dividends.

*   *   *

Pakistani Incursions Into India: The War Begins

By November, the fighting between the *Mukti Bahini* and the Pakistan Army in Bangla Desh had led to several border incursions

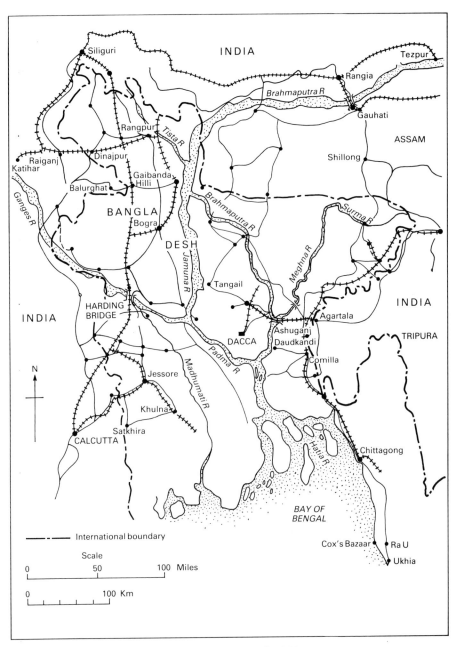

MAP XI   Bangla Desh 1971.

into India by Pakistani troops, either in hot pursuit of guerrillas, or in the course of attacking bases adjacent to the Indian border. In addition there had been a number of violations of Indian air space, and shelling of Indian villages by Pakistani forces. Many of these incidents had resulted in casualties to Indian civilians and soldiers. Indian forces did not do more than push back these attacks, and on one occasion advanced a few kilometres into Bangla Desh, before retiring again. However, on 3 December 1971, preceded by an ineffective attempt at a pre-emptive air strike on Indian airfields, Pakistan attacked in the Poonch and Chhamb sectors on the Western Front. The Indians, who were not taken by surprise, halted these attacks, and followed up with a series of limited, but bitterly contested offensives. They succeeded in pinching off a number of salients, and gained some key features overlooking Indian positions. In this way they neutralised the Pakistan Army in the West, leaving the way clear for an Indian offensive in the East.

The Indians Prepare to Invade

General Aurora, the commander of India's Eastern Command, had three corps with which to attack: 2nd Corps between Calcutta and the western border of Bangla Desh, 33rd Corps on the north-west border, and 4th Corps on the eastern border. In addition he had a communications zone headquarters on the north-east border which he intended to use as a mobile operational formation. It was clear to the Indians that speed was of the essence, the Pakistan Army in Bangla Desh must be defeated before there was diplomatic or physical intervention by Pakistan's two allies, the United States and China. Bearing in mind the need to impose the maximum delay, General Niazi, the Pakistan commander in Bangla Desh, had adopted a plan which involved blocking all routes of entry by India, by occupying strong defensive positions close to the border on all road approaches, and making best use of the terrain which greatly favoured the defender. The greatest threat lay on the western and northern sectors, because of the road approaches from India, and the direction of flow of the major rivers. Also, the Indians had located their major logistical and communications infrastructure in the West and the North-West. Communications on the Indian side of the border did not favour a thrust into the North-East of Bangla Desh. The threat to Bangla Desh from the East was not at first thought to be great, mainly because of the lack of logistic facilities in the Tripura area; or so Niazi believed. The railway and road communications were much as the British had left them, as described in Chapter 3, in the section on the Burma campaign, and the best of these were inside Bangla Desh. However, unknown to Pakistan intelligence until the end of October, Eastern Command had improved the existing roads and tracks, and built new ones; stockpiled supplies; and moved in logistic units.

Pakistani Defensive Measures

Niazi deployed in strength on the western border, opposite Calcutta, and in the North-West. As more information came in about the Indian build up in the East, Niazi built a string of strongpoints on the border with Tripura; his main concern the vital Dacca-Comilla-Chittagong road and rail link. The north-east sector was least strongly held. His policy of holding as much territory as he could, with the bulk of his forces committed forward in a rigid form of linear defence, was probably based on a belief that the *Mukti Bahini*'s aim was to carve out a belt of territory all along the inside of the border, and follow up by declaring a liberated Bangla Desh with its own government, as a way of gaining international recognition. He may have assumed that India would support this limited plan. He would have done better to have based his defence on the formidable river obstacles, finally concentrating on the close defence of Dacca.

The Indian Plan

The Indians well aware that time was not on their side, had to attack with such speed that the Pakistanis would be unable to fall back on the great river obstacles, and in particular to Dacca. The rivers Jamuna, Ganges and Meghna were very wide, and the approaches to them marshy. If the Pakistanis were allowed to withdraw in good order, they could turn Dacca into an island fortress. The Indians had an additional reason for a quick finish to the campaign in Bangla Desh; the mountain divisions must be back on the frontier with China as soon as possible. In the past the Indian Army had favoured the set-piece battle, a steady, phased advance, with re-grouping at appropriate stages. Niazi anticipated a similar approach on this occasion. However, Lieutenant General Aurora decided that he must get to Dacca within 15 days, before the Pakistanis could pull back and form a strong defensive position. His plan was to contain the Pakistan strongpoints on the border, and by-pass them with mobile thrusts. Each corps would strike in this way, with a minor thrust in the North-East. The objective of all three corps was Dacca. There was to be no rigid plan, he would exploit whichever axis looked the most promising. It was a bold concept to put into effect in terrain so unfavourable for mobile operations. The Pakistanis were a formidable enemy, at least as good as the Indians. Success would demand the highest standards of leadership, skill and logistical expertise.

The Indians Strike

On 4 December the Indian Army struck across the Bangla Desh border. From east of Calcutta, 2nd Indian Corps thrust for the Madhumati river, a tributary of the Ganges (Padma) linking it with the Sundarbans. This would serve two purposes: cutting off the Pakistanis from withdrawing across the river, and making for Dacca; and cutting the railway. The Pakistani static defence layout enabled the Corps to bypass opposition and press on fast. Infantry brigades moved off the main roads, across the paddy and using small tracks. Local transport in the form of rickshaws, bicycles and carts, willingly lent by the population carried some of the immediate supplies. Resupply was by airdrop. At times the troops ate local produce; harking back to the days of foraging, except that in this case the Bangla Deshis were only too happy to provide what they could. Jessore, a stronghold held by an infantry brigade group supported by tanks, was bypassed in this way. To everybody's surprise, the garrison fled.

On 33rd Indian Corps front, two brigades struck south, making for Dinajpur and Rangpur, critical road/rail junctions. 20th Indian Mountain Division thrust east through the salient opposite the Pakistan village of Hilli. Some of the strongest resistance by Pakistani troops was encountered in 33rd Corps's sector. In particular, while part of 10th Mountain Division raced ahead, having bypassed Hilli, it took four days of hard fighting to capture the complex of bunkers and pill-boxes. The Pakistanis had stocked their strongpoints with four weeks worth of ammunition, fuel, and rations; and had no plans for resupply.[6]

Logistical Problems

The account by the commander of 20th Indian Mountain Division of his logistic problems in India before his division started its advance is interesting. Once in Bangla Desh, the roads were far worse:

FIG. 7.1   Indian troops repairing the Jessore road—the flat terrain and primitive road communications are evident (*Evening Standard*).

'During October . . . we started moving to our concentration areas around Balurghat. The move posed a lot of problems and was carried out strictly by night only. We moved by road and rail as the T-55 tanks and medium guns could not be moved to Balurghat via Raiganj, owing to the weak bridges near Raiganj. T-55 tanks, medium guns and large quantities of combat engineer equipment were moved by train to Malda, while the rest moved by road and metre-gauge to Raiganj . . . The division took nearly twenty days to concentrate. The direct road from Siliguri to Balurghat could not take heavy vehicles or tanks. We had only twelve railway flats to move PT-76 tanks up to Raiganj, so the move had to be slow because of the shuttle service . . . ammunition had to be moved by road on the one-way road to Balurghat, and the availability of transport was limited. Owing to the narrow road from Raiganj to Balurghat, I had to enforce strict one-way traffic. The road *berms* (edges) were soft, and there were traffic jams whenever a vehicle tried to get off the road. Some of the existing bridges on this road had to be strengthened, while a number of rafts had to be constructed to take heavy tanks over rivers into the Balurghat area.'[7]

The Course of the Campaign

By 9 December, 20th Indian Mountain Division had taken Palashbari, a key road junction, and advanced to Gaibanda, a road/rail junction by the Jamuna river, thus cutting off the whole of the north-east sector of Bangla Desh. By 14 December, this division was fighting for the town of Bogra, and had swung a brigade north to join in the battle for Rangpur.

4th Indian Corps had perhaps the most difficult task of all, with the objective of bouncing the Meghna, and the smaller Brahmaputra, and racing for Dacca. The Corps Commander's subsidiary tasks were to cut the road/rail link from Dacca to Chittagong. The Meghna was about a mile wide at the most suitable crossing point, where there was a railway bridge at Ashuganj, but no road following the line of the railway. By 11 December 4th Corps had closed up to the Meghna on a broad front and, despite the railway bridge being blown, had bounced a crossing using helicopters and PT-76 tanks. The latter designed by the Russians for crossing European rivers, overheated after half-an-hour of swimming the wide, swift-flowing Meghna, by which time they were less than a sixth of the way across. Local boats were pressed into service pushing and towing these amphibious tanks.

The Defence Fragmented

By this time the bulk of the Pakistani Army was cut off from Dacca, except for a Pakistani brigade, commanded by Brigadier Qadir, east of the Jamuna river, north-east of Dacca. This brigade, together with the Pakistani forces withdrawing in front of 4th Corps crossing at Ashuganj, would be a considerable reinforcement to the Dacca garrison. Although the fall of Dacca was now only a question of time, General Aurora feared widespread destruction and loss of civilian lives resulting from a battle in the city; and to judge from Pakistani behaviour hitherto, savage reprisals. At Tangail, a small force held a bridge and a ferry site over a tributary of the Padma, to provide a withdrawal route for Qadir's brigade, which had received orders to pull back to Dacca. On the afternoon of 11 December, a battalion of the Indian Parachute Brigade was dropped just north of the river, and during the hours of darkness, seized the crossing sites in rear of Qadir's brigade as it withdrew towards Dacca. The Pakistanis made four attempts to cross the river, and finally, with another Indian brigade hard on their heels, Qadir's men melted away into the countryside.

This was not the only combined operation by the Indian forces on the Eastern Front. Aircraft from the Indian Navy aircraft carrier *Vikrant* bombed Cox's Bazaar airfield and Chittagong harbour and airfield on the first day of the war. It was then learned that Pakistani

FIG. 7.2   Marching infantry under load, with a difference; this soldier prefers
to carry his pack on his head (*Central Press*).

groups were escaping overland to Burma through Cox's Bazaar. An
amphibious operation was quickly mounted using a reinforced
battalion taken from 2nd Corps, and transported in an Indian
merchant vessel, SS *Vishwavijaya*, which happened to be anchored in
the river Hoogly. Off Cox's Bazaar, the battalion was transferred to the
only available Landing Ship (LST), which was at sea already, and
landed at Cox's Bazaar; the first ever amphibious operation carried out
by the Indian armed forces.

Surrender

On 16 December, with Dacca surrounded by the Indian Army,
General Niazi surrendered. It had taken 12 days for the seven
reinforced divisions of the Indian Army to liberate Bangla Desh, in the
face of four reinforced Pakistani divisions who had had ample time to
prepare, in terrain which favoured the defender. The major share of the
credit for this remarkable achievement must go to Lieutenant General
Aurora for his bold concept, and to his corps and divisional

commanders for maintaining the tempo of operations. Credit is also due to the Indian Air Force and Indian Navy, for providing close air support, and in particular for helicopters to 'air bridge' rivers. The success of many of the Indian bypassing operations were a direct result of the speed with which routes round Pakistani positions could be identified, thanks to the *Mukti Bahini*. But most critical of all, the Indians had time to plan and make the necessary logistic arrangements.

Conclusions

In 1971 the Indian Army was mainly an infantry force; for thirty divisions, there were only 1,500 tanks, 500 APCs, no self-propelled (SP) artillery and 250 helicopters. Transport was in short supply and mainly road-bound. The principal road and rail transport links had been constructed for commercial or strategic purposes before 1947, when the sub-continent was one country. Therefore, they did not necessarily run in directions suitable for operations within the sub-continent. Without sufficient transport capable of cross-country movement, the Indians were faced with the problem that moves off the main communications axes were difficult to support logistically.[8] With eight months to prepare for the war, particularly in the demanding terrain of Bangla Desh, the Indian Army was able to take steps to offset some of their logistic shortcomings, for example by requisitioning civilian transport, and re-allocating transport to formations that were short. However, these expedients did not always prove satisfactory.[9] Had the Pakistanis opted for a different operational plan, the Indians might have found themselves expending more ammunition, and the war might have lasted longer, with accompanying logistic difficulties. A combination of time to prepare, and an inept Pakistani plan, allowed Indian logistic shortcomings to be overcome. The shorter the time there is to prepare, the more important logistic mobility becomes. Armour, infantry, and guns can be moved relatively swiftly off the main communications network to meet the unexpected, or carry out moves in response to the operational situation. But without ammunition and fuel, they will rapidly become ineffective. So their logistic support must also be capable of keeping up with them in terrain with few, or no roads. This requires large numbers of suitable load carriers, preferably a combination of helicopters and rough terrain vehicles, even at the expense of cutting down on teeth arms.[10] The problems of logistic mobility were to show themselves to be the key issue in the land battle, in the campaign described in the next chapter.

PART THREE

8

Amphibious Logistics—Falklands 1982

He had forty-two boxes, all carefully packed,
 With his name clearly painted on each:
But, since he omitted to mention the fact,
 They were all left behind on the beach.
Lewis Carroll, 'The Landing' from the Hunting of the Snark.

'The plan of embarking mules and men in the same ships, was in the first instance
objected to on the ground that some ships were better able to carry mules than others,
and that the comfort of the troops would be greater if all animals were placed in
separate vessels; but this objection was overruled by the Commander-in-Chief, who
stated that he was convinced by history, that the governing principle in preparing
such expeditions, was so to embark the force that every portion of it should be able to
disembark, completely equipped from the ship or ships conveying it. This, he stated,
was absolutely necessary if the landing was likely to be opposed, and was the best
means of preventing confusion and delay even if there were no opposition.'
British Egyptian Expedition 1882.[1]

From 29 March 1982, the Staff at Fleet Headquarters in Northwood had been taking precautionary measures in case the Argentines invaded the Falklands.[2] On the same day, Admiral Fieldhouse, the Fleet Commander, ordered Rear Admiral Woodward, the Flag Officer First Flotilla, then at Gibraltar exercising with sixteen frigates and destroyers, to prepare plans for the detachment of a task group to the South Atlantic. On 31 March, intelligence was received in London that the Falklands would be invaded on 2 April. The Prime Minister, conferred with the Secretary of State for Defence, John Nott, two junior Foreign Office Ministers and Admiral Leach, the First Sea Lord, representing the Chief of the Defence Staff, who was out of the country. As a result of this meeting, Admiral Leach was ordered to 'prepare a force which he had advised would be required to retake the islands "without commitment to a final decision as to whether or not it should sail"[3]

3rd Commando Brigade: Preliminary Moves

While all these preliminary moves were taking place, 3rd Commando Brigade Royal Marines, the force which would have to land and retake the islands, and without whom the sailing of a task force, except as a gesture, would be nugatory, were blissfully ignorant that their services might be required. The commanding officer of one commando,[4] it is true, had been warned in vague terms that his commando might have to travel to the Falkland Islands, to pre-empt an invasion. Soon the requirement was reduced to a company. However, he was not allowed to make any preparations, including bringing his men to shorter notice, nor was it revealed how the commando, or the company, would get to the scene. Even in a ship steaming all the way at 30 knots, the journey would take over eleven days, and a more realistic time would be fourteen to sixteen days. The airfield at Port Stanley was too small to take long range transports, and at that time British C-130 aircraft, capable of landing at Stanley airport, were not fitted with air-to-air refuelling (AAR) probes. The only way to Stanley by air would have been via Argentina. Soon the commando was stood down. However, part of the Commando Brigade Air Defence Troop, with their Blowpipe shoulder-launched surface-to-air missiles, was warned that they might be needed. The problem of their method of transport to the Falklands was also left unresolved, leading to facetious speculation that they might travel on Argentine civilian airlines, posing as musicians, with their Blowpipes in double-bass cases. By 31 March, the day that the Prime Minister held her meeting, the Air Defence Troop had been stood down. That evening the commander, 3rd Commando Brigade returned from a reconnaissance in Denmark for a NATO exercise, to be informed, for the first time, of the orders and counter-orders issued to some of his units over the preceding two days; and that none of his brigade was required. The brigade staff, also unaware of what had been going on in England, remained in Denmark to complete the reconnaissance. On 1 April, two carriers, HMS *Hermes* and *Invincible*, were ordered to come to 48 hours notice for sea.[5] Third Commando Brigade was still at their normal seven days notice for operations and starting to go on leave. Whether deliberate policy or an oversight, failure to issue any kind of warning order to 3rd Commando Brigade was unpardonable. Even if a limited number of key people had been told, the four days before the Argentine invasion could have been put to good use, and avoided some of the scramble that ensued, particularly logistically.

The Lack of a Mission, Contingency Plans and Adequate Warning

On 2 April, the order did come, at first in the form of a telephone call to reduce the notice of the Brigade to 72 hours, and eventually in a signal ordering it to load into shipping and sail South with all despatch. At this stage no mission was given, and the problem of translating political intent into military action, that was to persist until well after the landing on 21 May, first reared its head. There were no formal plans to cater for the possibility of having to retake the Falkland Islands after their seizure by the Argentines, or anyone else. A contingency plan is useful because although it is unlikely to provide the planners with all the data required when the emergency arises, it is quicker to amend an existing plan than design one from scratch. This particularly applies when time is short, which was the case with 3rd Commando Brigade, whose key staff did not return from Denmark until the evening of 2 April.

Loading: The Price of Expediency

Loading for an amphibious operation is best carried out in the following sequence: identify the mission, find out as much as possible about the enemy (intelligence), make the plan, and stow the ships so that men and loads will come off in the sequence required to meet the plan. Unlike a peacetime sea-transported move to a port, where the marrying up of men and equipment can be done on arrival, ships for an amphibious operation must be combat loaded. Men, their equipment and ammunition must travel in the same ship, in formed units, thus enabling them to start fighting without delay on arriving at the beach or landing zone. The unit must be able to disembark in the right tactical sequence and grouping. Contrasted with non-tactical, or administrative loading, combat loading tends to make less economical use of the space available in transporting ships.

No mission had been given, and there was little intelligence about the enemy. For good political reasons, there was no time to do anything other than load ships quickly, and get them away as early as possible, with as sensible a mix of stores and troops as could be achieved based on the little information available. For lack of anything better, the plan for the reinforcement of Northern Norway in a time of tension was used as a planning guide. However, as units were added to the order of battle of 3rd Commando Brigade, the need arose for more ships than had at first been allocated by Fleet Headquarters. There was also the matter of the War Maintenance Reserve, the fuel, ammunition, food and spares needed to supply the Brigade in battle. This amounted to 9,000 tons. However, the Brigade was not the only formation outloading. The Royal Navy and the Royal Air Force also needed stores to be moved from depôts in various parts of the United Kingdom. With the Brigade's war maintenance reserve, this amounted to 1,260 tons of petrol, oil and lubricants (POL), 8,260 tons of ammunition, and 3,880 tons of ordnance stores (all types of stores, including spares). Most of this was outloaded within the first 72 hours.[6] Because the move of stores was over the weekend, and at short notice, the outload could not be completed by British Rail, as envisaged in the Northern Norway contingency plan.[7] The bulk was lifted by road transport using virtually all the United Kingdom-based Regular Army Transport Units, as well as several Territorial Army Transport Units called up for service. Commercial operators also provided a substantial lift. During this period, one unit travelled more than 510,000 miles, performed 293 tasks with 1,231 vehicles, moved more than 15,000 tons of materials, and consumed 249,000 litres of fuel.[8]

In the first eighty hours, the full 30 days War Maintenance Reserve (WMR) of all items, and first line scales consisting of two days ammunition and five days rations for 3rd Commando Brigade had been loaded into shipping. By an unlucky coincidence, the crisis caught the Royal Fleet Auxiliary storeship that was permanently loaded with the War Maintenance Reserve for one commando, in the process of unloading in order to turn-over her stocks; an event that occurred only once every four years.

The Influence of Terrain on Logistic Planning

An important logistic decision to take a minimum of wheeled vehicles was made early in planning, resulting from a study of the terrain in the projected area of operations. Terrain usually has a profound affect on land force logistics, far more so than Naval and Air logistics. Most of the ground in the Islands, particularly in East Falkland is peat bog, with, in places, large areas of hummocky tussock grass. Stone runs also abound, up to hundreds of yards wide and several miles long. These are like rivers of stone consisting of boulders varying from the size of a man's head to that of a car. The mountains, although not high, and more akin to moorland hills (the highest, Mount Usborne being 2,300 feet), were almost all crowned with great, craggy castles of rock, which stood up like the spines of some vast prehistoric reptile. These crenellated bastions, with deep fissures, sudden sheer drops, and great buttresses were obstacles to any type of vehicle, wheeled or tracked. Few were less than 500 metres long, and some in excess of 2,000 metres. In 1982, apart from the environs of Stanley, and a surfaced track to Fitzroy, there were no other roads, or tracks. A lightly loaded Landrover would be lucky to cover four miles in the hour; provided it kept off tussock and stone run, and did not follow the tracks of a predecessor which had broken through the light crust and reduced the going to a black slurry. A wheeled vehicle loaded with ammunition or towing a gun would not move at all. The Brigade did have seventy-six of its BV202 tracked oversnow vehicles in Britain, the remainder being stockpiled in Norway. Although designed to operate over snow, it was assessed that these vehicles with a ground pressure of only about one-and-a-half pounds per square inch, about that of a man on skis, would be able to motor across the peat bog. All were taken. Fortunately, the commanding officer of the Logistic Regiment persuaded the Brigade commander to allow him to take ten trucks equipped with fuel pods, and nine Eager Beaver four-wheel-drive rough-terrain fork-lift trucks. Without these late additions to the order of battle, the logistic situation would have been difficult, to say the least.

The Weather Factor

The weather was also an important consideration. Although the Islands lie on the same latitude south of the equator, as Britain lies north, the great Southern Ocean, with no equivalent of the Gulf Stream to warm the sea, and the proximity of the vast frozen continent of Antarctica, Cape Horn, and the Andes, combine to make the climate significantly different. Icebergs regularly come within 200 miles of the islands, and if a huge tabular berg grounds on the Burdwood Bank to the South, it can alter the weather pattern in the Falklands. Snow, rain, fog, and brilliant sunshine follow each other with bewildering rapidity at all times of the year, even in summer; the only constant is the wind. The average windspeed throughout the year in Britain is 4 knots, in the Falklands it is 15 mph. It would be approaching mid-winter when the landing force was likely to arrive.

As Units Are Added, the Complications of Loading Increase

As units were added to the Commando Brigade, the tonnage of supplies to be taken south increased accordingly. Because of the need to load within three days, there was insufficient time to move ships to convenient ports. There was insufficient suitable shipping, and as more and more was crammed into the vessels made available, combat loading had to be forgone in the interests of meeting the requirement to get south. Some ships were down below their loading marks, others had mixed loads of packed fuel and ammunition in the same space. Normally, every effort is made to keep a unit's assault pack together on one ship. This did not happen on this occasion. Types of ammunition and rations were difficult to identify when they reached the docks, and were sometimes put on the wrong ships. Once aboard, it was not possible to establish exactly what had been loaded where. In an effort to produce a comprehensive inventory of each ship's load, the Commanding Officer of the Logistic Regiment placed an NCO from the Regiment on each ship with orders to complete a detailed load state, and signal it back to Regimental Headquarters. By 6 April, it was decided that the scaling of supplies being taken would be insufficient, therefore the balance of the Brigade's War Maintenance Reserve of ammunition was loaded in the container ship *Elk*.[9] A re-stow before any landing took place was absolutely essential. This would be done at Ascension Island, just over half way to the Falklands.

The Task Force: Preliminary Measures

Meanwhile the Royal Navy's logisticians had also been busy. Storing the warships was the easy part, although done at twice the normal speed, at least it was a familiar task. Storing and making the necessary conversions to the Ships Taken Up From Trade (STUFT), of which there were ultimately 54, was a different matter. Converting merchantmen for war required a wide range of stores from communications fits, life-jackets, anti-flash gear, and code books, to helicopter decks and replenishment at sea (RAS) rigs.[10] The conversions usually involved more than just providing the equipment. For example, fitting a flat steel deck on which a helicopter can land on a ship is only part of the job. Communications must be provided to enable the ship to speak to the helicopter, and a small flight deck party to marshal it and, if necessary lash it down if the ship is rolling or pitching. Many ferries, designed for short passages of up to only 24 hours, had no fresh water make-up equipment, carrying what was needed in tanks. This would not meet the needs of ships on long passages, spending weeks at sea, usually carrying far in excess of their peacetime passenger load. Most ships needing this facility were fitted with reverse osmosis (RO) plants. Similarly, ferries designed for short-haul work do not need to carry great quantities of fuel. To avoid the need for a daily RAS of fuel

FIG. 8.1 *Atlantic Conveyor* about to RAS(L) from an RFA oiler (*IWM*).

(RAS(L)), the ballast tanks in some ferries were converted to take fuel, which involved major pipework to allow the fuel to be embarked at sea and transferred to the engines. In the case of ships that were to be used essentially in their peacetime role, some of the tankers and dry store ships, the conversion was limited to radio equipment and RAS rigs. Where the role was changed, conversion was more complex and almost all done in the Royal Dockyards. At first, attempts were made to carry out major conversion in a commercial yard, but the volume of labour and skilled resources required swamped the available facilities. Ships in the Royal Dockyards were converted on average in four days and nights.

Some Specialist Conversions

In Gibraltar, the SS *Uganda*, normally a schools cruise tour ship, having disembarked her load of schoolchildren, was converted in two-

and-a-half days to a hospital ship. She was fitted with a helicopter pad, and had all the public rooms converted to provide an operating theatre, wards, intensive care unit, burns unit, X-ray department, ophthalmic department, dental surgery, dispensary and pathology laboratory. Two special de-salination plants were fitted. Her hull and superstructure were painted white with large red crosses, and extensive external lighting was fitted. The 13,000 ton ferry *Norland* was converted to a troop ship and fitted with two helicopter pads, flight and communications facilities, extra fresh water make-up, and RAS gear. One of the most unusual ships to be converted was the *Stena Seaspread*, designed as a 9,000 ton multi-purpose North Sea oil rig support ship. Her new role was as a forward repair ship, so she was fitted with workshops, machinery, a mobile crane on deck, extra generators, air compressors, spares and other stores. Additional accommodation was added for the Fleet Maintenance teams who were added to her ship's company, together with messing facilities for 500 men. Two helicopter pads were fitted, and 100 tons of additional ballast. Such was the speed of the operation, that she arrived in Portsmouth from the North Sea with divers still in the decompression chamber.

Aircraft Transporters

Four large container ships were converted to aircraft transporters. First was *Atlantic Conveyor* (15,000 tons and longer than a light fleet carrier), converted in 5 days to a Harrier and helicopter transporter. The main work consisted of clearing obstructions from the upper deck and strengthening hatch covers, provision of protection from the elements for aircraft on deck by using containers in the form of pens, two helicopter landing spots, accommodation for 100 additional people, and RAS and RO equipment. Fuel cells were installed in the adapted containers, and provision made for refuelling aircraft on deck, liquid oxygen for the Harriers, and fresh water for washing down all aircraft. *Atlantic Conveyor* was intended as the aircraft repair ship with a team from the Royal Navy's Mobile Aircraft Repair Transport and Salvage Unit embarked. The huge space below decks was filled with stores, including engineer plant and equipment to build an airstrip within the beachhead in the Falklands, and tents for 4,500 men. It was the intention that this should be offloaded in the beachhead anchorage through the stern doors. These had been strengthened to enable them to be opened at sea and used as platforms for helicopter transfers. Three further ships, *Atlantic Causeway*, sister ship to the *Conveyor*, *Contender*

Bezant (18,500 tons), and *Astronomer* (28,000 tons), were converted in a similar way, but with increasingly sophisticated facilities.

Beans, Bullets and, Especially, Fuel

Fitting, loading, and despatching ships was only the beginning. At the height of the war, a total of 26 warships and 54 STUFT were deployed in the operational area, with a total of 25,000 men ashore and afloat. Every bean, bullet, and drop of fuel had to come down a line of communication 8,000 miles long. Naval spares, food, and stores constituted in excess of 900,000 different line items (i.e.: over 900,000 different types of equipment and spares—from socks to screws). To these must be added the lengthy list of land force items. RAS(L) by day and night enabled ships to remain at sea for weeks without coming off station. On one occasion a RAS by a Royal Fleet Auxiliary (RFA) fleet tanker lasted for twenty-six and a-half hours, refuelling a succession of warships. RAS(L) lasting several hours were commonplace. But the fleet tankers themselves needed replenishment. The Task Force sailed on 6 April 1982 with sufficient fuel for its immediate needs. However, the fuel 'pipeline' 8,000 miles long needed to be kept filled. There were two problems: to procure a sufficient volume of fuel, and to find shipping to transport it. The first was solved easily; the glut of oil on the market at the time enabled the speedy purchase of the necessary large quantities. Eventually fourteen commercial tankers were chartered to provide the supply chain. All were fitted to receive the RFA tankers' abeam rigs, enabling them to replenish from the commercial tankers. As with fitting helipads, it was not sufficient just to supply the RAS rigs to commercial tankers; communications fits operated by RFA officers, and RFA deck and engineering officers were also needed.

Repair of Battle Damage at Sea

Battle damaged ships, 8,000 miles from home need repair if they are to survive, especially in the great Southern Ocean, the roughest waters in the world. After South Georgia was retaken, *Stena Seaspread* initially called in at the old whaling stations of Leith and Stromness, abandoned twenty years before. Stromness had been the repair base for the whale catchers, and there was a wealth of steel and other repair material for the taking. *Stena Seaspread* eventually moved forward up to the Carrier Battle Group operating area.

The Vital Contribution of the RAF

The inherent flexibility of a sea-borne logistic system, alluded to in an earlier chapter, was amply demonstrated in this war. Of course the right ships must be available, or suitable substitutes taken up from trade and converted, and the techniques must be well established and frequently practised.

However, the Royal Air Force also played a vital part. The first problem that required their assistance was the storing to war scales of warships already at sea, and diverted from other tasks. To this end, a forward logistic base was set up at Ascension Island, over 3,700 nautical miles from the United Kingdom and 3,300 nautical miles from the Falkland Islands. It was possible to deliver an urgent item to a ship in 24 hours if she was within helicopter range of Ascension Island, and for those further south airdrops could be delivered within two days. This service was carried out by RAF C-130s and VC-10s operating from the United Kingdom, Royal Navy helicopters from their ships, and, eventually, RAF Chinooks based on Ascension Island.

Since the end of the 1960s, the Royal Air Force, in common with the other Services, had reduced its capability for long-range intervention operations, in accordance with the policies of successive governments, which had orientated the Nation's defence requirement to NATO, to the exclusion of almost everything else. Although a small force of tanker aircraft had been retained, its task was to prolong the endurance and range of air defence fighters. There was no NATO requirement to refuel the large longer-range aircraft. The Vulcan bomber had an Air-to-Air Refuelling (AAR) capability in the 1960s, but this had not been maintained when the aircraft's role had been changed from nuclear strike to low-level delivery of iron bombs some years before 1982. All Vulcans were within three months of being removed from service. So when it became apparent that the nearest available airfield to the Falkland Islands was Wideawake on Ascension Island, the Air Force was presented with a considerable challenge. It was clear that the RAF could assist in three ways. First, by flying men and equipment to Ascension for transfer to ships. This would allow ships to sail from the United Kingdom without having to wait for last-minute items of equipment, or a specialist who was not immediately available; the principle of saving time by maximum concurrent activity. For example two companies of 45 Commando Royal Marines were flown to Ascension while an empty Landing Ship Logistic (LSL) was steamed across the Atlantic from Belize. Second, RAF Harriers and helicopters would be needed to supplement the Naval aircraft. Third, by deploying Victor tankers, Vulcans, Nimrod maritime patrol aircraft, and C-130s, to bring air power to bear as far South as possible; but this would require the rapid addition of an AAR capability, including one to the Harriers.[11]

Ascension Island: The Role of Wideawake Airfield

Wideawake was leased by Britain to the United States Government, and managed by Pan American Airways. It had a 10,000 foot runway, but the usual number of aircraft using it hardly ever exceeded four a week, which never put a strain on the island's supply of aviation fuel, accommodation, or aircraft parking space. Within a day of the start of the airbridge to Ascension, up to fourteen aircraft a day were landing and departing from Wideawake; and this was only the beginning. Between 2 April and 4 June 1982, the average number of aircraft movements per day was 94.8, including helicopters. The record was reached on 16 April when there were over 300 aircraft movements, making Wideawake the busiest airport in the world, on that day. Aviation fuel was suddenly needed in huge quantities. A tanker had to be permanently anchored offshore to pump fuel through a floating pipeline into the bulk fuel farm at Georgetown, the capital and only town on Ascension Island. Initially, fuel bowsers were used to transport the fuel from Georgetown to the airfield, but this method could not meet the consumption rate, and eventually the Royal Engineers laid a pipeline from the bulk fuel farm to the aircraft hardstandings.

Chinooks

The Chinook helicopters were employed on logistic tasks from early in the operation, starting by flying stores from Culdrose in Cornwall to ships up to 100 miles out at sea. Thus vital stores, that could not be embarked before the deadline for sailing, were delivered to the ships and the political impact of the immediate sailing of a task force was not diminished by embarrassing delays in the full glare of publicity. Perhaps the most striking example was the flying out of a 5-ton propeller bearing for HMS *Invincible*. It was a closely guarded secret that she had a defective bearing on one shaft, reducing her to one propeller, with a consequent limitation on speed. Repairs were effected at sea. To have *Invincible* creep back to port after the euphoric send-off of the task force carriers from Portsmouth, would have been mortifying for the Navy and the government, apart from delaying her passage south. Five Chinooks were embarked in *Atlantic Conveyor*, one being flown off at Ascension to assist with lifting stores to ships as they passed. In one day 350 tons were taken out; the main limitation to Chinook operations was the inability of ships' crews to clear the deck of such huge loads before the arrival of the next.[12]

. . . and Tankers

Nine RAF Harriers (GR3s), fitted with AAR probes, flew from the United Kingdom to Ascension, fuelled by Victor tankers *en route*. The journey took nine hours and fifteen minutes. They, and eight Sea Harriers (SHARs) which had flown out, supported by air tankers earlier, joined *Atlantic Conveyor* at Ascension. Air tanking also made possible the two Vulcan attacks on Stanley airfield, the Nimrod patrols as far south as South Georgia and off the coast of Argentina, and the C-130 air drops to the ships in the Total Exclusion Zone (TEZ), within 200 miles of the Falkland Islands. The surveillance sorties by the Nimrods lasted for between seventeen to nineteen hours and required up to twelve Victor tankers to provide fuel twice outbound, and a top-up during the return trip. The Nimrod could spend about four hours on station. The air tanker proved itself a significant force multiplier.

A Council of War

Having glanced at the logistics of the air and sea war, it is time to return to the landing force, and their logistic problems. Starting on 17 April, the ships of the Amphibious Group began arriving at Ascension Island. Among the first was HMS *Fearless*, a Landing Platform Dock (LPD), the headquarters ship of Commodore Clapp, commander of the Amphibious Task Group, and Brigadier Thompson, commander of the Landing Force Task Group.[13] The same day, Admiral Fieldhouse arrived by VC-10 with Major General Moore his land deputy and Air Marshal Curtiss his Air Commander. Admiral Fieldhouse chaired a council of war on board HMS *Hermes*, at which a number of matters were raised, and decisions taken on some. It was decided that:

> 1. Admiral Woodward was to press on with the Carrier Battle Group to attempt to win the air and sea battle before any amphibious landing took place. He was also responsible for inserting special forces patrols to reconnoitre a number of locations at the behest of Clapp and Thompson. Meanwhile, the Amphibious

Task Group would remain at Ascension and carry out a much needed re-stow of men, stores and vehicles.

2. Any landings would be carried out on East Falkland, and proposals for landing on West Falkland were rejected. Exactly where the landings on East Falkland would take place depended on a number of factors, including beaches and enemy locations. Special forces patrols would be tasked to report on these, among other things. Meanwhile Clapp and Thompson would prepare various options for landing areas.

3. The Commando Brigade should be reinforced, and arrangements for this were already in hand. The reinforcements included another parachute battalion, another battery of light guns, more medics, another troop of engineers, more Blowpipes, and another flight of light helicopters. The Brigade strength with these reinforcements would be around 5,500 men, including five commandos or battalions, twenty-four 105 mm light guns, eight tracked armoured reconnaissance vehicles, a battery of Rapier surface-to-air missiles (SAM), fifteen light helicopters, and a logistic regiment.[14]

4. The air battle would be won before the amphibious operation took place. This was categorically stated by the Task Force commander, Admiral Fieldhouse, not for the first time.

It was agreed that:

1. The Amphibious Group needed more ships, some of which were *en route* already, but others, such as another LPD, should now be sent south.

2. With the Argentine forces on the Islands assessed as being around 10,000 strong, of which about 7,500 were believed to be in the Stanley area, at least another brigade was required to even up the numbers. This would require a divisional headquarters to come south to take command of the two brigades. The second brigade was the 5th Infantry Brigade, stationed in the United Kingdom.

At this meeting, Woodward stated that from about the end of May the severe South Atlantic weather and pace of operations would begin to take their toll on ship serviceability. He forecast that by mid-to-late June, equipment failure on the majority of warships with the original task groups would cause severe restrictions on their operational capability. This naval sustainability limitation was ultimately to have a profound effect on the land battle.

The Chain of Command

By this time the chain of command had been established as follows:

All task group commanders reported direct to CTF 317 at Northwood. Admiral Woodward was NOT the task force commander, although he was senior task group commander, and had some co-ordinating responsibility.

The table below does not show two other task groups which do not concern us: the South Georgia Task Group, and the Sub-surface Task Group.

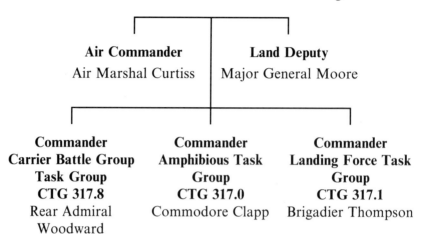

Commander Task Force 317
Admiral Fieldhouse at Northwood throughout

Air Commander	**Land Deputy**
Air Marshal Curtiss	Major General Moore

Commander Carrier Battle Group Task Group CTG 317.8	**Commander Amphibious Task Group CTG 317.0**	**Commander Landing Force Task Group CTG 317.1**
Rear Admiral Woodward	Commodore Clapp	Brigadier Thompson

The missing link in this command chain was a task force commander of three star rank, near the scene of the action to command and co-ordinate the task group commanders, and to deal with the Commander-in-Chief at Northwood, leaving each free to concentrate on his own task. The lack of such a commander led to some friction and a lack of control of logistic assets once all task groups had arrived in the Falkland Islands area.

Problems of Sorting and Identification of Stores

One immediate logistic problem that emerged concerned the administrative organisation on Ascension Island; a willing but over-worked Naval Party, dedicated to ensuring that ships passing through would lack nothing. Stores for the Commando Brigade started to pour in, reacting to signalled demands. These piled up and were not distributed to the units concerned for two reasons. First, if they were addressed to a particular unit, the Naval Party had no idea on which ship, or ships, the addressee was embarked (some units were embarked on several ships). Second, if as often happened, there was only a demand number on the package, the Naval Party was even more perplexed. In either case they usually did nothing, or at a pinch, despatched the item to a ship, any ship. Some ships which had no landing force units embarked, were surprised to receive equipment and spare parts whose purpose was a total mystery. There was a need for a team of Royal Army Ordnance Corps personnel to 'recognise' (to use the army expression) the item, and arrange for helicopter transport to deliver it to the correct recipient. When an ordnance team was sent out from the United Kingdom, the Officer Commanding the Naval Party unfortunately sent them back on the next aircraft, on the grounds that there was insufficient accommodation and a water shortage on the island. Eventually, after strong representations by the Brigade Commander, an Ordnance team from the Brigade, who could ill be spared from the job of re-stowing the ships, was sent ashore, and a modicum of order was restored. But not before some stores had gone missing completely, including special ammunition and weapons for the Brigade, which had been appropriated by an SAS Squadron passing through Ascension *en route* to South Georgia, who, seeing them lying about, had taken a fancy to them. More were sent out, but arrived after the Amphibious Group had sailed. Chaotic logistical practices lead to a piratical, devil-take-the-hindmost attitude, which in turn results in wasted effort. However, among the stores consigned to 3rd Commando Brigade which happily did arrive, were variable time fuzes for the 105 mm high explosive shells. These (VT) fuzes, that enable the shell to burst above the ground, were not included in the Artillery Regiment's first line ammunition, and had to be sent out separately. Only 18 per cent of the fuses were VT, and bearing in mind the very soft ground in the Falklands, there was concern that conventional shells bursting even near the enemy would only cover him in peat, not splinters. It was decided to send out a large percentage of the 105 mm VT fuzes held by the British Army of the Rhine. These also caught up with the Brigade at Ascension.

Ascension: The Re-Stow

A considerable effort was made by the Logistic Regiment NCO embarked in each stores-carrying ship to locate the supplies in his ship in the ten days between leaving Britain and arriving at Ascension. A comprehensive list was eventually produced, but not without difficulty, and not before arrival at Ascension. The only means of communication between stores carrying ships was often by signal, the lists were long and signal traffic was 'minimized' (a technical term meaning that only essential signal traffic was allowed to be sent from each ship, to avoid swamping the communications system. The definition of 'essential' was left to the judgement of the captain of each ship, and many viewed logistics as below that category). Some ships' captains were unwilling to allow anybody into the cargo areas while at sea, frustrating their embarked Logistic Regiment NCO in his task of compiling an inventory. In some ships the cargo holds were packed so tightly that only the top layer could be identified.

A thorough examination of the stores lists and the contents of each ship in the Amphibious Group, by the logistic staffs of 3rd Commando Brigade, resulted in a plan being drawn up for the re-stow, to make better use of hold and deck spaces, and achieve combat loading where possible. Rigorous questioning of the senior landing force officer on each ship revealed room for more men in every ship, jealously guarded in the interests of comfort. Spare corners were ruthlessly filled up, even if Board of Trade regulations on the maximum number of passengers on civilian ships, often invoked as a last resort, had to be broken. Nevertheless, because of lack of shipping space and purpose-built amphibious ships, not everybody could travel south from Ascension Island in the ship from which they would be taken ashore by helicopter or landing craft. Some cross-decking of men and equipment would be necessary just before the landing, to marry up teams, such as engineer reconnaissance and artillery forward observation parties, with the units they were supporting. There were other compromises. It was clear that the Rapier battery would be required ashore as early as possible. The only means of lifting the firing posts to their operating sites was by helicopter. Therefore Rapier equipment should be loaded in the most accessible place in the LSL in which it was travelling; the upper vehicle deck. However, the electronics and other sensitive equipment associated with each Rapier firing post were likely to be badly damaged by salt spray, so the Battery was stowed in the lower vehicle deck. There was insufficient space to leave the upper vehicle deck free to speed up the unloading of Rapiers, and this was occupied by a light gun battery, which would have to be lifted ashore first, notwithstanding its lower priority. This would allow the LSL's crane to plumb the hatchway to the lower vehicle deck, lifting each firing post to the upper vehicle deck. Helicopters would not be able to approach, however, until the crane had been stowed. This laborious and time-consuming process is described in detail to give some idea of the problems facing staffs planning an amphibious operation with insufficient purpose-built amphibious ships and ship-shore movement assets.[15]

The re-stow at Ascension Island would have been far easier, and accomplished in less than the twelve days it took, had there been a port with slipways to accept the roll-on-roll-off (Ro-Ro) ferries and LSLs, and room to unload most of the vehicles and stores; and thus start again more or less from scratch. There was no port. The operation was conducted at anchor in Georgetown roads, which is subject to the ceaseless mid-Atlantic swell, deceptively smooth when viewed from the deck of a large ship, but demanding great skill on the part of the coxswains of landing craft and Mexeflotes heaving up and down at the stern ramps and bow doors of Ro-Ros and LSLs, while vehicles were gingerly edged on and off; or alongside while ships' cranes plumbed over the side dangling loaded trucks or light tanks. The logisticians had to play a complex puzzle game, the movement of one 'piece', truck or equipment, from ship to ship, almost invariably required several other 'pieces' to be moved first. All over the anchorage, floating 'parks' of vehicles and stores on Mexeflotes could be seen, bobbing in the swell, while they awaited their turn to come to the ship, or ships, to deliver their loads, and take more.

Helicopters were used for the lighter, and accessible loads, but their use was restricted by two considerations. First, the need to conserve engine hours against the day when helicopters would be required for the assault landing, and subsequent tactical and logistic tasks. Second, they were in demand for rehearsals and trials. These were necessary, mainly to establish parameters for timings in preparation for the eventual landing. The planning staffs were familiar, through long practice, with the time needed to fly off a given number of men from a purpose-built amphibious ship. But nobody knew how long it would take to lift, say, a battalion from the two helicopter decks recently fitted to the *Canberra*, each one-spot.[16] Timings, including routes for troops and loads to reach flight decks, must be established for each STUFT. For the same reason, rehearsals with landing craft were necessary, particularly as some troops, principally the two parachute battalions, had no experience in landing craft. Logistical requirements took priority, however, and rehearsals and trials were reduced to the minimum; each battalion and commando achieved one by day and one by night, except for 2 Para, who arrived at Ascension too late for anything except one daylight practice loading into landing craft. There was no time for a full scale rehearsal, even a turn-away landing.[17] Anyway, there was no beach large enough, and the only landing zone for helicopters, because of dust ingestion problems everywhere else, was busy Wideawake. Finally, frustrating the logisticians, by preventing night working, all the ships weighed anchor and steamed out to sea as a precaution against attack by Argentine submarines or, more likely it was thought, frogmen delivered by a merchant ship.

The Logistic Concept

The logistic concept was based on keeping supplies afloat in the beachhead area in order to save time, ship-shore movement assets spent in unloading, and to avoid a large dump ashore. Hardstanding and space was at a premium, even at the most promising location, Ajax Bay. Furthermore, it was the Brigade Commander's intention to make maximum use of the sea flank for the movement of supplies, to cut down on helicopter lift. As part of the re-stow, the Logistic Regiment loaded two Landing Ships Logistic (LSLs) *Sir Galahad* and *Sir Percivale* with two days' stocks of combat supplies for the Brigade, mainly ammunition of all natures, packed fuel, and rations. (One day's supply for the Brigade was based on the Daily Combat Supply Rate, one DCSR weighed 95 tons). A further four days and sixteen days were held on RFA *Stromness* and MV *Elk*[18] respectively. Once *Stromness* had offloaded 45 Commando, she and *Elk* could, if necessary, be held off, at the outer edge of the TEZ, until their stores were required. At which point empty LSLs could steam out to meet them to replenish, or *Stromness* and *Elk* could enter the beachhead and replenish the LSLs there. This allowed a flexible logistic plan, providing for two possible landing options, as well as dividing the assets in case one of the LSLs was sunk. SS *Canberra* was designated as the Main Dressing Station for the Brigade. Casualties would be evacuated to her by helicopter, and subsequently to the *Uganda*. However, a Field Dressing Station (FDS) was to be landed, capable of holding casualties for up to six hours, and carrying out stabilisation and resuscitation of casualties, should immediate evacuation to the Main Dressing Station from Regimental Aid Posts (RAPs) be impracticable for operational or other reasons. This was the grand conception; we shall see how it worked in practice.

*   *   *

Five LSLs with the majority of the Brigade's logistic personnel, and the Commanding Officer of the Logistic Regiment embarked, sailed from Ascension on 30 April. The main body of the Amphibious Group waited for the arrival of 2 Para Battalion Group, coming south in the MV *Norland*, MV *Europic Ferry*, and a follow-up contingent of the Commando Logistic Regiment, under the Regimental Second-in-Command, in HMS *Intrepid* (the second of the two Landing Platforms Dock (LPD), the specialised assault ships. Headquarters 3rd Commando Brigade was embarked in the first, HMS *Fearless* (see

FIG. 8.2   LPD docked down, stern gate open, two Sea King helicopters on flight deck (*IWM*).

FIG. 8.3   Fork-lift truck and LCU (*IWM*).

page 272). These ships are specifically designed to provide good command facilities in addition to the carriage of heavy vehicles and equipment needed in the assault upon a beach. A complement of large landing craft (Landing Craft Utility (LCU)) is carried in the special internal dock of the ship from where they are launched, fully laden, through the ship's stern doors. A number of smaller craft (Landing Craft Vehicle and Personnel (LCVP)) are carried at davits. For lack of space, and against the advice of the Air Defence Battery Commander, the Brigade Commander decided to leave the Rapier optical repair vehicle and second-line repair fitters at Ascension to follow on as soon as possible. This was an error, because they were delayed for six weeks.

*   *   *

Closing the Falklands

The main body sailed from Ascension on 7 May, by which time it was clear that it was highly unlikely that the air battle would be won before the landing. However, it was too late to change the logistic concept or the loading of the ships based on a commitment that the air battle would be won, which was now proving to be false. Although Admiral Woodward, and his Carrier Battle Group, and the Vulcans, all did their utmost to reduce the strength of the Argentine Air Force. The Vulcan raid on Stanley airfield on 1 May, and follow-up by Sea Harriers (SHARs) the same day, made it impossible for the Argentines to operate Mirages or Skyhawks from the Falkland Islands, which would have been feasible after a modest improvement to the airfield. On this and subsequent days, several Argentine aircraft had been shot down while attacking ships of the Carrier Battle Group, mainly those close to the Falklands on bombardment duty in daylight. SHAR and GR3 attacks, and bombardments continued to harass the airfield.

The Air Threat

However, the Argentine Air Force plainly intended to reserve its main effort for attacks on the Amphibious Group. This was sensible, because the Carrier Battle Group could not win the war, although they could lose it in an afternoon if not properly handled. Unless raids were mounted against mainland Argentine bases, which was understandably politically unacceptable, the air battle could not be won before the amphibious operation was carried out. In retrospect, statements about the air battle being won before landing, were misleading, because there was little prospect of achieving such a situation. It would have been less confusing if all concerned had been told from the outset that the landing would go ahead anyway; since this was obviously the intention. With hindsight, Thompson, who was perfectly capable of working this out for himself, should also have ensured that the logistic plans catered for an off-load into the beachhead on arrival, which in the event is what happened. The operation would have been better served had there been more frankness from the beginning. This would have allowed more open discussion of the problem with the Headquarters at Northwood, in the course of which, among other things, it could have been made plain that an offload would buy up all ship-shore movement assets for several days, precluding any tactical moves out of the beachhead, thus avoiding subsequent acrimonious discussion on the satellite communication system. Plain speaking would have avoided misunderstandings about how quickly Rapier firing posts would have been in action. It was exactly this situation, among others, that called for a higher level overall commander forward with the three task groups.

However, at least the naval surface threat to the amphibious group was nil. The sinking of the *Belgrano* led to the Argentine Navy returning to port for the rest of the war.

D-Day: 21 May

Meanwhile the Brigade Commander had given orders on 13 May, for a landing on three beaches inside San Carlos Water on a day and time to be confirmed. These orders were repeated to the Commanding Officer of the Commando Logistic Regiment on 16 May when the main body of the Amphibious Group made their rendezvous with the LSLs. Ajax Bay was designated the Brigade Support Area, because there was more room behind that beach than in rear of any of the others in San Carlos Water. An added attraction was the disused mutton factory, which would provide overhead cover from the elements for the FDS, advanced workshop and ordnance detachments and some technical stores. On 19 May D-Day was confirmed as 21 May, with an H-hour of 2.30 am local time.

The Effect of Argentine Air Attacks on Logistics

The landings went well, with some delays. There was no opposition on the ground and all objectives were secure halfway into the morning.

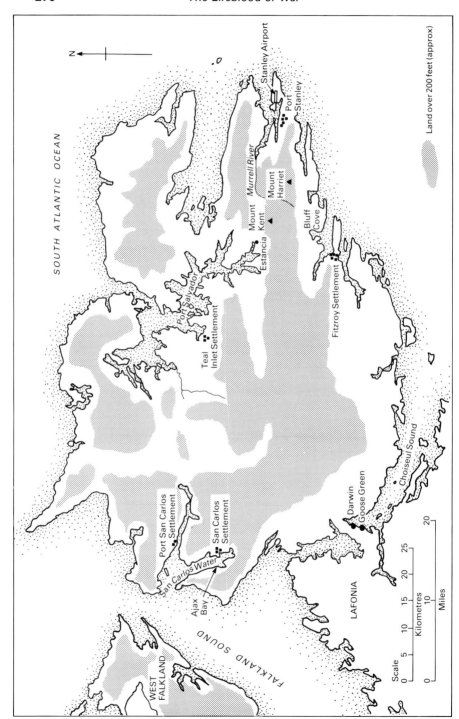

Land over 200 feet (approx)

N

SOUTH ATLANTIC OCEAN

Stanley Airport

Port Stanley

Murrell River

Mount Kent

Mount Harriet

Estancia

Bluff Cove

Port Salvador

Fitzroy Settlement

Teal Inlet Settlement

Port San Carlos Settlement

San Carlos Settlement

San Carlos Water

Ajax Bay

FALKLAND SOUND

WEST FALKLAND

Darwin

Goose Green

Choiseul Sound

LAFONIA

Scale

0   5   10   15   20   25

Kilometres

0   5   10   15   20

Miles

MAP XII   East Falkland 1982

However, the number of Argentine air attacks throughout the day led to the decision that all non-essential ships, including *Canberra* and *Norland*, would be sent out of the anchorage under the cover of darkness, to join the Carrier Battle Group well to the east. The LSLs were to remain, offload, and sail to the East on completion. The plan to use *Canberra* as a floating FDS had to be abandoned. Before she sailed, as much as possible of the FDS had to be unloaded to the mutton factory at Ajax Bay, the only possible place in the beachhead. *Norland* offloaded the Parachute Clearing Troop (PCT) of 16 Field Ambulance. There was insufficient time to get all the medical personnel off *Canberra*, and she sailed off with part of a dressing station and a complete Surgical Support Team (SST). One SST belonging to the Commando Brigade was still in HMS *Hermes*, where they remained until the end of the war. *Canberra* and *Norland* also took with them the unit stores of two commandos and both parachute battalions. They did not see most of them until after the war was over. These stores ranged from vital replacement battle batteries, to first line stocks of ammunition not carried on the men, such as mortar, Milan and Wombat anti-tank rounds, and a complete resupply of small arms ammunition. Also in *Canberra* when she sailed were 90,000 rations, enough to feed the Brigade for eighteen days. As a consequence the Logistic Regiment immediately had to start meeting the urgent demands of units deprived of their own back-up supplies, while at the same time working round the clock to offload the LSLs and STUFT.

. . . and Hence on the Final Outcome

Fortunately, on the first day, the Argentine Air Force concentrated their attacks on the warships in San Carlos Water, and Falkland Sound. Not one logistic ship, STUFT or troop carrrier was hit; had the Argentines sunk several of these, the logistic situation would have been very serious; although it is difficult to be specific about what effect such sinkings would have had on the eventual outcome. Major factors to take into account in any assessment, would have been the types of ships sunk or destroyed, numbers of casualties, quantities and types of supplies lost, how many craft and Mexeflotes were damaged or destroyed, and the effect these losses had on British public opinion, and hence on the Government's will to continue the war (the most damaging to the landing forces would have been substantial losses of fuel). Once the bulk of the men, equipment, SAMs, and guns were ashore, with enough ammunition to defend the beachhead, and with naval gunfire and air support, the Argentines would have found it difficult to dislodge them. Therefore, depending on the scale of losses, and providing these did not lead to faltering, either at political or military level, the British would still have had a chance to win. However, there is little doubt that such a situation would have led to a much longer war, while more supplies, further back in the line of communication, were brought up and offloaded.

The Assault and Subsequent Advance

Meanwhile, the offload proceeded as best it could, with the limited ship–shore movement assets available. To begin with, STUFT was only allowed into the anchorage during the hours of darkness, which, allowing passage time to and from the eastern edge of the TEZ, restricted offloading time to four hours. Helicopters could not operate from STUFT at night, so all unloading was by Mexeflote and LCU. In darkness, in swell up to six feet in height, the difficulties of unloading ships that were not purpose-built for amphibious operations became even more apparent. In many cases the Ro-Ro ramp would not match the Mexeflote height, and at times, one end of the raft was lifted out of the water by the Ro-Ro ramp as the ship pitched, endangering the vehicles, men, and fork-lift trucks as they busily shuttled to and fro from ship to raft. The situation was made no easier by the cross-decking of landing force stocks by the Navy, without reference to the Logistic Regiment. This led to ships being called in because they were thought to have specific stores on board, only to discover that they were now somewhere else. The Logistic Regiment took to sending teams on board every STUFT as soon as it arrived in the anchorage, to pick over the stores to see what was on board, and to interrogate the first officer on what, if anything, had been transferred, and to whom. This was both time-consuming and extremely frustrating for the logisticians.

Problems Arising from a Lack of Centralised Command

To add to their problems, the ships that they had requested did not always arrive at the anchorage. Each night the commanding officer of the Commando Logistic Regiment would visit Commodore Clapp aboard *Fearless*, and give him a list of ships to be steamed into the anchorage the following night from the holding position east of the Islands. Clapp, always co-operative, would signal Woodward to ask him to send them in. Often, for operational reasons, the ship, or ships asked for would not arrive. A substitute might come in, sometimes arbitrarily picked and containing none of the stores needed in the beachhead at that particular time. This confusion was a direct result of the lack of an overall commander in the theatre of operations to allocate priorities. From D-Day there were two different battles in progress simultaneously, and when the landing force moved away from the immediate beachhead, there would be three. Drawing together the operational and logistical threads of these battles, miles apart, and usually with conflicting priorities, could not be, and was not, satisfactorily achieved from a headquarters 8,000 miles away, by a commander and staff whose information was frequently out of date by the time it was received.

The command system was further muddled by being altered to that shown below, to reflect the impending arrival of General Moore with another brigade.

COMMAND CHAIN FROM 20 MAY

CTF 317

Admiral Fieldhouse at Northwood England

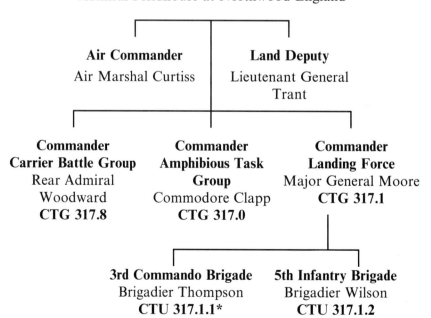

Air Commander	**Land Deputy**
Air Marshal Curtiss	Lieutenant General Trant

Commander Carrier Battle Group	**Commander Amphibious Task Group**	**Commander Landing Force**
Rear Admiral Woodward	Commodore Clapp	Major General Moore
CTG 317.8	**CTG 317.0**	**CTG 317.1**

3rd Commando Brigade	**5th Infantry Brigade**
Brigadier Thompson	Brigadier Wilson
CTU 317.1.1*	**CTU 317.1.2**

* Task *unit*, a curious way to describe a formation of 5,500 men, with eight major *units*, and sixteen *sub-units* under command.

Fortunately signals to Moore were copied to Thompson, who acted on them as if he were the action, rather than the information addressee. The change was made on D-1, when Moore joined the liner Queen Elizabeth at Ascension. In retrospect, Moore believes he and a small tactical headquarters, should have joined the amphibious task force by parachute from a C-130 just before D-day.[19] He could have used the command facilities in the other Landing Platform Dock, HMS *Intrepid*. The change of command structure required him to command a land battle, 4,000 miles away, although getting closer daily, from a passenger liner with no command facilities. The concept might have suited naval command by remote control, designed for operations at sea, but was less than satisfactory for a land battle. A further complication arose, as soon as the *Queen Elizabeth* sailed from Ascension. It transpired that for technical signals reasons, Moore could not communicate with Thompson, and, except for scraps of information gleaned from the maritime communications network, was almost totally ignorant about what was happening in the beachhead, and unable to influence events, until he arrived on D+9.

*   *   *

Helicopter Tasking

For the first few days, helicopter assets were very short. Of the eleven Sea Kings and five Wessex with which the Amphibious Group arrived, one Sea King was permanently allocated to supporting the twelve Rapier sites with fuel for their generators, and providing an immediate maintenance team to keep them in action. Four of the remaining Sea Kings were fitted to allow them to be flown at night with Passive Night Goggle equipment. They spent most of each night inserting Special Forces and other patrols, and, except in an emergency, were not used by day, to allow crew rest and servicing. This left a total of six Sea Kings and five Wessex for logistic and tactical tasks every day. However, many more helicopters at this early stage would have led to another problem. Until the Emergency Fuel Handling Equipment (EFHE), could be installed ashore, helicopters were restricted to refuelling on the one-spot decks of LSLs, or the two-spot decks of the two LPDs in the anchorage. This was time-consuming, and frequently interrupted by air raids. The twenty-one light helicopters of the Brigade Air Squadron were also competing for this fuel.

Fuel Distribution

There was no shortage of bulk fuel, the problem was to get it ashore and distributed. The EFHE had departed in the holds of the STUFT on the evening of D-day, and was subsequently distributed to other ships. When the ships were sailed back to the anchorage off the beachhead, not all the parts could be found. It was eventually assembled, thanks to the ingenuity of the Royal Engineers, initially using just a towed Flexible Fuel Barge (Dracone), connected to the shore by pipeline. Work-boats towed the empty dracones out to a tanker in the anchorage to be re-filled. Eventually the combat engineers of the Commando Engineer Squadron were able to install a system of flexible tanks on shore to which the fuel could be pumped from the dracone, and stored. When the airstrip was established at Port San Carlos, this facility dispensed up to 50,000 gallons of aviation fuel (AVCAT) to Harriers and helicopters each day. However, it was not to achieve this fuelling rate for some time, and all fuel, not just AVCAT, formed the 'critical path' in the whole pattern of supplying the land battle. At Ajax Bay, which held all types of fuel, including drummed AVCAT, there were other problems. The Logistic Regiment's Petrol Troop, being Reservists, were not mobilised, so other men had to take their place, and learn about fuel management on the job. To them fell the time-consuming business of filling jerricans from the bulk containers on the podded trucks. The podded trucks would be embarked on Mexeflotes, and taken to a ship carrying the relevant fuel, diesel oil (dieso), petrol (CIVGAS), or AVCAT. This would be pumped over in a hose to the pods. On completion, the podded trucks would be driven off the Mexeflote into the beach support area (BSA) at Ajax Bay, where the logistic organisation was established under the Commando Logistic Regiment. Despite the shrewd move by the commanding officer of the Commando Logistic Regiment, in insisting on taking 4,000 additional jerricans from the depot at West Moors before leaving the United Kingdom, an acute shortage of these cans was yet another obstacle to be surmounted in the struggle to keep the landing force supplied. Although the most voracious consumers of fuel were helicopters and Harriers, others needed CIVGAS or dieso. On rough terrain, the BV202s drank fuel at a high rate; even when stationary, the engines in command BVs had to be run frequently to keep the radio batteries charged. Raiding craft, used for a multiplicity of tasks, mainly, although not exclusively, tactical, needed frequent re-fuelling. The generator by each of the twelve Rapier firing posts had to be kept

FIG. 8.4　Chinook re-fuelling from rubber bladders at Port San Carlos.
These could be lifted forward (*IWM*).

running, if the missile system was to stay in action. All these, BVs, raiders and Rapiers, could only be refuelled by jerricans. The ability to hold CIVGAS and dieso in bulk at Ajax Bay, became severely limited when the only 10,000 litre rubber pillow-tank available, was holed by aircraft cannon shells, as was the Mexeflote transporting it ashore.

Problems of Lift and Movement

Lack of dedicated assets to move supplies was another problem. The organisation of the Logistic Regiment, and indeed all the plans for the brigade's employment on NATO's Northern Flank, had assumed that road movement of supplies would be possible. The supply system was based on trucks, all under the direct control of the Logistic Regiment, and hence the Brigade Commander. Helicopters and craft were a bonus or adjunct. Now they were all that was available, but remained under the control of Commodore Amphibious Warfare (COMAW) through-out the war, and could be arbitrarily removed, without warning, even if half-way through a task. Furthermore, there were insufficient Mobile Air Operations Teams (MAOT) to spare one for the Logistic Regiment. So there was no means of joining the helicopter control radio net, to receive warning of incoming helicopters, and tell them to switch to the logistic regiment's VHF frequency in order to direct them to loads, and brief them on the task. The means to move every pallet of ammunition, box of rations and drum of fuel, had to be fiercely bid for against a number of other conflicting demands. The result was that ammunition, particularly gun ammunition, took absolute priority over all other loads. Troops often went short of rations or found themselves without sleeping bags and replacement dry clothing, for lack of helicopters to move their large rucksacks forward. As one experienced rifle company commander saw it:

'All comments and lessons from the logistics of the campaign should be leavened with the fact that this must be one of the few campaigns fought by a regular force since the internal combustion engine became generally available, where the widespread use of wheeled transport was not possible. This, combined with the speed with which it was necessary to put the whole act together, and the enemy's efforts to disrupt the act, makes it arguable that we were fortunate to have any logistics at all!'[20]

Until the logistic offload had been completed, and more helicopters had arrived, any ideas of advancing to the high ground overlooking Port Stanley, the Mount Kent area, had to be postponed. The infantry could advance on foot, but major battles, or repelling counter-attacks on the key positions near Stanley, would require the heavy expenditure of ammunition—shells and mortars in particular. In this terrain, the only way to lift these was by helicopter and there were insufficient helicopters to maintain a substantial force, in contact with the enemy, over the distances involved.[21] The distance could be reduced by taking stores round to Teal Inlet in Port Salvador by LSL, and there was every intention of doing just this. But Port Salvador was overlooked by the very high ground that also overlooked Port Stanley. Until this was in friendly hands, any ships using Port Salvador would be seen, and subjected to air attack at the very least.

Vulnerability to Air Attack

A further consideration was the vulnerability to air attack of the line of communication as the Brigade moved away from the air defence umbrella around San Carlos Water. As well as mainland based fighters, the Argentines had several Pucara ground attack aircraft based on East Falkland. The Amphibious and Landing Forces could not risk losing even a few of the small number of medium helicopters to air interdiction. More helicopters were on the way in *Atlantic Conveyor*, due into San Carlos on the night 25/26 May. But the crucial battle, fought by the ships and Harriers, under Commodore Clapp's control, was for control of the air, so that large-scale ground operations could be conducted outside the air defence umbrella. Until then, movement forward was restricted to a comprehensive reconnaissance programme, designed to prepare the way for the advance to the high ground, including seizing Teal Inlet as an advanced Brigade Maintenance Area.

A Devastating Loss

On the night of 25/26 May, *Atlantic Conveyor* was due to arrive in the beachhead, with her valuable cargo, including four Chinook and five Wessex helicopters, and the engineer plant and equipment intended for the construction of the airstrip at Port San Carlos. The heavy lift helicopters would allow the move of the Brigade to the Mount Kent area to begin the next night. The reconnaissance was in place, on Mount Kent, at Teal Inlet, and on key high ground overlooking the route. As the Brigade staff were putting the final touches to the plan for the move, they were informed that *Atlantic Conveyor* had been sunk, only one Chinook, away on a mission, survived. This helicopter spent the night on HMS *Hermes*, and flew into the beachhead the next day, although it was not made available for landing force tasks until 29 May. With this Chinook arrived a detachment to support and maintain it. However, the maintenance they could effect was minimal since they arrived without spares, tools and documentation; all these were at the bottom of the sea. Two night-qualified crews came ashore, and they and their one helicopter were to provide a sterling service. The aircraft flew 109 hours without servicing, and carried impressive loads. For example, one Chinook could lift three 105 mm guns, and 22 soldiers in one sortie. Other loads included 81 men, all standing up as in the underground in the rush-hour, and on another occasion, 64 casualties. Four of these aircraft would have made an enormous difference to the waging of the land battle.

The sinking of *Atlantic Conveyor* was the most serious loss of the war. Because of the ship sustainability problem alluded to earlier, and the effects of weather on the landing force, it was essential to bring the war to a successful conclusion as soon as possible. The means to do so, trebling the helicopter lift, and the plant and material for speedy construction of a forward airstrip, were removed at a stroke, as were large quantities of tentage to provide cover from the elements for the landing force. Finally, she could have provided a back-up deck in the event of one of the carriers suffering damage, or at a pinch, acted as a carrier, if *Hermes* or *Invincible* was sunk. So her loss, while removing the means to speed up the operation, made an early termination even more imperative.

The airstrip at Port San Carlos was eventually built, thanks to the ingenuity of the Royal Engineers, using matting intended for runway repair at Stanley; a commendable effort without the plant for construction.

The Land Battle Continues

Notwithstanding these drawbacks, the orders to move out of the beachhead were not rescinded, and a raid on the settlements of Darwin and Goose Green, cancelled through lack of helicopter lift was ordered to be re-mounted and amended to include the capture of these places. This is not the place to discuss the wisdom or otherwse of the demand that the two settlements be taken, suffice it to say that it was a diversion from the aim of getting forward to the high ground west of Port Stanley, and delayed that move considerably, because during the two nights and two days that the battle, and the preliminary moves occupied, most medium lift helicopter effort was diverted in support of the battalion engaged in the fighting. Nevertheless, a commando and a parachute battalion moved out from the beachhead on foot, at the same time that the other parachute battalion set off for Darwin and Goose Green. Fortunately they were not involved in any fighting, nor did the Argentines attempt even the smallest attack on the long files of marching infantry. If they had, the logistic support of troops engaged in fighting would have been very tenuous. As it was, many men ran out of rations, not for the last time.

A Damaging Airstrike in the BSA

The logistic support for the Goose Green battle was interrupted by an Argentine air strike on the BSA, which apart from killing 7 men and wounding 32, demolished all of 45 Commando's Milan missiles and firing posts. Of more immediate importance logistically, the air strike destroyed 200 rounds of 81 mm mortar, and 300 rounds of 105 mm in netted loads waiting to be lifted down to the gun and mortar positions supporting the battalion. The outcome was that the battalion's mortars ran out of bombs at a crucial stage in the battle, and there were grave shortages of 105 mm ammunition on the gun position, resulting in the weight of fire laid down being far less than that required to be effective. The shortfall could not be made good during the battle, in daylight, because Argentine Pucara aircraft, based on the Falklands, dominated the air line of communication for a vital few hours, while mist at sea kept the British Harriers deck-bound. This air strike also underlined the need for the BSA and other logistic installations to have adequate air defence. The BSA was at least within the air defence umbrella in San Carlos Water, others which were about to be established would not be so fortunate. An air strike against the landing force logistic assets was potentially far more damaging than any other form of enemy action.

Ammunition Expenditure Mounts

The Goose Green battle showed that the ammunition rates for which the commando brigade's reserves had been stocked were unrealistically low. In fairness, this had been recognised for some years, but Treasury parsimony had prevented an increase in stocks. As a hang-over from its

FIG. 8.5 '. . . heavy expenditure of ammunition'. 105 mm gun and ammunition stack (*IWM*).

days in the Far East and before, the brigade was provisioned to Limited War Rates of ammunition, perfectly adequate for the brush-fire wars on which it had been engaged in the recent past. The small arms ammunition expended at Goose Green and Darwin was four times that of the daily ammunition expenditure rate (DAER) allowed for in limited war, and that of 105 mm guns and 81 mm mortars, five times. This represented an expenditure higher by a factor of 25 per cent than General War Rates (the rate for the most intense operations envisaged in a war against the Warsaw Pact). Not for the first time was the rate at which ammunition was actually expended in war to exceed expectations. Fortunately, the Commanding Officer of the Commando Logistic Regiment, Hellberg, and Baxter, Moore's chief logistician, had agreed during the meeting at Ascension on 17 April, that 30 days worth of ammunition at Limited War Rates might not be sufficient. They estimated that the entire stock of 105 mm and 81 mm ammunition would last only about a week at intense rates of fire. Baxter accordingly arranged for a further 30 days stocks of War Maintenance Reserve, taken from holdings earmarked for other formations, to be sent South well before the landing force arrived in the Falkland Islands. This included additional 30 mm Armour Piercing Discarded Sabot ammunition for the Scimitar light tanks (at that time still trial ammunition), and extra VT and other fuses for 105 mm shells.

The Forward BMA Established

By 2 June, establishment of the Forward Brigade Maintenance Area (BMA) for 3rd Commando Brigade at Teal Inlet was well under way. A Distribution Point (DP) was established at Estancia, the head of the creek nearest to the positions occupied by the Brigade. LSLs could now bring supplies to the Forward BMA, and from there they could be lifted by boat to the DP for collection by units by BV, or a requisitioned farm tractor, or taken by helicopter direct to unit locations from Teal Inlet. This system saved a great deal of helicopter lift, and resulted in a better service to the Brigade than provisioning direct from Ajax Bay. AVTUR in drums was positioned at Teal Inlet, which became the Forward Fuelling and Re-arming Point (FARP) for the Brigade's light helicopters, dispensing with the need for them to fly a 90–100 mile round trip every time they needed replenishment. The use of Port Salvador in this way, capitalising on the amphibious capability and expertise of the Brigade and Clapp's force of ships and craft, had been planned weeks ago, before sailing from Ascension. It was a source of much satisfaction to see it being put into effect and working so well.

A Severe Case of Cognitive Dissonance

The logistic situation in 5th Infantry Brigade (who arrived on 2 June), through no fault of theirs, was less happy. They brought

FIG. 8.6   Chinook lifts load off LPD starboard after spot (*IWM*).

stocks, and the men of two Ordnance companies, but little else; no podded vehicles, no more craft, no Eager Beaver fork-lift trucks; in short, nothing with which to ease the key problem: distribution. Even their stocks were deficient, their 5,000 jerricans were loaded empty, because peace-time regulations were invoked in Britain. Although Board of Trade rules on the carriage of ammunition were waived to allow first line to be carried with troops on passenger ships. But most cargo was not combat loaded, being stowed in the order in which it had arrived at the dockside.[22]

The reason for this paucity of logistic assets was rooted in the uncertainty that attended 5th Infantry Brigade's deployment south.

FIG. 8.7 Forward Arming and Re-fuelling Point (FARP) at Teal Inlet Settlement—Scout helicopters re-fuelling from 40 gallon drum (*IWM*).

The Brigade's primary mission was the 'Intervention Role', a euphemism for the protection and rescue of British Nationals from countries overseas in time of crisis. This, it was assumed, because it was convenient to do so, would be by invitation on the part of the country concerned, or at worst, in the face of very light opposition; a few dissidents equipped with small arms. In short, operations against the sort of enemy that constituted the sole experience of the majority of British servicemen. The Brigade was equipped accordingly. This 'Intervention Role' was a glance in the direction of recognising that something might occur outside the NATO area, requiring a response by the British. Unfortunately it was only a glance, resulting from an over-inflated confidence on the part of officials, politicians, and many military, in their powers of foreseeing the future, and predicting the nature, timing, and place of the next conflict. Although to be fair, there is evidence that before the Falklands war, the Ministry of Defence (MOD), had been planning improvements to the 5th Infantry Brigade's capability; but these had not been implemented by May 1982.[23] Nevertheless, there was plenty of time to make good deficiencies in the Brigade's logistic organisation and equipment, by borrowing from other formations. However, another factor came to the fore; possibly linked to the aforesaid confidence by some in their expertise at operational crystal-ball gazing, and perhaps symptomatic of disbelief in some quarters that there would actually be a war which had not been legislated for in some contingency plan. Apparently, when the formation sailed, there were doubts about whether or not it would be used to fight. It was a view held by some, not by anyone in the original landing force, that 5th Infantry Brigade would only be employed in a garrison role. Why this should be so is a mystery, which will only be explained, when the files are opened to the public, which will not be for another 22 years at the time of writing. It was made perfectly clear, or so Thompson thought, at the council of war at Ascension on 17 April, that the reason that another brigade was required was to reduce the numerical odds from 2:1 against, to about evens. If the reinforcing brigade was not to fight, then what? The reluctance to recognise that it would be used in combat can only be ascribed to a severe case of cognitive dissonance somewhere.

The upshot of this muddled thinking was that the Commando Logistic Regiment, originally established to support a brigade of 3,000 plus, and actually supporting a brigade of 5,500 plus, suddenly found itself supporting a two brigade formation of 9,000, with less movement assets, and manpower, than it would expect for its task of supplying a dependency one-third that size.

Fitzroy

Following the orders to 5th Infantry Brigade to move on the southern axis to Stanley, 3rd Commando Brigade having moved on the northern route, it was decided to establish another forward BMA at Fitzroy, and a DP at Bluff Cove, south-west of Port Stanley to support 5th Infantry Brigade. The supplies for this forward BMA were steamed round to Fitzroy in two LSLs. They remained there in daylight, without any air defence, other than the machine-guns of the troops ashore. Unfortunately, the anchorage was overlooked by high ground to the North-East, not yet secured by British troops. Reports of activity in Fitzroy were sent back to Stanley by the Argentine regiment on Mount Harriet, the high ground referred to earlier. These messages were intercepted by 3rd Commando Brigade's electronic warfare troop, but too late to warn Divisional Headquarters, who in any case could have done little about it, except perhaps warn the LSLs. The ships were bombed with the loss of 43 dead and over 200 wounded; the price for lack of air defence, and committing the military sin of venturing into a valley, in this case a cove, before securing all the dominating high ground. However, despite the loss of stocks, and 5th

Brigade's FDS, all was not gloom. The activity at Fitzroy served to confirm the Argentine assessment that the main thrust for Stanley would come from the South-West; the easier route. Whereas it would come from the North-West and West, by 3rd Commando Brigade.

It must be said that the risky operation at Fitzroy was the result of pressure to conclude the war before the ship sustainability situation became irreversible, with the Navy having to withdraw ships from the theatre. 'Backseat driving' from Northwood was a contributory factor in the losses incurred. They forbade Clapp to send an LPD on a third trip to the south of Fitzroy to unload by landing craft at night. Had there been an overall commander nearer the scene of operations, much of this might have been avoided.

The Final Build-Up: More Problems for 5 Brigade

The logistic build-up for the final battles, aimed, among other things, at stocking gun positions with 480 to 500 rounds per gun. After the first night battles, on the night 11/12 June, when 3rd Commando Brigade seized all their objectives, it was intended that 5th Brigade should attack the Phase 2 objectives the following night. The Commanding Officer of the Commando Logistic Regiment attended the orders group of Commander 5th Brigade. For some reason no Gunners were present (probably another result of the *ad hoc* nature of this brigade, which had no artillery regiment on establishment, and thus no regimental commander to advise the Brigade Commander). After listening to orders, the Commanding Officer of the Logistic Regiment stated that following the attack by 3rd Commando Brigade the previous night, the gun positions were extremely low on ammunition, and it would take at least another day to re-stock, and then only to about 250–300 rounds per gun. After some deliberation, the Commander 5th Brigade asked the Divisional Commander for a 24 hour postponement, which was approved. This proved a blessing to his battalion commanders, who had not had sufficient time to study the ground. In the event, one battery almost ran out of ammunition during the attack on the night of 13/14 June, and only some expert flying by the 3rd Commando Brigade's light helicopter squadron commander, leading in the Sea Kings with underslung loads of ammunition in darkness and a snow storm, enabled the battery to come into action again. Before the attacks started that night, the only bridge over the Murrell River collapsed under the weight of an armoured recovery vehicle loaded with ammunition, closing 3rd Commando Brigade's only land main supply route (MSR) by which BVs could reach the forward units. The Royal Engineers mounted an ingenious operation which involved building an air-portable bridge at Fitzroy and flying it under a Chinook to replace the damaged bridge and re-open the route.

After the Argentine surrender, fuel continued to dominate the logistic scene for some time, mainly because 3rd Commando Brigade requisitioned all the Argentine transport on arrival in Stanley for logistic use on the network of roads and tracks within and around the town. The Rapier generators too were voracious consumers of CIVGAS, and on one occasion, there were only 90 jerricans of fuel in Port Stanley, 85 allocated to Rapier. Again, distribution, not bulk stocks, was the problem.

Four Lessons

The Ministry of Defence in their report to Parliament highlighted four lessons from the Falklands war.[24] First, the high expenditure of ammunition, including missiles and anti-submarine weapons. Second, and following from the first, that the level of logistic support for operations outside the NATO area needed to be reviewed. Third, the importance of air-to-air refuelling. Fourth, the significance that civil resources can make to defence. On the first and second, one can only comment by saying that they fall into the blinding glimpse of the obvious department; being lessons that did not need to be 'learned', there were plenty of examples in the past to go by, but as Hegel has said:

> 'What experience and history teach us is this—that people and governments never have learned anything from history, or acted on principles deduced from it.'

On the third lesson, the comment might be, 'fair enough', but 'ditto above'. On the fourth lesson, at the time of writing, the merchant navy has been allowed to run down to the extent that a Falklands type operation might be impossible to repeat,[25] without using ships under flags of convenience. Certainly there is no ship that lends itself to being used as a hospital ship. It is even difficult to find enough of the right type of merchant ships to meet the comparatively modest demands of NATO exercises. Again, 'ditto above'.

It was fortunate that the commander of 3rd Commando Brigade was blessed with a highly competent staff, whose achievements are hard to overrate. Herein lies another lesson, a first class, well trained staff can make bricks from very little straw. Conversely a poor staff would have lost the battle for their commander. Lieutenant Colonel

Hellberg, the commanding officer of the Commando Logistic Regiment, deserves special mention. His regiment, like most military organisations, reflected their commanding officer's competence. That they achieved what they did is proof enough of the level of his professionalism.

The Missing 5th Lesson

The Ministry of Defence report alluded to above fails to spell out the most important lesson of all; the relationship between logistics and operations. For all that it is so obvious, it is so often forgotten; if ever learned in the first place. The reasons for 3rd Commando Brigade being unable to advance out of the beachhead on D-day, and for several days after, have been explained, they were above all logistic reasons. Apparently this was never fully understood in Northwood and Whitehall, partly because of the command structure. But also, we contend, because there were few, even the most senior among the military and civilians in the United Kingdom with personal experience of amphibious operations at higher rank, i.e. one star or above. Even the handful at the top of the tree, with considerable experience in the Second World War, had been junior officers, and concerned with leading their platoons and companies, or equivalent tasks. The logistics and movement problems of amphibious, or any other, operations had been no concern of theirs. So when one distinguished Cabinet Minister, interviewed for a television programme after the Falklands war, likened the beachhead at San Carlos to Anzio, by implication that there was lack of drive, he was falling into a trap. In attempting to prove his point by the selective use of military history, he demonstrated his ignorance of the actual reason, and of the logistic imperatives at the operational level. The majority of senior officers and their staffs were handicapped by a dearth of understanding of the logistic realities of fighting a conventional war. Brush-fire wars and Northern Ireland had provided few logistic problems, and most peacetime exercises, with their emphasis on tactical movement, teach false logistic lessons. Commanders on these exercises are seldom faced with the choice between moving men, and moving beans, bullets and fuel. In war, if helicopters are in short supply, and for some reason other means of movement are not available, or cannot be used, the men will walk carrying some of the beans and bullets, and the helicopters will be almost exclusively employed carrying the rest.

Logistics the Driving Factor

In the Falklands, as in previous wars, logistics was the principle factor driving planning. The high rate of expenditure of ammunition was offset by the relative shortness of the battles within what was, itself, a short campaign, and because such a small proportion of Britain's land forces (only two brigades) was involved. Because Britain was not embroiled in a war elsewhere, resources earmarked for other formations could be diverted to sustain this campaign. Total expenditure rates would be vastly higher in a general war, or a conflict on the scale of the Iran/Iraq war. The logistic unpreparedness noted in the chapter on Korea, based on a flawed perception of future conflict, was repeated in the Falklands in the case of 5th Infantry Brigade. Despite there being time to make up the leeway, little was done. The flexibility of sea power was again demonstrated, not only at tactical level, but also logistically, as it had been in antiquity by Alexander the Great, in the Middle Ages by Richard the Lionheart and, in our own era, in North Africa, Italy, Korea and Vietnam, to name but a few examples from the last fifty years.

9

Supplying the War That Never Was—Yet

'I don't know what the hell this logistics is that Marshall is always talking about, but I want some of it.'

Fleet Admiral King USN

'Without the combat readiness of the Soviet Armed Forces Rear Services there is no troop combat readiness. War may begin, but without a well prepared rear, without precise and comprehensive rear support, it would end sadly a few days later. That is why we must make every effort to see that the Soviet Armed Forces Rear Services are always combat ready as the forces they are supporting.'

Marshal Grechko[1]

'That's the reason they're called lessons' the Gryphon remarked: 'because they lessen from day to day.'

Lewis Carroll, Alice's Adventures in Wonderland

As the author said in the Preface, some readers may wonder why this chapter is included. The clue lies in the last quote above. Collective and individual memories are short, and in the flush of the West's victory over the Soviet Union without a shot being fired, two points may be overlooked.

First, despite its economic weakness and commercial and industrial inefficiency, the Soviet Union possessed mighty and highly competent armed forces. Indeed, they were probably one of the few efficient parts of the Soviet Union. They included, and include, some excellent brains, and, as will be discussed, a system of analysis, that made for a very different approach to war-fighting from that in NATO.

Second, despite its ideals, the NATO Alliance had a number of drawbacks. The most serious, as will be explained, being its lack of sustainability. As the author contends, the Soviet Union was deterred by the deterrent, not by NATO's conventional strength. Without nuclear weapons, however gallant a show the West made, and provided the Soviet Union had performed reasonably competently, after a few days, the West would have lost for lack of anything with which to continue fighting. This lack of sustainability had a spin-off in NATO exercises, many of which were 'military minuets', where the forces involved went through the motions as a demonstration in Alliance solidarity. The logistic wonderland behind the facade was evident only to the professionals, and not to all of them. So what? A time may come when an alliance is being constructed, where the imperfections of NATO might serve as a lesson.

Van Creveld in his book *Supplying War*, states that the logistic aspect of war is nothing but an endless series of difficulties succeeding each other. He goes on to wonder how armies managed to move at all, how campaigns were waged, and victories occasionally won. This endless series of difficulties, and things that go wrong is a commonplace, and is exactly what Clausewitz meant when talking about the 'friction of war'.[2] He surmises that logistics makes up as much as 90 per cent of the business of war, and the staff-work involved requires hours, days, and sometimes weeks, of calculations.

From Alexander the Great at one end of Asia, to Giap in Vietnam at the other, there are a host of examples where logistics were the overriding factor in the success or failure of the plan. Bearing this in mind, it would seem, says van Creveld, that the trick is to work out what is the optimum logistic organisation for a given set of circumstances; advance, defence etc. But as he notes:

'In practice there is scant evidence that the task has been attempted by the majority of twentieth century (not to mention earlier) operational planners. Rather *most armies seem to have prepared their campaigns as best they could on an ad hoc basis, making great, if unco-ordinated, efforts to gather together the largest possible number of tactical vehicles, trucks of all descriptions, railway troops, etc., while giving little, if any, thought to the "ideal" combination which, in theory, would have carried them the furthest.*'[3]

We will look at some aspects of NATO and Soviet logistic planning for war in the light of this assertion. Soviet, because, without the Soviet Union there would be no Warsaw Pact. The Warsaw Pact is (or, in the light of recent events, one might say 'was') an extension of the Soviet General Staff, taking its orders directly from that staff. NATO Headquarters in Brussels, consisting of a collection of officers and civilian officials representing all the members of the Alliance, receives its authority from the governments of sixteen sovereign nations acting collectively through the machinery of the North Atlantic Council, and the civil and military structures. So it would not be true to say that without the United States there would be no NATO; almost inconceivable, but not totally, if the threat was sufficient, and the political will was there. But first we need to remind ourselves of some of the logistic trends covered earlier.

Two Logistic Watersheds

The major watershed in military logistics occurred in 1914, with another, during the Second World War. The first watershed was reached when it was no longer true to say, putting it crudely, that logistics are easier when you keep moving, because when you stop, you quickly exhaust the local resources of food for men and the fuel for prime movers, i.e., fodder for your animals. From 1914 onwards the reverse has applied. The reason; the vast increase in ammunition expenditure and the consequent huge expansion in transport to lift it, and, once taken to a chosen spot, the great effort required to relocate it.

The second watershed alluded to was the arrival of the all-mechanised and motorised army, and, since 1953, the use of helicopters. With mechanisation/motorisation, of course, fuel for the horses, in the form of fodder, was replaced by petrol and oil for vehicles, commodities which, regrettably, do not grow in the fields for collection by foraging parties, or provide grazing for vehicles, something which, in horse-drawn days, went some way towards reducing the load of fodder that needed lifting forward. Most Soviet sources agree that in a major offensive, 50 per cent of all supplies by tonnage will be fuel.[4] But, as we shall see, foraging is not completely dead, in some armies.

The Effect of Movement on Logistics

So, static warfare is usually easier to supply than mobile warfare, because ammunition can be stocked, and fuel expenditure reduced. This was as true in the Falklands as in the First and Second World Wars, and in Korea. A rapid advance or pursuit will use fuel, but ammunition expenditure wil usually fall. Whereas a slow, grinding advance will usually use both in large quantities. Soviet tank armies advancing at a rate of between 16 and 45 kilometres a day in 1944–45 suffered only one-third the losses in men and two-thirds the losses in tanks of tank armies advancing only 4.5 to 13 kilometres a day; and consumed a third of the fuel and one sixth of the ammunition.[5] And of course we must remember Clausewitz and his 'friction': weather, terrain, snow, dust, frost, and 'General Mud', will tend to clog the wheels literally and figuratively, making nonsense of the logistic calculations of the staffs, without any effort on the part of the enemy. Erroneous forecasting as to the nature of the battle may have an equally catastrophic effect. If, for example, having prepared logistically for a battle of movement, the opposite happens; as was the case in Russia in July 1941 when Rundstedt's Army Group South, having loaded its supply vehicles with ammunition and fuel on a ratio of 1:2, found itself fighting hard and moving slowly, which led to drastic shortages of ammunition. By 1 August, this Army Group had only about one sixth or one seventh of its basic ammunition load.[6] Alternatively, the Soviet Army Rear Commander who commits his vehicles to the road loaded with ammunition for a planned artillery barrage in preparation for a breakthrough will look very foolish if, at the last moment, no breakthrough is needed, but instead the enemy withdraws and a rapid pursuit commences, as happened to 6th Guards Tank Army in Manchuria in 1945.[7]

In the Second World War the Germans were, generally speaking, better disciplined and less prone to the wasteful habits of the United States and, to a lesser extent, of the British Armies. They were, therefore, able to exist on far fewer supplies than the British and Americans. A German division, albeit smaller, consumed 200 tons per day, compared with about 700 tons per day for a British or American division. Even so, a major reason why the final German offensive in the West, in the Ardennes, ground to a halt, was the lack of fuel (although, at one time, they were, in fact, within a few hundred yards of 3 million gallons of fuel on the Walmes–Malmedy road, which would have gone a long way towards solving their POL problem).[8] Enough of historical examples.

NATO Logistic Planning

Let us turn to NATO logistic planning as it stood at the time of writing (Summer 1990). It is not the intention to dwell on the problem of outloading stocks and moving them and personnel across to mainland Europe, SACEUR's Rapid Reinforcement Plan (RRP). A recent study,[9] concluded that *if adequate time is available* (some would say a big 'if'), the RRP will work; although the figures are impressive, with 1,000 American sailings to Britain and Europe, 2 million tons of freight to the United Kingdom and 10.5 million tons of freight and

1.4 billion gallons of fuel to Europe. However, there are still some snags. Studies carried out on the effects of activities that would have had to be carried out concurrently with the RRP, such as the evacuation of dependants from the British Army of the Rhine, and the recall of units away on training, at Suffield in Canada and in other locations, throw doubts about whether the system would have borne up under the strain. For example, the British national option for reinforcing Germany with the 2nd Infantry Division in advance of SACEUR's RRP, might have clashed with the arrival of the III United States Corps—an event that would have tied up a great deal of rolling stock in Germany during the movement of pre-positioned stocks. It was not known whether this meant that 1st British Corps would have been unable to load their stocks on to wagons until the American corps had completed its moves. There was therefore a paradox which could apply in the future—the greater the speed and success with which the United States reinforced Europe, the greater the potential clash of priorities.

But on the whole, the staff work has been done, and provided the potential enemy did not interfere (another big 'if'), and the weather is reasonably kind, what is in effect a 'get you in service' logistic plan would probably have worked. But, one has misgivings that for a plan made in peacetime, without the pressures associated with planning in war, the result is not all that convincing. It has that 'shop window' look about it which permeates so many NATO plans and activities. Behind corps' rear boundaries, where the national Lines of Communication of five member nations pass through the Low Countries, with an alternative through France, the 'tram' lines, are more like a 'big bag of spaghetti', according to a recent Quartermaster General of the British Army. Having arrived, would the logistic plan have worked when battle was joined? The first problem was, and is, the lack of a NATO operational doctrine from which the logistic doctrine should flow. But the matter of an operational doctrine is outside the scope of this book. Instead we will ask three questions in the present tense, since, at the time of writing, the forces were still in place:

a. Is the logistic command and control satisfactory?
b. Is the logistic system satisfactory?
c. What is the sustainability of NATO forces?

Command and Control

First, command and control.

'Operational planning consists of an intimate blend of tactical and logistic thinking to carry out strategic concepts. This unity and coherence is essential to swift, decisive military action in any type of human conflict . . . in combat the logistic support that may be considered inadequate by a timid or mediocre commander may be adequate for a bold and competent commander who understands the nature and source of flexibility, provided he has adequate control of a flexible logistic system.'[10]

Does a NATO commander of a multinational force have unity of command and adequate control of the logistic system, let alone a flexible one? The NATO Logistics Handbook lays down two principles which were set out in two sentences in the North Atlantic Council Resolution of 23 February 1952:[11]

First sentence: 'The responsibility for logistic support to national component forces will, in general, remain with the responsible authorities of the nations concerned.'
Second sentence: 'The responsibility for co-ordination will, however, rest with the Supreme Commander and with his major subordinate commanders at the appropriate levels.'

At first glance these are comfortable words because any unease that might be engendered by the opening sentence, with its implication that national authorities have a free hand to decide on the level of support for their components, is assuaged by the mention of co-ordination in the second sentence; and it is this that we will address first. Co-ordination can mean all things to all men: from the mere passing of information, to the issue of firm direction, but as the NATO handbook says, both are wrong. Under the NATO agreed definition of co-ordination, the co-ordinator has the authority to require consultation between the agencies involved, but does not have the authority to compel agreement. It is not therefore surprising that without the power to enforce agreement, logistic co-ordination is at best patchy, and at worst non-existent. And logistics is, after all, the creation and sustained support of forces and weapons to be tactically employed in order to gain strategic objectives.[12]

So, for example, if one corps's national logistic capacity becomes critically low, the Army Group headquarters may recommend a reallocation of stocks between National Logistic Support Commands (NLSCs). If the other national authorities involved refuse to transfer stocks, the Army Group Commander has to refer it to the Commander-in-Chief Central Region (CINCENT), who then negotiates with the Ministries of Defence concerned. Thus tactical and logistical responsibilities are separated and command is divided, contrary to lessons learned from previous campaigns. It is proper to ask how plans can be made without control of logistic support. The problems which arise from the lack of comprehensive planning may result in the deferment or even abandonment of a military operation. Because neither CINCENT or the Army Group Commanders in the Central Region have at their disposal logistic command elements, logistic units, logistic troops or stocks. Despite the fact that tactics and logistics are inseparable, neither the Army Group Commanders, or any other NATO land commanders commanding more than one national component, have the power to employ or re-deploy nationally provided operational support capabilities or resources. They can only monitor them. The same is applicable in the Southern and Northern Regions. So in fact the Army Group Commanders may command the troops, but they do not have under their hands the 'beans, bullets, and fuel', or the means of moving these commodities. Therefore they do not command the troops in the full sense of the word. They are commanders in name only.[13] Only national corps commanders have the wherewithal with which to plan and conduct their parts of the land battle. The Army Group Commanders may be forced into reacting rather than acting. Alternatively, the Army Group Commanders may arrive at decisions by considering only tactical facts with no logistic input: or may obtain information from National Logistic Support Commands who cannot apply any tactical weighting to their advice and data. The result is likely to be that the redeployment of formations to maintain cohesive balance or build-up for a counter-attack, for example, will be made almost impossible because higher commanders, that is the Allied commanders, do not have adequate logistic information on which to base redeployment and reinforcement decisions; and even if they had, they lack the means, and as we shall see shortly, the system and stocks.

Problems of Incompatibility

We now return to the first of those two sentences from the NATO logistic handbook; 'Logistics is a national responsibility'. What started as an obligation to provide adequate resources to support operations in particular NATO Regions and Allied Commands has, with the passage of time, become an excuse for NATO inaction and national failure to meet their commitments. Incompatible logistic systems abound.

There are two points of view, and one grey area. The first point of view is held by those who consider logistics so inextricably involved with national sources of money and material that it can never be collectivised. The second is adhered to by those who agree that the doctrine of national responsibility for logistics 'has long seemed inefficient and wasteful in an area like the Central Front in Europe, where forces of neighbouring countries are due to operate side by side, and where lines of communication pass through each other's territories and sometimes cross.'[14]

EUROLOG has now produced 'Principles of Co-operation in Logistics', approved by the Ministries of Defence of Belgium, the United Kingdom, Germany, and The Netherlands. Thus four nations in Northern Army Group, but not in the Central Region, or the Alliance as a whole, aim to achieve the 'closest possible integration of logistic systems'. But this is the grey area, what does it mean? The document does admit that progress is dependent upon

> 'fundamental changes in the arrangements for financing the procurement of equipment and also on the achievement of a much greater standardisation of weapons and equipment than exists at present.'

These financial and equipment rearrangements can only be effected over a long period of time.

> 'But logistics has traditionally been the Cinderella of military science. Operational plans remain on paper and do not involve expenditure until the emergency begins, whereas logistic plans require immediate translation into materials and money.'[15]

The result is that national corps operate on their own 'logistic tramlines'. Cross-corps boundary logistics is at best difficult, and at worst impossible. Routes for cross-corps boundary reinforcements are already pre-planned and movement control centres will be established. But, for example: there are three different types of tank-gun ammunition; some artillery shells are the same, but the fuzing and charges are different, requiring different tables and computer settings. Fuel is interoperable, but the methods of resupply are different; the United States and the British use bulk fuel resupply, whereas the Belgians use a jerrican pack system. And there are no plans for an interoperable logistic support system for Airmobile operations, of which much is being made at present; one detects the hand of the tacticians with their sweeping moves across country with the stroke of a chinagraph pencil. Again, taking Northern Army Group as an example, there are differences in all Corps in the level to which the push/pull logistic system operates, i.e. how far forward supplies are delivered automatically, and how far back units have to go to collect. There are other differences.[16]

All this militates against a cohesive Army Group battle, let alone Central Front, Northern or Southern Flank battle.

Sustainability

We now come to the third question, sustainability. NATO does not have an agreed definition of the term, but SACEUR has approved the following for circulation by the Military Agency for Standardization (MAS) for comment and approval by nations:

> 'Sustainability: the ability of forces to maintain the necessary level and duration of combat activity to achieve their objectives. This requires having sufficient personnel, equipment and stocks on hand and also having the ability to resupply and reinforce on a continuous basis. Sustainability is normally expressed in days. It then reflects the commander's subjective assessment of the overall capabilities of his command to sustain military operations.'[17]

Most nations in the Alliance would agree that sustainability is important. But the last part of that definition makes it clear, once one had unravelled the 'NATO-speak' in which it is pronounced, sustainability in NATO is an educated guess, which of course depends upon the standard of military education of the commander.

The Soviet Approach to Logistic Planning

How long would the war have lasted and at what intensity would it have been fought? There are no official NATO pronouncements on this subject, but, as will become clear later, the levels to which Alliance members stock, indicates a belief, or perhaps a hope, that the war would be short. Perhaps an answer will emerge by looking at the other side. The enemy thinks too! How long does he believe it might have lasted? There are indicators in Soviet military writing that they have envisaged a longer war than some in NATO might imagine. Colonel General Gareyev, in 1985, then the Chief of the General Staff's Military Science Directorate, criticised earlier Soviet military theory which had stressed the inevitability of escalation to massive nuclear use. He asserted that Soviet writers of the 1960s and 1970s had failed to foresee that the 'accumulation and modernisation' of nuclear arsenals would reach such proportions that 'a mass use of these weapons in a war would bring catastrophic consequences for both sides.[18] This fact, coupled with Western and Soviet efforts to spur the development of high-accuracy conventional weapons systems, led him to the conclusion that the 'possibility of a comparatively long war with the use of conventional weapons is increasing.' The long war theory is not new, the Soviets have acknowledged for some years the need for being prepared for a war that lasts for at least a year. Soviet military scientists appear to see no contradiction between the anticipation of an extended conflict on the one hand, and the likelihood on the other, that the new systems would dramatically increase the tempo of conventional operations. They have apparently concluded that the combination of attrition, interdiction of forward-deploying forces, disruption of control, and simply, the increased complexity of operations, may entail shorter and more intense battles, but longer wars. There is no contradiction in this assumption. Consequently, regardless of whether the war is nuclear or conventional, 'it is necessary to be prepared for a long, stubborn, and bitter armed struggle.' One could argue that the recent pronouncements by Mr. Gorbachev, and events in Eastern Europe, have made this so unlikely as to be no longer worthy of consideration. However, the NATO military have to prepare to face the likely enemy's *potential* to wage war, dealing in capabilities and possibilities. Whatever Gorbachev says or does, the Soviet General Staff's duty will be to continue to be planning to fight and win a war.[19] Furthermore, the path of *perestroika* is a rocky one and even the boldest optimist would not deny that Gorbachev's own position is highly vulnerable.

Viability

Assuming that the Soviets retain a war-fighting and offensive capability, would they propose to support a long war? What is their Sustainability? There is no such word in the Russian language. The word most closely equated to the NATO definition is 'Viability', and they use it in a much broader context to include (and the list is not exhaustive): training; the quantity and quality of weapons and equipment; the organisation of formations, and the various arms and services; as well as supply, reinforcements and repair. The word 'Sustainability' carries a connotation of the supplying of material needs. Whereas in the Soviet Army a whole range of subjects, that in NATO armies are the exclusive domain of the operational staffs, are closely integrated with logistics to constitute the *viability* of the army. Differences in the Soviet approach to assessing the problem go further than that. They rely on a scientific system of battle planning to reduce to a minimum the uncertainties of conflict, in all the disciplines, including logistics. They also take great pains to use military history, or military experience, to analyse wars, post-1941, including the various Arab/Israeli encounters, the Falklands and their own operations in Afghanistan. By a combination of historical and technical analysis they arrive at a detailed and quantitive assessment of battlefield needs, including the stress of battle on the men. They also have a comprehensive and common military doctrine, and standing operating procedures throughout the Warsaw Pact. None of these advantages, as we have already seen, are enjoyed by NATO.[20]

Categorisation of Reserves

Based on their past experience, the Soviets divide their reserve stocks into four categories: emergency, mobilisation, strategic and state reserves. Emergency reserves are located with deployed ground forces, and are to be used for the immediate conduct of military operations. Mobilisation reserves are to be used to replace combat losses. Strategic reserves are under the control of the General Staff, and are not planned for early use. State reserves are those resources over and above the stockpiles under military control. Strategic and state reserves must be adequate to supply the armed forces continuously until industry is able to expand its production and meet wartime demands. Based on their Second World War experience, this is likely to be 90 days supply of ammunition, fuel, technical supplies and other items.[21] The expense is enormous. Translated into NATO terms, the cost of one day's worth of ammunition for 1st British Corps is in the order of £200 million.

The System of Supply

Do they have a supply system? Is it still as reported by Fitzroy Maclean in 1945?

> '... we emerged on to the main road and joined a continuous stream of Red Army trucks, tanks and guns flowing northwards into battle. One thing in particular struck us now, as it had struck us from the first, namely, that every Soviet truck we saw contained one of two things: petrol or ammunition. Of rations, blankets, spare boots or clothing there was no trace. The presumption was that such articles, if they were required at all, were provided at the expense of the enemy or of the local population. Almost every man we saw was a fighting soldier. What they carried with them were materials of war in the narrowest sense. We were witnessing a return to the administrative methods of Attila and Ghengis Khan.'[22]

Soviet divisions still have a mobile, streamlined, logistic tail. The bulk of logistic resources are held at Army and Front level, whose headquarters have the responsibility for supply forward, 'two down' if required. But this centralised control gives the senior commander a great deal of flexibility in deciding which axes to support, and which to abandon, and it enables him to concentrate his effort on the chosen axes very quickly indeed—rather different from NATO Army Group commanders. Soviet priorities for supply are: ammunition, POL, spares and technical support, food and medical supplies and clothing; in that order. Reflecting their doctrine they regard the supply of fuel as the greatest challenge, and have evolved a system of tactical pipelines to cope with the problem. But it is interesting to see that they still include in their principles of the rear services, that of making maximum use of local resources. Foraging for food and for POL particularly, is still considered to be of great importance if the length of the battle exceeds the planned period. The intendence or quartermaster service has butchery and grain grinding facilities. All units have cooks well used to dealing with totally unprepared foodstuffs, raw grain, cattle on the hoof and such like. Their engineers of the fuel service are equipped with pumps which could be used to evacuate the tanks of service stations overrun intact. In this respect they have retained a capability as old as warfare itself. As a consequence of their doctrinal approach, viability is not a subjective evaluation. The Soviet commander is able to establish his combat requirement before the war starts. He does not have to make a subjective judgement, or in plain English, guess, whether he can sustain his battle. It may be some consolation to reflect that the Soviets themselves are becoming worried that their 'sums' may be inadequate for accurate prediction, or too long-winded to permit rapid reaction. Furthermore, they do not always implement their system very well due to national inefficiency.[24]

Fighting Hard and Moving Fast

However, the Soviet commander would not have had it all his own way. Committed to a doctrine which demands a high tempo of operations, fighting hard and moving fast, he would have been consuming huge quantities of ammunition and fuel. It has been assessed that in order to provide these supplies the Soviet Army would have had to use every wood, village, and town to hide them, and every road and track to move them up. These areas should be well known to NATO and, we assume, had already been targeted. Some assessments predict that, as a result, Soviet formations would have been unable to maintain this tempo, calling for an advance averaging fifty miles a day. Although, as Donnelly has pointed out, these figures are based on calculations to determine the capacity of roads, and other routes. The saturation of the battlefield, and resulting immobility is a strong reason in Soviet eyes, for reducing force density on both sides in order to return the advantage to the offensive, i.e. to them.[25,26] The Soviets have given this a great deal of thought in the light of historical study, including the Yom Kippur War of 1973, and, it is safe to assume, the Iran/Iraq war. Their logistic system to cope with the war they have envisaged is discussed below.

As Donnelly has pointed out, the Russian word 'TYL' meaning 'rear', embodies two very wide-embracing concepts. First, it denotes the homeland with all its industrial production capacity, its human and material resources from which the state draws its military strength. Second, it refers to the entire rear services of the Armed Forces.[27]

The Rear Services

To co-ordinate and control the Rear Services in peace and war, the Soviets have a Chief of Rear Services, a Deputy Minister of Defence. He has direct responsibility for logistics planning, procurement, resource allocation and administration. In war, his responsibilities included Warsaw Pact logistics. It is as if the American Deputy Secretary for Defence had a controlling and co-ordinating function over the whole of the NATO Alliance, with the authority to go with it. This centralised logistic control permeates down through the Soviet Army, again in contrast to NATO, where each national corps or group of corps has its own logistic system.

Fitzroy Maclean's description, quoted earlier, of the Soviet logistic system is as apposite in a general sense today as it was forty-five years ago. The Soviet Army still maintains a strict control of supply priorities, and a ruthless determination to maintain its aim in any operation. Nevertheless, as tactics and equipment have changed, so have the rear services. The Soviets believe that success in future war against a major opponent, NATO or China, will depend on their ability to achieve surprise and maintain a continuous high-speed offensive. To meet the first requirement, surprise, the main objectives must be attained by the forces in being, with only the minimum of pre-war reinforcement. To achieve the second requirement, the armies of the Soviet first strategic echelon must be capable of continuous sustained combat over the whole period of the strategic operation, two weeks or more. They do not under-estimate the difficulties involved, and recognise that these will certainly be greater than in the past.

Organisation of Rear Support: Guidelines

They have laid down broad guidelines for the organisation of rear support, listed below. Although broad, they are, nevertheless, considerably less broad-brush compared with the British and American logistic principles (Chapter One).

1. The organisation of the rear must reflect the character of the war and the nature of the fighting.
2. Reserves must be echeloned in depth and deployed before the war starts.
3. The higher command is responsible for supplying lower formations, units, and sub-units.
4. *All* available forms of transport must be used.
5. Equipment repair assets must be deployed to those areas with the greatest number of repairable vehicles or weapons.
6. The medical services must deploy as near as possible to the areas of the largest number of casualties.
7. Foraging for local supplies must be undertaken wherever possible.

The first principle may seem obvious, but has been broken on numerous occasions in the past by other armies. As will be seen, the Soviet Army tailored its logistic organisation especially for the war in Afghanistan.

The second principle, which demands the establishment of supply bases well forward along all axes of advance, may conflict with the Soviet need to preserve surprise, unless considerable pains are taken to camouflage the pre-positioned stocks in concert with a comprehensive deception plan. The movement of stocks forward could provide an indicator of Soviet intentions.

The third principle, supply forward, has led to considerable underestimates in the West of the logistic capability of the standard Soviet division, leading to the erroneous conclusion that it is not logistically viable. In fact, most of the division's support comes from Army or Front, and the logistic resources are held, and controlled by these formation commanders. Army vehicles will deliver not only to the divisional rear, but also to the regimental rear when battle permits. So instead of operating on corps-level 'tramlines', backwards and forwards along national layers of the sponge-cake style NATO deployment, the Soviet commander can switch support along his desired axes very quickly.

The fourth principle demonstrates the Soviet realisation that the main problem will be moving stocks along congested roads. Their analysis of the rates of expenditure of ammunition and fuel in the Arab/Israeli and Iran/Iraq wars has reinforced the need to use every means possible, including captured transport, to lift supplies forward.

The fifth and sixth principles are proof that the Soviets recognise the nature of the battle they would fight, and flow from the first principle. The battle they intend would be fought on narrow axes. There will be no secure rear areas, and no forward edge of the battle area, or front line. Deep penetrations would result in great distances from the spearhead to the relatively safe rear bases behind the initial start lines. Therefore the Soviet response is to move repair and medical assets well forward. Immediate attention would be given to those men and equipments that are only lightly affected, so that they can be returned to the battle as soon as possible. Equipment needing more in-depth repair would be left for recovery by higher formation workshops, and badly wounded men evacuated to advancing field hospitals. It is a misconception that the Soviet Army has a 'use and throw away' attitude to men and equipment. On the contrary, the Soviets constantly aim to reduce the attrition rate by returning as many lightly wounded soldiers and easily repairable equipment as possible to the battle, in order to keep up the strength of the formation for as long as possible. However, once the formation is badly mauled, it would be replaced by a fresh one; the Soviets do not believe in 'topping up' with reinforcements. The Soviet attitude to casualties, both human and equipment, and its effect on viability, is so important that we will return to it later.

The final principle, making use of local resources, has been alluded to before. The Soviets must be one of the few armies that include it as a principle of logistics; by doing so, they demonstrate their professional and level-headed approach to war-fighting.[28]

A Mix of Movement Resources

The Soviets are clear in their own minds that despite the abundance of cargo vehicles and stocks at their disposal, giving them the potential to support a long war, the main problem will be getting the supplies to where they are needed. Their own experience in war and on exercises, and their study of the Arab/Israeli wars has impressed upon them the voracious consumption of ammunition and fuel in modern war. As a consequence, they are prepared for the effort involved. Their tables and daily estimated requirements take these factors into account.[29] As has been noted earlier, the Soviets still place considerable reliance on the use of railways to assist with the huge movement problem. They recognise that railways are vulnerable to interdiction and have a repair system to cope with damage. Although the capacity of the Soviet Military Transport Aviation (VTA) combined with Aeroflot, is considerable, the tonnages it can move are a drop in the ocean when seen in the context of the vast logistic requirement, in the order of 35,000 tonnes per day per Front;[30] and most of the VTA is likely to be earmarked for airborne operations. Nevertheless, it is probable that airlift would be used to move vital supplies, such as fuel, to formations to maintain momentum, and where there is no other way possible. To this end, the old MI-6 Hook helicopter had been converted into a flying fuel bowser for the rapid refuelling of forward mobile units. In order to spread the load and avoid putting all their eggs in one basket, Soviet commanders and their staffs are trained in formulae which enable them to arrive at the right mix of road, rail, air and pipeline for the movement of men and material to ensure that they arrive at the right place on cue.[31]

Fuel Supply

It was noted earlier, the Soviets believe that fuel would form well over 50 per cent by weight of all supplies in an offensive, about 20,000 tonnes per day per Front. According to Russian press comments, a Soviet commander's nightmare is to have his successful advance or pursuit halted at a critical moment because he has run out of fuel. To cater for this problem, the Soviets have an efficient system which reflects their concern that fuel, or lack of it, should not be a limiting factor in their operational style. Over the last few years they have used a range of rubber fabric reservoirs from 4,000 to 260,000 litres capacity, which can be loaded on to ordinary task vehicles. Some of the larger trucks can carry twelve times as much fuel in these reservoirs as in cans or drums. If a crane is available, the reservoir can be lifted off and dumped, freeing the truck for another task. Fuel economy is taught at all levels, from drivers of all types of vehicle, to officers planning deliveries of supplies, to ensure that whenever possible, vehicles with the lowest fuel consumption are employed for logistic loads.[32]

To move fuel to Army dumps and airfields, tactical fuel pipelines are employed. Specialist Pipeline Laying Troops are dedicated to this task. Pipelines can be laid across country, but it is more common to lay them alongside roads and tracks. Weather and terrain will have a considerable effect on the speed at which the system can be constructed. In favourable conditions a pipeline battalion employing a tracked pipelayer could lay up to 25 kilometres of pipeline a day. With three or four battalions supporting an army (a typical allocation), each laying pipe in its own sector, a total of 75 to 100 kilometres a day could be achieved. The Soviets acknowledge that laying, operating, and maintaining a fuel pipeline in an operational environment is considerably more difficult than might appear at first glance. Action by the enemy, or damage to the pipeline by their own vehicles are but a few of the problems to be overcome. In mountainous terrain, pipe sections have to be shorter, and steep gradients demand special pumping techniques. Additional hazards include rock and snow avalanches, sections washed away by streams and rivers in spate, and pumps freezing. In other situations sand and gravel may cause pump failure. However, despite these and other challenges to be overcome, the pipeline can deliver 20,000 gallons of fuel per hour over considerable distances, leaving roads and transport assets free for the movement of other supplies. Where roads are few, and very congested, as they are on the Northern Flank, the effort involved in laying and protecting a pipeline might well be repaid.

An Accent on Conservation of Supplies

The need to conserve all manner of supplies, and to make do, is inculcated into every Soviet soldier. What appears to be a programme of constant nagging to reduce waste in peacetime is probably good training for thrift in war. Despite the rising expectations of the Soviet citizen and soldier, they would not expect the lavish supplies of non-essentials enjoyed by the United States Army in Korea or Vietnam. And one suspects that in the Soviet Army, in wartime, the sort of logistic vandalism encountered by General Gale in Africa, described in an earlier chapter, would end in the offenders being summarily shot. The Soviet literature on logistics in war is constantly ramming home the message that there will never be enough of the essentials, nevertheless, the mission must be accomplished.

Foraging has been mentioned earlier. The Soviets do not plan on the use of captured weapons and ammunition, it is so difficult to predict how much will fall into their hands in working order, and because of the problems, alluded to earlier, of training men to use all but the simplest unfamiliar equipment in the time available. However, stocks of captured food, fuel, transport, engineer plant, accommodation, and water are very important ingredients in Soviet logistic planning. They do not see repair and maintenance of captured vehicles and plant posing much of a problem over the short period for which they would be used. Again, their planning is based on Second World War experience. Donnelly points out that despite the Wehrmacht having a serious fuel shortage in 1945, in the battle for Berlin almost half the Soviet 1st Guards Tank Army's fuel was provided from captured stocks.[33]

Repair and Maintenance

The repair and maintenance system in the Soviet Army has been briefly mentioned earlier. It was arrived at as a result of the Soviet demand that battalions, regiments, and divisions should be highly mobile with great firepower. They also recognise that rear support is essential if momentum is to be maintained. So, although the organic logistic support at division and below is light, considerable support facilities are concentrated at a higher level, with all the advantages discussed earlier. Repair and maintenance and, as will become apparent later, medical support, is also centralised to a degree that is unusual in other armies. Because they failed to appreciate this, the Germans in the Second World War underestimated the repair facilities available to the Soviets on their main axes.[34]

In designing their repair system, the Soviets have used the analytical approach noted earlier. One conclusion they have reached is that it will be very rare for fresh equipment to be fed into their formations at any level during the course of a battle. The only source of replacement for damaged equipment will be from operational reserves, or equipment repaired on the battlefield, or at higher formation. The repair rate achieved in the Second World War was remarkable. It was not unusual for a formation to end a battle with more armoured fighting vehicles (AFVs) than it had at the beginning. Each vehicle having been knocked out on average two or three times, and each time been repaired to fight again. Overall figures from 1941–45 show that 60 per cent of all AFVs bringing armies up to strength just before an operation, and 85–90 per cent joining during battle, came straight from repair workshops.[35] Within all formations at all levels, there is a reserve of AFVs which can be deployed to restore the viability of a unit or formation. Repair bases will be well forward, and move to keep pace.

Medical

As with equipment repair, medical battalions would be moved to the areas of greatest casualties. It is Soviet policy to treat casualties as far forward in the casualty evacuation chain as possible. Although medical supplies have the lowest priority in the Soviet Army, it is not true, as was noted earlier, to say that casualties are left to die for lack of a system. There are medical orderlies at company level, and medical personnel at every level above. The Russians realise that it is important to treat the wounded quickly and efficiently, not only to maintain morale, but also in order to return as large a percentage of treated men as they can to the battle as quickly as possible.[36] The medical evacuation system is not unlike that practised in Western armies.

A Soviet View of NATO's Equipment Repair Policy

With this equipment repair policy in mind, it is interesting to look at the equipment design and maintenance practices, and NATO strategy in the Central Region through Soviet eyes. They draw three conclusions. First, in their view, an army whose policy is to withdraw, or is forced to, will be unable to recover its equipment for repair, and will therefore lose combat viability far quicker than an advancing army suffering the same, or greater rate of loss. Second, it is counter-productive to have equipment that needs much maintenance at unit level, because in war at high tempo there will not be time to carry out maintenance. Once this is accepted, equipment can be designed in such a way that overall costs are cut, and units can be more 'teeth' heavy. Third, and flowing from the first conclusion, a defensive strategy aimed at wearing down a Soviet attack, could end in defeat for the defender, unless his capacity for restoring combat losses greatly exceeded the attacker's. In Soviet eyes, it is the rate of combat losses which is critical. Which is why the only capability possessed by NATO which has ever worried them is a successful mass use of nuclear weapons.[37] If NATO were to acquire improved conventional weapons well ahead of the Soviets, that also would cause them considerable concern.

Soviet Logistics in Afghanistan

Before turning to look at NATO sustainability, it is worth glancing at Soviet logistics in the recent Afghan campaign. It is interesting for two reasons. First, because it shows that the Soviets are capable of tailoring their logistic system to reflect the actual situation, in accordance with their first principle of rear support; while adhering to the principles of centralised planning, forward positioning of support units, and a priority system of supply. Second, they are continuing to supply the Afghan army; the latter are trained in Soviet methods, and the success or otherwise of the government will turn to a large extent on their ability to keep their forces supplied and that part of the population under their control.

The battle in Afghanistan was, and is, for control of the lines of communication. At its peak, the combat forces of the Soviet 40th Army in Afghanistan consisted of 103rd Guards Airborne Division, 201st Motorised Rifle Division, 5th Guards Motorised Rifle Division, an air assault brigade, three motorised rifle brigades, two attack helicopter regiments, two transport helicopter regiments, three motorised rifle regiments, and a rocket launcher regiment. These amounted to 80,000 men out of the estimated total of 130,000 Soviet troops in Afghanistan at their peak strength. The 40th Army Deputy Commander for the Rear, with Army Headquarters in Kabul, was responsible for the entire logistics and supply operation in Afghanistan. He was also responsible for rear area security, tasking support units, and allocating deployment areas to these units. He co-ordinated rear area command and control with the Chief of the Rear of the Soviet Armed Forces in Moscow.[38]

Centralised planning did not preclude flexibility in the Soviet logistic system in Afghanistan. Indeed it enhanced it. Soviet logistics were adapted to meet tactical changes resulting from much experimentation. As we have seen, the Soviet priority of supply for general war is: ammunition, fuel, technical supplies, rations, medical supplies and clothing. This priority was amended to reflect the situation, and expenditure rates, as follows: fuel, technical supplies, ammunition, rations, medical supplies and clothing. Mechanical handling equipment, improved palletisation and packaging, and containerisation, all enhanced the logistic capability of 40th Army. Rear Area Command of 40th Army was also responsible for the support of the Afghan Army, and a large slice of the civilian population. Virtually every item had to come from the Soviet Union, including wood for cooking.[39]

There were, and are, virtually no railways in Afghanistan. The limited road network was, and still is, subject to ambush and demolition by the Mujahideen rebels and impassable in winter in many areas. The Soviet use of both long and short range air transport was therefore of prime importance. Many outposts depended entirely on helicopters for supply. However, there was also extensive use of road transport in areas where this was possible. The characteristics of the campaign—a high rate of movement, mainly logistic, and a lower intensity of combat, led to fuel being the most important commodity, and so assuming top priority. Fuel consumption was some 30–50 per cent higher in the mountains of Afghanistan than on the Russian steppe. To meet this high consumption, the Soviets built a tactical pipeline from the Soviet Union to Kabul. But convoys of fuel bowsers and helicopter-lifted pillow tanks were also needed to supplement the pipeline, and transport fuel to locations in the field.[40]

The principle of forward repair also operated in Afghanistan, and only a minority of vehicles were back-loaded for repair in the Soviet Union. Damaged vehicle collection points were established whenever possible. If evacuation was not feasible because of the tactical situation, every effort was made to destroy the equipment by fire to avoid it falling into the hands of the Mujahideen.[41]

Because of the sensitivity of the Soviets to reports on casualties in Afghanistan, the medical services received little publicity, and it is difficult to judge their effectiveness. However, reports were received that the standards of hygiene of the ordinary Soviet soldier were so low that outbreaks of hepatitis and dysentery reached epidemic proportions. This led to special measures being taken to control health and hygiene in Soviet units.[42]

On the whole the Soviet logistic system performed well in Afghanistan. There were no rear areas, which in itself is not unlike the Soviet perception of modern combat elsewhere. Sustaining an army of 120,000 men in such a hostile environment, as well as coping with an upsurge in demand for specialised items such as flak jackets, water purification tablets, and manpack radios, to name but a few, would pose a challenge to any logistic organisation. The point is that the Soviets did not withdraw because they were unable to support their force in Afghanistan logistically. Their system showed itself to be inherently flexible.[43] The Afghan Army, which has inherited the system, seems to be confounding those who prophesied a quick collapse following the Soviet withdrawal. The Soviets learned many lessons from the Afghan experience, and no doubt, using their analytical system, will discard those they feel inappropriate to a war against NATO, retaining or modifying those that they judge to be apposite.

NATO'S SUSTAINABILITY

How much sustainability has NATO? The agreed stock level is 30 days. Many nations do not stock to even that level, but to examine them all would take too long. In addition, all have different ways of arriving at such basic data as Daily Ammunition Expenditure Rates (DAER). So let us take a brief look at the British who do stock to 30 days, or purport to. In common with all the European members of NATO, they have no plans, at least none that are made public, for gearing up their industrial base to replace the equipment and stocks expended in war. Once the thirty days worth has gone, there is no more, and as will become apparent, at high intensity, stocks will not last thirty days. The major item, of course, is gun ammunition, but the sustainability of the guns themselves, and other equipments such as AFVs of all types is also relevant. Studies have been carried out with a view to arriving at a figure for the ammunition stocks in the War Maintenance Reserve (WMR), to enable 1st British Corps to fight a six day battle at intense rates, plus two days at normal rates. At the end of this they were to assume that a large percentage, in the order of half the Corps, would not be fit to fight. They were also told to assume that the rate of intensity of battle, particularly in the Central Region would be greater than the NATO rate for which the thirty days stocks were designed to last. This should come as no surprise when it is remembered that in some Falklands battles the British expended five times the 'conventional' war rate in one day. The latest study indicates that ammunition stocks need to be even higher. Even though the first study took account of the attrition of equipment, the new study assumes that after ten days fighting, an even lower percentage of units will survive; and though there will consequently be even less guns and tanks to fire the ammunition, there will be logistic losses caused by attrition of the logistic chain with some losses perhaps as high as 50 per cent.

The Ammunition Problem

Some idea of the scale of the problem can be seen when it is realised that one British armoured division needs nearly 4,000 tons of ammunition of all types per day, by far the largest proportion being artillery ammunition. Guns will be expected to move several times a day to have a chance of surviving counter-battery fire. If they leave ammunition behind, it must, if possible, be picked up. This compounds the already huge problem that the transport will have in servicing the current gun positions and stocking the next, as well as clearing those just vacated. With 48 batteries in 1st British Corps, there could be up to 940 locations a day to service. Each 155 mm has to be prepared to fire 450 rounds per day. The guns move from ammunition point to ammunition point, some will fire very little on some days, so the ammunition situation will become lopsided. 1st British Corps is not alone in having these testing transport problems.

The False Lessons of Peacetime Training

NATO has a plan to fight an identified enemy in Europe in a certain manner, but the only way the Alliance can test its plans, including its logistic preparedness, is on Field Training Exercises (FTXs) and Command Post Exercises (CPXs). As noted before, an FTX consists of plenty of movement, but little firing. Hence the lessons, particularly on ammunition expenditure, are not necessarily applicable to war. This unreality probably applies even so on CPXs designed to practise international procedures and communications. It is easier to co-operate with one's allies on a CPX than in an actual war situation, because it is less painful to give away 'paper stocks' than real resources.

NATO's Lack of Standardisation and the Ability to Inter-Operate Equipments

A long war, or even a relatively short, high intensity war, is likely to leave the individual members of the Alliance shorn of supply, thus unable to continue fighting. Lack of interoperability, standardisation, co-ordination, and a common system will result in the inability of Allies to support each other. One is led to the conclusion that in common with armies in the past, the armies of the NATO Alliance, unlike their potential enemy, have prepared for the likely campaign as best they could on an *ad hoc* basis, making great, but unco-ordinated efforts to gather together the largest possible number of tactical vehicles, trucks of all descriptions, and other equipment, while giving little, if any thought to the ideal combination which, in theory, would have carried them the furthest, or, one might add, enable them to last the longest.

THE OTHER SIDE OF THE HILL

On the other side of the hill, despite the Soviet preparation, standardisation of equipment, and the seamless garment of a doctrine with a logistic organisation to match, perhaps they would not have advanced as far and as fast as they imagine; at least in the initial stages. However, since their stocks are at least three times those of NATO, the chances are they would have had something left with which to continue fighting, long after the soldiers of the Alliance were reduced to using their rifles as expensive clubs for lack of anything to fire. It is for precisely this reason that the only NATO capability the Soviets feared, and fear, is its battlefield and strategic nuclear weapons. Without these, the Soviet Army could have overrun Europe long ago. According to Donnelly, they also have an inferiority complex about the West in technical matters.[44] If the West can develop the technology to produce a new family of weapons and equipment, which enables it to guarantee mass destruction of Soviet equipment by conventional means, and if the West can integrate new technology on command, control, and movement so that it can get within the Soviet 'command and control cycle', to bring the new family of weapons to bear in the right place and time, the Soviets would have little chance of success. But this technical lead has not yet been achieved by the West.

Some Implications of Force Reductions

For this reason a zero option on battlefield nuclear, and chemical weapons is very much in the Soviet interest. As indeed are conventional force reductions. As pointed out earlier, mutual force reductions which would reduce force density on the battlefield favour the attacker. Economies can be achieved by the Soviets while actually enhancing their relative capability. There may be no point in them building more tanks. It might be better to invest the time, research and development, and funds in the search for new weapons and equipment; faster and more lethal helicopters, precision guided munitions, better command and control systems, and so forth. By reducing manpower in their fully deployed first category formations, there will be savings in equipment. The stockpiling of this modern equipment will allow their 2nd and 3rd category mobilization formations to be better equipped.

Conventional force cuts should in no way reduce the Soviet ability to form mobile and air-mobile groups. If NATO and the Soviet Union agree to a zero option on battlefield nuclear weapons, and mutual force reductions, the Soviets would still have the capability to penetrate as far as the Rhine, if not further. The likelihood of this and other implications for the West is discussed in the next chapter.

10

Crystal Ball Gazing—Future Wars and Their Support

'To prepare for war in time of peace is impracticable to commercial representative nations, because the people in general will not give sufficient heed to military necessities, or to international problems to feel the pressure which induces readiness.'
Mahan

'It would be nice to say that we won the war (the cold war) because we are so good, but we won because the other guy had so many problems.'
Commander-in-Chief Allied Forces Central Europe addressing the Royal United Services Institute 20 June 1990

An Unequal Contest and an Unchanged Threat?

We have now seen how logistics has an impact on the conduct of wars in the past, and the possible influence on a war that never happened. In order to look at logistics in armed conflict in the future, it is first necessary to examine the possible shape and size of armed forces, and likely strategic, operational and tactical concepts.

If conventional war between NATO and the Warsaw Pact had broken out in the days before the Non-Soviet Warsaw Pact powers had so clearly shown their reluctance to become involved, the Soviets could have won merely by sustaining the conflict long enough at sufficient intensity, to ensure that the West ran out of supplies. It is likely that they would have done more than that, and the NATO strategy of holding forward in response to understandable German political pressure, would have served to speed up the process of defeat. In short, as has been discussed in the last chapter, NATO did not, and still does not have, the logistical capability to win a

313

conventional war against the Soviet Union, and using short-range nuclear forces in order to stave off defeat seems, to the author, to have lacked credibility years ago, and is now probably out of the question, given the situation in Eastern Europe. Yet all the recent experience, including the Iran/Iraq War, points to high expenditure of conventional weapons, and highlights the West's reliance on battlefield nuclear weapons. It appears that the only way NATO could reduce this dependence, would be to increase its stocks of conventional weapons and the size of its armies.

However, the question had to be asked what is the threat from the Soviet Union? Intentions can change quickly; capability, both in hardware and training terms takes years to build up; whereas the ability to deploy one's capability is subject to changes which may be outside one's control. As an example of this last point, because of the situation in Eastern Europe the ability of the Soviet Union to deploy its armies in a surprise attack on the West, has disappeared in a matter of months. Nevertheless, it is worth pursuing the matter of capability in hardware terms, because there can be little argument that far from abating the production and modernisation of equipment, the Soviets have increased it. For example, Soviet tank production for the years 1986–88 ran at an average 3,400 per year, compared with 2,800 per year from 1982–84.[1] Although the 1989 production is estimated at 1,700 tanks:[2] from which one can conclude that either the modernisation run is nearing completion, or that the Soviets are cutting their overall tank numbers; depending on what one wishes to believe. General Galvin, the Supreme Allied Commander Europe (SACEUR), has said that the Soviets have merely replaced old tanks with new, so although the number of tanks is not greater overall, the tank fleet has been modernised, and therefore presents a greater potential threat. On the other hand, the Chief of the Main Directorate of the Soviet General Staff was quoted in October 1989 rejecting these allegations, claiming that not one single new tank had reached Soviet troops situated on the territory of Hungary, East Germany, Poland, and Czechoslovakia.[3] SACEUR has not so far replied, but stated in a speech in May 1989 that:

'Over the last 10 years or so, the Soviets have engaged in a very sophisticated modernisation programme with their entire short-range missile force. They have continued to replace FROG with the SS-21; in fact, they have doubled the number of SS-21s that were in Europe when President Gorbachev took office. They have improved the accuracy and range of the SCUD. Indeed they have incorporated accuracy and range improvements in all of their missile systems. In addition, there are a number of other systems that are being developed that will have a significant effect on European security such as the AS-15 (an air-launched cruise missile) and the SS-N-21 (a submarine-launched cruise missile).'[4]

There is also the matter of 530,000 Soviet troops still stationed in Eastern Europe, of which 300,000 are in East Germany alone. At the time of writing (June 1990) the withdrawal of these has stopped.

Whereas NATO has modernised some systems, including dual-capable aircraft, it has not modernised Lance, the one ground-to-ground missile in the West's armoury, nor is it likely to; and tank production in the United States fell from 938 in 1987 to 610 in 1989. Therefore, despite the claim and counter-claim, there is no reason to assume that the Soviet Union has changed its offensive capability, or concepts at all. Furthermore, there is no clear picture of the future shape and size of Soviet forces, and when they will restructure for 'defensive defence', an expression which can mean all things to all men, since any defensive strategy must include plans to restore the situation by counter-offensive; ergo possessing the means to effect an offensive: the equipment, doctrine, and training.

Problems for NATO in CFE

Talks on reduction of Conventional Forces in Europe (CFE) appear to offer the prospect of reducing that capability. However, it is easy for one nation as well equipped as the Soviet Union, to reduce its overall number of equipments, and, at the same time, retain the most modern items in the armoury. The sixteen nations of the NATO Alliance will find it far more difficult to manage reductions in step with keeping the most modern equipment. The Supreme Headquarters Allied Powers Europe (SHAPE) plan to shuffle equipment among Alliance partners; to ensure that the most modern weapons in the NATO arsenal escape cuts resulting from any arms reduction agreements is known as 'cascading'. CFE is a treaty between nations, not alliances, although co-ordination must be done on an alliance basis. Nevertheless, individual nations, certainly within NATO, are free to implement the agreement as they see fit. Redistribution could be very difficult. For example, to reduce NATO's overall total of combat aircraft, should Belgium hand over some of its 108 F-16s to Turkey, in exchange for the latter disposing of an equal number of its ageing aircraft; thereby reducing the Belgian Air Force below a viable level, and doing little to enhance the Turkish Air Force? Such a move, and others like it, are unlikely to commend themselves to national governments.

Paradoxically, but for different reasons, the plan is also likely to cause resentment amongst public opinion in the West, particularly among nations with a strong peace lobby; West Germany, Holland, Belgium and Denmark. The man in the street, however misguided on defence matters, perceiving disarmament to be on hand, may be thoroughly dismayed at the sight of what could be portrayed as NATO attempting to cheat. On the other hand the Soviet Union and the Non-Warsaw Pact Nations have to take account of the political, social, and economic consequences of disposing of some 24,000 tanks, 22,000 troop carriers, and 6,000 aircraft and helicopters, in addition to demobilising one third of a million men. There is, therefore, considerable potential for upheaval, and hence dangerous instability. So there is no guarantee that CFE will succeed, and yet there is pressure from a number of directions, not least economic for further reductions in the West's readiness.

The Threat

What about intentions? It is hard to believe that the Soviet Union has any desire at present to go to war with the West. Even the most hard-line Soviet soldier has far too much to distract him at home. Unrest and violence in the non-Russian republics abounds. Army morale is reported as being low. Recent British military visitors have discerned a ground-swell of resentment among officers of the rank of Colonel and below against the increasing unpopularity of the Soviet Army at home, coupled with a perception that their seniors are doing little about it. Many officers of all ranks would like to see a smaller Soviet Army of Russian regulars, purged of ethnic minorities. It is also hard to believe that even if the most hard-line Leninist leader succeeded Gorbachev (who is an avowed Leninist himself), he would indulge in an attack on the West as a means of distracting the population from the growing economic and social problems. He would, after all, have the example of Lenin himself, surrendering vast tracts of land and resources to the Germans at the Treaty of Brest Litovsk in 1918, in exchange for peace, and thereby gaining a breathing space in which to tackle his country's problems, without the unwelcome burden of a war with a foreign power. The way in which Gorbachev allowed the Eastern European nations, that provided the Soviet Union with a 'glacis' against the West, to slip out from Soviet control is a similarly pragmatic move. So he, or a successor, is unlikely to attack through the buffer of neutral states that have replaced the 'glacis'. Provided, that is, the West maintains a level of deterrence which Gorbachev, or any as yet un-named hardline replacement, perceives as sufficiently high to deter him.

The question of the ability of the Soviet Union to deploy its capability has partly been covered already. There must also be doubts that the capability exists at present in terms of training, morale, and the willingness of the people to support a war. Therefore, despite its undeniable capability in hardware, the threat from the Soviet Union has all but disappeared for the moment. At the same time the Soviet Union is a formidable nuclear power, and will remain so. It will continue to exert a major geopolitical influence on Europe. It is unlikely to become a democracy in the Western sense for several years, if ever. Taking these points into consideration, it will be some time before the West, or anyone, can have total confidence in the Soviet Union's peaceful intentions.

We in the West have lived so long, the lifetime of anybody under 50 years old, with the notion of one clearly perceived enemy and a tailor-made defence solution to face him, that many see this as 'normal'. It is not. We are actually returning to the 'normal' state. Historically, the enemies of any nation, particularly the British located offshore, waxed and waned in the scale of the threat they posed; changing places in the order of menace—some dropping out, as new ones appeared.

One of the results of the unshackling of Eastern Europe, has been the re-nationalisation of Eastern European politics, and the emergence of such unwelcome manifestations as racism and even fascism. In the not too distant future, Eastern European nations might look to the West for security guarantees. This could include calling for action in the event of pressure being exerted by the Soviet Union, perhaps extending to incursions into the neutral belt; or if there is conflict between two Eastern European states.

The Response

Because there is so much uncertainty, it is important that NATO should retain certain characteristics and capabilities. First, adequate forces and the integrated military structure must be kept. Second, Germany must remain a full member of the Alliance, including remaining part of the integrated military structure. Third, NATO must remain a transatlantic alliance, the involvement of the Americans is crucial. Any notion of acceding to demands from the Soviet Union for total withdrawal of United States troops should be resisted. Fourth, it is necessary to keep the nuclear deterrent. Fifth, as well as United States forces, other national contingents must continue to be stationed in West Germany.

Certain features of the Alliance will probably have to change. It is likely that for political reasons the strategy of Forward Defence will be abandoned. Forces stationed in West Germany will have to be acceptable to the local population. In this respect, multinational formations have the best hope of acceptability. Furthermore, these formations benefit smaller nations who find difficulty in providing large contingents, and at the same time they avoid the singularisation of Germany. For such forces to make military sense, the smallest building brick should be brigade or division, with the exception of the covering force discussed below. Furthermore, interoperability must become more than just a catchword. There will be a need for logistical systems, weapons, ammunition and equipment to be standardised, or at least compatible. Multinational forces will cost money to begin with, which is why, if they are adopted, there will be no peace dividend.

With the abandonment of Forward Defence, should go the 'layer-cake' deployment of NATO forces in West Germany, to be replaced by what has been described as the 'currant bun' deployment. Most forward would be a multinational Covering or Guard Force consisting of units from all the present nations represented in the Central Region. The purpose of this Covering Force would be to signal vigilance and NATO solidarity. It would require a surveillance and reconnaissance capability. Further back would be a Rapid Reaction Force consisting of multinational formations, able to deploy to areas identified by the covering force. In depth, based well back, in many cases on their own soil, in Belgium, Holland, France and the United Kingdom, would be the national formations of the Manoeuvre Force. Finally, Reinforcement Forces would be based in the United States and Canada. Because the threat of regional conflict in Eastern Europe has increased, an uprated re-inforcement capability outside the Central Region is required. In addition, the need to reinforce both the Northern and Southern Regions remain, particularly the latter for reasons which will be explained later.

In addition, each member of NATO is likely to perceive some threats through a different set of strategic spectacles from its neighbour, or allies. There will be threats that are perceived to be common to all, for which common security measures will be necessary. But there will be others which will not fall into this category. Some nations may find common cause therein. For example, the United Kingdom and France, who is not even a member of the military structure of NATO, as the only two European powers with a nuclear capability, and each with a healthy out of area intervention capability, might wish to pursue a common theme; different from, although not necessarily at odds with other European countries. To put it bluntly, we simply do not know what will happen; not that we ever did. But later in this chapter we will discuss what and where these threats might be.

The ability to meet the deployment outlined above, pre-supposes three key elements: mobility, flexibility, and reservists. To meet the unexpected, a nation must have forces that are flexible. It will be too late to change organisations, let alone equipment, when the threat materialises. To design forces for this situation requires a nice judgement. Let us look at the problem through the eyes of the United Kingdom.

Focusing on the United Kingdom

If the United Kingdom, as part of a defence alliance, is to maintain its readiness in the face of growing pressure on defence budgets, coupled with increasing public demand for force reductions, it is faced with some questions. Does it strive to improve present systems, in support of current strategy and operational concepts, including considerable expenditure on enhancing the key area of sustainability, in which in company with the rest of NATO it is so weak? As we have seen, modern war is such a voracious consumer of material, that it is probably beyond the economic capability of the West to maintain present standards of living and expectations, and at the same time stock for the level of sustainability needed to have a chance, using conventional means, of containing Soviet aggression in Europe, even vouchsafed a far longer warning time than hitherto. Any Western government attempting such a policy would be committing political suicide. Does the United Kingdom, recognising that there are insufficient stocks of ammunition, to service all the weapons it plans to deploy, reduce 'teeth' without cutting the present 'tail', thus avoiding the need to increase stock holdings and turning CFE to its advantage? Does the United Kingdom do nothing, other than meet NATO CFE proposals? In which case it should be borne in mind that as presently organised, forces and equipment withdrawn from Western Europe, and perhaps disbanded and disposed of, would be impossible to reconstitute, let alone re-position in time to counter aggression. There could be advantages in withdrawing equipment from continental Europe but not disposing of it. For example, there have been suggestions that the

USAF at Hahn air force base could maintain the same sortie rate by keeping 36 of their F-16s in Germany, despatching the remaining 36 to the United States, and plan for rapid re-inforcement in time of war. Or does the United Kingdom, perhaps recognising its special geographical position, restructure its armed forces along new lines, aiming to maintain capability, while reducing size, including logistic overheads? At the same time, examining ways to shorten any future conflict, by seeking to reach a decision sooner; the aim would be to reach a situation where the potential opponent is persuaded, by non-nuclear means, that further aggression would be non-productive. Simpkin in *Race to the Swift*[5] goes into this in detail, and it is not intended to repeat it here. Suffice it to say that the shorter the war, in general terms, the less logistic effort required. And as a means of cutting costs, this is a worthwhile aim.

Political Considerations: A Scenario

In order to discuss the logistic support of future war and come to some conclusions about policy, it is necessary to write a short political scenario. For convenience, and to reduce the problem to manageable proportions, the play will be viewed totally from a British perspective. It is early in the twenty-first century.

In Scene One, talks on CFE have resulted in some troop withdrawals by NATO and the Warsaw Pact from Central Europe. For convenience, we will call this CFE I. As far as the British are concerned this amounts to one armoured division returning to the United Kingdom, where it disbands. There are plans for further withdrawals. In Scene Two, further reductions under CFE II have taken place. The new United Germany has remained within NATO and the Common Market. As a confidence building measure, NATO troops are stationed on West German soil, West of the old inner German border. Only German troops are stationed in the old East Germany. For a time some Soviet troops are stationed in what was East Germany. How long this situation will remain is open to question. Both sides possess a limited number of nuclear weapons. Even if a time should come when all foreign troops are stationed on their own soil, all members of NATO are committed by treaty to go to each other's assistance, if threatened by an aggressor on the continent of Europe and the British Isles. The British commitment includes a contribution to the Covering and Rapid Reaction Forces in the Central Region and the Manoeuvre Force, as well as reinforcing the European mainland in the Northern and

Southern Regions. The siren song of the Maritime Only strategists has been resisted, and Britain has recognised the need to apportion her resources between the demands of a Continental and a Maritime Strategy.

Threats to World Peace and Stability

Throughout the play there is a growing threat to world peace, stability, and harmony, from a number of directions other than Soviet Russia.

First, militant Islam, with a small, but expanding number of Islamic nations possessing nuclear weapons and the means of delivery. Countering this threat is an additional reason for both NATO and the Soviet Union to retain nuclear weapons. There is also continuing instability and bitterness in the Arab world following the humbling of Iraq in 1991. The situation is exacerbated by an increasingly strong Iran, with a well-equipped army, air force and navy and aspirations across the Gulf.

Second, unrest in the Mediterranean basin, the leading players being Syria, Libya and Algeria; with, as an added distraction, Greece and Turkey almost on the point of open war with each other following border clashes over a period of years. Stability is further threatened by the demographic trend in the countries on the southern rim of the Mediterranean. The economies of the countries of the southern rim are in disarray. Both factors have led to a flood of illegal immigration into Spain, France, Italy and Greece, and, since the abolition of frontier controls, from these countries into the rest of the EEC. The economic and ecological situation in the countries of the southern rim and their southern neighbours, has led to seething unrest and bitterness in the whole of Africa north of latitude 10. The pressure thus engendered threatens to spill over from the 'have-nots' of the southern rim into the 'haves' of the northern rim and beyond.

Third, the muscle and influence wielded by those involved in the drug trade, increasing to the point of taking over governments in some parts of the Third World. (This pre-supposes that nations have not legalised drugs).

Fourth, and linked to the preceding two points, the growth of guerrilla movements and terrorism worldwide. In some cases funded by, or connected with, the drug trade, in others, as a result of the demographic trends in the Mediterranean basin alluded to earlier. Greece, with inadequate security, provides a favourite entry point for terrorists into Europe. As a *quid pro quo* for allowing free passage, Greece is left undisturbed by any but her own indigenous terrorist groups. To assess these last two as a threat to world peace and stability, is over-egging the cake, but they do pose a threat to harmony, which we define as a state of good order in which all inhabitants of all nations regardless of creed, colour or race may go about their lawful business, in peace and quietness, enjoying the fruits of their labours.

All these factors have led NATO to re-align some of the Alliance's contingency plans on to a South–North axis, while retaining a capability to meet an East–West threat.

The British Reaction

To meet the scenario outlined above, the British began to restructure their army along the lines suggested by Richard Simpkin.[6] It will be apparent to anyone who has read Simpkin, that the author has drawn heavily on this work. He makes no apology for doing so. In examining the support required for the war of the future, one has to start somewhere, and Simpkin has produced by far the best appraisal of the likely shape of future war. The British re-organisation began as soon as one armoured division was withdrawn from Germany, the necessary planning having been put in train well before. The opportunity for a complete re-think of the size and shape of the Army, and indeed the Royal Navy and Royal Air Force, at this watershed in history was too good to miss. Fortunately, servicemen, officials and politicians with the courage and intellectual ability to take the necessary steps were in place at the time. The suggested new organisation is discussed in outline below. The changes are radical, but it is nonsense to imagine that the army we have today can be retained intact, if withdrawn from Germany. There simply is not enough room for another 55,000 troops and their equipment in the barracks and camps in the United Kingdom, let alone the training areas. The sheer impossibility of maintaining a Corps of armoured and mechanised formations in the United Kingdom alone calls for a different organisation. Should, post Scene Two, an eventual withdrawal from Germany not come about, there is still a need to restructure the Army to take advantage of the increasingly greater power and potential provided by imaginative use of the helicopter.

A New Look for the British Armed Forces?

The early gurus of armoured warfare in the 1920s, especially Fuller and Liddell Hart, conjured up visions of fleets of armoured fighting vehicles (AFVs), manoeuvring over the ground like battle fleets at sea. The Second World War, and other wars since have shown this notion to be largely an illusion. The flaw in the AFV-playing-ships-at-sea theory is that seas are flat. Except in the roughest weather, ships can, within the constraints of navigational hazards, go where they like without diminishing their speed and changing their tactics only to meet the imperatives posed by the threat. Very few parts of the world's land surface present a sea-like appearance. The Russian steppe might do so, but, as the Germans discoverd between 1941 and 1944, even the rolling steppe can be transformed into a sea of mud by spring thaw and autumn rain, and in winter, the snow brings its own problems to ground-borne vehicles. Some deserts may have considerable stretches of flat, firm going, which allow vehicles to manoeuvre at high speed. But they also have much larger areas where the terrain is intersected by deep wadis, rocky escarpments, boulders, salt marshes, and huge sand-seas. These last may look like the sea, but there the similarity ends. The trafficability over the rolling dunes, to all but specialised vehicles, varies from difficult to impossible. The terrain of Europe bears no similarity to the sea whatsoever; rivers, woods, hedgerows, banks, forests, mountains, large conurbations, and in the North, fjords, present an endless series of obstacles that range from trivial to challenging.

The Increased Role of the Helicopter

The arrival of the helicopter has given the soldier the opportunity to move over the ground, in the way that a ship moves across the sea (only rather better and at a higher speed), riding over the 'waves' of the terrain, mountains, woods, rivers, marshes, conurbations, and so forth. As Simpkin says, the helicopter allows troops to use the ground tactically without depending on it for mobility. To date, the drawback of the helicopter has been its vulnerability, and limited payload. However, recent developments in helicopter design point the way to considerable improvements in both these areas. Experience with succeeding generations of helicopters since their arrival on the scene in the early 1950s, has led many military men to think in terms of what helicopters can do now, rather than what they will be able to do very soon, and the quantum jump that might be possible in the early part of the next century. The imaginative use of the helicopter might also drastically improve the linear speed of a land force, which van Creveld discusses in such an interesting way in *Supplying War*.[7] We shall return to this point later.

Where Now With the Tank?

This is not to suggest that the tank has had its day; yet. But its future is probably limited. Sheer economics alone militate against wholesale scrapping of all British AFVs in one fell swoop. But it is important to decide whether or not the present generation of tanks should be replaced with what amounts to just a 'better tank', or by something absolutely different. What should be done, it is suggested, is a gradual re-organisation along the lines suggested below, over a period of years. Clearly the scenario will be politically driven, but by intelligent reading of the play, it should be possible to ensure that changes in the British defence posture are timed, so that although they might not exactly synchronise with shifts in policy, they are at least not too far behind the game. The first step is to start thinking the unthinkable now.

Thinking the Unthinkable

The Royal Navy and the Royal Marines

The Royal Navy would retain its present roles, but there would be a move for more ships, including, eventually, carriers and assault ships to be built with the ability to go sub-surface. Naval manpower would be reduced by having smaller crews in warships, following the trend that still continues as technology improves, and ships progressively become less man-power intensive. As suggested by Simpkin, there would be two Marine brigades, although the overall manpower strength of the Royal Marines would not increase. Each brigade would consist of an assault helicopter commando, a light mechanised regiment (army cavalry), a light commando, an artillery regiment (army), engineer squadron (army), and a logistic regiment (marine/army mix). The manpower for the additional brigade would be achieved by rationalising training, dispensing with landing craft crews when these are no longer required, disbanding bands, and reducing the number of officers in units. All helicopters, except those with a strictly maritime role, would be flown by the Army Air Cavalry (see below). It could be argued that the Royal Marines should become part of the Army, and this possibility should not be ruled out, especially if economies could be made, particularly in training; and career opportunities increased.

The Royal Air Force

The Royal Air Force would retain its present roles, except that it would hand over all its helicopters to the Army Air Cavalry. It would need modernised tactical transport aircraft, of the type envisaged by the European Future Large Aircraft Group (EUROFLAG), the FLA tactical transport (tactran), about which more later.

The Regular Army

The Regular Army would start to structure itself as suggested by Simpkin, but modified, and would, following total withdrawal from Germany, eventually consist of something along the following lines:

▷ A corps headquarters.
▷ Three divisional headquarters.
▷ One Special Forces Brigade, consisting of an SAS regiment and an SBS regiment, the latter from the Royal Marines.
▷ Two parachute brigades.
▷ Assault helicopter brigades (number to be decided but one provided by the Foot Guards).
▷ Light infantry brigades (number to be decided but one to be provided by the Light Division).
▷ Three light mechanised brigades (one Household Cavalry).
▷ Four artillery brigades.
▷ Four engineer brigades.
▷ Logistic groups.

Definitions

Before going further, it is necessary to establish a few definitions to clarify terms used in later discussion. The term 'air mobile' will refer to a force that rides to battle or fights in helicopters. An 'air-landed' force is one which is taken to its destination by fixed-wing transport aircraft, which lands on arrival and disgorges its load. A 'parachute' force is self-explanatory. 'Airborne' will be used as an all embracing term for a combination of two or more of the forces described above.

Re-organisation

Brigades would have organic artillery, engineer, and logistic support. Infantry battalions would be much smaller than at present, but with fire-and-forget, all-weather, hand-held missiles capable of more 'punch'. Cavalry regiments not included in the light mechanised formations, would form part of the new Army Air Cavalry, which would take over the Army Air Corps, and change its name (but, by sheer coincidence, not its initials). The Army Air Cavalry would fly and service all helicopters involved in the land and amphibious battle. They would not, as in the United States Army, provide the 'bayonets', the troopers. These would be from those guards and infantry regiments retained on the regular establishment. The logistic services would amalgamate into a Logistic Corps.

The Reserve Army and a New National Service

The remainder of the infantry would become territorial battalions, solely for home defence, but not organised as the Territorial Army is now. There would be a regular cadre of officers and NCOs, but there the similarity would end. The bulk of officers, NCOs and soldiers would be conscripted part-timers, as part of an overall scheme for compulsory universal service in a variety of public services, for all men and women in the country. As far as the new territorial forces were concerned, after a period of initial training, part-time soldiers would be required to attend evening drills, week-end camps, and longer periods of training. These would not, as now, be voluntary events, with the only sanction being non-payment of bounty for back-sliders, or discharge for persistent non-attenders. Offenders would be charged under suitable legislation, and fined or imprisoned. The period of service would be for five years.

Officers

Again, as suggested by Simpkin, the officer corps of the Armed Forces, particularly the Army and Royal Marines, would be drastically reduced to 5 or 6 per cent of total strength, instead of 15 per cent or more. Handing all helicopters to the Army would not reduce the overall number of aircrew. However, provided that the Army retained the NCO aircrew category, it would reduce the officer numbers in the Royal Air Force, and overall officer aircrew at a stroke. Careers guaranteed up to fifty-five years of age should be abolished. The notion of a second, third, fourth, and so on, career is already accepted as 'normal' throughout the nation. There should be more 'sackings' for culpable failure or incompetence. This would allow fast promotion for those with real ability. A smaller officer corps, and shorter careers, should release funds to pay salaries competitive with industry and commerce, thus attracting first class men and women. There should also be fewer generals and their equivalent. For example all brigades could be commanded by colonels, as in the Israeli and German armies. One argument put forward for retaining such a high proportion of general officers, or their equivalent ('stars'), is first, to provide a worthwhile career structure in terms of status and cash, to aid recruiting, and second, to persuade the better officers to remain. The first point is probably lost on potential officer recruits, few of whom join with their sights set on high rank. Whereas quick promotion for the gifted few, and good salaries for all, would satisfy both those who place a higher value on the 'brass' in their pockets than the brass on their shoulder or sleeve, and those who put job-satisfaction above monetary reward.

Reducing 'Stars'

The 'star' reduction should start at the top. To have a five-star officer as Chief of Defence Staff, the only one in NATO, devalues the rank enough. But to hand a marshal's baton, or its equivalent, to every Chief of Staff of Navy, Army, and Air Force on retirement, after honourable but uneventful service, makes a mockery out of a rank that should only be awarded as a result of successful command of an army, navy or air force in a protracted campaign of national importance in a major war: a Wellington, Montgomery, Tedder, or Cunningham. In the recent past, and increasingly in the future, most, although by no means all, of the recipients of the marshal's baton, or the naval or air force equivalent, have not, and will not have commanded so much as a platoon, aircraft, or ship's boat, in any sort of campaign throughout their career.

Organise for the Most Dangerous Threat

All the formations described below, and the marine commandos, must be capable of operations at all levels of intensity. It will be noted that there are no specialist 'Out of Area' troops. The concept of formations earmarked and equipped solely for low intensity operations is a relic of post-colonial days, and is inappropriate in the face of potential enemies with well trained and lavishly equipped armies. A formation on the lines of the pre-1982 British 5th Infantry Brigade (see Chapter 8), has political sex-appeal, because it is cheap. It is of no use in anything other than an internal security situation; it lacks punch and staying power for lack of equipment and logistic support.

A Parachute Capability

The rationale for maintaining two parachute brigades is for operations that require the seizure of an objective beyond the range of helicopters. The brigades would include light mechanised vehicles, and so obviate the need for parachute soldiers to land right on, or close to, their objective; necessary at the moment, because once down, parachute soldiers have the mobility of the boot, and the firepower and protection of non-mechanised infantrymen. In essence, an airborne operation would begin by dropping one or two battalions, with a few light mechanised vehicles, to seize an airstrip, or suitable flat area, into which would fly FLA tactrans with vehicles, guns, helicopters, and men. The brigade would then set off for its objective(s). FLA tactran will be designed to carry in the order of 25 tonnes over a range of 2,000 to 2,550 nautical miles, and with air-to-air re-fuelling (AAR), over far greater distances. This aircraft is not vastly different in size to the RAF's stretched Hercules Mark III, but would achieve much greater airlift and efficiency through modern technology and design. It is possible that an Osprey type tilt-rotor aircraft with the same payload and range capability as FLA tactran, including AAR, will be developed in the future. If this happens, the need for parachute soldiers, except in small numbers for special operations, will disappear.

Air Assault Brigades

Air assault brigades could comprise around two thousand men (including supporting arms), with about 130 helicopters. The heli-copter force consisting of sixty attack machines (tank equivalent), forty assault machines (infantry fighting vehicle equivalent), and twenty fire-support helicopters. At first the attack helicopter would be the Apache AH-64, or its equivalent. However, this aircraft only goes part of the way to meeting the requirement to replace tanks by helicopters. Eventually it should be superseded by the Main Battle Air Vehicle (MBAV), a true replacement for the AFV. As Simpkin explains,[8] modern technology in the form of centrifugal contra-rotating rotors to reduce rotor diameter and eliminate the tail rotor, and the increasing payload of helicopters, allowing selective armouring, should make an MBAV more than just a science-fiction pipe-dream early in the next century. The principle task of the air assault brigade would be to spearhead counter-attacks, seize ground of tactical importance, and mount deep operations.

The infantry fighting helicopter should be able to carry a section, be selectively armoured, and be equipped with weapons to lay down suppressive fire, and possibly be able to defend itself against an attack helicopter. Fire support helicopters could be equipped with multi-barrelled rocket launchers.

Light Infantry Brigades

The light infantry brigades would consist of three infantry battalions, with artillery, engineer, and logistic support. Helicopter lift for the infantry would be in the form of forty unarmoured helicopters of the Blackhawk type, per brigade. The type of gun with which the artillery was equipped, would dictate both the type and number of the remaining helicopters within the brigades. If the artillery regiments in these brigades were equipped with the new Ultra Light 155 mm howitzer being developed by Vickers Shipbuilding and Engineers Ltd, additional Blackhawk type helicopters would suffice for lifting both guns and ammunition. However, if a gun as heavy as the present FH-70 was retained, there would be a need for more heavy-lift helicopters of the Chinook variety. The role of the light infantry brigades would be as follow-up forces in amphibious and airborne operations, or to tackle light opposition in minor out of area operations.

Light Mechanised Brigades

Light mechanised brigades would consist of a mix of tracked light AFVs and infantry fighting vehicles, all capable of being slung under a heavy-lift helicopter, or transported in FLA tactrans. Their fighting vehicles would have a mix of fire-and-forget missiles, conventional guns, and heavy machine guns (these possibly of the chain gun type). These brigades would have no organic helicopter support, other than reconnaissance machines. They would have artillery and engineer support. The gun selected for the artillery supporting the light mechanised brigades would depend upon whether a track-mounted heavy mortar or light howitzer, for example the ultra light 155 mm, can be developed. Another solution would be a towed piece, which could be lifted by a Chinook as an alternative means of moving it into position.

Artillery

The artillery brigades, necessary to thicken up the fire-power, of the other brigades, would be equipped with Multiple Launched Rocket System (MLRS). The rockets would include 'smart' ammunition capable of destroying armour. Smart ammunition would also form a proportion of the shells and bombs with all artillery and mortars organic to brigades. MLRS can be lifted by Chinook.

Engineers

The cry 'in war there are never enough sappers', is more than just a cliché. In every conflict, at whatever intensity, engineers are at a premium. It could be argued that with a greater use of helicopters, the need for ferries and bridging equipment, and mine clearing will be reduced. This is so, and is why the savings to be made by reducing heavy armoured units, will include the equipment which gives them mobility; including tank transporters. However, there will be a need to lay and clear mines, and sappers and plant will be required for rapid construction, of helicopter and VSTOL aircraft hides, short strips, fuel and logistic installations, rapid light bridging (of the Medium Girder Bridge type that can be lifted in under a Chinook), clearing booby traps, and in out of area operations, digging wells for water, and construction tasks, perhaps in support of the civil power. Engineer brigades would be equipped with plant, and rapid mine dispensing and mine-clearing systems. As much as possible of these equipments should be capable of being underslung beneath a heavy-lift helicopter, or transported by FLA tactran.

Heavy Lift

There would be a need for a heavy-lift helicopter force to be held centrally for logistic support. Aircrews and maintenance personnel, as with all other helicopters in support of the land battle, would be provided by the Army Air Cavalry. But the heavy-lift helicopter force would be part of the transport of the Royal Logistic Corps (RLC).

Meeting the Cost

The total helicopter requirement for the British Forces would be about 1,000 compared with about 700 at present.[9] How this increase would be funded is beyond the scope of this book, but suggested areas for savings include: dispensing with all main battle tanks; reducing the size of the Regular Army, including disbanding all Gurkha units; reducing the size of the Royal Air Force by removing all helicopters, and re-roling much of the cavalry to fly helicopters; shorter careers for officers, within a reduced army fewer officers as a percentage of the total, and less senior officers; reduced naval manpower. If Britain had a force of around 1,000 helicopters, and not counting the 60 Chinooks which do not rate as combat helicopters, this would represent 49 per cent of the number (1900) of combat helicopters, that each group of countries belonging to the same treaty of alliance, is allowed to station in Europe under the proposals on CFE, submitted by the member nations of the NATO Alliance, at Vienna on 13 July 1989.[10] The final allowance would depend, among other things, upon the political and military position of the re-unified Germany; the agreements on the size of her armed forces, and their role.

Time Now for a Radical New Appraisal

While continuing to be stationed in Germany, following withdrawals under a CFE agreement, the members of the NATO Alliance should grasp the opportunity to implement a radical revision of plans for the employment of the new-look British Army of the Rhine (BAOR), and some of the other national corps, including changes in deployment areas. This should be made possible once the withdrawals of portions of other national contingents have taken place; perhaps one American corps, the Canadians, a French division and so forth. The present peacetime location of BAOR is an accident of history; the British were on the left flank of the Allied advance through North–West Europe, all the way from the Normandy beachhead in 1944 to the surrender of the Germans in May 1945. The British Zone of Occupation became the British deployment area, which it shares with three other corps, Belgian, Dutch, and West German. Deployed, as was alluded to earlier, like a layer-cake, with no operational doctrine to bind them together, these corps offer a would-be attacker the opportunity to direct his assault at the weaker layers, or between layers. The Soviets regard the British, Belgian, and Dutch corps as the weaker members, and the Germans and Americans as the more formidable.[11] Northern Army Group (NORTHAG), which contains the three weaker corps, and one strong one, is deployed on the most likely axis for a Soviet attack. It would make strategic sense to adopt the 'currant bun' deployment, again alluded to before in this chapter, to balance the distribution of strength, between Central Army Group (CENTAG) and NORTHAG, at the same time creating a strong reserve with excellent mobility; the lack of which has always been one of NATO's most serious weaknesses.

At present it takes 96 hours to commit a reserve corps to battle, and while it is moving, on tracks and wheels, across the rear of other corps to its battle position, crossing their main supply routes (MSRs), it effectively shuts down their logistic support for up to 36 hours, thereby endangering the very formations it is endeavouring to support. Moving on six major routes, and with no enemy interference (a pious hope in war!), a corps takes more than 24 hours to drive past a point in columns nearly 400 kilometres long.[12] There is a further problem, inherent in the time it takes to deploy the reserve corps: the commander has to decide 96 hours (four days) in advance where he wishes to commit it. One's only comment is that if the members of the Alliance seriously believe that this was ever a viable operation of war, then here is yet another example of collective cognitive dissonance. Airmobile formations, for the reasons discussed earlier, provide the key to unlock the problem of increasing the linear speed of armies, which has remained low hitherto, despite the invention of the internal combustion engine and the track. So, once rotary-wing equipped, the British brigades, including the parachute brigades, would be better employed by being held back as part of an Allied Airborne Army, which supported by fighter-ground-attack fixed wing aircraft, would move fast to block and destroy enemy thrusts.

The Need for a Drastic Overhaul of Logistics

What is also clear is that the 'logistics is a national responsibility' doctrine must change as soon as possible. It never made military sense, for the reasons explained in the previous chapter. If the currant bun operational concept is adopted, national formations will be reliant on each other for support, including logistics, which as was shown earlier, is not possible even as things stand today. To rectify this, a twin track approach is required.

Standardisation and Compatibility

First, a far greater emphasis on co-operative defence equipment manufacturing projects. Costs of equipment should thereby be cut, which, in itself, is reason enough for going in this direction without delay. But there are also compelling operational arguments for such a move. Without standardised equipment, compatible spares and interoperability, tighter co-ordination of logistics within the Alliance can only be marginally improved. The picture in the area of co-operation has not, up to now, been particularly happy. In the last two years alone, six major NATO collaborative defence projects have run into difficulties, mainly through one or more partners dropping out.[13] The sorry state of co-operation within the Alliance is well illustrated by the lack of any airborne battlefield radar system within the armouries of any of the nations. The Alliance suscribed to the concept of Follow-on-Forces-attack (FOFA), to hit the Soviet ground forces well back, with non-nuclear means. But without airborne battlefield radars to identify and locate the enemy while he is well back, the Alliance paid lip service to the idea, because NATO commanders were effectively blindfolded and unable to put the concept into practice. The technology exists to produce a system, or range of systems, but there has been little progress towards production, although the requirement has existed for about 15 years. Hand-in-hand with more collaborative arms production, is the need to develop the industrial means to produce ammunition in large quantities, at short notice. Stockpiling is expensive, prone to obsolescence, and may be forbidden by CFE agreements.

A Tighter and More Integrated Structure

However, the provision of NATO forces with standardised, or compatible equipment, does not of itself guarantee a co-ordinated logistics system, able to react to the army group commander's operational plans, although it will be vastly easier to accomplish than it is at present. So the second track, running parallel to greater collaboration in defence manufacturing, is a need to institute a far tighter and more integrated structure, to tie up the logistic support of the Alliance. This will require wholehearted support by all nations in the Alliance, because it will mean some loss of national control over resources.

The Emphasis on Reinforcement Rather than Stationed Forces

The political advantages of smaller, multinational forces stationed in Germany must not be overlooked. There will undoubtedly be an increasing resentment among the local population at the continuing presence of large, high profile national formations. Most of this resentment can be defused by the deployment covered earlier. However, if the bulk of national forces are based in their own countries, rapid re-deployment will be necessary if the concept is to be credible. As far as the United Kingdom is concerned, the ability to fulfil the commitment to reinforce the mainland of Europe, would be enhanced by possessing a largely rotary-wing army, with a substantial airborne element, and no heavy AFVs. Helicopters can fly across the Channel, the North Sea, or for that matter across Europe to the Southern Flank, while shipping for the light mechanised brigades, artillery brigades, and engineer brigade would be a fraction of that required for the reinforcement of BAOR now. We will be turning to intervention outside the NATO area later. But to continue with the re-inforcement of Europe, the use of helicopters and airborne forces could not only permit a faster reaction, but a more flexible one.[14] The plan could be amended to fit the threat as it actually comes to pass, instead of as it is thought it will; which, of course, it most certainly will not.

The British Expeditionary Force: Stockpiling

The system of logistic support of the British Expeditionary Force (BEF), no longer BAOR, because it may not be fighting on the Rhine, or anywhere near it, would partly depend on whether or not stockpiles of equipment were positioned on the mainland of Europe. In future cuts under CFE, the matter of stockpiles may be addressed, and if pressure is brought to bear on the Soviets to withdraw theirs behind national boundaries, it is reasonable to assume that NATO nations will be required to follow suit as a *quid pro quo*. Although it can be argued that taking supplies forward from Soviet Russia to support an advance into Germany is less of an undertaking than transporting them across the Channel, let alone the Atlantic. So there may be room for some give and take on this matter, and it is worth briefly examining the value, or otherwise, of stockpiles in the context of what has been discussed so far.

The advantages of pre-positioned stocks, particularly heavy items such as ammunition, AFVs and fuel, are obvious; provided that they are in the right places, and are not destroyed by the enemy before they can be outloaded. Even if they are not exactly in the right place, by being on the right continent, or area of that continent, much movement effort can usually be saved. 'Usually', because in the case of a country like Norway, with limited communications, a stockpile for use by the United Kingdom/Netherlands Amphibious Force, located in the 'wrong' place could be more inaccessible than having it, say, in the United Kingdom. It is therefore a matter of weighing up the balance of advantage to be gained by pre-positioning stockpiles in the projected area of operations, against the possibility that the next war will not be fought in that area at all. For the immediate future, the best answer is to maintain the stockpiles where they are, while examining the most favourable deployment for them in the longer term, taking into account possible international agreements that might in years to come limit, or even forbid, the positioning of war-like material on another nation's soil in the continent of Europe. However, it must be realised that stockpiling is an expensive measure calling for constant care and inspection of the equipment in the stockpiles and for regular activation.

The consequences of dependence upon defective stockpiles do not bear thinking about, for it could spell nothing short of disaster.

The Flexibility of Air Supply

If stockpiles in likely deployment areas in Europe are forbidden, there is a need to ensure, as far as the United Kingdom is concerned, an adequate number of both ships and tactical and long-range transport aircraft, to lift supplies to the deployment area. Aircraft of the FLA tactran type allow far greater loads than is possible at present to be taken over considerable distances, to positions reasonably adjacent to the battle area. Once supplies have arrived at the forward airhead, the problem of moving them nearer the customer arises. The closer that ammunition and fuel can be located to the consumer, the better. No commander wants his Main Supply Route (MSR) clogged with, for example, AFVs, and artillery vehicles driving for miles against the flow of traffic, seeking ammunition and fuel points. In the initial phase of a reinforcement operation, both in and outside the NATO area, there is likely to be a shortage of vehicles to lift loads forward to Distribution Points (DPs) close up behind the customers. This is where the flexibility of a rotary-wing force comes to the fore. Because the helicopter can cover the ground fast, and without clogging up the MSRs, it can come back some distance to refuel and rearm, possibly all the way to FARPs located near the forward airhead, or fuel pipe-line outlet. So your 'tank', now an MBAV, your 'SP gun', now a fire support helicopter, comes back to the 'supermarket', rather than delivery vans having to go to the customer. Chinooks can lift fuel and ammunition forward to those units which cannot move back. Chinooks, too big to be lifted by FLA tactran, can fly considerable distances direct from the UK base using AAR.

Fuel

One of the biggest requirements for a rotary wing army will be fuel. All over Europe, stocks of AVCAT on airfields, and fuel tank farms in likely deployment areas could be earmarked for military use. If possible, the existing NATO fuel pipeline should be left in place, despite its being designed to support a war in Germany, and nowhere else. Fuel outside Europe can be provided either by requisitioning by the supported nation on behalf of the intervention force, or alternatively, if the operation is near the coast, by fleet auxiliary tankers carrying the correct fuel, which might be re-routed, and pump-over to EPHE type installations flown in for the purpose. Fuel for amphibious operations should pose less of a problem, provided that the necessary tankers and pumping equipment exist, and are in the right place.

Ammunition

Ammunition would be another major item. Again, it is less of a problem in an amphibious operation, with the proviso that enough of the right shipping and ship-shore movement assets are available. Within Europe there are a number of options for moving the back-up supplies of ammunition, not flown in with the force. Resupply could be by air, road, rail, or sea; depending upon the operational deployment area. With a move away from tank ammunition, and towards smart artillery and mortar ammunition requiring less expenditure to damage the target, there is a possibility that ammunition tonnages will be reduced in future.

Countering Instability Both In and Out of Area

In areas where there is little or no logistic infrastructure and poor communications, and accessible by sea, an amphibious force based on shipping with its heavy lift capacity may provide the answer. These forces, provided that they are correctly configured and stocked, are inherently more flexible logistically than airborne forces, or ground forces supported by airlift, or on long overland lines of communication. It is here that the marine brigades would come into their own. However, in many instances a combination of amphibious and airborne forces would be the best solution, with the bulk of the heavy lift being seaborne.

The increasing threat to world stability and harmony posed by some nations around the Mediterranean basin, and in the Middle East, has been touched on earlier. The threat varies from the support of international terrorism, which is at the bottom end of the spectrum, and is a menace to harmony, rather than world stability, to nuclear or chemical blackmail which carries with it considerable perils for peace. We will return to terrorism later, and consider the upper end of the spectrum first.

In Area

The Southern Flank of NATO is particularly vulnerable for the reasons touched on earlier. Because it is only possible to hazard a guess at the place and timing of a threat to a Southern Flank nation, it is difficult to draw up detailed contingency plans. The answer is the rapid reaction and flexibility conferred by a rotary wing and parachute capable force, supported by a tactical air transport force. If there has been sufficient warning time, a marine brigade could be deployed by sea to stand-off the threatened area, either to make the initial landing in support of the threatened region, or reinforce the airborne force.[14] There will be no question of stockpiling, so logistic supply is likely, in the first instance, to be by air. Later, both sea and overland lines of communication may be usd.

Out of Area

For operations 'out of the NATO area', the methods of supply discussed above would still hold good. In addition, the United States has pre-positioned stocks in Diego Garcia to support operations in the Indian Ocean littoral. Provided these continue to be maintained, and there is compatibility and standardisation, there is no reason why the British, or any other NATO nation should not use them if taking part in an operation alongside the Americans in this area. Both here and elsewhere, these operations might include combating guerrillas, possibly at the behest of a state whose existence is threatened by a guerrilla movement, and because it is in the West's interest to become involved. Although such suggestions are not fashionable at present, political fashions change, as do economic imperatives, and it would be foolish to state categorically that it would never happen.

Guerrillas and Terrorists

It is necessary to distinguish between guerrillas and terrorists, because confusion exists in some minds as to which are which. This is because in both official pronouncements and in the press, the terms 'terrorist', 'guerrilla', 'commando', 'urban guerrilla', 'gunman', 'urban terrorist', and others, are sometimes used in the same statement or article as if they were synonymous. As Walter Lacquer says, the main culprits in this respect are the '*simplificateurs terribles*' in the media. He goes on to say:

> 'The essence of guerrilla warfare is to establish foci, or liberated areas, in the countryside and to set up small military units which will gradually grow in strength, number, and equipment—from squads to companies and regiments, eventually to divisions and armies, as in Yugoslavia and China in the Second World War (and Vietnam, he might have added)—in order to fight battles against

government troops. In the liberated areas, the guerrillas establish their own institutions, conduct propaganda and engage in other open political activities.

None of this applies to terrorists, whose base of operations is in the cities, and who have to operate clandestinely in small units. Any major concentration would immediately expose them to retaliation by the government. The terrorists may be part of a political movement that engages in propaganda and other political activities (such as the IRA and the Basque ETA), but there is a strict division of labour between the legal and the military arms of the movement. Terrorists no more engage in political propaganda than spies, as their chief assignment is to remain under deep cover.'[15]

The logistics of a typical guerrilla movement were examined in the chapter on Vietnam, including the problems that can beset a guerrilla commander because of the inherent inflexibility of his supply system. The logistics of forces fighting a guerrilla movement have also been comprehensively covered in the same chapter. Suffice it to say that, although the advent of the rotary-wing vehicle opened up new possibilities for operations and tactics, the campaigns in Vietnam and Afghanistan (and others not covered such as Borneo and Dhofar), proved that the possession of a substantial force of helicopters will not in itself confer success on a conventional army engaged in a campaign fighting guerrillas, unless the operational concepts and tactics are correct. But without helicopters, supply would have been even more difficult, and at times impossible. They allowed armies to conduct far more ambitious operations than was possible in the pre-helicopter age. So the restructured British Forces would be well placed to fight a campaign against guerrillas, in any type of terrain.

Terrorist Logistics

In this chapter on the logistics of future wars, it is worth glancing at terrorist logistics. Because terrorists have been, are, and will continue to be, an enemy of harmony, and therefore an ingredient of future wars. Just as we examined the logistics of another potential enemy, the Soviet Union; a look at the terrorist logistical system and its problems, may provide one clue that might be worth following up in greater detail, as part of the battle to defeat, or at least contain terrorism at a bearable level. Neither space, nor time, permits an analysis of terrorist logistics, even one that equates with the brief treatment accorded to Soviet supply in this book. We are dealing with a multitude of terrorist organisations, with a host of differing aims, and operating areas. However, there do seem to be some common themes.

'Modern terrorists, unlike their predecessors do not live by enthusiasm alone; they need a great deal of money. The preparation for major operations is usually expensive; money is needed for logistic purposes, for arms, for information and, generally speaking for paying the expenses of the militants who have no other incomes. Cars can be stolen, but frequently it is less risky to buy them. Safe houses cannot be stolen and money is also needed for bribes and various emergencies.'[16]

The necessary funds can be obtained from a variety of sources, from robbing banks and post offices, from donations by sympathisers and friendly governments, and from the drug trade. The Provisional Irish Republican Army (PIRA) is a typical example. The Irish Northern Aid Committee (NORAID) in the United States is the most well known, although not necessarily always the most generous, funder of the PIRA. There is evidence that they have found support in more than twenty other countries, including West Germany, Holland and Scandinavia. Support ranges from cash to training. In addition, the PIRA runs a number of business operations, some legal, some not: a fleet of taxis in Belfast, protection rackets under the guise of 'guarding' buildings and construction sites, 'kick-backs' from contractors in return for frightening off the opposition when tendering for contracts, and unofficial taxes on drink in public houses in Catholic areas, to name but some. Opinions vary widely on the subject of how much is made by terrorist organisations throughout the world. But there is no doubt that the PIRA are in a small-time league compared with Abu Nidal whose income in 1985 was estimated as US$30–40 million at 1980 prices. And this, in its turn, looks small beer beside the drug funded terrorists (narco-terrorism) of the Colombian group M19, whose income in 1985, was estimated at US$50–150 million at 1980 prices.[17] The collection of funds can in itself be an indicator that a terrorist group is planning an operation. For example, the German Red Army Faction (RAF), not one of the richer organisations, had to rob banks to obtain funds for the purchase of weapons and explosives, and other requirements, before each operation. If forced to steal explosives, the terrorist may give a clue to the authorities that he is preparing for an operation. The need for the terrorist to hide weapons and explosives, and subsequently collect them before use, can also be a weakness in his logistic system, sometimes leading to his capture.

Setting up a terrorist operation requires a great deal of logistical and other preparation, and time. Which is why fears in some circles that the Libyans might immediately react to the United States bombing of Tripoli with a massive terrorist campaign in Britain were ridiculous. Unless the means for such a campaign had already been in place, the sheer size of the logistic problem involved made such a reaction impossible. Logistics will also dictate the scale and complexity of operations that a terrorist organisation will attempt. For example after the Mogadishu hi-jack, which failed, the Red Army Faction never again tried hi-jacking. It requires special weapons, supporters (possibly in more than one country), and hide-outs; so usually only the bigger organisations, such as the PLO and other Arab groups attempt hi-jacking. Sometimes the smaller groups will assist each other logistically. The French group *Action Directe* set up a logistic front to provide weapons, papers, money and safe houses which they not only used themselves, but provided assistance to the Italian Red Brigades hiding in France. Before the Belgian group, the Fighting Communist Cells (CCC), went into action on its own account, it provided arms and explosives for more active groups.[18] Support for terrorist operations by governments is at the other end of the scale. The leaders in this respect recently, have been Syria, Iran and Libya. Syria has provided Hizbollah with Soviet Sagger anti-tank missiles, and Grad missiles and launchers. State sponsored terrorism is, however, not a new phenomenon; for example, the assassination of King Alexander of Yugoslavia in Marseilles in 1934 was set up by the Italians, and the murder of Trotsky in Mexico in 1940, by the Soviet Union. It is likely to continue for the foreseeable future, and become more, rather than less, violent, if those who practise it belong to sects who are as careless of their own lives as of their victims.

The drug barons run terrorist organisations for profit. The forces at their disposal are often far greater than most terrorist groups could achieve, both in terms of size and quality of equipment; in some areas controlling large tracts of countryside and operating overtly, which puts some of them into the guerrilla bracket. There is evidence that drug traffickers, and indeed terrorist groups, in Central and South America, have been equipped with vast quantities of arms and ammunition by Cuba, much of this is American equipment abandoned in South-East Asia, or taken from the ARVN in 1975 and subsequently acquired by Cuba from the Socialist Republic of Vietnam in return for agricultural produce and shell-fish. These totalled over 2 million small arms of different types. In addition, Cuba distributed a wide range of Eastern Bloc weapons to insurgent groups in Nicaragua, along with Portuguese weapons abandoned in Mozambique and Angola.[19] To crush such powerful groups is likely to require an armed response, unless the subtler, and cheaper, approach of legalising all drugs is adopted.

SUMMARY

Although, at the time of writing, the prospect of war with Soviet Russia seems to be receding, there are no grounds for the West to disarm. From the top end of the threat spectrum, right to the bottom, there is a need for Western nations to maintain armed forces, and the means to supply them. The NATO Alliance will be needed until the Soviet threat diminishes to an acceptable level. It is difficult to say what that level is because it will depend on so many factors, including the nature of the government in the Soviet Union and the correlation of forces in Europe. Outside NATO, no one can tell where or when the next conflict will be, the form it will take, and whether or not it will involve the West. What is certain, is that unless the West remains strong, with modern weapons and equipment, with the logistic organisation and stocks to support its forces, a situation will eventually arise which involves abandoning something territorial, economic, a point of principle, a permutation of any of these which the West would wish to maintain. Therefore it would be wise for the West, either through the existing machinery or NATO, or some new European grouping, to examine means of maintaining collective security against new threats, however dimly perceived at present. As ever, logistics will play an important part, and the temptation to set up shop-window forces with no sustainability will need to be resisted if they are to provide the necessary deterrence.

It would be advisable for the new grouping, or the old Alliance, to examine its logistic requirements and organisation in tandem with its operational targets from the outset; starting at the industrial base, and working forward to the front-line. In this way the *ad-hoc* approach that NATO adopted from its inception could be avoided in future. The changing patterns of threat, and the shape and size of forces to meet it, offer an opportunity to provide the logistics that really do cater for the force levels required. We started by listing logistic principles. The five principles of administration: foresight, economy, flexibility, simplicity, and co-operation still provide as good a set of points to march by when planning the whole matter of logistics for the next few decades, whether at the level of the Alliance's (or its replacement's) strategic sustainability, or the operational and tactical organisations to cater for a whole range of situations and force levels.

TAILPIECE

As this book was about to go to press. we have seen a stunning display of power projection by the United States and its Allies in the Gulf. The demonstration of readiness by the United States military, based on years of meticulous planning, contrasted favourably with the uncertain political direction by the State Department. The latter was largely responsible for sending the wrong political 'signal' to Saddam Hussein, precipitating his invasion.

The rapid appearance of two airborne divisions, squadrons of fighter/bombers and air defence fighters, and the redeployment of carrier battle groups and amphibious groups showed convincingly the need for such forces, along with their means of mobility. The activation of the stockpiles at Diego Garcia during the first days when only light forces were available to deter an Iraqi attack into Saudi Arabia, was crucial. Heavier weapons and substantial logistic support were provided infinitely more quickly than a long sea-lift from the United States would have allowed.

Eventually, the United States moved in enough stocks to last 60 days of combat; provisioning against the eventuality of what General Schwarzkopf, the Allied commander-in-chief, called a 'slug-fest'. In this area, as in others, he showed himself a worthy successor to the great captains of the past. The logistics of the great armoured and air-mobile outflanking thrust were daunting enough. Indeed General Schwarzkopf is said to have over-ruled doubters on his staff that it could be done. Only a commander who understands logistics can push the military machine to the limits without risking total breakdown. Although it must be said that the expenditure of tank ammunition, and possibly artillery rounds, was lower than it would have been had the Iraqi army fought hard. But providing fuel for an armoured corps totalling six divisions, motoring 325 kilometres across the desert in two days, was a notable feat in itself; let alone the fuelling of the great air-mobile thrust to the west.

The conception and handling of what Simpkin has called the 'club sandwich battle' was a classic in itself. It included the seizure of the forward supply base deep in Iraqi territory by airmobile troops of 101st Airborne Division. This provided the hinge for the swinging level arm of a mix of armour, mechanised and air-mobile forces to plug the Iraqi withdrawal routes across the Euphrates. Inside this lever, a mass of armour raced to engage the Iraqi Republican Guard.

The genius of Schwarzkopf's plan was in recognising that Saddam Hussein had put his army in the Kuwait Theatre of Operations (KTO), including southern Iraq, in a bag. One side was the sea, the bottom was the defences they had created to keep the Allies out. The western side was open. The trick was to feint an amphibious landing, tying down six Iraqi divisions, and punch hard on the right and centre, to keep him looking that way. VIIth Corps zipped up the western side and squeezed. The way out of the bag lay over the Euphrates bridges, damaged by airstrikes. The swinging arm closed off the neck.

Air power was indispensable. It came nearer than at any other time in history to bringing victory unaided. Despite all the efforts by the airmen, the logistics of the Iraqi army seem to have continued working. Until they were brought to battle on the ground, they could have survived, still in possession of Kuwait. Slessor's words (see Chapter 3), 'In short, it (air power) cannot absolutely isolate the battlefield from enemy supply or reinforcement', are as true in 1991 as they were in 1944.

It was the prospect of a ground offensive that led to Saddam Hussein's frantic attempts to fudge a cease-fire. It needed the ground offensive, by 15 Allied divisions to utterly destroy 42 Iraqi divisions in 100 hours. It was a ground offensive that forced Saddam out of Kuwait, and brought his generals to the table at Safwan airbase, courtesy of the 'Big Red One', the 1st United States Infantry Division. Against a backdrop of the Division's colours, adorned with battle streamers, signalling the United States Army back in all its power and glory, General Schwarzkopf announced the unconditional terms he had dictated to a defeated enemy. The poison had, at last, been drawn from the wounds inflicted by Vietnam; bringing gladness to the friends of the United States, and confounding the detractors and whingers—notably backward-looking media marshals and amateur generals in the halls of academe.

The British 1st Armoured Division played a starring role in this victory on land, thanks to its general, and all under his command. It is too early to comment in full on all the aspects of the handling of the British 1st Armoured Division. But two stand out.

First, the imaginative handling of the artillery as a brigade. Thus General Smith was able to minimise his tactical weakness, only two armoured brigades, and maximise the crushing power of his artillery, particularly the Multi-Launched Rocket System (MLRS). Iraqi prisoners are reported as saying that the bombing was bad enough, but the artillery was devastating.

Second, the logistic expertise of the Division. At the end of its advance, it had enough fuel and ammunition to take it to Baghdad.

All the partners in the coalition land force, made up of major contingents from seven nations, and several minor contributions from others, played their part in the success of the 100 hour land battle.

It is also too soon to list all the logistic lessons. But one stands out already. Thanks to British parsimony with military resources over the previous decade, it took half the logistic resources of 1st British Corps, and a slice of the Army in the United Kingdom to make the Division battle-worthy. There were no operational Warrior AIFVs and only about 10 running Challengers left in the whole of Rhine Army, not to mention a host of other equipment left useless by cannibalisation. Herein lies a lesson for the future. Only those forces that are demonstrably capable of conducting sustained operations at the end of long lines of communications will be of the smallest use in deterring threats posed by latter-day adventurers on the international scene.

This has been a new kind of war. A war in which technology brought unprecedented levels of accuracy in both airborne and ground-based weapons, new levels of destructive power and, above all, a revolution in the availability of information to the Allied commanders. Finally, what many feared would prove a weakness, the development of strategic and tactical plans for the command and control of a force containing elements of so many nations, was to prove a triumph—the credit for which must finally go to their dynamic commander—described by Lieutenant General Sir Peter de la Billiere as 'the man of the match'. Behind all this however, lay the necessity for immense logistic support—the lifeblood of war.

CHAPTER NOTES AND BIBLIOGRAPHY

Chapter Notes and Bibliography

Chapter Notes

Where full publishing details are not given, they can be found in the Bibliography following the Chapter Notes.

Part One

Chapter 1: Principles: The Disciplines of Wars

1. Thorpe, G. C., *Pure Logistics* (National Defense University Press, Washington DC), p. xi.
2. Thorpe, p. 1.
3. Clausewitz, *On War*, edited and translated by Michael Howard and Peter Paret (Princeton University Press), p. 339.
4. Clausewitz, *On War*, p. 131.
5. Clausewitz, *On War*, pp. 337–338. The allusion to a 'G. Snob' dates from the old British Army staff system (pre-dating NATO standardisation) by which operations staffs at all levels above battalion or regiment, were part of the General (G) staff, hence Major General Staff, heading the operations branch at army level, Brigadier General Staff at corps, General Staff Officer Grade One, a lieutenant colonel, at division, to the General Staff Officers Grades Two and Three, majors and captains at all levels; who did all the work; so they claimed. The Quartermaster General's branch were responsible for administration, and the Adjutant General's branch for personnel. Each had their own hierarchy of Vice Quartermaster General, Vice Adjutant General, Deputy, Assistant, and Deputy Assistant, down to brigade where one officer combining both administrative and personnel functions, rejoiced in the title Deputy Assistant Adjutant and Quartermaster General. At all levels, from brigade to army, there were Staff Captains, who, according to them, did most of the work. A 'G. Snob' was an operations officer who took no account of logistics in his planning, or affected a disdain of such mundane matters as supply.
6. Clausewitz, *On War*, pp. 330–340.
7. Clausewitz, *On War*, p. 133.
8. Jomini, *The Art of War*, translated by Captain G. H. Medel and Lieutenant W. P. Craighill, U.S. Army (Greenwood Press), p. 69.
9. Jomini, *Op. cit.*, p. 253.

10. The *Shorter Oxford Dictionary Vol. II* gives the origin of the word Quartermaster as a naval petty officer who attends to the stowing of the hold. By 1600 the military meaning was an officer attached to each regiment with the duties of providing quarters for the soldiers, laying out the camp, and looking after the rations, ammunition, and other supplies of the regiment. Now logistics is taken to cover all supply, movements, and administrative matters, including medical and welfare.

Chapter 2: The Assyrians 700 BC to the Armistice AD 1918

1. Shaw, *Supply in Modern War*, p. 1.
2. Engels, *Alexander the Great and The Logistics of the Macedonian Army*, pp. 23 and 119. Marius reduced the numbers of animals by having the soldiers carry their own cooking utensils and provisions, and hence they were called Marius's Mules. Both Marius and Philip made these reforms for similar reasons; to increase their armies' speed and mobility and to reduce the numbers of animals in regions where they were difficult to acquire *and feed* (Author's addition).
3. Josephus, *The Jewish War*, p. 196. In his account of the Jewish War of AD 66 to 73, having described the weapons with which a Roman infantry soldier was equipped: 'together with saw and basket, axe and pick, as well as strap, reaphook, chain, and three days rations, so that there is not much difference between a foot-soldier and a pack mule!' As Marius had carried out his reforms (Note 2 above), about a hundred years before Josephus was writing, it is unlikely that this comparison was original!
4. Engels, p. 24, Note 39. If the Macedonians carried their arms and armour on pack animals, and if the average weight of the soldier's panoply was 30 lb., and there were 50,000 troops in the army, their combined panoply would weigh 1,500,000 lb. This would require 6,000 animals to carry it, and 240 additional animals to carry their grain ration for one day. All these additional animals, or their equivalent in carts were not required by Alexander.
5. Engels, p. 24, Note 40. According to Xenophon, carts would not only require drivers, but a quantity of lumber for replacement parts, skilled carpenters and tools for repairing them, and a shovel and mattock per cart, probably for road building. Only a limited number of these would be needed by Alexander's force.
6. Lane Fox, *Alexander the Great*, p. 280. Before leaving Meshed on his march to Afghanistan and the Hindu Kush, Alexander set an example of reducing baggage loads: 'all excess baggage was piled on to wagons and massed in the centre on the camp: Alexander then set fire to it, his own wagon first, the others only when his example had been observed. From now on, pack-animals would serve as transport on roads too rough for wheels. The army acquiesced in the sudden loss of their luggage, knowing that Alexander had suffered too; at least they were allowed to keep their native concubines'. *Author's comment* Many armies in antiquity appear to have had a commonsense approach to the question of the needs of the soldiers, regarding it as perfectly normal that healthy young, and indeed not so young, men, need regular intercourse with women, not just the sexual variety, but for the special companionship that a woman provides, which enriches and fulfils. In this respect ancient armies were less burdened by the baggage of hypocritical values which have been, and are, borne by later armies.
7. Engels, p. 26, Note 3.
8. Engels, pp. 21–22.
9. Engels, p. 61.
10. Lane Fox, p. 133.

11. Lane Fox, p. 140.

12. Engels, p. 112.

13. Engels, p. 19, has excellent tables showing the correlation between the numbers of pack animals and the endurance of armies in antiquity. He concludes that nine to ten days is the maximum that an army could exist without resupply, and before men started to starve. It would, for example, take 40,350 animals to carry 15 days ration, and 107,600 for 20 days. It is doubtful if that number of suitable animals existed in the whole of Greece. One day's supply of grain for 40,350 horses would weigh over 200 tons, and unless it could be transported by water, there would be little possiblity of it reaching the animals overland, since it would have to be carried by other pack animals who would be consuming the supplies they were carrying.

14. Keegan, J., *The Price of Admiralty*, pp. 46–47. 'HMS Victory was designed to store enough biscuit, beef and beer for 850 men for four months and enough powder and shot for estimated expenditure in a three-year commission. A great deal of necessary maintenance—repairs to sails and "setting up" the rigging—was carried out daily at sea as a matter of course.' Keegan goes on to illustrate how fast, potent and logistically sustainable a man-of-war was compared with contemporary armies:

> 'Napoleon's Army of the North of 1815, that destined to give battle at Waterloo, took 366 guns of 6-pounder to 12-pounder calibre into the field. The force of artillerymen needed to work this cannon park numbered 9,000 and the train of horses to draw it, its ammunition limbers and its supply wagons at six horses to a train some 5,000. Horse fodder, at 20 lb per horse per day, amounted to 50 short tons (*2,000 pound tons, rather than 2,240 pound tons—Author's note*), a supply which also had to be collected and transported at heavy additional cost in human and animal labour. By contrast, Nelson's Trafalgar fleet of twenty-seven ships mounted 2,232 guns, of which the *lightest* was 12 lb. in calibre and the heaviest 68 lb. The force of men needed to work this cannon park, at twelve [men] to two guns (since only one broadside was manned at a time) was some 14,000, their daily supplies, some 3 lb. per man (liquids, which had to be transported at sea as they did not on land, added another 8 lb.), while the motive power to manoeuvre the whole artillery force and its crews (though not the attendant capital costs) came free. In short, the gun power of Nelson's Trafalgar fleet exceeded that of Napoleon's Waterloo army six times; and if it had had to be transported by land—at a speed five times less—it would have required over 50,000 gunners and 30,000 horses, as well as a daily supply of some 300 short tons of fodder and 75 tons of food; the comparable daily intake of solids and liquids aboard Nelson's fleet was 70 tons. In brief, six times as many guns, of much heavier calibre, could be transported daily by Nelson's fleet as by Napoleon's army, at one-fifth of the logistic cost and at five times the speed.'

15. Keegan, p. 119.

16. This can be useful, even in peacetime; for example just in the Author's experience alone, in 1967/68 after the British withdrawal from Aden, a task force of never less than one strike carrier with a full complement of aircraft, one LPH (aircraft carrier converted to carry 700–800 marines, guns, vehicles and helicopters), and escorts was kept at sea in the vicinity of South Arabia on two separate occasions, each of two months. All supply was by the underway replenishment group (URG). On the second occasion, the task group was out of sight of land from clearing the Malacca Straights to returning. In the Falklands warships were at sea for considerably longer.

17. Oman, Charles, *History of the Art of War in the Middle Ages* (Methuen, London 1898, reprint 1979), p. 83.

18. Oman, p. 222–223.
19. Oman, p. 250–252.
20. Van Creveld, *Command in War*, p. 27.
21. Clausewitz, *On War*, p. 320. 'Baggage, in point of fact, rarely had any influence on movements; . . . so the Seven Years' War produced marches that have still not been surpassed: Lascy's, for instance, in 1760, in support of the Russian diversion towards Berlin. He covered the 220 miles . . . in ten days—a rate of 22 miles per day which would be astounding even nowadays for a corps of 15,000 men.'
22. *The War of the Rebellion, Vol. XIX, Part 1*, pp. 10–11 and 13–14. In both armies, from regimental/battery level upwards, excellent records were kept, a combination of what we today would call war diaries and after-action reports. The Confederate Official Records were captured at the end of the war, and with their Union equivalents, compiled into 70 volumes forming what must be the most comprehensive account of any war in history, in one publication, as seen through the eyes of commanders on both sides from army commanders down.
23. *The War of the Rebellion, Vol. XIX, Part 1*, pp. 97–98. A report on p. 96 in the same volume, by Brigadier General Rufus Ingalls, the Chief Quartermaster of the Army of the Potomac, speaks about the problems of supply at long distances from railheads of rivers:

    'Our trains (wagon trains) at this time could not carry supplies of provisions and short forage for the army, with the necessary ordnance, hospital stores, camp equippage, etc. for more than six or eight days. A wagon drawn by six mules over good roads can haul 1,200 short rations of provisions (bread, sugar, coffee, salt, and soap) and six days of grain for mules. Over hilly or muddy roads the weight would be correspondingly reduced. It can thus be easily seen how far from depots an army can be supplied by wagons. When supplies in trains (wagon trains) become exhausted, an army must be at or near another source of supply as a matter of course.'
24. One of his soldiers remarked years after the war that whereas it took Moses forty years to get the children of Israel through the wilderness, 'Old Jack' would have double-timed them through in three days on half rations!
25. *The War of the Rebellion, Vol. XXV, Part I*:

    p. 197. The Report by Brigadier General Warren, Chief of Topographical Engineers describes the route and the weather; 'the road was a crooked one, through forests, and very muddy . . . at about the same time it began to rain'.

    p. 298. Colonel Dana commanding the 143rd Pennsylvania Infantry includes in his report the observation; 'The experience of the late movement, if I may be pardoned to remark, furnishes strong evidence that only in critical emergencies should men be compelled to carry, in addition to their usual equipments, including 60 rounds of cartridge, eight days' rations.'

    p. 396. Rations on the man were; three days cooked rations in his haversack, and five days' hard bread, coffee, sugar and salt in his knapsack.

    (*Author's comment, the rations must have been fairly sparse, or amazingly light, or both. A present day infantry soldier carrying eight days rations and his ammunition load would have around 100 lbs on his body*). Five days' beef on the hoof marched with Hooker's army (p. 396. This was about 312 head of beef cattle per corps). The reserve ammunition was carried on pack mules. Only a small number of wagons crossed the Rappahannock to Chancellorsville. Hooker stipulated (*Part II of Volume XXV*, p. 262) that trains (wagon trains) were to be left behind, only two ambulances and one battery were to accompany each division, and the few wagons were only to carry forage for the animals.
26. *The War of the Rebellion, Vol. XXV, Part I*, p. 551, report by Brigadier General Taylor, commander 1st Brigade, 3rd Division, 5th Corps.

27. Luvaas, *A Prussian Observer With Lee.*
28. Luvaas, *G. F. R. Henderson and the American Civil War.*
29. Luvaas, *A Prussian Observer With Lee,* p. 116. The work was entitled *Der Burgerkrieg in den Nordamerikanschen Staaten.*
30. Although the Austrian musket was vastly inferior to the Prussian needle gun. The latter was actually inferior to the French Chassepot rifle.
31. Luvaas, *A Prussian Observer With Lee,* p. 112.
32. Van Creveld, *Supplying War,* p. 106.
33. Van Creveld, *Supplying War,* p. 102.
34. Van Creveld, *Supplying War,* p. 118.
35. Kennedy, *The Rise and Fall of the Great Powers,* p. 240.
36. For a very full account of the difficulties encountered by the Germans, and an analysis of the causes see Van Creveld, *Supplying War,* pp. 109 to 141.
37. Even then, the Confederates were unable to use captured Spencer repeating carbines in any numbers, once any captured ammunition was expended, because they lacked the special cartridges and had no metal for their manufacture.
38. Lachhman, Singh, *Indian Sword Strikes in East Pakistan,* p. 166. In the 1971 war in East Pakistan, Major General Singh commanded the Indian 20th Mountain Division, which experienced some of the hardest fighting. He records: 'It is of interest to know that shell injuries, compared to the bullet injuries, were high and most of these injuries were the result of air bursts'. At one stage, when his division had 634 wounded, there were 316 shell, and 262 bullet injuries. The Pakistan Army in East Pakistan was not particularly lavishly supplied with artillery.
39. *The Story of the Fourth Army in the Battle of the Hundred Days,* p. ix., discussing the advisability of accepting the Armistice before the Germans, falling back on their own frontiers, stiffened their resistance, and prolonged the war; 'it was a physical impossibility for at least the British Armies to continue their advance rapidly and in strength and to immediately follow-up their successes. Had they done so, they would have starved'.
40. It is difficult to express it better than van Creveld, *Command in War,* p. 190, 'Strategically, the rise of the gasoline-powered motor vehicle meant that armies were now released from the tyranny exercised over them by the railways since the days of Moltke and Grant. The result was a tremendous gain, not so much in the linear speed or in the number of ton/miles lifted (for both of which purposes the railways, so long as they are free from air interdiction, have retained their superiority to this day), as in the flexibility it provided'.

Chapter 3: Three Campaigns in a Global War

1. Donnelly, *The Sustainability of the Soviet Army in Battle (SSRC C53),* pp. 233–236.
2. Alstead, *Ten in Ten, A Study of the Central Region Transport Capability in Crisis and War.*
3. Terraine, *The Right of the Line,* p. 263 quotes Richards and Saunders, *The Royal Air Force 1939–45* (HMSO 1974).
   '. . . with the approach of D-Day a rapidly spreading paralysis was creeping over the railway network of the Region Nord. When that day dawned, 21,949 British and American aircraft had cast down a total of 66,517 tons of bombs on eighty chosen targets . . . The movement of German troops and material by rail had thus become a matter of very great difficulty and hazard, and this well before any landings had been made. Such trains as ran moved very slowly, were forced to make long detours and travelled only at night. The enemy had no freedom of movement in a large part of France and Belgium.'

4. *Supply Problems of 21 Army Group and American Expeditionary Force 1944–45.*
   (The Liddell Hart Centre for Military Archives, King's College, London.)
5. Terraine, p. 370.
6. Van Creveld, *Supplying War*, p. 144.
7. Van Creveld, p. 145.
8. War Office series *The Second World War, 1939–1945, Army Movements*, p. 303.
9. War Office series *The Second World War, 1939–1945, Army Supplies and
   Transport*, Vol. I, p. 221. The initial troop allocation in the Assault Convoy was:
   Algiers
   > Two platoons of 3-ton trucks for temporary beach maintenance (i.e. moving
   > stores off the beach), then to Philippeville and Bone when relieved.
   > Two platoons of 6-ton trucks for port maintenance at Algiers.
   > Two platoons, less three sections, of tipper trucks, to carry fuel for the airfield,
   > then to be employed on road and airfield repair.
   > One platoon of ambulances.
   > One Bailey Bridge platoon.
   Bougie
   > One platoon of 3-ton trucks for temporary beach and port maintenance.
   > Arriving on D+4:
   > One platoon of the Armoured Brigade Transport Company.
   > One Bailey Bridge platoon.
   > One troop carrying company.
   > One tank transporter company.
   > One platoon, less two sections, ambulance car company.
   > One platoon water truck company.
   > One heavy anti-aircraft regiment company.

   The above would constitute the total *planned* transport for the force until the third
   convoy due on D+14 or 18 arrived.
   Petrol, oil and lubricants (POL) was allowed for as follows:

MT spirit (petrol)	5 galls/veh/day
Derv (diesel)	50 galls/tank or AFV/day
Lubricants	6% of total petrol or diesel

   45 days reserves were to be built up by D+90. Thereafter there would be a
   build up to 60 days reserves.
   At this stage in the war, the British Army was still using the old fashioned petrol
   tins instead of the 'Jerrican' which was to prove so successful later. The former were
   so flimsy that when stowed in ships in stacks more than 12 feet high they crushed,
   and leaked. Some ships arrived in North African ports with cans stacked up to
   50 feet high, having leaked up to 40 per cent of the contents, and the holds many
   feet deep in petrol. Up to a further 25 per cent was lost in transit from these cans.
   The losses from leakage was not only hazardous, but also very wasteful of
   transport effort (S. & T., Vol. I, p. 233). Lieutenant-General Sir Francis Tuker,
   Approach to Battle (Cassell 1973), p. 17, as commander of 4th Indian Dvision in
   8th Army assessed that about 50 per cent of fuel carried in these ineffective cans was
   lost in transit.
10. *Movements*, p. 372, claims that the beaches used in Normandy were the worst ever
   for a combined operation from the point of view of the beach gradient. Because of
   this, fully laden stores ships had to remain up to five miles offshore, which resulted
   in considerable turn-round times for ferry craft and amphibians (DUKWs). The
   tonnages were:

   D Day Nil because of bad weather
   D+1   4,600
   D+2   Nil because of bad weather

D + 3   2,924
D + 4   6,049
D + 5   9,911

Total   23,484 tons unloaded over 4 days = an average of 5,871 tons per day on which unloading was possible

11. Terraine, p. 389. In the campaign in Cyrenaica and Tripolitania the Desert Airforce was soon to solve the problem of pushing fuel forward to newly captured airfields.

'. . . valuable aid in the form of the US 316th Troop Carrier Command, with its admirable DC-3s, the famous Dakotas which were to transform Allied air transport problems. It was impossible to carry the grossly inefficient standard British four-gallon commercial tin inside an aircraft (*see Note 9 above*). The alternative was 44 gallon steel drums, but the RAF did not have the carrying capacity for these. The Dakotas could do it, and did, to the tune of 130,000 gallons lifted for the Desert Air Force for the El Agheila operation in mid-December, and 153,000 gallons of petrol as well as 9,500 gallons of oil lifted to Marble Arch landing ground alone during December and January— the equivalent of the total tank capacity of 1,575 Hurricanes, or 1,240 Kittyhawks, or 355 Bostons (aircraft types used in close support of 8th Army)'.

The lessons learned by 8th Army and the Desert Air Force about army/air co-operation took some time to be hoisted in by their counterparts planning and operating at the other end of the North African littoral.

The Germans, however, were well ahead of the Allies in the techniques of supply by air. Terraine, p. 751:

'In January (1942) when Rommel launched his counter-offensive, the Luftwaffe had only enough fuel for two weeks offensive operations. "Had not air transport carried enough fuel to meet daily consumption, the GAF units would have been grounded within a fortnight" (Air Historical Branch/II/ 117/8(B) pp. 290–291). "Even after the attacks from Malta upon the sea route to North Africa had dwindled to almost nothing, the Germans made great use of their numerous transport aircraft to carry men and stores from Crete to Cyrenaica". (Playfair, *Official History, The Mediterranean and the Middle East* (HMSO, 1954).' See also Note 12.

Thanks to flawed tactical and strategic thinking in The Royal Air Force before the Second World War, cogently portrayed by Terraine in *The Right of the Line*, the British possessed nothing to compare with German or American air transports.

12. Terraine, *op. cit.*, p. 115. As far back as the invasion of Norway, in 1940, the Germans had shown how they outstripped the British in the bold and imaginative use of air transport.

'For the initial invasion the Luftwaffe deployed 500 combat aircraft and another 571 Ju 52/3M transports. It was the latter which brought in the six companies of airborne troops who captured the Norwegian capital with its 250,000 inhabitants; it was Ju 52s again which dropped the 120 paratroops who captured Stavanger aerodrome shortly before eight o'clock on the morning of the first day. By that evening, 180 Ju 52s arriving with clock-work regularity, had touched down in Stavanger. In the course of the whole campaign (but their chief use was in the early stages) these invaluable aircraft flew 3,018 sorties, carrying 29,280 personnel, 259,300 imperial gallons of fuel and 2,376 tons of supplies.' Quoting William Green, *Warplanes of the Third Reich*, p. 410.

13. *S. & T.*, *Vol. 1*, pp. 229 and 230. The situation was aggravated because, at the last

minute, a total of 400 vehicles were shut out of convoys arriving up to, and including, the one on D + 18, caused by the limited quantity of commercial ships capable of carrying a worthwhile load of sizeable trucks. In 1942 there were few of the specialised ships for moving large quantities of trucks that were available for later operations. Also, not only were the second line transport companies operating at light scales, but some units to be supported, such as the commandos and parachute battalions operating in a conventional infantry role, had practically no first line transport, let alone second line. (First line transport consists of the vehicles organic to the unit. Second line transport is sent forward from brigade, or division, depending on the system being worked in the theatre, to support units for a specific task).

Added to this was the steadily increasing flow of US combat troops forward, without an increase in transport at the same rate. So that for example: two infantry brigade companies designed to maintain 9,000 men, found themselves supporting 17,000 to 20,000 men up to 80 miles in advance of the railhead, with only one tank transporter company to assist. 78th Division's third line company did not arrive until early December, and 6th Armoured Division's third line company did not arrive until well after that.

14. *Movements*, p. 314, provides a summary as follows:

	Tons per day	
Into Tunisia		
Eastward from Bone by road, rail and craft	500	
Eastward through Souk Arhas by rail:		
a. From Bone	750	
b. From Algiers	500	
Eastward through Tebessa by metre gauge rail	750	
	2,500	tons
Into the Constantine Area (Airfields and Advance Base)		
From Philippeville by road and rail	500	
From Algiers by rail	750	
	1,250	tons

15. *War Diary of Chief Administrative Officer Allied Force Headquarters.* (The Liddell Hart Centre for Military Archives, King's College, London).

5 January 1943:

'Generally speaking this HQ is improving, but is still far from being the perfect running machine it could be. Merging the American and British Staff organisation is rather like screwing a metric nut on to a Whitworth bolt— however we may get the threads sufficiently well crossed to ensure security.'

26 February 1943:

'Visits to forward areas have revealed the following indications of the attitude of our Allies towards Supplies:

(a) Pilfering at OULED RAHMOUN became so bad that a CMP (military police) raid in force became necessary. Numerous court martials are resulting. In one instance the US locomotive battalion removed 42 cases of compo (composite rations packed so that each case provided 14 mens' rations for one day) at pistol point.

(b) At TEBESSA the 85 QM Company hold 1,000,000 rations. They describe this as 21 days for 23,000 men—or two rations per day per man!

(c) Of accounting, in our sense of the word, there is none. To understand this it is necessary to remember, firstly, that Americans in the USA, have never known want, privation or real poverty. There is always "plenty more where this came from". An appeal to them to consider shipping space or the needs of others is of no avail because it has never been brought home to them.

Secondly, they regard TEBESSA, in all seriousness, as being "in the front line." (*Author—perhaps Gale is being a trifle scathing. Although the German breakthrough at Kasserine, 14–22 February 1943, did not reach Tebessa, it nearly succeeded in doing so, and the Americans from Eisenhower downwards were considerably alarmed. 10,000 tons of ammunition and fuel were captured or destroyed in the retreat of US II Corps).* The result of these two principles, if such they can be called, is that they act on the following maxim. "Our boys are fighting the battle for the Allied cause. Whatever they want they must have. If they are hungry then we must give them all the rations that we can. And the boys sure can eat a hell of a lot." A ration scale to them is meaningless.

In the American Army a supply officer—Quartermaster to them—is judged by his ability to amass as great a quantity of supplies and stores as possible by any means whatsoever. His value as an officer is judged by the magnitude of his "dump". The following examples may be quoted:

A unit representative came to draw, and presented an indent showing the unit strength as 84. He was handed 84 cases of compo (i.e. enough to feed 1,176 men). Another unit indented for a quantity of petrol which comprised five days supply. After two days the unit reported that they had none left. An inspection of the unit location revealed that men were sleeping in dug-outs composed of walls of full petrol tins. Expostulations were met with the reply, "it's OK these boys are non-smokers".

The viciousness of this attitude is too obvious to be enlarged upon. No wonder we have difficulties with shipping, railways and road transport.

After dinner had a further discussion with General Miller (Major General Administration 18 Army Group) and Brigadier Philipe on our problems. I think we shall build up our reserves for the battle but it will be a tight squeeze, especially on the U.S. side.'

The British, although better disciplined, could also overbid, as demonstrated from a memo produced by the Major General Administration 18 Army Group on 7 April 1943, one month before the end of the campaign (with Gale Papers):

'(a) First Army demands for "build-up" in Army Area prior to offensive action were based on 2,500 rounds per 25-pr (pounder) field gun in Army Area over and above 1st and 2nd line holdings. This was the estimate given by the "G" staff (operations) to "Q" (logistics) and accepted by the latter, although after some demur. The battle of Alamein was fought over a period of over 10 days with an expenditure of well under 1,000 r.p.g. (rounds per gun) 25-pr. 2,500 r.p.g. for an estimated 10 day battle is of course fantastic. (Readers will no doubt remember from Chapter 2 that, the expenditure which Miller thought so fantastic, i.e. 250 rounds per day per gun, was greatly exceeded in the course of battles in the Falklands compaign. But at Alamein, and indeed in most major battles taking several days and over a great area (at Alamein a 25 mile front), all guns are not firing all the time) . . .

(c) The RAF have been bad offenders in the past . . . U.S. Airforce do not appear to do much more at present than to make a wide safe guess. In one case in this theatre enough fighter aircraft ammunition was moved to a forward airfield to last the fighter force squadrons at intensive rates daily for one year! On another occasion I was asked to provide transport to withdraw 5,000 tons of 100 octane from a forward airfield when threatened by an enemy advance. Both these examples [which] show complete lack of appreciation of the administrative situation in relation to operational requirements and situation, caused a waste of limited transport resources and proved that there was no proper staff control of priorities.'

Gale, who went on to become Eisenhower's chief of administration at Supreme Headquarters Allied Expeditionary Force (SHAEF) for the invasion of North West Europe and the subsequent campaign, was not anti-American, although the tone of the entries in his diary would suggest otherwise. As an outstanding logistician, he was outraged at what he saw. On the whole, the Americans were the worst offenders. But at this stage of the war their army, mostly consisting of not particularly well trained and disciplined draftees, under inexperienced officers, had a great deal to learn about the realities of tactics and logistics. Tactically, they improved to become as good as any under some outstanding generals such as Patton, Collins, Ridgeway and Gavin, to name but a few. This was not always the case logistically. As late as 1944, there were instances, particularly in Patton's U.S. 3rd Army, of employing highly unorthodox methods to obtain supplies, including hi-jacking trucks and removing the fuel, see Van Creveld, *Supplying War, op. cit.*, p. 221 for comments on waste.

16. Daily maintenance means exactly what it says: the ammunition, fuel, food and other supplies needed to maintain operations on a daily basis. This will be based on the size of the force (in technical logistic terms: 'the dependancy'), and the anticipated intensity and type of operations, and hence the rates at which: ammunition will be expended, fuel consumed, vehicles and equipment needing repair or replacement. Almost the only commodity which can be provided for with absolutely guaranteed accuracy is rations, for obvious reasons. If the staffs underestimate the intensity of operations, and are mistaken about the form they will take, some commodities will run short, and reserves, if there are any, will be consumed. The rate of build-up of reserve stocks, to meet the higher expenditure rate of intense operations associated with an offensive, will be critically affected if there is insufficient margin in the transport system to allow both daily maintenance supplies and an element of reserve supplies to be lifted forward each day. Hence the importance of improving the lines of communication from the situation in the first two months of the campaign when only 3,750 tons a day could be lifted forward, 1,750 tons a day short of the lowest daily maintenance requirement in April, let alone the need to move a daily average of 2,040 tons of reserve stocks forward at the same time.

17. *S&T* Vol. 1, p. 283. As an aside it is interesting that the standard resupply of 17th United States Airborne Division at the Rhine Crossing in March 1945, was 270.54 tons a day, of which ammunition of all natures including mortar and gun ammunition for guns up to 105 mm calibre, made up 214.94 tons, i.e. 79 per cent ammunition. (HQ 1st Allied Airborne Army Report on Operation VARSITY, The Rhine crossing—Appendix 9—Resupply and Casualty Evacuation).

18. Terraine, p. 594, and p. 598. He is quoting here from *Air Historical Board/ II/116/22* p. 111, and *Appendix to Air Historical Board/II/117/11(A)*, as well as Slessor, *The Central Blue*. A recent re-assessment of the effects of Operation STRANGLE (Edward Male, New Look at Strangle, *Military Affairs, Vol. 52, No. 4, October 1988*, pp. 176–184), does not undermine Slessor's argument, summarised in his final sub-paragraph. Research by Male shows that the Germans faced serious logistic problems, but admits that STRANGLE did not achieve what it set out to do: to force the Germans to abandon Rome for lack of supplies. He offers the following reasons:

(a) The Allies, [not for the first or last time—author's comment], underestimated the German reaction, which included making most of their moves at night. On one occasion Von Senger moved the whole of his Corps across the entire front of German 14th Army, to check the advance of the

U.S. Vth Corps. On another the Herman Goering division made a move by daylight in response to an urgent operational situation, and air attack failed to stop them.

(b) The Allies overestimated the supply requirements of the Germans, who were able to exercise economy measures, particularly in rear units.

(c) There was no co-ordination between Allied ground operations (DIADEM), and air operations (STRANGLE), to ensure that maximum pressure was exerted at a time when the enemy was having maximum logistical difficulties.

(d) The Allies underestimated the road transport available to the Germans. Daily transport returns, passed by signal and picked up by ULTRA, only included figures for divisional and corps transport. Returns giving figures of road transport under the control of the headquarters of the two field armies, 10th and 14th, were not passed by signal, and were not, therefore, picked up by the intercepts.

(e) Bad weather grounded the medium bombers for at least half the time.

(f) Finally, the terrain favoured the defence, and delaying actions, which could be conducted without high ammunition expenditure.

Therefore there was no collapse of the German logistic system, despite it being virtually defenceless against air attack, having almost no fighters, and flak protection only around a few strategic bridges.

19. The British found themselves in the same position on the Western Front in the period 1914–17, and indeed to a lesser extent until the end of the First World War. To begin with, they were so vastly inferior numerically to the French that there was no question of pursuing a private strategy, they simply lacked the means. From 1917, following the French Army mutinies, and the need for the British to shoulder the major burden of the offensives on the Western Front, they had more say in strategy, but were not in any sense able to conduct it in isolation.

20. *Admin. Planning*, p. 40. 'The absence of a decision during most of 1944 was to present a series of administrative (logistic) problems that seemed almost insoluble. In fact, during this period the Principal Administrative Officers Committee on more than one occasion deemed it necessary to warn the Chiefs of Staff that, unless a decision could be given, there was a risk that the necessary administrative preparations could not be made for either course in time.' The Principal Administrative Officers Committee was a sub-committee of the British Chiefs of Staff, consisting of the Fourth Sea Lord, the Quartermaster General, the Air Member for Supplies and Organisation, and a representative of the Civil Ministries. They were responsible for advising the Chiefs of Staff on all inter-service logistics matters, except personnel, medical, and legal.

21. *Transportation*, p. 180. Because of the Japanese threat in early 1942, Calcutta was virtually closed as a port for a time, throwing an additional burden on the other ports and railways in India.

22. *Admin. Planning*, p. 42.

23. *Admin. Planning*, p. 79. The roads to the Arakan front were also difficult to build. There is a story, probably apocryphal, but nevertheless making the point, that when the Quartermaster General (a four star general), visited the Arakan front in 1944, on leaving his car at the road-head, he was informed by the Corps Commander of the order that everyone going forward was required to carry a basket of bricks to help in the making of the road; he complied.

24. *Movements*, p. 420.

25. Wingate is alleged to have decreed that: 'no patrol is ever to report that the jungle is impenetrable, until they have penetrated it.'

26. *S. & T., Vol. II*, p. 93 gives the following dates for the progress of 14th Army:

Kelewa taken 2 December 1944.
Shwebo and Ye-U taken 2–10 January 1945.
Mandalay taken 20 March 1945.
Rangoon taken 3 May 1945.
27. *S. & T., Vol. II*, p.102 gives the reasons:
 (a) It was expensive in tonnage, as one-third of the weight was supply dropping equipment, and the percentage of breakages and losses rose to as much as 25 per cent.
 (b) It was expensive in aircraft, owing to the time spent circling over the dropping zone, and the fatigue of the pilots.
 (c) It required a very high standard of training and co-operation from the pilots.
 (d) It took a long time to collect a large drop.
 (e) Troops were necessary to protect the personnel collecting the drop and also possibly as labour.
28. *S. & T., Vol. II*, p. 100.
29. Terraine, p. 365. In October 1941, on the eve of the British CRUSADER. Rommel had lost 63 per cent of his supplies crossing the Mediterranean.
30. Kennedy. *The Rise and Fall of The Great Powers*, pp. 443–444.
31. *Army Administration Vol. I*, p. 62.

Part Two

Chapter 4: Unpreparedness and Speedy Recovery

1. Appleman, Roy E., *The United States Army in the Korean War, South to the Naktong, North to the Yalu*, p. 182.
2. Appleman, p. 488.
3. Schnabel, James F., *United States Army in the Korean War, Policy and Direction: The First Year*, pp. 63–64.
4. Gough, J., *US Army Mobilization and Logistics in the Korean War*, p. 24, however, quotes a claim by Colonel Curtis, U.S. Army (Retired), who was in the plans division of G-4 (Logistics), Army General Staff, stating that in 1948, a series of logistic studies were prepared that included one for an invasion of South Korea across the 38th Parallel. According to Curtis, he prepared a strategic concept that called for a 'retreat to and defence of the Pusan perimeter, build-up and break-out, *and an amphibious landing at Inchon* to cut the enemy supply lines'. The purpose of these strategic logistic studies was to 'ascertain in advance what unusual logistic requirements could be expected in various potential theatres of operations'. Curtis claims that other sections of the General Staff concurred in his strategic concept, but does not make clear whether logistic plans were ever made to support it. Only thorough archival research will prove whether or not there were logistical plans for the Korean War. If there were, it seems strange that they were not pulled out and dusted off. Furthermore, for there to have been such plans, operational plans, or at least concepts, would have had to have been written first. The logistician does not, as a rule, plan in an operational vacuum.
5. *Lessons from Korea, 1954* (The Infantry School Fort Benning, Georgia), (TDRC No. 4259), starts:
 'The infantry has learned many lessons from its military operations in Korea. These lessons were learned mainly through mistakes made on the battlefield. It is enlightening—and disheartening—to note that these errors were often the same as those described in World War II combat reports, which suggests that this article might be more aptly titled "Lessons Relearned in Korea." '

and continues by cataloguing the shortcomings of the United States infantry in Korea, including: poor standards of training; a universal distaste for night operations (a shortcoming quickly recognised and seized on by the NKPA and CCF); lack of discipline; lack of aggressive patrolling; and poor ammunition conservation. It also notes that for lack of spares, helicopter serviceability was poor; some aircraft being downed for months, so that out of the five helicopters per division, it was normal to have only two available.

6. Schnabel, p. 60. Appleman, p. 180, also notes the same in rather more detail, when discussing the performance of the 24th Infantry Division in the first months of the war.

> 'The basic fact is that the occupation divisions were not trained, equipped, or ready for battle. The great majority of enlisted men were young and not really interested in being soldiers. The recruiting posters that had induced most of these men to enter the Army mentioned all conceivable advantages and promised many good things, but never suggested that the principle business of an army is to fight.'

The author's comment on this is to say that recruiting posters rarely portray the truth in this respect. Herein lies a potential problem in most volunteer armies, or navies for that matter. A number of British naval ratings when war looked likely in the Falklands in 1982, were on record as saying that they had not joined the Navy to go to war! No such remark was recorded in the case of the commandos and parachute battalions. It would seem therefore that the 'I'm only here for the beer' syndrome can be overcome by training. This, of course, is the responsibility of officers at all levels.

7. Schnabel, *op. cit.*, p. 59. Also Appleman, *op. cit.*, pp. 113/115 for examples of the shoddy state of U.S. Army equipment, and lack of stocks.

Some vehicles would not start, and had to be towed on to the LSTs when units loaded for Korea. The worn tyres and tubes were soon destroyed by the rough Korean roads. The 25th Infantry Regiment reported that it had only 60 per cent of its establishment of radios, and that four-fifths of them were inoperable. The 1st Battalion of the 35th Infantry had only one RCL, instead of six; none of its companies had spare barrels for machine guns, and most of its rifles and carbines were unserviceable. Some categories of ammunition were in short supply.

There were no C Rations (ration packs designed to be stowed in the soldier's equipment and provide one day's meals for one man) in Korea, and very small stocks in Japan. Arrangements were hurriedly made to ship ration packs from the United States. Meanwhile, the United States troops in Korea existed on Second World War K rations.

8. Victory, P, *The Commonwealth Artillery in the Korean War 1950-53* (TDRC No. 8137), p. 1.
9. Hastings, Max., *The Korean War*, p. 85.
10. Appleman, pp. 248–249.
11. For example, in October 1810, Wellington falling back deliberately on the Lines of Torres Vedras and supplied through the port of Lisbon. And, Rommel operating at the end of a long line of communication against the British Eighth Army on the Alamein position in July 1942.
12. Gough, p. 17. Pusan was an excellent harbour with deep-water dock facilities. It could berth nearly thirty deep-draught vessels, and unload twelve to fifteen LSTs at once. This produced a daily discharge potential of 40,000 to 45,000 tons, but problems of cargo handling and inland transportation reduced the actual capacity to about 28,000 tons daily. Over the period of a year, 1951, the port cleared an average of 14,000 tons per day (Huston). Masan, twenty miles west of Pusan, could provide deep-water berthing for only two ships. Inchon, when it was

captured, was the second busiest port used by the United Nations (see below for its unattractive characteristics). The tidal basin built by the Japanese could berth up to nine shallow-draught ships, but deep-draught ships had to be unloaded into lighters offshore. Other Korean ports came nowhere near Inchon's capacity.

13. Badly trained or inexperienced troops will often carry too much when first committed to battle. The peace-time habit of not carrying a full ammunition load on field training has much to blame for this. Without the weight of live ammunition, for which blank is a poor substitute, because it is lighter, the soldier gets a false idea of how much space he can allocate to personal comforts as opposed to essentials. As he hardens under operational conditions, he finds he can do with fewer and fewer extras, learning to exist with the minimum—food, water, weapon and ammunition, and enough clothing and protection from the weather to survive; this last will vary according to the climate.

14. Appleman, pp. 259–261.

15. Gough, p. 24. As noted above, Colonel Curtis claims to have thought of it first. However, if the Inchon landing had been studied, as Curtis claims, all the factors in its selection should have been available to the planners, obviating the discussion which took place at various levels when MacArthur proposed the amphibious hook. Unless, of course, the study had become lost in the mass of paper in Washington, which seems highly inefficient, but not beyond the bounds of possibility; and not only in the Pentagon.

16. Appleman, pp. 498–499. There are no beaches in the landing area, only wide mud flats at low tide and stone walls at high tide. The flats would not support a man on foot. The main approach from sea is by two channels 50 miles long, and only 36–60 feet deep. The Flying Fish channel, used by big ships is narrow and twisting, hazardous even in daylight. Tides in the restricted waters of the channel and the harbour have a maximum range of more than 31 feet. Some of the landing craft required 23 feet of water to clear the mud flats. The larger landing ships (Landing Ships Tank LST) needed 29 feet. The Navy settled for 23 feet of tide as the critical point needed for landing craft to clear the mud flats and reach the landing sites. This meant that men and supplies could be landed only from the time the incoming tide reached 23 feet, until the outgoing tide dropped again to that level; a period of only about three hours. Troops ashore would then be unable to be reinforced until the next high tide about eleven to twelve hours later.

   The combination of the right tide and daylight, needed for the transit of the channel, occurred only on 15 September, 27 September and 11 to 13 October. The sea walls that fronted the landing sites were 16 feet high above the mud flats. Except at high water, these presented a scaling problem. As the first waves would land before high tide in order to use the last two hours of daylight, ladders were needed, as were grappling hooks, lines, and cargo nets.

   The initial objective of the landing force was to gain a beachhead at Inchon city (population 250,000). A battalion would land on Wolmi-do, an island which dominated the approaches to the main landing sites, at 06.30. An eleven hour pause would follow, to allow the right tidal conditions, before the main landing at 17.30. The Inchon area was very heavily built-up, and easily defended.

17. Appleman, pp. 493/495, a message from MacArthur to Washington on 8 September included the following:
   'The envelopment from the north will instantly relieve the pressure on the south perimeter and, indeed, is the only way that this can be accomplished . . . The seizure of the heart of the enemy distributing system in the Seoul area will completely dislocate the logistical supply of his forces now operating in South Korea and therefore will ultimately result in their disintegration. Indeed this is the primary purpose of the movement. Caught between our northern and

southern forces, both of which are completely self-sustaining because of our absolute air and naval supremacy, the enemy cannot fail to be ultimately shattered through disruption of his logistical support . . .'.

18. Huston, pp. 156–157. Probably no single item of supply received more attention in the support of operations in Korea than ammunition. Total stocks often fell below the ninety day level of supply, and sometimes well below the safety scale of sixty days. There were three contributing factors:

(a) The very high rate of fire needed to break up mass attacks.

(b) That there were no ammunition production lines of any consequence in the U.S.A. For example, no 105 mm ammunition had been produced since 1945.

(c) It took about 18 months to establish production lines.

19. Appleman, pp. 639–640. For example the Imjin River rail bridge spanned a river 1,600 feet wide, and requird a length of several thousand feet of earth fill in its approaches. To provide a road bridge across the Han River, seventy C-119 aircraft flew in a pontoon bridge from Japan. This made up a 50 ton floating bridge, 740 feet long.

20. Schnabel, pp. 260–261. Xth Corps staff had prepared a study discussing the Marine advance which read:

'As the 1st Marines move towards Changjin (Chosin) they will tend to be extended. The left flank of the Marines will be on the mountainous ridge that divides the watersheds of the peninsula. It is generally impassable for heavy military traffic. However prisoner reports show that the 124th CCF (Chinese Communist Forces) Division entered Korea at Manpojin and is now in the Chosin Reservoir area. If the 1st Marine Division attacks north beyond this route well ahead of the Eighth Army it will be vulnerable to attacks on its flank and rear.'

In the light of this assessment, it is difficult to understand why Almond pressed Smith to advance without due precaution.

Smith had no illusions. Speaking to Rear Admiral Morehouse, the chief of staff to the Commander Naval Forces Far East, he expressed frank concern over what he considered General Almond's unrealistic planning and his tendency to ignore enemy capabilities when he wanted a rapid advance. In a letter to the Commandant of the Marine Corps he admitted that he felt that Almond's orders were wrong. 'Our orders require us to advance to the Manchurian border. However we are the left flank division of the Corps and our left flank is wide open.' He pointed out that there was no Eighth Army unit closer to his flank than eighty miles south-west. While Xth Corps, according to Smith, could assure him, 'when it is convenient', that there were no Chinese on his flank, he observed, 'if this were true, there would be nothing to prevent Eighth Army from coming abreast of us. This they are not doing.'

21. Schnabel, p. 273.

22. Ridgway, M. B., *The Korean War*, pp. 85–87.

23. At this point it is convenient to refer to the non-communist forces in Korea, as the United Nations forces. By June 1951, all ROK formations were under command of Eighth Army. The only major non-U.S. or ROK formation was the Commonwealth Division, made up of British, Australian, Canadian, New Zealand and Indian formations and units; 24,000 strong at its maximum. At between 4,602 and 5,455 strong, the Turkish contingent was the next largest after the Commonwealth Division. For similar reasons of convenience the North Koreans and Chinese are referred to as Communist Forces, unless it is necessary to distinguish between the two.

24. Schnabel, p. 399.

25. Hermes, W. G., *The United States Army in the Korean War, Truce Tent and Fighting Front*, p. 105.
26. See Chapter 3.
27. Hermes, p. 195, quoting *COMNAVFE, Command and Historical Report, Feb. 52*, pp. 1–4.
28. Hermes, p. 319, quoting USAF Historical Study 127, *United States Operations in the Korean Conflict 1 July 52–27 July 53*, p. 26.
29. Hermes, p. 196, quoting Air Interdiction Program in HQ Eighth Army, General Administration files, March 52, Paper 21.
30. Hermes, pp. 511–512.

Chapter 5: Insufficiency and Superabundance

1. French Indo-China consisted of the present countries of Laos, Cambodia and Vietnam.
2. Roy, *The Battle of Dien Bien Phu*, p. 315.
3. The French Army in Indo-China was a colourful mixture, reflecting its peculiar heritage and tradition of colonial service. Historically French conscripts served only to defend their country. Forces to serve outside Metropolitan France were raised either from Frenchmen, and, in the case of *La Légion Étranger*, other Europeans as well, volunteering specifically for service overseas, or from volunteers from France's numerous colonies. The regiments of the French Foreign Legion; *Régiment Étranger d'Infanterie (REI)*, and *Régiment Étranger Parachutiste (REP*, need no introduction. But for example: *Bataillons de Parachutistes Coloniaux (BPC)* were manned by Frenchmen; *Régiment d'Infanterie Coloniale du Maroc*, by Moroccans; *Infanterie de la Marine*, by Frenchmen serving in a regiment that had long since severed its connexion with the sea, and was exclusively recruited for service overseas. The officers for these 'colonial' forces, including the Legion, were exclusively French regulars, products of the French Military Academy, St Cyr. In this book, the term 'French troops' includes men of all nationalities serving in the French colonial army, from Moroccans, Vietnamese, Laotians, Cambodians, Europeans of every race, including ex-SS Germans, to Frenchmen. The term Vietnamese troops refers to the Vietnamese National Army.
4. The Vietminh, and later the North Vietnamese and Viet Cong, had three categories of fighting units. Although the proportions of man and woman-power assigned to each group was to change as the years passed, the groupings never did. They were:
    (a) The Main Force units, in Round One, the regular units of the Vietminh fighting the French. In Round Two, the regulars of the North Vietnamese Army and the Viet Cong engaging the Americans and the South Vietnamese. These units were well led, well trained, and brave. Their size grew from platoons in 1944, to divisions, corps and Fronts (a Soviet expression denoting a group of armies operating on a particular front). Eventually, they were equipped with armour, artillery, aircraft and anti-aircraft guns and missiles. They always came directly under the commander-in-chief of the army, or a Front or area commander.
    (b) The Regional or Local forces were second line troops found from a province or district. The Regional forces were further subdivided:
        (1) Provincial forces, about battalion size, reasonably well armed, recruited from, and operating in, their province.
        (2) District forces, less well armed, recruited from and operating in their district.

Local forces were commanded by the Commander-in-Chief and controlled through the Interzone which included several provinces. Early in Round One, the Vietminh had five Interzones, but later redesignated them Military Regions (MRs): four in North Vietnam, and one, MR V, in the north of South Vietnam. In Round Two, another nine MRs were set up in the rest of South Vietnam. The Regional Forces varied in performance, but were essentially light infantry, carrying out reconnaissance and screening tasks for Main Force units, and ambushing and attacking enemy troops when they invaded their tactical area.

(c) Guerrillas or Popular Forces, raised by hamlets and villages and sub-divided:

> (1) The Dan Quan, consisting of both sexes and all ages, and without any fighting capability.
> (2) The Dan Quan Du Kich, consisting of men aged 18–45 which carried out combat operations. They were without uniforms, and ill equipped. They worked in the fields by day, and occasionally attacked enemy outposts at night.

Controlled by the Commander-in-Chief through the Interzone/MR, province and district, the main task of both groups of Popular Forces was to lay booby traps, and act as intelligence gatherers and porters for the Main and Regional Force units.

The recruiting and training system was interesting, and innovative. All soldiers started as guerrillas. The best men were sent to Regional Forces for further 'blooding', the most capable being further promoted to the Main Forces. So Main Forces received a trained, and often very experienced recruit. Its disadvantage was that when Main or Regional forces had taken heavy casualties, guerrilla units were milked to provide reinforcements, sometimes at the expense of their own fighting capability.

5. Davidson, p. 35, *The Military Art*, p. 79.
6. Fall, *Street Without Joy*, p. 17.
7. Personnel—G1; Intelligence—G2; Operations—G3; Logistics—G4.
8. At least at those attended by the Author, both as a logistic staff officer in the British Army Far East Land Forces Headquarters in the period 1966/67, and as an Assistant Secretary to the British Chiefs of Staff Committee in 1970/71.
9. Davidson, pp. 59–60. Giap's figures for loads are interesting, quoting O'Niell, *General Giap—Politician and Strategist*, p. 72:
   'A man could lift . . . 55 lbs of rice or 33–44 lbs of arms and munitions over 15.5 miles of easy country by day, or 12.4 miles by night; 28 lbs of rice or 22–33 lbs of munitions over 9 miles of mountainous country by day, or 7.5 miles by night. A buffalo cart could move 770 lbs over 7.5 miles per day. A horse cart could move 473 lbs over 12.4 miles per day.'
10. O'Ballance, *The Indo-China War 1945–54: A Study in Guerrilla Warfare*, p. 118 and Fall, *Street Without Joy*, p. 33, who gives mortars.
11. Davidson, pp. 76–77, gives late 1949 as the date when Giap organised his regiments into divisions. Although the Author would respectfully submit that Davidson's statement that the division is the smallest unit to combine all ground arms, to maintain itself, and to fight independently, is not strictly correct; a brigade group can do all these things. Giap formed five divisions, of which the 308th became, in Davidson's words, 'one of the élite divisions in the military world'.
12. Fall, *Street Without Joy*, p. 33.
13. De Lattre's strategy was aimed at increasing French offensive strength to enable him to seize the initiative from Giap. Because the French Government would not provide additional troops, he had to reduce the number of French troops in static

defensive positions within the Delta. His plan was to build a fortified line (the de Lattre Line), around the perimeter of the Delta, and increase pacification operations within the enclosed area. He proposed turning over the static defence duties to the Vietnamese National Army under the Emperor, Bao Dai. In step with this, he aimed to increase military aid from the United States. The de Lattre Line ran from the sea north of Haiphong, west to Viet Tri, and then south-east to the sea near Phat Diem. It enclosed a salient about 75 miles wide where it rested on the sea, about 15 miles wide at its narrowest around Viet Tri, and about 110 miles long. Its defence consisted of small, mutually supporting fortified infantry positions. By mid-summer 1951, 600 posts had been completed, and a further 600 by the end of that year.

In the end, the overall concept never worked properly because it depended on Vietnamese National Army troops taking over the Line—very expensive in manpower (over two infantry divisions worth of men)—and successfully pacifying the area. Unfortunately the Vietnamese Army was never effective.

14. Davidson, p. 124, gives the rationale for these timings.
15. Fall, *Street Without Joy*, p. 31.
16. Spector, *Advice and Support; The Early Years: The US Army in Vietnam 1941–1960*, pp. 142–143. Page 143 quotes the record of the meeting on 20 September 1951 with de Lattre saying:

   'If you lose Korea, Asia is not lost; but if I lose Indochina, Asia is lost. Tonkin is the key to Southeast Asia, if Southeast Asia is lost, India will "burn like a match" and there will be no barrier to the advance of communism before Suez and Africa. If the Moslem world were thus engulfed, the Moslems in North Africa would soon fall in line and Europe itself would be outflanked.'

   This was a somewhat extreme version of the Domino Theory, even by the standards of the time! Although, according to Spector, p. 144,

   'the American leaders were willing to accept the de Lattre concept of one war, they were unenthusiastic about taking any practical steps toward establishing a unified Franco-American war effort in the Far East'.

17. Spector, p. 145: only 444 jeeps out of 968 and 393 6 × 6 trucks out of 906 were delivered in the summer of 1951. See p. 153 for maintenance standards.
18. Spector, p. 148; and p. 118 where he gives the example of Brigadier General Brink, Commander USMAAG, flying to U.S. Far East Command headquarters in Tokyo to obtain critical supplies for the French during the Vinh Yen battle in January 1951. Again, in June of that year, when the French ran dangerously short of 105 mm gun ammunition during the Phat Diem battle during Giap's Day River offensive, Brink arranged for the French to draw ammunition directly from the stockpiles of the U.S. Far East Command.
19. Fall, *Street Without Joy*, p. 94, gives the figures as 2 Soviet Molotava trucks, a U.S. jeep, 150 tons of ammunition, 500 rifles, 100 sub-machine guns, 22 machine guns, 30 Browning automatic rifles, 40 light mortars, 14 medium mortars, 2 heavy 120 mm mortars, 23 bazookas, and 3 recoilless anti-tank guns. Davidson gives higher figures which are the same as those given in the footnote to Fall p. 94, where he is quoting Captain Marion of the French Army. But neither figure constitutes a haul worth the effort expended by the French. What was significant, and a portent for the future was the Soviet trucks, as Fall says, positive proof that the Soviet bloc was starting to pour equipment into Northern Vietnam. By 1954, nearly 800 Molotavas would have been delivered to the Vietminh, a vital factor in the battle that decided the outcome of the War. These trucks were of a better design for the terrain than the American models used by the French. Trucks, artillery pieces, and other equipment supplied by the Soviets, steadily closed the technological gap between the French and the Vietminh.

20. Davidson, p. 188.
21. These were not from the ineffective Vietnamese National Army, but colonial troops, Vietnamese commanded by Frenchmen. They were excellent soldiers who fought well, on the whole.
22. In 1954, even the most modern helicopters were not capable of moving large numbers of men, over the sort of distances involved in the fighting in Indochina. Neither did they have even a medium lift capability, let alone a heavy lift. Not until the next generation of helicopters came into service was there any prospect of air-mobile operations.
23. Davidson, p. 218, quoting JCS Study, The Khe Sanh Study, Annex B, p. 4 and MACV Study of the Comparisons Between the Battle of Dien Bien Phu and the Analagous Khe San Situation, March 1968, comes to a figure of 60–70 aircraft, but the author has chosen to apply the 75 per cent serviceability rate. Hence his lower figure is less than Davidson's.
24. At the battle of Arnhem, the air force delivered to 1st British Airborne Division over a period of eight days, 1,431 tons of supplies in 601 sorties; 84 aircraft were shot down, only 106 tons were collected.
25. Davidson, p. 219.
26. Fall, *Street Without Joy*, p. 322.
27. Fall, *Street Without Joy*, p. 385.
28. Spector, pp. 258/259. For example, in the central maintenance depot near Saigon, thousands of tons of equipment lay scattered in disorder over thirty-two acres of open fields, where it was subject to the ravages of the humid South East Asian climate in which deterioration set in very rapidly.
29. Spector, pp. 285/286, in 1956 the Quang Trung basic training centre was capable of handling over 9,000 recruits at a time in a sixteen week course, and there was an eight week course for reservists.
    An American adviser reported that:

> 'One day during practice firing the 60 mm mortar, I was rather appalled at the lack of organisation of the class. For example there would be ladies, in their large straw conical hats, out selling bowls of soup and other things to nibble on right in among the class . . . that type of thing.' When the Vietnamese officer in charge was challenged by the American adviser on this and other slack habits, and asked which was better, the way he carried out the instruction or the way he had seen at Fort Benning, from where he had just returned, he replied, 'Oh, it was much better at Fort Benning.' On being asked why, he said, 'Well sir, that was Fort Benning and this is Vietnam.'

30. Spector, p. 354.
31. Heiser, *Logistic Support, Vietnam Studies*, p. 14.
32. Tolson, *Airmobility 1961–1971, Vietnam Studies*, pp. 70–71.
33. Heiser, p. 154; in 1967, helicopters lifted a total of 828,000 tons. Fixed wing transport lifted 780,000 tons. In 1968, the figures were 1,123,032 tons by helicopter and 997,174 tons by fixed wing aircraft.
34. Cochran, *First Strike at the River Drang*, p. 50 quotes Kinnard giving helicopter losses during his time in command of 1st Air Cavalry Division. His helicopters flew over 161,000 combat hours (400,000 individual sorties), and one helicopter was hit per 274 hours, one shot down per 4,500 hours, one hit and destroyed per 11,500 hours, one crew member killed per 6,000 hours, one wounded per 1,200 hours. Over 60 per cent of all helicopters shot down were recovered and repaired.
    Author's comment: *These figures demonstrate what a friendly air environment the U.S. forces operated in over South Vietnam. There was also no threat from*

mobile, surface-to-air missiles. If there had been, the Americans could not have operated in the way they did.

35. Ploger, *US Army Engineers 1965, Vietnam Studies*, pp. 115 and 124. In 1969, 70,000 tons of rock were used by U.S. Army engineers every week. This rate more than doubled in 1970. See also Dunn, Base Development in South Vietnam 1965–1970, pp. 99–112. The U.S. Army carried out considerable work to improve the rail system. By 1971 about 60 per cent of the original railway was in use again. Increasing amounts of freight were carried each year—until the U.S. withdrawal.

36. Heiser, *Op. cit.*, p. 41. There were, for example, three push packages and fifteen increments for an airborne brigade. Each one had 24,000 separate items and a varying amount of each item depending on the estimated consumption. Together they were intended to provide 240 days' supply. In 1965, the cost of one such package was over $19 million.

37. Heiser, p. 107.

38. Bowers, *Tactical Airlift in the United States Air Force in South East Asia*, p. 209, admits this: 'The Air Force airlift support of the cavalry division in the first weeks at An Khe was inauspicious.'

39. Bowers, pp. 213–214.

40. Starry, *Mounted Combat in Vietnam, Vietnam Studies*, pp. 181–182.

41. Burke, *Corps Logistic planning in Vietnam*, pp. 3–9.

42. Davidson, p. 400.

43. Davidson, p. 551.

44. Shore, *The Battle for Khe Sanh*. The B-52s, particularly, wielded an awesome power. Each carried a 27 ton payload of 108 mixed 500 and 750 lb bombs. The bombs churned up strips of terrain several thousand yards long, and the ground for miles around shock from the concussion alone. In some instances, NVA soldiers were found after a B-52 strike wandering around in a daze with blood streaming from their noses and mouths. Often, the internal haemorrhaging induced by the concussion was so severe that it resulted in death. To catch the stunned survivors above ground, the gunners inside the base put down fire missions into the target area for 10 to 15 minutes after the last B-52 had gone.

45. Shore, pp. 85–87. Often as many as 16 helicopters were used up to four times in one day during the Super Gaggle without loss. Before the introduction of this technique, as many as three helicopters were shot down in one day around Khe Sanh.

46. Tolson, pp. 226–227. Captured records indicated that the 'City' supported the 7th NVA Division.

47. Davidson, p. 627. The total haul included: 23,000 individual weapons, enough to equip 74 full strength NVA battalions: 2,500 crew-served weapons, 25 battalions worth; 16,700,000 rounds of small-arms ammunition—one year's expenditure; 14 million lbs of rice; 143,000 rounds of mortar, rocket, and recoilless rifle ammunition; and about 200,000 rounds of anti-aircraft ammunition.

48. Thompson, *Peace Is Not At Hand*, p. 77.

49. Khuyen, *RVNAF Logistics*, p. 200.

50. Khuyen, p. 238. NVA reinforcements could be in South Vietnam in three days. Large truck convoys moved along this route and the infiltration corridors into South Vietnam by day and night. ARVN intelligence estimated that the amount of supplies stored at NVA rear service bases actually in South Vietnam, were enough to support their troops for 13 to 18 months at the 1972 tempo of activity.

51. Khuyen, pp. 264, 346, 376 and 418. The effect of the cut back in U.S. aid in 1973/74 can be seen from the examples in the table below which shows the piece-by-piece replacement of critical equipment. These are only extracts, the whole table contains eight items, and the average replacement rate is one sixth of that requested:

Type of Equipment	Total Losses	Called Forward	Received
Tactical wheeled vehicle	8,514	2,466	843
Armoured tracked vehicle	240	143	95
Artillery pieces	163	143	51
Machine guns	2,377	2,260	267
Small arms	35,829	30,756	5,100

Also Khuyen, pp. 414, 416 and p. 420. 'History has it that the U.S. Congress chose to ignore the survival package and opt for humanitarian aid for those who survived'. Khuyen is alluding to the final requests for aid as the survival packages for the RVNAF. The use of individual clothing and jungle boots was extended from 6 months to 9–18 months for combat troops. In the author's experience as a logistician in the Far East, a pair of jungle boots could be worn out on one ten day patrol. The state of mind of the U.S. Congress can be judged by the fact that they allocated a Congressional conference room to Jane Fonda, and her husband Tom Hayden, where they could work to promote the North Vietnamese agitprop programme. These two persons gave lectures in the Capitol itself, attended by at least sixty Congressional aides. A group of thirty-five of these aides formed the Capitol Hill Coordinating Committee, whose purpose was to end all aid to South Vietnam.

52. Sharp, *Strategy for Defeat, Vietnam in Retrospect*, pp. 256–258 has an account of what is meant by 'the will to win', as related by an American Navy pilot, prisoner in the 'Hanoi Hilton' for seven years:

'If our escalation, our creeping up the panhandle with graduated bombing raids, our bombing pauses, conveyed any message to the enemy, it was lack of commitment . . . The guards were wide-eyed and particularly hostile after the raid, but the city was back to normal within minutes. The street sounds picked up, patriotic music bleated from the speakers at every corner, the interrogators strutted about the prison yards defiantly. By nightfall an almost carnival atmosphere could be sensed. Songfests went off as scheduled in the guards' quarters and in the city parks . . . So it was in the latter half of '66, '67, and '68 till the bombing stopped. These were the darkest days for the prisoners—when the brutality was of the sort you've read about.

A totally contrasting atmosphere swept the city on that December night in 1972 when the raids didn't last ten minutes but went on and on—when the B-52 columns rolled in, and the big bombs impacted and kept on impacting in the distance—when the ground shook, and the plaster fell from the ceiling, and the prisoners cheered wildly, and the guards cowered in the lee of the walls, cheeks so ashen you could detect it even from the light from the fiery sky. Some of this light was from the burning B-52s (I'm told that the losses were almost as predicted—low, but the important fact was that they kept coming). This was commitment. This was victory for the United States, and doomsday for North Vietnam, and we knew it and they knew it. By day, interrogators and guards would enquire about our needs solicitously. The streets were silent. The centre of Hanoi was dead—even though like our prisons, thousands of yards from the drop zones. We knew the bombers knew where we were, and felt not only ecstatically happy, but confident. The Vietnamese didn't. Night after night the planes kept coming in—and night after night the SAMs streaking through the sky were fewer and fewer (the naval blockade worked). The shock was there—the commitment was there— the enemy's will was broken. You could sense it in every Vietnamese face. They knew they lived through last night, but they also knew that if our forces moved their bomb line over a few thousand yards they wouldn't live through tonight. Our planes were transmitting the message of the utter futility of further resistance.'

Chapter 6: Into Africa—Sinai to Suez

1. Perlmutter, *Israel's Fourth War, October 1973; Political and Military Mispercep- tions.* Decision makers misperceive events when they try to fit incoming information into their existing theories and images, particularly when the latter play a large part in determining what is expected. Under these circumstances, reality is screened and the person perceives what he expects. Thus, most misperceptions, though not all, may be defined as instances of cognitive dissonance. Dissonance of cognition takes place, according to Leon Festinger, in his work *A Theory of Cognitive Dissonance*, when behaviour is incompatible with a person's values. Misperception then becomes a cognitive process misrepresenting the current state of affairs and moulding events according to personal cognition. Reality is misrepresented in order to adapt those events to the person's cognitive map.

2. Herzog, *The Middle East War 1973*, p. 11.
3. Kiesewetter, *Golan Tank Graveyard*, Wehrkunde 2/74 (TDRC No. 2314), p. 7.
4. Dupuy, *Elusive Victory*, p. 501.
5. Van Creveld, Two Years After: The Israeli Defence Forces 1973–75, p. 31, referring to Israel, '. . . the nation's resources are stretched to breaking point . . .' and later, on p. 34, Israel maintains '550 first line aircraft and more tanks than Britain and France put together'. This state of affairs persists today—see *The Military Balance 1989–1990* (IISS and Brassey's (UK)). France pp. 59–62, United Kingdom pp. 78–82 and Israel pp. 102–104. See also Corddry, *The Yom Kippur War: Lessons Old and New*, p. 506. The war cost Israel $250 million a day. The Israelis spent 40 per cent of GNP on defence.
6. Alford, *The Israeli Approach to Defensive Tactics. A Study of the 1973 Arab–Israeli War* (TDRC No. 3977), p. 245.

    '. . . there were never more than 600 soldiers on the Canal itself, and the number had been reduced to about 450 on 6 October 1973, as a result of an apparent lull in the fighting along the Canal. These were from a reserve (JERUSALEM) Brigade, and spread through 20 forts overlooking the water. In fact there seems to have been very little attempt to think through exactly what the Bar Lev Line could achieve in a situation on a major crossing of the Canal by the Egyptians in open war. It was probably too weak to prevent a determined attempt to force a crossing, and could only hope to direct artillery fire. The quite widely separated fortifications were easily masked by smoke and neutralised by Egyptian artillery. Had all the supporting tanks reached their prepared positions (many moved too late and were caught on the move by the first waves of Egyptian anti-tank crews), they would have brought considerable fire-power to bear on the obstacle, but it is difficult to see how 20 men every 5 miles, even with armoured support, could altogether upset Egyptian plans . . . No provision was made to evacuate the posts which had identified aggression and were about to be over-run. They remained a source of embarrassment for many days, diverting forces to their relief, and confusing the higher echelons of command . . . the Israelis—uncharacteristically—had failed to think through the role of the posts in a war.'

7. Sellers, *The Defeat of 25 Egyptian Armoured Brigade by 162 Armoured Division 17 October 1973* (TDRC No. 6002), p. 10.
8. Alford, *ibid.*
9. Herzog, *War of Atonement*, p. 272, says that the Israelis would do well to develop the internal rail system in order to speed up reinforcement and mobilisation.
10. Van Creveld, *Command in War*, p. 190.
11. Shazly, *The Crossing of Suez*, p. 31 and pp. 165–169.

12. Alford explains why they did not.
13. *The Military Balance 1989–1990*, pp. 78–82 and 102–104. For example, at present, the United Kingdom, at full mobilisation (which has not occurred since the Second World War) would put 1.12 per cent of her population into uniform (from a population of 57,013,000, the total armed forces mobilised numbers 636,650, consisting of 311,650 active list and 325,800 reservists). The Israeli Defence Force on full mobilisation consists of 645,000 men and women, which out of a population of 4,542,000 represents 14.20 per cent.
14. Dupuy, p. 396.
    'Rising abruptly from the east edge of the Canal was a high embankment along the entire east bank, southward from Kantara. This was based upon nearly a century of Canal dredging residue, which had been made higher and wider by the Israelis ... In the first place this was to conceal Israeli movements just east of the Canal. Second, its 45 degree slope from the water ensured that no amphibious vehicle could possibly climb it. See also diagrams in Shazly, pp. 208–9.
15. Dupuy, p. 480, based on interviews with Generals Bar Lev, Gonen, Sharon and Adan.
16. Alford, p. 244.
17. Shazly, pp. 170–174, not everyone was deceived, according to Shazly. He says that he recognised the attack for what it was, and wanted to withdraw armour and anti-tank missiles from the East Bank to pinch off the Israeli lodgement. He was over-ruled by Sadat and Ismail. The piecemeal attacks by the Egyptian Army that followed were, according to Shazly, the inevitable outcome of Sadat's decision.
18. Heikal, *The Road to Ramadan*, p. 220, claims that the Egyptians were deceived for up to four days.
19. Monroe and Farrar-Hockley, *The Arab-Israeli War, October 1973; Background Events*, p. 28.
20. This farm had been built before the 1967 war by a Japanese agricultural mission to Egypt, and abandoned when the Israelis overran the Sinai. The Israelis mistook the inscriptions on the walls for Chinese, hence the name.
21. Shazly, pp. 173–175, argued against 25 Armoured Brigade attacking in this manner, and forecast its destruction. Whether or not this is hindsight on his part is difficult to say. In his book, he says that Adan sprung the trap with three armoured brigades, whereas he actually used two.
22. Sellers, p. 4, unkindly describes this bridge as a 'typical sapper folly'.
23. Magan replaced Mendler, the original commander, who had fought the holding action on the Sinai front on the first day of the war. Mendler was killed on 13 October.
24. Shazly, p. 191, claims that 3rd Army needed 150 tons of supplies per day to 'stay alive'. This is a very low figure for an army in contact, and one wonders what he means by 'stay alive'. The incomparably more efficient German Army in 1944 needed 200 tons per day per *division* when in contact; American and British divisions considerably more (700 tons per day). The Egyptian 3rd Army consisted of eight infantry brigades, one armoured brigade, and ten tank battalions, the equivalent of three or four divisions.
25. Viksne, *The Yom Kippur War in Retrospect*, p. 28 gives the following figures:

Country Aircraft	Missions	Average Distance (Km)	Total tonnage	Total tonne/km (million)
U.S.				
C-141	421 ⎱	11,700 (a)	⎧ 11,632	136.4
C-5	145 ⎰		⎩ *10,763*	126.21 (b)
Total	566		22,395	262.61

Israel

720, 707, 747　　140　　　　11,350 (a)　　　5,500　　62.50 (b)

Notes:

(a) The discrepancy is possibly explained by most Israeli flights being routed from Eastern U.S.A.

(b) As an indication of the lift provided by purpose-built transport aircraft, the 145 C-5s produced twice as much tonne/kilometres as the 140 Israeli civil airliners. A tonne/kilometre is a means of expressing the ability of any movement resource, truck, train, etc. to lift one tonne (2,000 lbs) over one kilometre.

26. Dupuy, pp. 501–502.
27. Keisewetter, p. 7.
28. Dupuy, pp. 566/571.
29. Van Creveld, *Command in War*, p. 30, and in conversation with the author. This accords with Herzog's observation, *War of Atonement*, p. 279, that there was a lack of administrative discipline in the Israeli Army. Van Creveld says that, in an attempt to get the logistic system right in the Lebanon invasion of 1982, the Israelis over-corrected, to the extent that the narrow roads were clogged with ammunition vehicles to the detriment of follow-up units trying to get forward to maintain the momentum of the advance. This was one, but not the sole, reason for the Israeli failure in Lebanon to secure all their objectives before the cease-fire could be imposed.
30. Corddry, p. 508.
31. Chari, *Military Lessons of the Arab–Israeli War of 1973; A Re-Evaluation*, p. 564.
32. Herzog, *War of Atonement*, p. 277.
33. Herzog, *War of Atonement*, pp. 289/290.

Chapter 7: War in A Snipe Marsh

1. Palit, *The Lightning Campaign*, p. 166.
2. Lachman Singh, *Indian Sword Strikes in East Pakistan*, pp. 19–21. See also Palit, pp. 59 and 154. No denigration of the *Mukti Bahini* is intended here, some of their operations were very successful. Palit quotes some examples; at Belonia, 450 Pakistani troops were killed in a battle in which the *Bahini* lost 70 dead. Eventually, the Pakistanis had to deploy a whole brigade to clear the area. Near Satkhira the Pakistanis lost 300 soldiers against guerrilla losses of about 20.
3. Lachmann Singh, p. 4.
4. Palit, p. 59. Over a hundred important road and rail bridges, and nearly a thousand minor bridges and culverts were blown up.
5. Palit, p. 69, a heartfelt comment from a soldier!
6. Lachman Singh, p. 42.
7. Lachman Singh, p. 57.
8. Rikhye, *The Indian Army: Lessons Learned From 1971*.
9. Lachman Singh, pp. 162–169. Because of the tasks given to Major General Lachman Singh, commanding 20th Mountain Division, who comes across as a highly competent divisional commander, he was reinforced to an overall strength of 30,000 men. Corps Heaquarters allotted him 300 3-ton military vehicles and 300 civilian vehicles.

   'Because of breakdowns, mechanical difficulties, "malingering" by some civilian drivers and owners, the average civilian vehicles available to us were not more than 150 on any day. Civilian transport posed us a lot of other problems also. It was not easy to get spare parts for necessary repairs for the multitude of varieties of vehicles in the forward areas ... Some of our mechanics were not trained to repair the different varieties of transport. Most of the civilian transport was not fit for movement on *kacha* (rough, rudimentary) tracks.'

Singh gave priority to gun and tank ammunition, and to mortar bombs and machine gun ammunition. He found that small arms ammunition expenditure was low. Not surprisingly in a fast moving battle, fuel expenditure was high, and gun ammunition was not particularly high (between 2,500 and 3,000 rounds per battle).

10. *Military Balance 1989–1990*, pp. 158–160. At present India has 33 divisions and 14 independent brigades, including, among other equipments, 3,150 Main Battle Tanks, 1,150 APCs (700 MICV, and 450 APCs), 130 SP guns (80 × Abbot and 50 × 130 mm), and 442 helicopters (280 army and 152 air force). No figures are given for load carriers, and it would be interesting to see if the increase in 'teeth' in the Indian Army has been matched by an equivalent increase in 'tail'. The author's guess would be to say that it has not. However, the Indians have clearly learned the value of amphibious forces, because they now have one regiment of marines (1,000 strong), with another forming (p. 160).

Part Three

Chapter 8: Amphibious Logistics—Falklands 1982

1. Stokesbury, *British Concepts and Practices of Amphibious Warfare—1876 to 1916.* Quoting *Frontier and Overseas Expeditions from India, Vol. VI*, pp. 28–30.
2. Brown, *The Royal Navy and the Falklands War*, p. 65.
3. Brown, p. 53.
4. A Royal Marines Commando is equivalent to a British non-mechanised infantry battalion in size and composition.
5. Brown, p. 65.
6. *The British Army in the Falklands 1982*, p. 25.
7. The main problem was lack of time to pre-position rolling stock.
8. *The British Army in the Falklands 1982*, p. 23.
9. Some assault packs (a complete 30 days' WMR for a unit group constitutes one assault pack) were loaded complete into one ship (RFAs). On other occasions, mainly in the case of the LSLs and the STUFT, loads were stowed where there was space. MV *Elk* had all the ammunition (698 tons) from three assault packs, and some 4,800 anti-tank mines. These and a large quantity of defence stores, barbed wire, sand-bags and metal pickets, were stowed in one vast pile in *Elk's* lower vehicle deck. She was effectively a floating bomb. See Note 18 below.
10. Supporter, *Logistic Support for Operation Corporate.*
11. Curtiss, *The RAF Contribution to the Falklands Campaign*, pp. 24–25.
12. Curtiss, p. 27.
13. Under the naval task organisation system the Task Force (TF) is given a number, in this case 317, so Fieldhouse was Commander Task Force (CTF) 317. Task Groups (TG) are allocated a number after a decimal point, for example TG 317.1, and the commander is CTG 317.1. Below Task Group, is Task Unit (TU), which are numbered with two decimal points, TU 317.1.1, and the commander is CTU 37.1.1.
14. 3rd Commando Brigade consisted of the following:
    Brigade Headquarters including Signal Squadron (a)
    Two troops B Squadron RHG/D The Blues and Royals (b)
    29 Commando Regiment Royal Artillery (a)

Three gun batteries, each of six 105 mm light gun (a)
One gun battery of six 105 mm light gun (c)
One Naval Gunfire Support Observation battery (a)
One air defence battery (RAPIER SAM) (b)
59 Commando Engineer Squadron Royal Engineers (reinforced) (a)
40 Commando Royal Marines (a)
42 Commando Royal Marines (a)
45 Commando Royal Marines (a)
2nd Battalion The Parachute Regiment (c)
3rd Battalion The Parachute Regiment (b)
Special Boat Squadron Royal Marines (b)
Headquarters and D and G Squadrons 22 SAS (b), (c)
Mountain and Arctic Warfare Cadre RM (Brigade Reconnaissance) (a)
3 Commando Brigade Air Squadron RM (light helicopters) (reinforced) (a) (b)
3 Commando Brigade Air Defence Troop (BLOWPIPE) (reinforced)
Commando Logistic Regiment RM (a)
Ten other minor units, such as a Field Record Office and a Force Reinforcement
    Holding Unit (a) (b) (c)

Notes:
(a) Original Units of 3rd Commando Brigade Royal Marines.
(b) Added to the Brigade before sailing from the U.K. in early April 1982.
(c) Joined the Brigade at Ascension Island before 7 May 1982 or at sea just before
    D-Day 21 May.

15. Ship-shore movement assets are craft, helicopters, and ferries for moving men,
    equipment, and supplies ashore. They include hovercraft, amphibious armoured
    vehicles, and amphibious wheeled vehicles such as the Second World War
    DUKW, none of which the British possessed. The only amphibious vehicles in
    3 Commando Brigade were two Combat Engineer Tractors, tracked and
    armoured plant, on loan. The type and numbers of ship-shore assets available to
    the Amphibious Task Group Commander, under whose command they came,
    were as follows:

Craft available for Logistics

Type	*Load*
8 Landing Craft Utility (LCU) (4 in each LPD)	100 tons cargo or 140 men or two tanks
8 Landing Craft Vehicles and Personnel (4 in each LPD)	5 tons of cargo or one landrover and trailer or 35 men
5 Mexeflote Pontoons (a)	120 tons (but loaded with up to 200 tons in this campaign)

Helicopters

Type	*Typical loads*
11 SEA KING	20 fully loaded men (b) or one 105 gun or one landrover or two pallets 105 ammo (48 rounds)
5 Wessex	10 fully loaded men (c) or one pallet 105 ammo (24 rounds)

Notes:
(a) Five was the maximum number available. On D-day, 5 × 120 foot rafts were
assembled, one was subsequently holed by cannon fire and was unuseable. A
further raft, the only other Mexeflote possessed by the British anywhere in the

world, arrived in the beachhead on 4 June. Mexeflotes can be assembled as 60 ft or 120 ft rafts. Driven by two large outboard engines.

(b) This could be exceeded for short moves depending on the load carried on the men, and the fuel load in the helicopter, but 20 fully loaded infantry is the planning figure.

(c) Can take up to 15 men, depending on fuel state and load on men. The planning figure is given.

16. Flight decks are marked with a circle to indicate where helicopters should land. A one-spot deck means that only one helicopter can land on that deck at a time. LPDs had three-spot decks, although the clutter of stores usually allowed only two to be operated.

17. A Turnaway Landing is a form of amphibious rehearsal, in which all ships approach the rehearsal beachhead, first waves of helicopters and landing craft are launched, but turn away without landing. The purpose is to test communications, boat and helicopter assault lanes, and check timings, allowing amendments to be made before the actual event. It is the absolute minimum rehearsal recommended by the pamphlets before any amphibious operation!

18. At Ascension, the amount of ammunition in *Elk* was reduced by transferring 129 tons of unit first line ammunition, including gun ammunition, to the ships in which units were travelling, so it could be issued before, or be immediately available on, D-day. The sixteen days supplies in MV *Elk* included 2,000 tons of ammunition, defence stores, and much besides; so much so, that when stores could not be located in other ships, it was always worth looking in *Elk*. This led to the Commando Brigade logisticians' cry of 'it's on the *Elk*!' The quantity of ammunition she carried also led to a reluctance to allow her into the anchorage off the beaches until the air threat had been reduced. Had she been hit and exploded, the damage to ships nearby and troops and equipment on the beaches could have been severe.

19. Conversation Thompson/Moore.

20. Gardiner, A Personal Account of Operations on the Falkland Islands, Appendix 1, p. 2.

21. The medium lift helicopter availability, all controlled by COMAW, for the period 21 May–1 June 1982 was as follows:

21–26 May
11 × SEA KING   less: 1 × SEA KING allocated to RAPIER support for fuel and spares
                 4 × SEA KING PNG for night use. Crew rest and servicing precludes day use except in emergency
5 × WESSEX
Therefore daily availability:
6 × SEA KING
5 × WESSEX
26 May–1 June
6 × SEA KING   remaining 5 × SEA KING allocated as above
5 × WESSEX
1 × CHINOOK

Example load:
To move a battery of 6 × 105 mm light guns with ammunition (480 RPG), 2 × half ton vehicles for battle battery charging, and men, takes:
82 × SEA KING Sorties
To lift 480 rounds per gun takes:
60 × SEA KING Sorties
    or

120 WESSEX Sorties

or

20 × CHINOOK Sorties

One pallet of 105 mm light gun ammo contains 24 complete rounds

SEA KING will carry 2 × pallets = 48 rounds

WESSEX will carry 1 × pallet = 24 rounds

CHINOOK will carry 6 × pallets = 144 rounds

Some example time and distance figures:

1. Distance San Carlos to Mount Kent gun positions flying tactically = 50 miles (40 miles in a straight line).
2. Turn-round time with underslung loads, including refuelling from one-spot decks in San Carlos Water = 1.5 hours.
3. First light 06.30 hours, last light 16.15 hrs.
4. Therefore, maximum number of sorties per day per hel = 7(1).
5. 6 SEA KINGS × 7 sorties = 42 lifts per day.
6. Therefore to lift one battery plus ammunition takes all available SEA KINGS two days.

Notes:

(1) Unlikely because of weather. Also, return trip of last sortie will be after last light—see below:

7 Sorties

(1)	(2)	(3)	(4)	(5)	(6)	(7)
06.30	08.00	09.30	11.00	12.30	14.00	15.30	17.00

6 Sorties

(1)	(2)	(3)	(4)	(5)	(6)
06.30	08.00	09.30	11.00	12.30	14.00	15.30

22. The 30 days stocks for 5th Infantry Brigade were put together by Headquarters United Kingdom Land Forces, and placed in a variety of ships. Although the Commanding Officer of the Commando Logistic Regiment was sent a signal telling him what had been loaded where, the Navy had busily cross-loaded much of it in and around South Georgia, and were never able to tell him where anything wss, from then on.
23. Implementing the Lessons of the Falklands Campaign, para 184.
24. The Falklands Campaign: The Lessons, pp. 25–26.
25. Implementing the Lessons of the Falklands Campaign, paragraphs 100 and 105.

Chapter 9: Supplying the War That Never Was—Yet

(To reduce the length of these notes, SSRC and TDRC papers have been given their full title the first time they appear only, thereafter only the page number is given thus: SRC C58, or TDRC 4567.)

1. Donnelly, *The Sustainability of the Soviet Army in Battle*, SSRC C53, p. 198.
2. Van Creveld, *Supplying War*, p. 231.
3. Van Creveld, *Supplying War*, p. 236.
4. Donnelly, *Rear Support for Soviet Ground Forces*, TDRC 4567, p. 28.
5. Donnelly, TDRC 4567, p. 20.
6. Van Creveld, *Supplying War*, p. 163.
7. Donnelly, TDRC 4567, p. 23.
8. *Supply problems of 21 Army Group and AEF 1944*, Liddell Hart Archives, file 15/15/48.
9. Alstead, *Ten in Ten*, a Study of the Central Region Transport Capability in Crisis and War.

10. Skinner, *NORTHAG, a Study of Organizational Structure.*
11. NATO Logistics Handbook.
12. Skinner quoting Eccles, *Military Concepts and Philosophy*, p. 69.
13. Compare this with the situation of a Soviet general commanding a front—the equivalent of a NATO army group. Although the example is taken from the Second World War, those who have made a close study of Soviet methods believe that they would operate in the same way now, with the necessary adaptations to fit the situation. (See Map XIII—taken from *Operativnaya Maskirovka Voysk* by Matsulenko, translated by Lieutenant Colonel Blandy).

    As part of the Soviet exploitation of their victory at Kursk (July 1943), the commander of the Voronezh Front (Vatutin), was ordered to attack in a south-westerly direction to break into the salient round Kharkov held by German Army Group South. Although there was plenty of railway track (some 856 km), in the sector allocated to Vatutin, all the lines ran laterally. There was not one railway track or road running direct to where Vatutin's Front, consisting of eight armies, was to mount the attack. The only line that ran in the right direction (Kastornaya-Kursk-L'gov) was outside his sector and belonged to Rokossovky's Central Front. However, by a prodigious effort of rail and road construction, the most important being the linking of the lateral rail system between Stariy Oskol and Rzdava, the distance from army bases was reduced by 184 km. This cut the movement times of trains from about two to three days to between 10 and 15 hours; doubling the supply capacity to the Front. As the Front advanced over terrain devastated by the Germans, six roads were built behind the advancing armies, to ensure that supply could keep pace.

    More remarkable, Vatutin took advantage of the lateral layout of the railway, to mount an elaborate deception plan. For several days before the operation began, trains steamed north-west on the line running to Sudzha and Lokinskaya loaded with troops, dummy stores and equipment, including tanks. Every night the trains returned with the troops, leaving the equipment and stores. This led the Germans into believing that a Guards Tank Army and a Tank Army were concentrating to mount the Front's main blow in a westerly and north-westerly direction. In fact, the main blow was actually on the south-westerly Belgorod–Kharkov axis. Deception (Maskirovka) is an important ingredient in any Soviet planning at operational level, and considerable pains are taken to make the bait more palatable.

    The switching of a NATO army group axis, let alone a deception plan based on a logistic dumping programme, would be beyond the capability of the layer-cake of national corps, each tied to their own line of communication carrying their largely non-interoperable range of ammunition and equipment.
14. Skinner, p. 81, quoting Burrows and Irwin, *The Security of Western Europe*, p. 92.
15. Skinner, p. 81, quoting Mulley, *The Politics of Western Defence*, p. 191.
16. The principal differences in the national systems for ammunition supply are:
    (a) Demanding procedures for ammunition, i.e., automatic or demand.
    (b) Methods of supply, i.e., 'PUSH' or 'PULL' or a combination.
    (c) The chain used for ammunition supply is often separate from other classes of supply.
    (d) Methods of determining initial and replenishment stocks.
    (e) Structure, organisation and manpower of ammunition units.
    (f) Responsibilities and tasks of units in the ammunition supply system.
    (g) Differences in the supply of the various natures of ammunition, e.g., artillery, Mines and Explosives.
    (h) Alternative systems for urgent resupply.
    (i) Extent of the use of Automatic Data Processing.

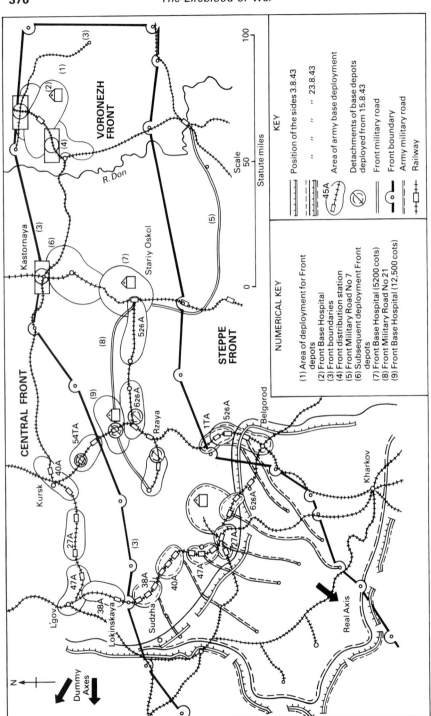

KEY

Position of the sides 3.8.43

" " " 23.8.43

45A

Area of army base deployment

Detachments of base depots deployed from 15.8.43

Front military road

Front boundary

Army military road

Railway

NUMERICAL KEY

(1) Area of deployment for Front depots
(2) Front Base Hospital
(3) Front boundaries
(4) Front distribution station
(5) Front Military Road No 7
(6) Subsequent deployment Front depots
(7) Front Base Hospital (5200 cots)
(8) Front Military Road No 21
(9) Front Base Hospital (12,500 cots)

VORONEZH FRONT

CENTRAL FRONT

STEPPE FRONT

R. Don

Kastornaya

Stariy Oskol

526A

Rzava

626A

54TA

40A

Kursk

27A

47A

38A

Lgov

Lokinskaya

Sudzha

38A

40A

47A

27A

626A

1TA

526A

Belgorod

Kharkov

Real Axis

Dummy Axes

N

Scale

Statute miles

0   50   100

MAP XIII The Rear of the Voronezh Front in the Belgorod–Kharkov Operation 1943.

(j) Extent of the use of standardised codes and packaging, i.e., NATO codes and pallets.

(k) Allocation and type of transport and Materials Handling Equipment at the respective levels of supply in formations and units.

(l) Different Daily Ammunition Expenditure Rates.

The lack of commonality in national systems has consequently precluded the full implementation of:

(a) Standardised logistic criteria for equipment and supply systems.

(b) Mutual logistic assistance.

(c) Interoperability.

17. Donnelly, *Soviet Use of Military History for Operational Analysis: Force Sustainability*, SSRC C58, p. 3.
18. Peterson and Trulock, *A New Soviet Military Doctrine*, SSRC C68.
19. Peterson and Trulock, SSRC C68, notes 44 (Sokolovsky) and 46. Also correspondence with Donnelly dated 30 October 1989.
20. Donnelly, SSRC C58, p. 6. See also *Rear Maintenance of Mobile Groups* by Colonel V. Odintsov and Colonel B. Ovsiyannikov translated by Lieutenant Colonel Blandy.
21. Turbiville, RUSI/RHAS Research Centre, *Soviet Logistic Support for Ground Operations*, RUSI 9/75.
22. Fitzroy Maclean, *Eastern Approaches*, p. 505.
23. Donnelly, TDRC 4567, pp. 6 and 32.
24. Donnelly, SSRC C58, and correspondence dated 30 October 1989.
25. Van Creveld, *Logistics Since 1945, From Complexity to Paralysis*, July 1989, p. 10.
26. Donnelly, *Red Banner, The Soviet Military System In Peace and War*, p. 226; and correspondence with Donnelly dated 30 October 1989.
27. Donnelly, SSRC C53, p. 198.
28. Donnelly, SSRC C53, pp. 214/217.
29. Donnelly, SSRC C53, p. 231 gives the following tables:

Divisional Daily Estimated Requirement Rates (tonnes)

(MR = Motor Rifle Division, TK = Tank Division)

	Heavily opposed or Major Axis		Lightly opposed or Minor Axis		Average		Totals max/min
	AMMO MR/TK	FUEL MR/TK	AMMO MR/TK	FUEL MR/TK	RATIONS MR/TK	SPARES MR/TK	MR/TK
Break-through	520/480	700/610	280/260	400/370	30/28	120/85	*1370/1200* 830/740
Defence	580/520	320/300	370/330	200/180	30/28	80/50	*1010/900* 680/590
Pursuit	66/63	900/810	44/40	590/550	30/28	60/40	*1055/940* 730/660
Reserve	140/120	230/200	88/80	160/140	30/28	32/35	*435/375* 315/275

30. Donnelly, SSRC C53, p. 231.
31. Donnelly, *Appendices to the Sustainability of the Soviet Army in Battle*, SSRC C54, pp. 604–618.
32. Donnelly, SSRC C53, pp. 256–258.

33. Donnelly, SSRC C53, p. 265.
34. Donnelly, SSRC C53, pp. 266–267.
35. Donnelly, SSRC C53, pp. 272–274.. Of a total of 738 Armoured Fighting Vehicles belonging to 1st Guards Tank Army requiring repair in the Visla–Oder operation in January–February 1945, 294 were repaired immediately by mobile tank repair detachments, 356 were repaired following inspection at the mobile tank repair base, and only 88 were backloaded to front workshops. (SSRC C54 pp. 624/625 and diagram of technical maintenance of 1st Guards Tank Army in the Visla–Oder operation January–February 1945 translated by Lieutenant Colonel Blandy).
36. Donnelly, SSRC C53, p. 281 and pp. 286–295.
37. Donnelly, SSRC C53, p. 283.
38. Donnelly, SSRC C53, pp. 406–407.
39. Donnelly, SSRC C53, pp. 408–409.
40. Donnelly, SSRC C53, p. 410.
41. Donnelly, SSRC C53, p. 411.
42. Donnelly, SSRC C53, pp. 411–412.
43. Donnelly, SSRC C53, pp. 413–414.
44. Donnelly, SSRC C53, p. 419.

Chapter 10: Crystal Ball Gazing—Future Wars and Their Support

1. *Jane's Defence Weekly*, 14 October 1989, p. 767.
2. *Jane's Defence Weekly*, 21 October 1989, p. 849.
3. *Jane's Defence Weekly*, 21 October 1989, p. 870.
4. *Journal of the Royal United Services Institute for Defence Studies*, Autumn 1989, p. 15, General Galvin (SACEUR), in the presence of General Lushev, Commander-in-Chief of the Joint Armed Forces of the Warsaw Pact.
5. Simpkin, *Race to the Swift*.
6. Simpkin.
7. Van Creveld, *Supplying War*, pp. 234/235.
8. Simpkin, p. 122.
9. A rule of thumb helicopter allocation might be as follows:

Army/Marines

Formation	*Helicopter type*	*Helicopters per formation*	Total
2 × Marine Brigades	Attack helicopters (MBAV?)	20	40
	Infantry fighting helicopters	20	40
	Fire support helicopters	20	40
	Recce	10	20
	Blackhawk	20	40
	Total all types	90	180
2 × Assault Brigades	Attack helicopters (MBAV?)	60	120
	Infantry fighting helicopters	40	80
	Fire support helicopters	20	40
	Recce	10	20
	Total all types	130	260
3 × Light Infantry Brigades	Infantry Blackhawk type	40	120
	Artillery Blackhawk type	40	120
	Reece	10	30
	Total all types	90	270

3 × Light Mechanised	Recce	10	30
Brigades	Total all types	10	30
4 × Artillery Brigades	Recce	6	24
	Total all types	6	24
Logistic	Heavy lift (Chinook) (a)	—	60
	Total all types	—	60
	Total Army/Marine Helicopters		824
Navy	Total all types		177
Air Force	Total all types		nil

Grand Total all types (b)   1001

Notes to table above:

(a) Does not qualify as a combat helicopter—see Note 10 below.

(b) See *The Military Balance, 1988–89*, pp. 81–83 for British helicopter strengths at the time of writing.

10. *Negotiation on Conventional Forces in Europe, Proposal Submitted by Members of NATO Alliance at Vienna, 13 July 1989*, p. 3 gives numbers of helicopters, and p. 6 gives types that qualify as combat helicopters.

11. Donnelly, *The Sustainability of the Soviet Army in Battle*, SSRC paper C53, p. 23.

12. MacKenzie, *The Counter Offensive*, script of address to working group at MOD/King's College seminar 19 July 1989, p. 7.

13. *Jane's Defence Weekly*, 14 October 1989, p. 783. The projects are:
   ▷ The Modular Stand-Off Weapon
   ▷ Intelligent Shelter Attack Submunition
   ▷ Short Range Anti-Radiation Missile
   ▷ Advanced Sea Mine
   ▷ Advanced Short Range Air-to-Air Missile
   ▷ NATO Frigate Replacement for the 1990s

As Major General Baxter, a recent British Assistant Chief of Defence Staff (Logistics), pointed out at the MOD/King's College seminar in July 1989, within NATO there are five different tanks with four guns of different calibres, and four different anti-tank helicopters with different missiles. The brief success with a common small arms round ended when 7.62 mm ceased to be the NATO standard calibre. Eleven firms in Alliance countries build anti-tank weapons, eighteen firms in seven countries design and produce ground-to-air weapons, and sixteen companies in seven countries work on air-to-ground weapons.

14. The flexibility of airborne forces equipped with the FLA Tactran and a mix of the present and next generation of helicopters can be briefly shown if we postulate the following scenario:

(a) A brigade to be flown 2,350 nautical miles from the U.K. (to Western Turkey for example), which we will call Airlift 1.

(b) Three days later a need arises for a rapid reinforcement of the mainland of Europe. The first phase of this reinforcement includes the insertion of an airborne force from U.K. at a radius of action of 800 nautical miles, to seize an airstrip which is held by heliborne forces of an advancing enemy army, designated Airlift 2.

(c) Concurrently with Airlift 1, stocks need to be flown from the United Kingdom to Europe at a radius of action of 400 nautical miles, designated Airlift 3.

Airlift 1

For the purposes of this scenario, the brigade in this move is not configured as envisaged in Note 9 above, but is more like an airportable brigade 1990 style. This enabled the figures to be validated by British Aerospace using data based on in-service, or existing equipment. The brigade consisting of 2,500 men, 5 light helicopters, 12 attack helicopters, 3,915 tonnes of freight, and 1,000 vehicles (including trailers, and light APCs) could be complete in Turkey by D plus 3 days 18 hours, taking 362 sorties. As a comparison, even using the C-130 J, still on the drawing board, but an improved version of the present C-130 H, this same lift would require 647 sorties by 65 aircraft and would not be complete until D plus 10 days 6 hours.

If the attack helicopters flew under their own power, the lift would be completed even quicker. The Apache AH-64A equipped with four drop tanks can fly UK–Western Turkey non-stop. So even if the brigade had its full establishment of attack helicopters (60), as in Note 9 above, their move would not impose further demands on the airlift. If the brigade was entirely heliborne (Note 9 above), the Blackhawks would replace many of the 1,000 vehicles in the FLA Tactran lift, and any attached logistic Chinooks could fly direct using AAR.

Airlift 2

The organisation of the parachute brigade in this operation is nearer that envisaged by the author, but has fewer light mechanised vehicles and more wheeled vehicles and towed equipments to allow the figures to be validated. It consists of:

    2,000 men
    25 light mechanised vehicles
    70 wheeled vehicles
    55 trailers and towed equipment
    2 light helicopters
    12 AH-64A Apache
    128 tonnes of ammunition on pallets
    73 tonnes of stores on pallets

with a daily resupply requirement of 64 tonnes of ammunition and 37 tonnes of other stores.

The assault is to be in three phases:

Phase One
Parachute assault by two battalions totalling 600 men to seize 3,000 foot strip.

Phase Two
On the strip seized in Phase One, airland 10 light mechanised vehicles (Scimitar type) and crews, and 2 light helicopters. AH-64As start arriving direct from U.K. each fitted with 2 external fuel tanks, 8 Hellfire missiles, 4 Stinger missiles, 1,200 rounds 30 mm.

Phase Three
Starting at H plus 45 minutes, airland:

    1,400 men
    15 light mechanised vehicles
    70 wheeled vehicles
    55 trailers/towed equipments
    32 ammunition pallets
    36 stores pallets

Phases Two and Three would be complete within 2 hours and 50 minutes of the Phase One drop, using 52 sorties of FLA Tactran. By comparison the C130-J would require 102 sorties and 8 hours 46 minutes to complete the same task.

Phase Four
Daily fly-in of 101 tonnes of ammunition and stores, requiring 5 FLA Tactran sorties, compared with 7 C-130J sorties.

Airlift 3

This requires a daily lift of 400 tonnes of logistic stocks to be flown 400 nautical miles, carried out concurrently with Airlift 1. It could be accomplished by 3 FLA Tactran in 24 sorties. By comparison, 5 C-130J would need 34 sorties to complete the same task.

All these ambitious tasks could be carried out by FLA Tactran with capacity to spare for the unforeseen, because on completion of Airlift 1, there would be lift available for 9,600 tonnes per day over a 400 nautical mile radius, or 2,160 tonnes per day over a 2,350 nautical mile radius. At the same point, there would be no spare capacity offered by a C-130J fleet.

The figures above and comparisons of FLA Tactran with C-130J assume the following:

    (a) 65 aircraft in the FLA Tactran or C-130J fleets.
    (b) Daily availability of aircraft:
        C-130J: 78 per cent (assumed 8 per cent improvement over current C-130)
        FLA: 90 per cent (1990s technology, better serviceability etc.)
    (c) Cruise speed (mean)
        C-130J 300 knots
        FLA 400 knots

15. Lacquer, *The Age of Terrorism*, p. 146–148 and footnotes.
16. Lacquer, p. 96.
17. Lacquer, pp. 102–103.
18. Dobson and Payne, *War Without End*, pp. 89–104.
19. Research by Dr Ezell, Director of the Institute for Research on Small Arms, in *International Security*.

Bibliography

To reduce the size of the bibliography, as a general rule only those published and unpublished works which have been quoted appear in this list. Some other works are quoted within notes. The mass of other books and papers researched for background material are not listed.

The following abbreviations are used in the bibliography:
   Royal United Services Institute For Defence Studies London—RUSI.
   Soviet Studies Research Centre The Royal Military Academy Sandhurst—SSRC.
   Tactical Doctrine Retrieval Cell at the British Army Staff College Camberley—TDRC.

Alford, J. R. *The Israeli Approach to Defensive Tactics: A Study of the 1973 Arab–Israeli War*, Defence Fellowship Paper, TDRC number 3977.

Alstead, F. A. L. *Ten in Ten: A Study of the Central Region Transport Capability in Crisis and War*, NATO Fellowship Study 1988.

Appleman, R. E. *South to the Naktong, North to the Yalu/The United States Army in the Korean War*, Office of the Chief of Military History, Department of the Army, Washington DC, 1961.

Bowers, R. L. *Tactical Airlift, the United States Air Force in South-East Asia*, Office of Air Force History, United States Air Force, Washington DC, 1983.

British Army, The, In The Falklands, Ministry of Defence (Army) 1983.

Brown, D. *The Royal Navy and the Falklands War*, Leo Cooper, London, 1987.

Burke, R. L. *Corps Logistic Planning in Vietnam, Military Review August 1969*.

Chari, P. R. *Military Lessons of the Arab/Israeli War of 1973, A Re-evaluation*, Institute for Defence Studies and Analysis Journal, April/June 1976.

Clausewitz, Carl Von. *On War*, edited and translated by Michael Howard and Peter Paret, Princeton University Press, 1976.

Cochran, A. S. *First Strike at the River Drang, interview with Major General Kinnard, Commanding General US 1st Air Cavalry Division*, for Military History.

Corddry, C. W. *The Yom Kippur: Lessons Old and New, National Defence, May/June 1974*.

Curtiss, J. *The RAF Contribution to the Falklands Campaign, Naval Review, January 1983*.

Davidson, P. B. *Vietnam at War*, Sidgwick & Jackson, London, 1988.

Dobson, C. and Payne, R. *War Without End*, Harrap, London, 1986.

Donnelly, C. N. *The Sustainability of the Soviet Army in Battle*, SSRC, paper C53. *Appendices to the Sustainability of the Soviet Army in Battle*, SSRC paper C54. *Rear Support for Soviet Ground Forces*, TDRC number 4567. *Soviet Use of Military History for Operational Analysis: Establishing the Parameters of the Concept of Force Sustainability*, SSRC paper C58. *Red Banner: the Soviet Military System In Peace and War*, Jane's Information Group 1988.

Dupuy, T. N. *Elusive Victory*, Macdonalds & Janes, London, 1978.

Engels, D. W. *Alexander the Great and the Logistics of the Macedonian Army*, University of California Press, 1978.

EUROLOG Ammunition Supply Study November 1987.

Exercise Babel, Staff College Camberley Exercise based on the Korean War, notes on administration of 29 (British) Brigade in Korea, TDRC number 6285.

Fall, B. *Street Without Joy*, Pall Mall Press, London, 1964. *Hell in a Very Small Place, The Siege of Dien Bien Phu*, Lippincott, New York, 1967.

Falklands Campaign, The Lessons, Presented to Parliament by the Secretary of State for Defence, Cmnd 8758, Her Majesty's Stationery Office, December 1982.

Gardiner, I. *A Personal Account of Operations on the Falkland Islands, X Company, 45 Commando Royal Marines, April–June 1982*, unpublished.

Gough, J. *United States Army Mobilization and Logistics in the Korean War: a Research Approach*, Centre of Military History, United States Army, Washington DC, 1987.

Hastings, Max. *The Korean War*, Michael Joseph, London, 1987.

Heikal, M. *The Road to Ramadan*, Collins, London, 1975.

Henderson, G. F. R. *Stonewall Jackson*, Longmans Green & Co., New York, 1961.

Hermes, W. G. *Fighting Front and Truce Tent/The United States Army in the Korean War*, Office of the Chief of Military History, Department of the Army, Washington DC, 1966.

Herzog, C. *The Middle East War 1973, Journal of The RUSI, March 1975. The War of Atonement*, Weidenfeld & Nicolson, London, 1975.

Huston, J. A. *Guns and Butter, Powder and Rice, US Army Logistics in the Korean War*, Associated University Press, London, 1989.

Implementing the Lessons of the Falklands Campaign, Fourth report from the Defence Committee Session 1986–87, House of Commons 6 May 1987, Her Majesty's Stationery Office.

de Jomini, A. *The Art of War*, Greenwood Press, 1971.

Josephus. *The Jewish War*, Penguin Classics, 1981.

Keegan, John. *The Price of Admiralty, War at Sea from the Man of War to the Submarine*, Hutchinson, London, 1988.

Kennedy, Paul. *The Rise and Fall of the Great Powers*, Fontana 1988.

Kiesewetter, H. A. *Golan Tank Graveyard. Wehrkunde 2/74*, TDRC paper number 2341.

Khuyen, Lieutenant General Dong Van. *RVNAF Logistics/Indochina Monographs*, United States Army Center of Military History, Washington DC, 1980.

Lacquer, W. *The Age of Terrorism*, Weidenfeld & Nicolson, London, 1987.

Lane Fox, Robin. *Alexander the Great*, Penguin Books, 1987.

Lessons from Korea 1954. The Infantry School, Fort Benning, Georgia, TDRC number 4259.

Luvaas, J. *A Prussian Observer With Lee, Military Affairs, volume XXI, Number 3, Fall 1957*.

Luvaas, J. *G. F. R. Henderson and the American Civil War, Military Affairs, Volume XX, Number 3, Fall 1956*.

Maclean, F. *Eastern Approaches*, Jonathan Cape, London, 1949.

Military Balance, The, 1988/89. The International Institute for Strategic Studies, London, October 1988.

Monroe, E. & Farrar-Hockley, A. H. *The Arab–Israeli War, October 1973: Background Events, International Institute for Defence Studies, Adelphi Paper 111*.

NATO Logistics Handbook, Senior NATO Logisticians' Conference Secretariat, NATO Headquarters, Brussels, June 1986.

O'Ballance, E. *The Indo-China War 1945–54: A Study in Guerrilla Warfare*, Faber & Faber, London, 1964.

Oman, C. *The History of the Art of War in the Middle Ages*, Methuen, London, 1898, reprint 1979.

Palit, D. K. *The Lightning Campaign*, Compton Press, Salisbury, U.K., 1972.

Perlmutter, A. *Israel's Fourth War, October 1973: Political and Military Misperceptions. Orbis Summer 1975*.

Peterson, P. A. and N. Trulock, *A New Soviet Military Doctrine*, SSRC paper C68.

Ridgway, M. B. *The Korean War*, Doubleday & Company Inc., New York, 1967.

Rikhye, R. *The Indian Army: Lessons Learned From 1971, Indian Army Quarterly, October 1972*.

Roy, Jules. *The Battle of Dien Bien Phu*, Faber and Faber, London, 1965.

Schnabel, J. F. *Policy and Direction: The First Year/United States in the Korean War*, Office of the Chief of Military History, United States Army, Washington DC, 1972.

Sellers, J. A. *The Defeat of 25th Egyptian Armoured Brigade by 162 Armoured Division 17 October 1973*, TDRC number 6002.

Sharp, U.S. Grant. *Strategy for Defeat—Vietnam in Retrospect*, Presidio Press, California, 1978.

Singh, L. *Indian Sword Strikes in East Pakistan*, Vikas Publishing, Ghazibad, 1979.

Shazly, S. *The Crossing of Suez*, Third World Centre for Publishing, London, 1980.

Shore, M. S. *The Battle for Khe Sanh*, Historical Branch Headquarters Marine Corps, Washington DC, 1969.

Simpkin, R. *Race to the Swift*, Brassey's, London, 1985.

Skinner, J. NORTHAG, *a Study of Organizational Structure*, Defence Fellowship paper held in Ministry of Defence Whitehall Library.

Spector, Ronald. *Advice and Support: The Early Years: The US Army in Vietnam, 1941–1960*, United States Army Center of Military History, Washington DC, 1983.

Stokesbury, J. L. *British Concepts and Practices of Amphibious Warfare—1876 to 1916*, unpublished PhD thesis, Duke University, U.S.A., 1968.

Supply Problems of 21 Army Group and AEF 1944, Liddell Hart Centre of Military Archives, King's College London, file 15/15/48.

'Supporter', *Logistic Support for Operation Corporate, Naval Review October 1982*. (Based on contributions from the staff of Chief of Fleet Support).

Terraine, John. *The Right of the Line*, The RAF in the European War 1939–1945, Sceptre, London, 1988.

Thompson, Sir Robert. *Peace Is Not at Hand*, Chatto & Windus, London, 1974.

Thorpe, G. C. *Pure Logistics*, National Defense University Press, Washington DC, 1986.

Van Creveld, Martin. *Command in War*, Harvard University Press, 1985. *Supplying War*, Cambridge University Press, 1986. *Two Years After: The Israeli Defence Forces, 1973–75, RUSI Journal March 1976. Logistics Since 1945. From Complexity to Paralysis*. Paper to working party at MOD (Army)/King's College, London seminar July 1989.

Viksne, J. *The Yom Kippur War In Retrospect, Australian Army Journal, April 1976*.

War Diary of the Chief of Administration Allied Force HQ, Liddell Hart Centre of Military Archives, King's College, London.

Vietnam Studies, Department of the United States Army, Washington DC: Dunn, Carroll, H. *Base Development in South Vietnam 1965–1970*, published 1972. Eckhardt, G. S. *Command and Control 1950–1969*, published 1974. Tolson, J. S. *Airmobility, 1961–1971*, published 1973. Heiser, Joseph S. *Logistic Support*, published 1974. Starry, D. A. *Mounted Combat in Vietnam*, published 1978. Ploger, Robert R. *US Army Engineers 1965–1970*, published 1974.

War of the Rebellion: a Compilation of the Official Records of the Union and Confederate Armies: Volume XIX, part I (reports), *Volume XXV, part I* (reports), *Volume XXV, part II* (correspondence).

War Office Series, *The Second World War 1939–1945, Army Movements* (referred to in Notes as MOVEMENTS), *Army Supplies and Transport* (S.&T.), *Army Transportation* (Transportation), *Administrative Planning* (Admin Planning), *Army Administration* (referred to in full).

Index